Also by the Editors at *America's Test Kitchen*

America's Best Lost Recipes
The America's Test Kitchen Family Baking Book
The America's Test Kitchen Family Cookbook
The Best of America's Test Kitchen 2007, 2008, 2009

The Cook's Country Series:

The Cook's Country Cookbook

The Best Recipe Series:

The Best Slow & Easy Recipes
The Best Chicken Recipes
The Best International Recipe
The Best Make-Ahead Recipe
The Best 30-Minute Recipe
The Best Light Recipe
The Cook's Illustrated Guide to Grilling & Barbecue
Best American Side Dishes
The New Best Recipe
The Best Cover & Bake Recipes
The Best Meat Recipes
Baking Illustrated
Restaurant Favorites at Home
The Best Vegetable Recipes
The Best Italian Classics
The Best American Classics
The Best Soups & Stews

The TV Companion Series:

Behind the Scenes with America's Test Kitchen
Test Kitchen Favorites
Cooking at Home with America's Test Kitchen
America's Test Kitchen Live!
Inside America's Test Kitchen
Here in America's Test Kitchen
The America's Test Kitchen Cookbook

834 Kitchen Quick Tips

To order any of our books, visit us at

http://www.cooksillustrated.com
or call 800-611-0759

Praise for the Best Recipe Series and Other *America's Test Kitchen* Titles

"Expert bakers and novices scared of baking's requisite exactitude can all learn something from this hefty, all-purpose home baking volume." Publishers Weekly on *The America's Test Kitchen Family Baking Book*

"An instant classic." Chicago Sun-Times on *America's Best Lost Recipes*

"This tome definitely raises the bar for all-in-one, basic, must-have cookbooks. . . . Kimball and his company have scored another hit." Portland Oregonian on *The America's Test Kitchen Family Cookbook*

"A foolproof, go-to resource for everyday cooking." Publishers Weekly on *The America's Test Kitchen Family Cookbook*

"A timesaving tome." The Chicago Tribune on *834 Kitchen Quick Tips*

"A moderate approach to lightening everyday dishes for the family." The Chicago Tribune on *The Best Light Recipe*

"Further proof that practice makes perfect, if not transcendent. . . . If an intermediate cook follows the directions exactly, the results will be better than takeout or Mom's." The New York Times on *The New Best Recipe*

"Exceptional renditions with thorough instruction . . ." Publishers Weekly on *Cooking at Home with America's Test Kitchen*

"Like a mini cooking school, the detailed instructions and illustrations ensure that even the most inexperienced cook can follow these recipes with success." Publishers Weekly on *Best American Side Dishes*

"Makes one-dish dinners a reality for average cooks, with honest ingredients and detailed make-ahead instructions." The New York Times on *The Best Cover & Bake Recipes*

"[The Best Meat Recipes] conquers every question one could have about all things meat." The San Francisco Chronicle on *The Best Meat Recipes*

"The best instructional book on baking this reviewer has seen." Library Journal (starred review) on *Baking Illustrated*

"A must-have for anyone into our nation's cooking traditions—and a good reference, too." Los Angeles Daily News on *The Best American Classics*

"If you've always wanted to make real Italian dishes as close to the Italian way as we can make them in America, here's a cookbook that shows you how." Pittsburgh Post-Gazette on *The Best Italian Classics*

America's
TEST KITCHEN

THE TV COMPANION COOKBOOK

2009

THE TV COMPANION COOKBOOK

2009

BY THE EDITORS AT
AMERICA'S TEST KITCHEN

ILLUSTRATIONS
John Burgoyne

PHOTOGRAPHY
Daniel J. van Ackere
Carl Tremblay

AMERICA'S TEST KITCHEN
BROOKLINE, MASSACHUSETTS

America's Test Kitchen
17 Station Street
Brookline, MA 02445

Library of Congress Cataloging-in-Publication Data
The Editors at America's Test Kitchen

America's Test Kitchen: The TV Companion Cookbook 2009
1st Edition

ISBN-13: 978-1-933615-35-6
ISBN-10: 1-933615-35-4
(hardcover): U.S. $34.95; Can. $37.95
1. Cooking. 1. Title
2008

Manufactured in the United States of America

10 9 8 7 6 5 4 3 2 1

Distributed by America's Test Kitchen,
17 Station Street, Brookline, MA 02445

Senior Editor: Lori Galvin
Associate Editors: Elizabeth Wray Emery, Kate Hartke
Test Cook: Megan Wycoff
Editorial Assistant: Elizabeth Pohm
Design Director: Amy Klee
Art Director: Greg Galvan
Designers: Matthew Warnick, Erica Lee
Photography: Daniel J. van Ackere, Carl Tremblay
Food Styling: Marie Piraino
Jacket Photographs: Christopher Churchill, Daniel J. van Ackere
Illustrations: John Burgoyne, Jay Layman
Production Director: Guy Rochford
Senior Production Manager: Jessica Lindheimer Quirk
Traffic and Project Manager: Alice Cummiskey
Imaging and Color Specialist: Andrew Mannone
Production and Imaging Specialist: Lauren Pettapiece
Copyeditor: Barbara Wood
Proofreader: Deborah Sosin
Indexer: Elizabeth Parson

CONTENTS

PREFACE

JUST LAST EVENING, I WAS DOWN IN THE BARN, standing in a horse stall looking out through the half-open Dutch door that leads into our lower pasture. Navajo, a horse we purchased from a riding stable up in the Adirondacks, was standing on the other side, eyeing me suspiciously. He has been at our place for about a year now and is starting to become more comfortable, but only gradually. So I held out a treat—an apple-flavored biscuit. He didn't move at first, but then shuffled his feet, moving his weight from side to side. He pretended to nibble at a hind foot and then got closer to my hand with his muzzle, near enough to breathe in the scent, to see if there was something he really wanted. Finally, he mustered the courage to get his mouth right up to the biscuit, but didn't bite at it. He just worried it a few times before using his tongue to lift it up into his mouth. By the third biscuit, he was friendlier and accepted a good scratch behind the ears.

Now this is a really long-winded way of saying that we are now on our ninth year of bringing you *America's Test Kitchen,* a show that is produced and filmed in our actual kitchens just outside of Boston. And, like our horse Navajo, you, the viewer, took a bit of time to get comfortable with our approach, our recipes, and our cooking advice.

We all know that there are a lot of cooking shows out there, a lot of flash and promise and, often, not a whole lot of substance. Our goal has always been to be both straightforward and eminently reliable in our advice and recipes. We think that a recipe ought to work the first time you make it. That is not, believe me, an easy promise to keep.

After all these years, we still surprise ourselves with what we don't know. We just learned how to make creamy tomato soup without the cream; which digital scale has a display that can be separated from the weighing platform (for ease of viewing); why you should brine your beans overnight for the best Tuscan Bean Stew; which beef broths are worth buying (most are not); why the traditional method for poaching salmon is a disaster (and how to do it right); that some hand whisks can take up to five minutes to whip cream and others only three minutes (yes, we timed it!); and why steaming sliced potatoes and rinsing them halfway through cooking makes fantastic mashed potatoes. These are only a few of the discoveries that we have made in the last year and that are included in this book.

For those of you who already know our show, thanks for coming back. It is always a pleasure to have you visit us through *America's Test Kitchen.* Newcomers, please give our recipes a try to see if we deliver on our promise of reliability. It is why we get out of bed in the morning!

Now, let me get back to our promise. We are not selling 20-minute recipes or fast and easy entertaining menus for eight that can be whipped together with minimal fuss. We think that you, our viewers, have both the intelligence and patience to take the time to do it right. There is something to know about good home cooking and that requires a bit of learning, a bit of time, and a bit of patience. That, of course, reminds me of a story.

President Hoover once remarked to Calvin Coolidge that he couldn't understand why his recovery programs had not yet produced results and why his critics were howling so loudly.

Coolidge replied, "You can't expect to see the calves running the field the day after you put the bull to the cows."

"No," replied Hoover, "But I would expect to see the cows contented."

Maybe none of us has either the patience of Coolidge or his sardonic wit, but we are willing to invest some time and effort to become good home cooks. It is a small investment that yields a terrific return, one that provides contentment not just for you, the cook, but also for anyone who shares your table. Overall, that sounds to me like a good long-term investment.

Christopher Kimball
Founder and editor, *Cook's Illustrated* and *Cook's Country*
Host, *America's Test Kitchen* and
Cook's Country from America's Test Kitchen

WELCOME TO AMERICA'S TEST KITCHEN

THIS BOOK HAS BEEN TESTED, WRITTEN, AND EDITED by the folks at America's Test Kitchen, a very real 2,500-square-foot kitchen located just outside of Boston. It is the home of *Cook's Illustrated* magazine and *Cook's Country* magazine and is the Monday-through-Friday destination for more than three dozen test cooks, editors, food scientists, tasters, and cookware specialists. Our mission is to test recipes over and over again until we understand how and why they work and until we arrive at the "best" version.

Our television show highlights the best recipes developed in the test kitchen during the past year—those recipes that our test kitchen staff makes at home time and time again. These recipes are accompanied by our most exhaustive equipment tests and our most interesting food tastings.

Christopher Kimball, the founder and editor of *Cook's Illustrated* magazine, is host of the show and asks the questions you might ask. It's the job of our chefs, Julia Collin Davison, Bridget Lancaster, Rebecca Hays, and J. Kenji Alt to demonstrate our recipes. The chefs show Chris what works and what doesn't, and they explain why. In the process, they discuss (and show us) the best as well as the worst examples from our development process: rubbery shrimp, tough biscuits, and fallen soufflés no one wanted to eat.

Adam Ried, our equipment guru, shares the highlights from our detailed testing process in equipment corner segments. He brings with him our favorite (and least favorite) gadgets and tools. He tells you which cutting board performed best in a dozen kitchen tests and shows how accurate measuring cups can produce better dishes.

Jack Bishop is our ingredient expert. He has Chris taste our favorite (and least favorite) brands of common food products—everything from hot salsa and bacon to Dijon mustard and dark chocolate. Chris may not always enjoy these exercises (black pepper and beef broth aren't always a whole lot of fun to taste), but he usually learns something as Jack explains what makes one brand superior to another.

Although there are just seven cooks and editors who appear on the television show, another 50 people worked to make the show a reality. Producer Melissa Baldino organized many aspects of filming to ensure that taping would run smoothly. Meg Ragland conducted all the historical recipe research. Guy Crosby researched the science behind the recipes. Along with the on-air crew, executive chefs Erin McMurrer and Keith Dresser planned and organized the 26 television episodes shot in May 2008 and ran the "back kitchen," where all the food that appeared on camera originated. Elizabeth Bomze organized the tasting and equipment segments.

During filming, chefs J. Kenji Alt, Kelley Baker, Matthew Herron, Suzannah McFerran, Paco Robert, Bryan Roof, Diane Unger, and intern Erwin Chuck were in the kitchen from early in the morning to late at night cooking all the food needed on set. Nadia Domeq was charged with making sure all the ingredients we needed were on hand. Kitchen assistants Maria Elena Delgado, Ena Gudiel, Ben Peskin, and Edward Tundidor also worked long hours. Chefs Lynn Clark, Charles Kelsey, Adelaide Parker, David Pazmiño, Yvonne

Ruperti, Cathy Wayne, and intern Jennifer Michalecko helped coordinate the efforts of the kitchen with the television set by readying props, equipment, and food. Meredith Smith led all tours of the test kitchen during filming.

The staff of A La Carte Communications turned our recipes, tastings, testings, and science experiments into a lively television show. Special thanks to executive producers Geoffrey Drummond and Nat Katzman; director and editor Herb Sevush; director of photography Jan Maliszewski.

We also appreciate the hard work of the video production team, including Stephen Hussar, Michael McEachern, Peter Dingle, Ken Fraser, Roger Macie, Gilles Morin, Brenda Coffey, Michael Andrus, Adam Ducharme, Aaron Frutman, Joseph Battista, and Stephanie Stender. Thanks also to Peter Tannenbaum, the second unit videographer.

We also would like to thank Hope Reed, who handles station relations, and the team at American Public Television that presents the show: Cynthia Fenneman, Chris Funkhauser, Judy Barlow, and Tom Davison. Thanks also for production support from DGA Productions, Boston, and Zebra Productions, New York.

Woodbridge by Robert Mondavi, DCS, Kohler, VIVA Towels, and Cooking.com helped underwrite the show and we thank them for their support. We also thank Demee Gambulos for handling underwriter relations and Deborah Broide for managing publicity. Fresh produce was supplied for the show by Olgo Russo at A. Russo & Sons of Watertown, Massachusetts. Meat was provided by Scott Brueggeman and Wayne J. Tumber of Brueggeman Prime Ltd. of Boston, Massachusetts. Fish was supplied by Ian Davison of Constitution Seafood of Boston, Massachusetts. Live plants and garden items for the show were furnished by Mark Cutler at Mahoney's Garden Center of Brighton, Massachusetts. Aprons for Christopher Kimball were made by Nicole Romano and staff aprons by Crooked Brook. All the props were designed and developed by Foam Props, Woburn, Massachusetts.

AMERICA'S TEST KITCHEN THE TV COMPANION COOKBOOK 2009

A high proportion of water to flour gives Pizza Bianca an exceptionally thick, chewy crust. And because the dough is so moist, there's no fussy rolling required. Simply place the dough on an oiled baking sheet and use your fingertips to press it from the center into the edges of the pan.

LUNCHTIME
specials

It's safe to say that the kid in all of us finds a bowl of rich, creamy tomato soup irresistible. Although the canned classic retains a certain charm, we wanted a lighter, fresher approach to this lunchtime favorite. Most versions of tomato soup include cream, not only for body, but also to round out the acidic flavor of the tomatoes. But we feel that cream tends to dull the flavor of the tomatoes. Thus, we made it our goal to turn out a fresh-flavored tomato soup with the same lush, creamy texture as the original—without the cream.

Tomato soup isn't the only lunchtime favorite for kids—and adults. Many of us in the test kitchen have been known to duck out for a slice of pizza around the noon hour—be it traditional Neapolitan or Chicago-style deep dish. So when we heard about Roman-style pizza—alas, not found in our neighborhood—we got busy in the kitchen to try and replicate it. This pizza, called *pizza bianca,* sports a crust that is crisp at the edges and soft and chewy in the middle and is traditionally topped with just olive oil and herbs, so that the wonderful flavor and texture of the crust can truly be appreciated. But the crust's remarkable texture is achieved through using a high proportion of water to flour and working with such a wet dough is no easy task. In addition to developing a workable method for preparing the dough, we also wanted to explore making the pizza with a modest amount of toppings. If we were going to eat pizza bianca for lunch, we'd need a heartier pie to hold us through the afternoon.

CREAMLESS CREAMY TOMATO SOUP

WHAT WE WANTED: Tomato soup can be thin and sharp. Adding cream—the usual stodgy solution—merely dulls it. We wanted to tame the tartness without losing flavor.

Tomato soup should have a bright, tomatoey taste balanced by the fruit's natural sweetness. But poor versions are the norm, featuring either an acidic, watery broth or an overdose of cream. Though cream is meant to tame tartness and lend body, we've found that it often mutes flavor. We wanted soup with rich tomato taste and a satisfying texture. Could we get there without the cream?

The first step in the process was to pass over fresh tomatoes for canned, which we find are almost always far better than your average supermarket tomato, boasting more consistently rich and concentrated flavor. We opted for whole tomatoes over diced or crushed for their bright tomato flavor. We then developed a simple working recipe, sautéing onions and garlic in butter, stirring in the tomatoes and a can of chicken broth, and then giving the whole thing a quick spin in the blender. The results were decent, but dull.

If cream subdues tomato flavor, could the milk solids in the butter be tamping it down as well? We substituted extra-virgin olive oil for the butter and found that the soup was brighter as a result. To compensate for the flavor the oil lost as it cooked, we drizzled a little more over the soup before it went into the blender. Most tasters also welcomed a couple of tablespoons of brandy.

Now that we had our flavor profile nailed down, we moved on to bigger problems: tartness and thin texture. Sugar is often used as a means to combat tartness. We preferred brown sugar to one-dimensional white sugar and corn syrup, but sugar could take us only so far—add enough to tone down tartness and the soup becomes unpalatably sweet.

We needed a thickener that would also help temper the acid. Flavor-dulling dairy ingredients were definitely out, but what about a starch? Cooking flour along with the onions to form a roux made for a thicker soup, but the texture turned slimy instead of creamy, and the flour did nothing for flavor. We scoured our cookbook library before finding inspiration in another tomato-based soup, gazpacho. At its most basic, this Spanish classic is made from tomatoes, olive oil, and garlic, along with a wholly unexpected element for thickening—bread. But gazpacho is served cold. Would bread work as a thickener for hot soup?

We tore several slices of sandwich bread into pieces and stirred them into the pot with the tomatoes and chicken broth as they simmered. When we processed the mixture in the blender, we ended up with bread chunks that swam in a sea of broth and resisted being sucked down into the blender's spinning blades. To cut back on the amount of liquid in the blender, we decided to try leaving out the broth until the very end. For our next batch of soup, we pureed the tomatoes with the aromatics and bread before returning the mixture to the pan and whisking in the broth. One taste and we knew we'd hit on just the right solution. Our tomato soup had the same velvety texture as the creamy kind, but with bright, fresh flavor. And, our soup contained a secret ingredient.

WHAT WE LEARNED: Choose canned tomatoes over fresh tomatoes—canned are simply more consistent in flavor than your average supermarket tomato. Whole tomatoes are preferred over diced or crushed for their concentrated flavor. To achieve a brighter, cleaner tomato flavor, cook the aromatics in extra-virgin olive oil instead of butter; and to combat the acid in the tomatoes, use full-flavored brown sugar. And for a soup with creamy body (but no cream), puree sandwich bread into the soup.

CREAMLESS CREAMY TOMATO SOUP

serves 6 to 8

If half of the soup fills your blender by more than two-thirds, process the soup in three batches. You can also use a handheld blender to process the soup directly in the pot. Serve this soup topped with croutons (recipe follows), if desired. For an even smoother soup, pass the pureed mixture through a fine-mesh strainer before stirring in the chicken broth in step 2.

¼	cup extra-virgin olive oil, plus more for drizzling
1	medium onion, chopped medium (about 1 cup)
3	medium garlic cloves, minced or pressed through a garlic press (about 1 tablespoon)
	Pinch red pepper flakes (optional)
1	bay leaf
2	(28-ounce) cans whole tomatoes
1	tablespoon brown sugar
3	large slices good-quality white sandwich bread, crusts removed, torn into 1-inch pieces
2	cups low-sodium chicken broth
2	tablespoons brandy (optional)
	Salt and ground black pepper
¼	cup chopped fresh chives

1. Heat 2 tablespoons of the oil in a Dutch oven over medium-high heat until shimmering, about 1 minute. Add the onion, garlic, red pepper flakes (if using), and bay leaf. Cook, stirring frequently, until the onion is translucent, 3 to 5 minutes. Stir in the tomatoes with their juice. Using a potato masher, mash until no pieces bigger than 2 inches remain. Stir in the sugar and bread; bring the soup to a boil. Reduce the heat to medium and cook, stirring occasionally, until the bread is completely saturated and starts to break down, about 5 minutes. Remove and discard the bay leaf.

2. Transfer half of the soup to a blender. Add 1 tablespoon more oil and process until the soup is smooth and creamy, 2 to 3 minutes. Transfer to a large bowl and repeat with the remaining soup and the remaining 1 tablespoon oil. Rinse out the Dutch oven and return the soup to the pot. Stir in the chicken broth and brandy (if using). Return the soup to a boil and season with salt and pepper to taste. Serve the soup in individual bowls, each portion sprinkled with pepper and chopped chives and drizzled with olive oil.

CROUTONS

makes about 1½ cups

3	large slices good-quality white sandwich bread, crusts removed, cut into ½-inch cubes (about 1½ cups)
1½	tablespoons olive oil
	Salt and ground black pepper

1. Adjust an oven rack to the upper-middle position and heat the oven to 400 degrees. Place the bread cubes in a medium bowl and drizzle with the olive oil. Toss well with a rubber spatula to combine. Season with salt and pepper to taste.

2. Spread the croutons in a single layer on a rimmed baking sheet or in a shallow baking dish. Bake the croutons, turning them over halfway through cooking, until golden brown and crisp, 8 to 10 minutes. After cooling, the croutons can be stored in an airtight container or a plastic bag for up to 3 days.

PIZZA BIANCA

WHAT WE WANTED: A replica of the Roman version of pizza—minimally adorned, with a crisp, extraordinarily chewy crust—and the option of adding toppings for a slice that makes a meal.

One of our test cooks returned from a trip to Rome, raving about a remarkable pizza he'd eaten, a pizza unlike anything he'd seen before. Glossed with just olive oil and flakes of salt, it looked, he said, more like focaccia than pizza. And after one bite into its crisp exterior and chewy, bubbly middle, he said he immediately forgot all about nomenclature—or even toppings. We had to try out this extraordinary-sounding pizza for ourselves.

We gathered together a few pizza bianca recipes and even spent a day working with Daniel Leader, owner of Bread Alone, a bakery in Boiceville, New York, who has spent time working in Italy to learn the craft of pizza bianca. We discovered it's made from the same basic ingredients as our familiar pizza crusts: flour, water, yeast, and salt (plus a little sugar). And the general method is no more difficult: Mix the ingredients, knead them until the dough forms (we use a standing mixer fitted with the dough hook), allow the dough to rise for a couple of hours, and you're good to go. So what's the difference?

As it turns out, there's a big one: Italians use significantly more water, creating a dough so wet it's impossible to roll out. Most pizza doughs don't exceed 60 percent hydration—meaning there are 6 ounces of water for every 10 ounces of flour—whereas pizza bianca dough ranges from 70 to over 100 percent. In Italy, pizza makers use a long-handled wooden "peel," or paddle, to deposit and stretch the gloppy dough across the far end of the oven.

There was no way we were going to try stretching out dough in our test kitchen ovens, no matter how good the resulting crust. But if we could simply press this very wet dough into a baking sheet—and add a few toppings to turn a snack into dinner—we might never go back to making any other kind of pizza crust again.

We were ready to get to work. We combined flour, water, yeast, sugar, and salt in a mixing bowl, opting for a hydration level around 90 percent. More water might make the dough sloshy and difficult to handle; any less, and we wouldn't get the bubbly interior we were hoping for. Though we knew a wet batter would require a lengthy kneading time (see "Pizza Water Works," page 9), we weren't prepared for the 30 minutes it took for the dough to form, even with the mixer on high. At high speed (a must for wet dough) we had to baby-sit the mixer to keep it from wobbling off the countertop. Unless we could cut down the kneading process to 5 to 10 minutes, as for other types of bread or pizza, this dough would be more hassle than it was worth.

We took a step back and thought about the mechanics of bread making. The goal in making any dough is to create gluten, the strong elastic network of cross-linked proteins that gives bread its crumb structure. Kneading facilitates gluten formation by bringing the protein molecules in flour into alignment so they can bind. But also, we'd learned from testing with our Almost No-Knead Bread (page 263) that a far different approach—a long rest—has the same exact effect. In this recipe, we let the dough sit for 8 hours, which produces so much gluten, it takes only a few seconds of kneading to create a loaf with a very open, chewy texture. We didn't want to wait around for a day just to make pizza, but what if we allowed the flour and water to sit for a modest interval—say, less than an hour? After experimenting, we found that a 20-minute rest was enough to reduce the kneading time to less than 10 minutes—a perfectly acceptable length of time to stand over a mixer.

Our next step was to transfer the dough to an oiled bowl and leave it to rise. Two hours later the dough had tripled in volume. Though sticky, the wet dough proved remarkably easy to shape. As we pressed it out over an 18 by

13-inch baking sheet, it showed little of the "spring-back" that can make firmer dough annoying to work with. And with no rolling out, we were avoiding the single biggest challenge of pizza making: getting the dough from the countertop onto the baking stone without tearing it and having to start over again.

Now ready to bake, we tried our typical protocol for pizza recipes: Let the dough rest 5 to 10 minutes, then place it on a preheated pizza stone positioned on a lower rack of a 500-degree oven. (We found that setting the baking sheet on a hot stone was a must for a crispy exterior.) But when we tried to remove the baked pizza, it stuck resolutely to the pan, leaving behind swaths of crust. The solution: We reduced the oven temperature to 450 degrees and baked the dough on the middle rack. The crust we pulled from the oven was golden and crisp on the outside, and chewy and flavorful on the inside—right in line with how our test kitchen colleague described the pizza he'd enjoyed in Italy.

Up to now we had been loyal to authentic versions, adorning our pizza with nothing more than salt, a handful of rosemary (added halfway through cooking to avoid burning), and a thin coat of olive oil brushed on at the end. As good as this was, we wanted a pizza we could serve as a meal. We settled on tomato sauce and mozzarella for a variation we knew would please even the pickiest eaters, and sausage for those who like a heartier pie. Adding these toppings halfway through baking was the key—spreading them over the raw dough at the beginning led to a gummy crust. Using a light hand was also essential, as too much of any one ingredient overpowers the flavor of the crust and detracts from its texture.

With the technique for dealing with wet dough perfected, and toppings successfully added, we had discovered how to adapt a classic Italian recipe for the home kitchen. This easy, all-purpose pizza crust is one we'll return to again and again.

WHAT WE LEARNED: For a pizza crust with crisp edges and a moist, chewy interior, dramatically increase the ratio of water to flour. Most American-style pizza doughs don't exceed 60 percent hydration (6 ounces of water for every 10 ounces of flour)—we aimed for 90 percent hydration, just as they do in Rome. To cut down the kneading time for the dough, let the dough rest before kneading it, which reduces the kneading time to just 10 minutes. Because the dough is too wet to roll out, shape it onto a baking sheet and then bake it on a hot pizza stone to encourage a crisp, browned crust. Use restraint with toppings to preserve the crust's subtle flavor and crisp, chewy texture.

PIZZA BIANCA

serves 6 to 8

Serve the pizza by itself as a snack, or with soup or salad as a light entrée. Once the dough has been placed in the oiled bowl, it can be transferred to the refrigerator and kept for up to 24 hours. Bring the dough to room temperature, 2 to 2½ hours, before proceeding with step 4 of the recipe. While kneading the dough on high speed, the mixer tends to wobble and walk on the countertop. Place a towel or shelf liner under the mixer and watch it at all times while mixing. Handle the dough with lightly oiled hands. Resist flouring your fingers or the dough might stick further. This recipe was developed using an 18 by 13-inch baking sheet. Smaller baking sheets can be used, but because the pizza will be thicker, baking times will be longer. If not using a pizza stone, increase the oven temperature to 500 degrees and set the rack to the lowest position; the cooking time might increase by 3 to 5 minutes.

3	cups (15 ounces) unbleached all-purpose flour
1⅔	cups (13½ ounces) water, room temperature
1¼	teaspoons table salt
1½	teaspoons instant or rapid-rise yeast
1¼	teaspoons sugar
5	tablespoons extra-virgin olive oil
1	teaspoon kosher salt
2	tablespoons whole fresh rosemary leaves

1. Mix the flour, water, and table salt in the bowl of a standing mixer fitted with the dough hook on low speed until no areas of dry flour remain, 3 to 4 minutes, occasionally scraping down the sides of the bowl. Turn off the mixer and let the dough rest 20 minutes.

2. Sprinkle the yeast and sugar over the dough. Knead on low speed until fully combined, 1 to 2 minutes, occasionally scraping down the sides of the bowl. Increase the mixer speed to high and knead until the dough is glossy and smooth and pulls away from the sides of the bowl, 6 to 10 minutes. (The dough will pull away from the sides only while the mixer is on. When the mixer is off, the dough will fall back to the sides.)

3. Using your fingers, coat a large bowl with 1 tablespoon of the oil, rubbing the excess oil from your fingers onto the blade of a rubber spatula. Using the oiled spatula, transfer the dough to the bowl and pour 1 tablespoon more oil over the top. Flip the dough over once so that it is well coated with the oil; cover tightly with plastic wrap. Let the dough rise at room temperature until nearly tripled in volume and large bubbles have formed, 2 to 2½ hours.

4. One hour before baking the pizza, adjust an oven rack to the middle position, place a pizza stone on the rack, and heat the oven to 450 degrees.

5. Coat a rimmed baking sheet with 2 tablespoons more oil. Using a rubber spatula, turn the dough out onto the baking sheet along with any oil in the bowl. Using your fingertips, press the dough out toward the edges of the pan, taking care not to tear it. (The dough will not fit snugly into corners. If the dough resists stretching, let it relax for 5 to 10 minutes before trying to stretch it again.) Let the dough rest in the pan until slightly bubbly, 5 to 10 minutes. Using a dinner fork, poke the surface of the dough 30 to 40 times and sprinkle with the kosher salt.

6. Bake until golden brown, 20 to 30 minutes, sprinkling the rosemary over the top and rotating the baking sheet halfway through baking. Using a metal spatula, transfer the pizza to a cutting board. Brush the dough lightly with the remaining 1 tablespoon oil. Slice and serve immediately.

TECHNIQUE:
Giving Shape to Pizza Bianca

Shaping the dough for pizza bianca couldn't be easier. Simply place the risen dough in the center of a large oiled baking sheet and, using your fingertips, press the dough from its middle toward the edges of the pan.

PIZZA BIANCA WITH TOMATOES AND MOZZARELLA

Empty a 28-ounce can crushed tomatoes into a fine-mesh strainer set over a medium bowl. Let sit 30 minutes, stirring 3 times to allow the juices to drain. Combine ¾ cup tomato solids, 1 tablespoon olive oil, and ⅛ teaspoon table salt. (Save the remaining solids and juice for another use.) Follow the recipe for Pizza Bianca, omitting the kosher salt and rosemary. In step 6, bake the pizza until spotty brown, 15 to 17 minutes. Remove the pizza from the oven, spread the tomato mixture evenly over the surface, and sprinkle with 6 ounces (1½ cups) shredded mozzarella cheese. Return the pizza to the oven and continue to bake until the cheese begins to brown in spots, 5 to 10 minutes longer.

PIZZA BIANCA WITH SAUSAGE AND FONTINA

Remove ¾ pound sweet Italian sausage from its casings. Cook the sausage in a large nonstick skillet over medium heat, breaking it into small pieces with a wooden spoon, until no longer pink, about 8 minutes. Transfer to a paper towel–lined plate and place in the refrigerator. Follow the recipe for Pizza Bianca with Tomatoes and Mozzarella, substituting 8 ounces shredded fontina cheese for the mozzarella and sprinkling the sausage over the pizza with the cheese.

SCIENCE DESK: Pizza Water Works

TO ACHIEVE ITS SUPREMELY CHEWY, BUBBLY TEXTURE, our pizza bianca recipe relies on very wet dough that has almost as much water as flour. But such a high proportion of water has implications for gluten formation. Gluten is the network of cross-linked proteins that gives bread its internal structure. Some extra water will facilitate the linking of proteins, but a lot will make it harder for the proteins to find

each other. Counteracting this requires one of two things: long and vigorous kneading or, on the other end of the spectrum, time. If water and flour are left to sit for hours, the proteins will align and bind on their own in a process called autolyse, without the baker ever having to lift a finger. For efficiency, we combined the two approaches, allowing the dough to rest 20 minutes before kneading it on high speed several minutes longer.

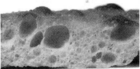

90% Hydration
More water, bubblier crust

60% Hydration
Less water, denser crust

EQUIPMENT CORNER: Digital Scales

AS HANDY AS THEY ARE, MEASURING CUPS WILL NEVER measure up to the accuracy of a digital scale. We've found that when measuring dry ingredients using a "dip and swipe" method, different cooks can be off by as much as 10 percent—a variance especially critical in baking, where measuring can mean the difference between a dense cake and a fluffy, tender crumb. To find the best scale for the job, we tested nine models, each measuring in 1-gram increments. As we placed 30-, 200-, and 500-gram lab weights on their surfaces—and moved them around to make sure readings were equal in every position—we found only negligible discrepancies (within 2 grams). We based our rankings, then, on how easy the scales are to use. Whether you choose a scale that measures in decimals (as the professionals use) or fractions (as most home recipes are written) is a matter of personal preference. We ranked scales most highly for roomy platforms (over 6 inches); at least 7-pound capacity; a large, clear readout display; and sensitive, accessible buttons. Our new favorite, the OXO Food Scale ($49.99), measures up all around.

Rating Digital Scales

WE TESTED NINE MODELS OF DIGITAL SCALES FOR ACCURACY AND EASE OF USE. BRANDS ARE LISTED IN ORDER OF preference. See www.americastestkitchen.com for updates to this testing.

HIGHLY RECOMMENDED
OXO Food Scale
$49.99; Capacity: II lb.; Measures in fractions
Exceptionally intuitive to use. The super-clear display offers an optional backlight and four easy-to-read buttons, and, unique to OXO, it can be pulled out from the large, removable (i.e., washable) platform when weighing bulky items.

RECOMMENDED
Polder Easy-Read Digital Kitchen Scale
$39.99; Capacity: 7 lb.; Measures in decimals
This scale boasts a smooth glass platform, easy-to-read buttons, and a jumbo readout display.

RECOMMENDED
Salter Aquatronic Glass Kitchen Scale
$59.95; Capacity: II lb.; Measures in fractions
Sleek and thin with a generous glass platform and four clearly marked buttons, this scale would need only a larger display to fight for first place.

RECOMMENDED
Soehnle 65055 Digital Scale
$29.75; Capacity: II lb.; Measures in decimals
Our previous favorite, this best-buy scale still impresses with its sexy design and recently slashed price, though its noncompact structure makes storage a challenge.

RECOMMENDED WITH RESERVATIONS
Soehnle Level 66200 Digital Scale
$34; Capacity: II lb.; Measures in decimals
This sibling to our former favorite scale made a disappointing comparison. Its large surface is a plus, but the display is tiny and the single button for all functions can be vexing.

RECOMMENDED WITH RESERVATIONS
Escali Pana Volume and Weight Scale
$64.95; Capacity: 6.6 lb.; Measures in both decimals and fractions
Measuring in both fractions and decimals is a definite plus, but the buttons on this relatively low-capacity, somewhat bulky scale felt a bit sticky and cheap.

RECOMMENDED WITH RESERVATIONS
American Weigh AMW-13 Digital/Postal Kitchen Scale
$29.95; Capacity: 13 lb.; Measures in decimals
Squarely compact and equipped with four clearly marked buttons, this scale had only one significant flaw: the irritating angle of its display window, which was impossible to read without crouching down.

RECOMMENDED WITH RESERVATIONS
My Weigh iBalance 5000 Digital Kitchen Scale
$46.90; Capacity: II lb.; Measures in decimals
Save for the too-small surface area, the clear decimal readings illuminated by a bright backlight and five super-clear buttons plus counting feature made this seem like a dream scale—until we went to load the four AAA batteries, which continuously popped out (on several models).

RECOMMENDED WITH RESERVATIONS
Terraillon Electronic Professional Digital Baker's Scale
$99.99; Capacity: 22 lb.; Measures in fractions
Its "baker's scale" capacity far exceeded that of the other models, but between the sticky buttons (including the vexingly tiny switch between grams and ounces on the underside), awkward frame, hefty price tag, and hesitation to turn on, we were less than impressed.

Julia and Chris discuss how brining the beans (soaking them overnight in salted water) for Hearty Tuscan Bean Stew helps them turn out creamy, tender, and intact, rather than mealy and broken.

SOUPS
CHAPTER 2
of the day

There is nothing as comforting as a bowl of really good homemade soup. But given the hectic pace of life today, a long-simmered soup like beef and vegetable seems out of reach. Building a rich beef stock takes a couple of hours—and shopping for the bones required to make the stock is no easy task, either. Even after the stock is done, it takes at least another hour to cook the meat and vegetables. But oh, how it's worth it. Our goal, therefore, would be to find a faster way to make this full-flavored soup. Maybe it wouldn't be as quick as the ultimate quick soup (canned), but it would taste so much better.

Tuscan bean soup is an Italian classic. Creamy, tender beans in a garlicky broth with tomatoes and greens—this is the soup you want on a cold winter's night. Our first goal was to make this soup more of a stew—a hearty one-pot meal that could stand on its own on the dinner table. Our second challenge would be working with dried beans, which can be finicky. Sure, we could use canned, but when the bean is the star of the dish, it's worth the extra effort; you simply can't coax buttery bean flavor from a can. The problem is that dried beans can turn tough—even after soaking—or they can explode into mushy bits during cooking. We needed to find a foolproof way to handle the beans so we could enjoy this satisfying stew all winter long.

QUICKER BEEF AND VEGETABLE SOUP

WHAT WE WANTED: Hearty beef and vegetable soup with old-fashioned flavor, in under an hour.

G iven enough meat, bones, and time, a great beef soup isn't all that hard to make. If you're willing to buy 6 pounds of beef shin meat and bones and invest 2½ hours, you can produce a fantastic stock (and a lot of leftover beef). Add another hour or so, and you have the ultimate beef soup. But we rarely have the time or energy to make this recipe.

When we want beef and vegetable soup in a hurry, we do what everyone else does—open a can of soup and complain about its lackluster flavor and mushy vegetables. But is this all-or-nothing approach really necessary? Could we collapse the two separate steps of making stock and then soup into one and develop bold beef flavor in just 60 minutes?

To get our bearings, we prepared several traditional recipes along with a handful of quick recipes. Every classic recipe yielded intense flavor, whereas the quick soups were uniformly disappointing and lacked any real beef flavor. Most used either cubes of "stew meat"—a butcher's catchall for any relatively chunky scraps of beef—or more tender cuts like strip steak or rib eye. Although stew meat contributed a pleasant beefy flavor, it was barely chewable after simmering for half an hour. The strip and rib eye, though more tender, tasted livery and had a chalky, dry texture. Our first and most important goal was to find a cut of meat that could give a quick beef and vegetable soup the same texture and flavor as one that cooked for hours.

After pulling out diagrams for beef cuts, we tried to find a cut of meat that would cook up to be fall-apart tender in a reasonable amount of time. We cooked through various cuts, chasing them around the chart as if it were a carousel. We discovered that those with a loose, open grain—including hanger steak, flank steak, sirloin tip steak (or flap meat),

and blade steak—had a shredded texture that fooled tasters into thinking we had cooked the meat for hours.

Of these four cuts, sirloin tip steaks offered the best balance of meaty flavor and tenderness. We just had to be careful how we cut the steaks. If the pieces of meat were cut too large, our soup seemed more like a stew. If we used too many small pieces, it resembled a watery chili. For six generous bowls of soup, we needed 1 pound of sirloin tip steaks cut into ½-inch pieces.

We had found a cut of beef that cooked quickly and had the right texture, but it didn't do much for the rest of the soup. We would have to start with store-bought broth and engage in some serious flavor doctoring. We tried reducing the broth to fortify its flavor, but when simmered down by half, it turned ultra-salty and made the soup so harsh that many tasters mistook it for canned. We were getting nowhere fast.

Several of the quick soup recipes we uncovered took an "everything but the kitchen sink" approach to the vegetables. Although these soups had flavor, it certainly wasn't beef flavor. We had better luck sticking to the basics: onions, carrots, and celery—safe, yes; exciting, not very. Then we remembered that many recipes for French onion soup rely on mountains of caramelized onions to up the meaty flavor of the broth. The liquid and sugars released by the onions leave a rich brown coating on the pan, contributing a depth of flavor that onions simply simmered in the broth can't attain. When we tested this idea, tasters praised the added complexity and sweetness, but we still had a long way to go before we were satisfied.

It was time to do some research into what constitutes beefy flavor. We discovered that beef flavor is accentuated by naturally occurring compounds called glutamates, which are found in numerous foods (see "In Search of Glutamates," page 17). Like salt, glutamates stimulate receptors on the tongue, making food taste richer and meatier. Mushrooms, it turns out, are high in glutamates and for that reason are often paired with (or even substituted for) beef in many dishes. Thinking this might help, we prepared soups with white button, portobello, cremini, and porcini mushrooms. Portobellos imparted an overly murky flavor, and earthy porcinis overwhelmed any beef flavor we had already developed. Utilitarian white buttons were OK but a bit bland. Cremini mushrooms were perfect, providing mushroom intensity without being obtrusive.

We wondered what other ingredients high in glutamates could do. Worcestershire sauce, Parmesan cheese rinds, and miso paste competed with the beefiness of the dish. Less-intense tomato paste and red wine boosted the soup's meaty notes, especially when we browned the tomato

paste with the meat and then deglazed the caramelized pan drippings with the red wine.

Though soy sauce is especially high in glutamates, we feared it might overpower the soup. But, to our surprise, it enhanced the beef flavor. We remembered, too, that soy sauce is a test kitchen favorite for quick marinades. Like a brine, the salt in soy sauce diffuses into the meat, allowing the individual muscle fibers to retain moisture while cooking. When we marinated the beef cubes with soy sauce for just 15 minutes, tasters commented on the improved flavor of the meat and also its tender texture.

We had now replicated the beef flavor of long-simmered soups but not the mouth-coating richness. This can be created only when collagen, the tough proteins in the meat and bones, breaks down into gelatin. Could we cheat and just add powdered gelatin instead? A tablespoon of gelatin softened in cold water and stirred into the finished soup provided the viscosity of traditional broths. This was an unlikely finish to a recipe that can stand up to soups that take hours to cook.

WHAT WE LEARNED: Using a cut of meat with great beefy flavor and a texture that will cook up tender in a reasonable amount of time is key. Sirloin tip steak is preferred over all other cuts—when the meat is shredded, its tenderness makes it seem as if it has been cooking for hours, and its meaty flavor imparts richness to the soup. In place of labor-intensive homemade beef broth, doctor store-bought beef broth with aromatics. To further boost the flavor of the beef, add browned chopped onions and ingredients like cremini mushrooms, tomato paste, soy sauce, and red wine (these ingredients are rich in glutamates, a naturally occurring compound that accentuates the meat's hearty flavor). And to mimic the rich body of a homemade meat stock (made rich through the gelatin released through the meat bones' collagen during the long simmering process), add a little gelatin dissolved in water straight to the soup.

BEEF AND VEGETABLE SOUP

serves 6

Choose whole sirloin tip steaks over ones that have been cut into small pieces for stir-fries. If sirloin tip steaks are unavailable, substitute blade or flank steak, removing any hard gristle or excess fat. Button mushrooms can be used in place of the cremini mushrooms, with some trade-off in flavor. If you like, add 1 cup frozen peas, frozen corn, or frozen cut green beans during the last 5 minutes of cooking. For a heartier soup, add 10 ounces red-skinned potatoes, cut into ½-inch pieces (2 cups), during the last 15 minutes of cooking.

1 pound sirloin tip steaks, trimmed of excess fat and cut into ½-inch pieces (see note)
2 tablespoons soy sauce
1 teaspoon vegetable oil
1 pound cremini mushrooms, stems trimmed, caps wiped clean and quartered (see note)
1 large onion, chopped medium (about 1½ cups)
2 tablespoons tomato paste
1 medium garlic clove, minced or pressed through a garlic press (about 1 teaspoon)

½ cup red wine
4 cups beef broth
1¾ cups low-sodium chicken broth
4 medium carrots, peeled and cut into ½-inch pieces (about 2 cups)
2 medium celery ribs, cut into ½-inch pieces (about ¾ cup)
1 bay leaf
1 tablespoon unflavored powdered gelatin
½ cup cold water
2 tablespoons minced fresh parsley leaves
   Salt and ground black pepper

1. Combine the beef and soy sauce in a medium bowl; set aside for 15 minutes.

2. Heat the oil in a Dutch oven over medium-high heat until just smoking. Add the mushrooms and onion; cook, stirring frequently, until the onion pieces are brown and dark bits form on the pan bottom, 8 to 12 minutes. Transfer the vegetables to a bowl.

TECHNIQUE: Building a Flavor Base

Before adding the beef to the pot, create a flavor base by browning chopped onions and cremini mushrooms. Stir frequently until the onions are really brown and dark bits form on the pan bottom. Don't shortcut this process or you will rob your soup of flavor.

GETTING IT RIGHT:
A Tale of Two Meats

We tested nearly a dozen cuts of beef before settling on sirloin tip steaks as the best choice for our quick soup. Texture was a deciding factor.

Too Dense

Tender cuts such as strip steak and rib eye become tough, livery, and chalky when simmered in soup.

Loose and Tender

Cuts with a loose structure, such as sirloin tip steaks, give the impression that the meat has cooked for hours.

GETTING IT RIGHT: Building Meaty Flavor Quickly

These four glutamate-rich ingredients boosted meaty flavors in our quick soup.

Mushrooms

Sautéed cremini mushrooms begin to build flavor.

Tomato Paste

Thick tomato paste caramelizes in the pot to create more flavor.

Soy Sauce

Strips of beef are marinated in soy sauce before being browned.

Red Wine

Red wine helps loosen flavorful browned bits from the pan bottom.

---

3. Add the beef and cook, stirring occasionally, until the liquid evaporates and the meat starts to brown, 6 to 10 minutes. Add the tomato paste and garlic; cook, stirring constantly, until aromatic, about 30 seconds. Add the red wine, scraping the bottom of the pot with a wooden spoon to loosen any browned bits, and cook until syrupy, 1 to 2 minutes.

4. Add the beef broth, chicken broth, carrots, celery, bay leaf, and browned mushrooms and onion; bring to a boil. Reduce the heat to low, cover, and simmer until the vegetables and meat are tender, 25 to 30 minutes. While the soup is simmering, sprinkle the gelatin over the cold water and let stand.

5. When the soup is finished, turn off the heat. Remove and discard the bay leaf. Add the gelatin mixture and stir until completely dissolved. Stir in the parsley, season with salt and pepper to taste, and serve.

SCIENCE DESK: In Search of Glutamates

IN GRADE SCHOOL WE ALL LEARNED THAT WE experience four primary taste sensations: salty, sweet, bitter, and sour. But what makes savory foods taste meaty? Japanese physics professor Kidunae Ikeda answered this question in 1909 when he extracted a white compound from the giant sea kelp used to give Japanese broths a savory and meaty flavor, even when meat is absent. This substance, called glutamate, has been found to stimulate the tongue's taste receptors, just like salt and sugar. Ikeda named the resulting sensation *umami,* which translates as "deliciousness" and "savory." The American cook interprets this as "full," "meaty," and "robust." Naturally occurring glutamates are found in a wide variety of foods, some of which we used in our Beef and Vegetable Soup.

GLUTAMATES IN COMMON FOODS

This scale shows the milligrams of glutamates per 100 grams (3½ ounces).

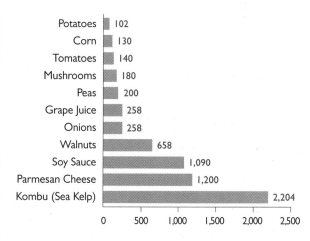

Food	Glutamates (mg per 100 g)
Potatoes	102
Corn	130
Tomatoes	140
Mushrooms	180
Peas	200
Grape Juice	258
Onions	258
Walnuts	658
Soy Sauce	1,090
Parmesan Cheese	1,200
Kombu (Sea Kelp)	2,204

HEARTY TUSCAN BEAN STEW

WHAT WE WANTED: A hearty version of classic Tuscan bean soup with creamy, buttery beans and chunks of vegetables, for a deeply flavorful one-pot meal.

The people of Tuscany are known as *mangiafagioli,* or "bean eaters," for the prominent role beans play in their cuisine. Cannellini (white kidney beans) are the region's most famous legume, and Tuscan cooks go to great extremes to ensure that these beans are worthy of star status. Simmering the cannellini in rainwater to produce a creamy, almost buttery texture is not uncommon. And putting the beans in an empty wine bottle to slow-cook overnight in a fire's dying embers is not unheard of.

When we set out to make a heartier stew version of the region's classic white bean soup, we wanted our cannellini to be as memorable as any you would find in Tuscany. Collecting rainwater and cooking in a fireplace would be one way to go about it—but we hoped to use a more practical approach.

The first task was to sort through all the contradictory advice given for dried-bean cookery. We began with the most hotly contested issue: how long to soak beans before cooking. Some recipes swear that a lengthy soak leads to beans with a more tender, uniform texture. Others insist that a quick soak—an hour-long rest off the stove covered with just-boiled water—is best. In the past, our recipes have maintained that no soak at all can be the way to go.

To judge for ourselves, we cooked up batches of beans using all three approaches. To our surprise, we found relatively minor differences. The biggest difference was in the cooking time: The no-soak beans took 45 minutes longer to soften fully than the beans soaked by the other two methods. But we were seeking perfection. And since the beans soaked overnight were, in fact, the most tender and evenly cooked of the bunch and had the least number of exploded beans, that's the method we settled on.

But while the beans' interiors were creamy, their skins remained tough, and overall they were not yet what we imagined a Tuscan cook would be proud to serve. Like length of soaking, when to add salt is another much-debated topic in bean cookery. Was there something to investigate here that could help us cook up perfect beans?

The conventional wisdom is that salt added to beans at the beginning of cooking will prevent them from ever fully softening. Paradoxically, other advice maintains that salting beans too early can create a mushy texture. When we added salt to a batch of beans at the outset of cooking, we found it made some of the beans mealy. We checked with our science editor and learned that the salt effect may be a matter of semantics. As beans cook, their starch granules swell with water, softening to a creamy texture and eventually bursting. The presence of salt in the cooking water causes the starch

granules to swell less, so that fewer reach the point of bursting. The result: beans that have a lot of starch granules still intact. To us, the texture of such beans is mealy; others may call the same effect gritty.

Though the texture of the beans was now inferior, their skins were exactly what we wanted: soft and pliable. Was there a different way to use salt to get the same effect? Our thoughts turned to brining, which we use in the test kitchen to help meat trap water and remain moist during cooking. Over the years, we've brined everything from poultry and pork to beef and even shrimp. Why not beans? Back in the test kitchen, we made a brine by dissolving a few tablespoons of salt in water and left the beans to soak overnight in the solution. The next day, we rinsed the beans thoroughly before proceeding with the recipe. Our experiment was a success: The cannellini now boasted tender, almost imperceptible skins with interiors that were buttery soft. Why the change? When beans are soaked in salted water, rather than being cooked in it, not as much salt enters the beans. Its impact is confined mainly to the skins, where sodium ions interact with the cells to create a softer texture (see "Brining Beans," page 22).

Although tasters were impressed with this technique, we knew that no Tuscan would stand for the number of exploded beans in the pot. Usually the culprit is an over-vigorous bubbling of cooking liquid, which disturbs the beans and causes them to blow out and disintegrate. We would need to simmer the beans very gently—with no perceptible bubbling and no stirring. Thinking back to the Tuscan technique of cooking beans overnight in a dying fire, we wondered if we might simply try cooking our beans in a 250-degree oven. In our next test, we brought the beans and water to a simmer on the stovetop, then covered the pot and placed it in the oven. This method required a little more time, but it worked beautifully, producing perfectly cooked beans that stayed intact.

With tender, creamy beans in our pot, it was time to work on the stew's other flavors. Salt-cured Italian bacon, or pancetta, is traditional in Tuscan white bean stew, lending depth and flavor. We still needed a few more ingredients to transform the dish into a one-pot meal. We settled on chewy, earthy-tasting kale, another Tuscan favorite, along with canned diced tomatoes, carrots, celery, onion, and lots of garlic. For extra richness, we also replaced some of the water in the stew with chicken broth (low-sodium, of course, to mitigate any impact on the beans).

We sautéed all the vegetables (except the kale and tomatoes) with the pancetta, added the beans and water, and placed the stew in the oven. The acid in tomatoes can toughen beans, so we waited until the beans were sufficiently softened, about 45 minutes, before adding the tomatoes to the pot, along with the kale. The final touch: a sprig of rosemary, steeped in the stew just before serving, which infused the broth with a delicate herbal aroma.

Borrowing from a classic Tuscan dish called *ribollita*—leftover bean soup thickened with bread—we made our stew even more substantial by serving it on top of slabs of toasted country bread. Drizzled with fruity extra-virgin olive oil, the stew was pure comfort food. And we hadn't even needed to collect rainwater or bank a fire to make it.

WHAT WE LEARNED: To ensure creamy beans with barely perceptible skins, brine the beans (soak the beans in salt water) overnight and then rinse before cooking. The conventional approach of soaking them in plain water and then cooking them in salted water softens the skins but also penetrates the interior, which turns the beans mealy. Rather than simmering the beans on the stove (the conventional approach), cook the beans in a 250-degree oven; this gentler method ensures the beans will cook through and remain intact. To complete the stew, add other traditional Tuscan flavors, including tomatoes, pancetta, kale, lots of garlic, and a sprig of rosemary. Add the tomatoes to the beans partway through the cooking process—if added early on, their acid will interfere with the beans' softening process. And to make this stew even heartier, serve it over a thick slice of toasted country bread, and don't forget to drizzle the stew with extra-virgin olive oil for an extra hit of Tuscan flavor.

HEARTY TUSCAN BEAN STEW

serves 8

We prefer the creamier texture of beans soaked overnight for this recipe. If you're short on time, quick-soak them: Place the rinsed beans in a large heat-resistant bowl. Bring 2 quarts water and 3 tablespoons salt to a boil. Pour the water over the beans and let them sit for 1 hour. Drain and rinse the beans well before proceeding with step 2. If pancetta is unavailable, substitute 4 ounces bacon (about 4 slices). For a more substantial dish, serve the stew over toasted bread.

Salt
1 pound (about 2 cups) dried cannellini beans, picked over and rinsed
1 tablespoon extra-virgin olive oil, plus extra for drizzling
6 ounces pancetta, cut into ¼-inch pieces (see note)
1 large onion, chopped medium (about 1½ cups)
2 medium celery ribs, cut into ½-inch pieces (about ¾ cup)
2 medium carrots, peeled and cut into ½-inch pieces (about 1 cup)
8 medium garlic cloves, peeled and crushed
4 cups low-sodium chicken broth
3 cups water
2 bay leaves
1 bunch kale or collard greens (about 1 pound), stems trimmed and leaves chopped into 1-inch pieces (about 8 cups loosely packed)
1 (14.5-ounce) can diced tomatoes, drained and rinsed
1 sprig fresh rosemary
Ground black pepper
8 slices country white bread, each 1¼ inches thick, broiled until golden brown on both sides and rubbed with a garlic clove (optional)

1. Dissolve 3 tablespoons salt in 4 quarts cold water in a large bowl or container. Add the beans and soak at room temperature for at least 8 hours and up to 24 hours. Drain the beans and rinse well.

2. Adjust an oven rack to the lower-middle position and heat the oven to 250 degrees. Heat the oil and pancetta in a large Dutch oven over medium heat. Cook, stirring occasionally, until the pancetta is lightly browned and the fat has rendered, 6 to 10 minutes. Add the onion, celery, and carrots. Cook, stirring occasionally, until the vegetables are softened and lightly browned, 10 to 16 minutes. Stir in the garlic and cook until fragrant, about 1 minute. Stir in the broth, water, bay leaves, and soaked beans. Increase the heat to high and bring the mixture to a simmer. Cover the pot, transfer it to the oven, and cook until the beans are almost tender (the very center of the beans will still be firm), 45 minutes to 1 hour.

3. Remove the pot from the oven and stir in the greens and tomatoes. Return the pot to the oven and continue to cook until the beans and greens are fully tender, 30 to 40 minutes longer.

GETTING IT RIGHT:
A Gentle Simmer Is Best
The bubbling action of stew simmered on the stovetop caused our beans to fall apart. Cooking the beans at a near-simmer in a covered pot in a 250-degree oven kept them intact.

Simmered on the Stovetop   **Near-Simmer in the Oven**

GETTING IT RIGHT:
Keys to Tender, Flavorful Beans

1. Saltwater Soak: Soaking the beans in salt water overnight helps them cook up creamy, with tender skins.

2. Low-Temperature Oven: Cooking the beans at a near-simmer in a 250-degree oven leads to fewer exploded beans in the finished stew.

3. Wait to Add Tomatoes: The acid in tomatoes can interfere with the beans' tender texture. Add them toward the end of cooking, after the beans have already softened.

4. Remove the pot from the oven and submerge the rosemary sprig in the stew. Cover and let stand 15 minutes. Discard the bay leaves and rosemary sprig and season the stew with salt and pepper to taste. If desired, use the back of a spoon to press some beans against the side of the pot to thicken the stew. Serve over the toasted bread, if desired, and drizzle with olive oil.

VARIATIONS
HEARTY TUSCAN BEAN STEW WITH SAUSAGE AND CABBAGE
This variation contains much more meat and is made with crinkly Savoy cabbage.

Follow the recipe for Hearty Tuscan Bean Stew, substituting 1½ pounds sweet Italian sausage, casings removed, for the pancetta; ½ medium head Savoy cabbage, cut into 1-inch pieces, for the kale; and 1 sprig fresh oregano for the rosemary. Cook the sausage in the oil in step 2, breaking the meat into small pieces with a wooden spoon, until no longer pink, about 8 minutes. Transfer the sausage to a paper towel–lined plate and place in the refrigerator. Proceed with the recipe as directed, stirring the sausage and cabbage into the stew along with the tomatoes in step 3.

VEGETARIAN HEARTY TUSCAN BEAN STEW
Follow the recipe for Hearty Tuscan Bean Stew, omitting the pancetta, substituting 3 cups vegetable broth for the chicken broth, and increasing the amount of water to 4½ cups. Combine ½ ounce dried porcini mushrooms with ½ cup of the water in a small microwave-safe bowl and cover with plastic wrap. Cut several steam vents in the plastic with a paring knife and microwave on high power, 30 seconds. Let stand until the mushrooms soften, about 5 minutes. Lift the mushrooms from the liquid with a fork and mince. Strain the liquid through a fine-mesh strainer lined with paper towels into a medium bowl. Stir in the mushrooms and reserved liquid with the broth in step 2.

QUICK HEARTY TUSCAN BEAN STEW
To speed up this recipe, we used canned beans and cooked the stew completely on the stovetop.

Follow the recipe for Hearty Tuscan Bean Stew, replacing the dried cannellini beans with 4 (15-ounce) cans cannellini beans, drained and rinsed well. Skip step 1 and omit the oven instructions from the recipe. Reduce the amount of chicken broth to 3 cups and the water amount to 2 cups.

SCIENCE DESK: Brining Beans

WHY DOES SOAKING DRIED BEANS IN SALTED WATER make them cook up with softer skins? It has to do with how the sodium ions in salt interact with the cells of the bean skins. As the beans soak, the sodium ions replace some of the calcium and magnesium ions in the skins. Because sodium ions are weaker than mineral ions, they allow more water to penetrate into the skins, leading to a softer texture. During soaking, the sodium ions will filter only partway into the beans, so their greatest effect is on the cells in the outermost part of the beans.

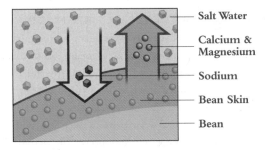

- Salt Water
- Calcium & Magnesium
- Sodium
- Bean Skin
- Bean

EQUIPMENT CORNER:
Deluxe Liquid Measuring Cup

TO USE A LIQUID MEASURING CUP, YOU TYPICALLY SET it on a level surface, pour in the ingredient, and crouch down to see if the liquid meets the line at eye level. Then you adjust. And readjust. To streamline this process, Cuisipro introduced a cup that can be read from above. The clear plastic measure, available in 2- and 4-cup sizes ($8.95 and $11.95), is dishwasher- and microwave-safe and features a removable clip fitted with a magnetized, dual-sided red plastic marker. When you slide the outer marker to the desired measurement line, the inner tab moves with it. Then

you fill to the level of the inside marker. We measured and weighed 1 cup of water to test for accuracy, then compared the results with our favorite Pyrex 2-cup glass measure. The Cuisipro, read from a standing position, measured even more accurately than the Pyrex, and we like its durability and easy-to-read markings.

THE BEST LIQUID MEASURING CUP
For a plastic measuring cup that can be read from a standing position, try the Cuisipro Deluxe Liquid Measuring Cup.

TASTING LAB: Beef Broths

WHEN WE SURVEYED THE BEEF BROTH FIELD IN 1998, tasters found every brand so dreadful that we all but banished supermarket beef broth from the test kitchen. The problem boiled down to an appalling lack of beef flavor. Lots of salt, plenty of vegetal flavors, a few metallic off-notes—but hardly anything that said *beef* beyond the brownish hue. When we learned that the U.S. Department of Agriculture requires only 1 part beef to every 135 parts water, we weren't surprised that most products came up short. (That translates to less than an ounce of beef for each gallon of water.)

Since our original tasting of beef broths, an impressive collection of new products has hit the supermarket shelves, so we decided to take another taste. We were especially intrigued by the increased availability of beef "bases," stock concentrates (just add water) that were once used almost exclusively by restaurants. Could any of these make us reconsider our boycott of beef broth?

Tasters sipped 12 beef broths—seven liquid broths and five made from concentrated bases—simply heated and served straight up. The top seven brands moved on to a full battery of tastings: plain (again), regular strength in a simple beef soup, and reduced in an all-purpose gravy.

The good news first: Some of these broths didn't taste half-bad! Even better, a few broths actually tasted like beef. Hints of mushroom, onion, other vegetables, and even chicken were still more common, but two brands elicited consistent praise for assertive beefiness.

So what makes a better beef broth? Our hopes of finding a clear pattern based on product type (that is, liquid broths versus concentrated bases) were quickly dashed after the final results were tallied. What about the presence of beef itself? Foiled again. Virtually every product in the lineup included some form of beef near the top of the ingredient list, and every manufacturer we contacted was unwilling to provide additional details. To get around this roadblock, we sent samples to an independent lab to be analyzed for protein content—but to no avail.

Frustrated, we canvassed industry experts to shed light on the beefy/not-so-beefy divide. The consensus was that it would be cost-prohibitive for broth makers to stray beyond the USDA's minimum beef-to-water ratio. Given that meager amount, manufacturers must rely on the magic of flavor chemistry to avoid a completely tasteless brew, which explains the blandness of the one beef broth that opted for the all-natural route.

In our lineup, every broth contained a generous amount of the most common additive—salt. Most contained some form of sugar. So far, so familiar. It was when we looked more closely at the less familiar ingredients that we stumbled upon our most important clues—namely, hydrolyzed vegetable protein and autolyzed yeast extract. Many sources we consulted lumped these additives together simply as "flavor enhancers," but more diligent digging revealed that they work quite differently.

Hydrolyzed vegetable protein (made by altering soybean, corn, or other vegetable molecules through a chemical

reaction, hydrolysis) merely adds flavor complexity, sort of like adding spices or salt. By contrast, autolyzed yeast extract (made by allowing yeast enzymes to feed on carefully chosen sugars and proteins until they release flavor-enhancing compounds) works like MSG (monosodium glutamate). Rather than contributing additional flavors, yeast extract amplifies flavors already present, especially savory and meaty ones. When yeast extract is included in the mix, that USDA

recipe of just 1 part beef to 135 parts water can taste like 20 parts beef instead.

Suddenly, the pieces were falling into place. As we scanned the ingredient lists of our beef broths, we spotted a definite pattern. Many of the products contained yeast extract, but they differed markedly in where it fell in the mix. In our top four brands, yeast extract was placed second or third (just after beef or salt). Moving down the ranks, the placement of yeast extract began to fall dramatically. What's more, our top five brands included no hydrolyzed vegetable protein (which can produce "metallic" off-tastes). The rest of the brands included multiple forms of hydrolyzed vegetable protein—and a few of them were indeed faulted for metallic off-notes. If yeast extract offers such a clear advantage in terms of flavor, why wouldn't all beef broth manufacturers opt to include it in the mix? Quite simply: cost. Yeast extracts are far more expensive than hydrolyzed vegetable proteins, in large part because the technology is so much newer.

So which broth to stock? Based on our tests, just note the first few ingredients listed on the label. We found the winning combination to be beef plus a flavor amplifier—in the form of yeast extract—near the top of the list.

Rating Beef Broths

TWENTY-FOUR MEMBERS OF THE AMERICA'S TEST KITCHEN STAFF TASTED SEVEN BRANDS OF BEEF BROTH AND reconstituted beef broth made from concentrated bases plain, in a simple beef soup (in both cases with the sodium levels adjusted to parity), and cooked in a simple gravy reduction (with sodium levels left as is). Brands are listed in order of preference. Sodium levels given are per 1-cup serving, based on package information. See www.americastestkitchen.com for updates to this tasting.

RECOMMENDED
Redi-Base Beef Base
$5.95 for 8 ounces (makes 2½ gallons);
Sodium: 690 mg

Tasters agreed on the presence of a "deep, dark, and hearty" character in the soup. Though many found the gravy salty, they also picked up a distinct beefiness, roasted flavor, and notes of onion and mushroom.

RECOMMENDED
Pacific Beef Broth
$2.69 for 32 fluid ounces; Sodium: 570 mg

In both the soup and the gravy, tasters found "toasty" or roasted notes, though the gravy was considered mild and in need of extra salt. But this was one of the rare products that tasted truly beefy.

RECOMMENDED WITH RESERVATIONS
Swanson Lower Sodium Beef Broth
$1.19 for 14 fluid ounces; Sodium: 440 mg

"Cardboard comes to mind," declared one taster, who then joined the nearly unanimous cry to "please pass the salt." Even the salt-corrected soup struck numerous tasters as "nondescript." At least there were no off-flavors.

NOT RECOMMENDED
Savory Basics Beef Flavor Stock Concentrate
$5.95 for 6 ounces (makes 1 gallon); Sodium:
570 mg

From "pallid" to "plain Jane," both the gravy and the soup were overwhelmingly decried as too light in color and too mild in flavor. One detractor groaned "not worthy of the name gravy," and many likened the flavor to that of chicken broth.

NOT RECOMMENDED
Orrington Farms Gourmet Beef Soup Base and Food Seasoning
$4.17 for 8 ounces (makes 2.8 gallons); Sodium: 570 mg

Detecting dried herbs and mushrooms, several tasters remarked that the bland gravy belonged on a TV dinner or grade-school hot lunch tray. "Archetypal cafeteria gravy," said one panelist. Others complained of metallic and "musty, stale" aftertastes.

NOT RECOMMENDED
Superior Touch Better Than Bouillon Beef Base
$4.99 for 8 ounces (makes 2.4 gallons); Sodium: 730 mg

Our 1998 "winner" suffered in the rankings this time around, thanks to stiff competition from the beefier newbies. In the gravy, tasters picked up on mushrooms, soy, and salt. In the soup, most tasters couldn't get past vegetal, artificial, and other off-flavors.

NOT RECOMMENDED
College Inn Fat Free & Lower Sodium Beef Broth
$0.99 for 14.5 fluid ounces; Sodium: 450 mg

This gravy was characterized as bland and "thin" by most tasters, several of whom also picked up distinct artificial flavor notes. Referring to plasticky and metallic aftertastes, one panelist griped that it "tastes like the can it came in."

EVEN LESS RECOMMENDED: In a preliminary round, tasters eliminated More Than Gourmet Glace de Viande Gold (base), Aromont Demi Glace Beef Stock (base), Bear Creek Beef Base (base), Campbell's Beef Consommé (liquid), and Health Valley Organic Beef Flavored Broth (liquid) from the final lineup. In general, tasters downgraded these brands for unpleasant aromas and bland, sour, winey, and plasticky flavors.

Because juices and textures vary among canned tomato products (whole, diced, and crushed), no single type fits all recipes. For our rich, thick Simple Italian-Style Meat Sauce, a combination of canned diced and canned crushed tomatoes works best. And for smooth, velvety Creamy Tomato Sauce, we reach for canned crushed tomatoes alone (they're easily pureed in a food processor).

PERFECTING
CHAPTER 3
pasta sauces

Real, old-fashioned tomato sauce seems to be an endangered species. Most of us simply don't have the time to keep vigil over bubbling pots of sauce for hours on end, or the patience required to prepare a well-rounded, flavorful pot of sauce. We turned our attention to two tomato sauces—Italian meat sauce and creamy tomato sauce—to see if we could somehow streamline their preparation and cooking times, without compromising their flavor.

For Italian meat sauce, hours of simmering aren't just for show. Most meat sauces require a long simmer to not only mellow and deepen the sauce's flavor, but to tenderize the meat as well. In many "fast" meat sauces, the meat turns out dry and crumbly or, even worse, rubbery. Without time on our side, we'd need to look for other ways to tenderize the meat and draw out its rich flavor.

Creamy tomato sauces always seem to be a gamble. Either the flavor is off—they taste acidic or too sweet—or the richness factor is out of whack. It's no wonder; each of the two main components—tomatoes and cream—has its own distinctive character. And though tomatoes have a vibrant flavor on their own, that flavor can be blunted when cream comes into the picture. With this issue in mind, we set out to develop a full-flavored tomato sauce that's accented, not overwhelmed, by cream.

SIMPLE ITALIAN-STYLE MEAT SAUCE

WHAT WE WANTED: A quick method for producing a thick, rich Italian meat sauce with all the lush texture and depth of flavor of a sauce that has simmered for hours.

In Italy, cooking a meaty pasta sauce is an all-day affair. Whether using ground meat for a *ragù alla Bolognese* or chunks of meat for a rustic sauce, one thing is for sure: These sauces slowly simmer for three or four hours—or even longer. This long simmer develops concentrated flavor and, more important, breaks down the meat, giving it a soft, lush texture.

In America, "Italian meat sauce" has typically come to mean a shortcut version in which ground beef, onions, garlic, and canned tomatoes are thrown together in a pot and cooked for half an hour. Although such sauces may be quick, their lackluster flavor and rubbery meat bear no resemblance to their Italian cousins. But the trouble is, when we crave pasta with meat sauce, we don't always have hours to spend on a Bolognese. Could we develop a meat sauce to make on a weeknight that tasted like it had been simmering for, if not all day, at least a good portion of it?

Our search started with analyzing Bolognese recipes, and we discovered right away that in the best ones the meat isn't browned. Instead, they call for cooking the ground meat until it loses its raw color, then adding the liquid ingredients one by one, slowly reducing each and building flavor before adding the next. One of the first liquids in the pot is usually some form of dairy, a Bolognese sauce's signature ingredient that imparts a sweet creaminess to the dish. In most American meat sauces, on the other hand, the beef is browned first—a step that adds flavor but toughens the meat. These recipes also skip the dairy in favor of tomato sauce, which doesn't provide the milk fat or the same layers of complex flavor.

Would eliminating the browning step and adding milk work better? We headed to the test kitchen to find out. After sautéing onion and garlic, we stirred in a pound of ground beef, breaking it up with a wooden spoon. As soon as it started to lose its raw color, we immediately added ½ cup of milk along with the tomatoes, and then simmered the sauce for 30 minutes or so. The results were disappointing: Some of the meat was tender and moist, but most of it was tough and mealy. And despite the milk, the sauce lacked flavor overall. If anything, without sufficient time to reduce, the milk actually overpowered the meat flavor in the sauce. It occurred to us that in order for the milk to develop the new flavor compounds that are its key contribution to a Bolognese sauce, a lengthy simmer was necessary. Would cooking the sauce a little longer—45 minutes instead of 30—help? Not enough to notice. Furthermore, the extra 15 minutes of simmering had little impact on the meat, which was still more rubbery than not.

It was time to look beyond Bolognese for ways to improve our simple weeknight sauce. Meat tenderizer seemed like an obvious place to start. A few teaspoons did soften the beef but also made it spongy. Would soy sauce work? Soy sauce is a base ingredient in many of our steak marinades, where it acts much like a brine, tenderizing meat by helping it retain moisture. But we quickly discovered that although soy minimizes moisture loss in large pieces of meat, such as steak, it has virtually no impact on tiny bits of ground beef. After a little research we found out why: Bigger pieces of meat contain more water, which takes a longer time to evaporate during cooking. The water in small pieces of ground meat, on the other hand, evaporates almost immediately, and not even soy sauce can help prevent this.

A colleague suggested a trick: mixing in a panade. This paste of bread and milk is often blended into meatballs and meat loaf to help them hold their shape and retain moisture during cooking. It was worth a try. Using a fork, we mashed up a piece of bread with some milk until we had a smooth paste and mixed it into the ground beef until well combined. We then proceeded as usual with the rest of the

recipe: stirring the beef mixture into the sautéed onions and garlic, adding the tomatoes, and simmering. We noticed a difference in the sauce even before we ladled it over pasta for tasters. The meat looked moister and, sure enough, tasters confirmed that it was. It turns out that starches from the bread absorb liquid from the milk to form a gel that coats and lubricates the meat, much in the same way as fat (see "Panade to the Rescue," page 31). But all was not perfect: Tasters were pleased with the meat's tenderness but complained that the sauce was too chunky and resembled chili. No problem. We pulsed the meat and panade together in a food processor to create finer pieces of supple, juicy meat.

With the meat issue solved, it was time to turn our attention to flavor. Without browning or a lengthy simmer to concentrate and build new layers of flavor, complexity and depth were noticeably lacking in our sauce. Could the type of ground beef we used enhance flavor? We bought four different kinds—ground round, chuck, and sirloin, as well as meat labeled "ground beef" (a mix of various beef cuts and trimmings)—and made four sauces. The ground round was bland and spongy, but tasters liked the other three equally well. Eighty-five percent lean beef proved to have just the right degree of leanness, adding richness without making the sauce greasy. Still, tasters were pressing, "Where's the beef [flavor]?"

Next, we tested a range of ingredients that are often used to boost meaty flavor. Beef broth ended up imparting a tinny taste to the sauce. Worcestershire and steak sauce overwhelmed it with their potent flavorings, and red wine lent a sour taste. Finally, we tried mushrooms—and at last we had a winner. The mushrooms brought a real beefiness to the sauce. After experimenting with different types, we discovered that plain white mushrooms worked just fine. The key was browning them. We minced a modest amount (about 4 ounces) and added them to the pan with the onions. Browning concentrated their flavor but left them tender and supple, allowing them to add complexity without otherwise letting their presence be known.

When it came to other components of the sauce, tasters liked a mix of diced and crushed tomatoes. The diced tomatoes brought a chunky texture, and the crushed provided a smooth foundation. We reserved a small amount of juice from the drained diced tomatoes to deglaze the pan after browning the mushrooms. This little trick gave the sauce's tomato flavor a boost, as did a tablespoon of tomato paste. Earlier, we had ruled against milk in the sauce (except for the couple of tablespoons in the panade), but we reinstated dairy in the form of a handful of grated Parmesan, which brought a welcome tanginess. With a dash of red pepper flakes and some fresh oregano, we were done.

We now had a sauce with meltingly tender meat that was as complex and full-bodied as any sauce simmered for under an hour could be. True, no one would mistake it for a Bolognese—but no one would ever believe we hadn't rushed home early to put it on the stove, either.

WHAT WE LEARNED: Browned chopped onions and mushrooms give the sauce a rich base of flavor. Deglaze the pan with tomato paste and tomato juice to further boost flavor. For sauce with tender meat, incorporate a panade—a paste of bread and milk—into the meat before cooking. Cook the meat mixture just until it loses its raw color; any longer, and the meat will turn dry and mealy. Then finish cooking the meat in a combination of canned diced and crushed tomatoes for the best mix of textures. A handful of grated Parmesan, added just before serving, lends the sauce a tangy, complex character.

SIMPLE ITALIAN-STYLE MEAT SAUCE

makes about 6 cups

Except for ground round (which tasters found spongy and bland), this recipe will work with most types of ground beef, as long as it is 85 percent lean. (Eighty percent lean beef will turn the sauce greasy; 90 percent will make it fibrous.) Use high-quality crushed tomatoes; our favorite brands are Tuttorosso, Muir Glen Organic, and Hunt's Organic. If using dried oregano, add the entire amount with the canned tomato liquid in step 2. The recipe makes enough sauce for nearly 2 pounds of pasta. Leftover sauce can be refrigerated in an airtight container for 3 days or frozen for 1 month.

4   ounces white mushrooms, cleaned, stems trimmed, and broken into rough pieces
1   large slice high-quality white sandwich bread, torn into quarters
2   tablespoons whole milk
    Salt and ground black pepper
1   pound 85 percent lean ground beef (see note and box on page 31)
1   tablespoon olive oil
1   large onion, chopped fine (about 1½ cups)
6   medium garlic cloves, minced or pressed through a garlic press (about 2 tablespoons)
¼   teaspoon red pepper flakes
1   tablespoon tomato paste
1   (14.5-ounce) can diced tomatoes, drained, ¼ cup liquid reserved
1   tablespoon minced fresh oregano leaves or 1 teaspoon dried (see note)
1   (28-ounce) can crushed tomatoes
½   ounce grated Parmesan cheese (about ¼ cup)

1. Pulse the mushrooms in a food processor until finely chopped, about eight 1-second pulses, scraping down the side of the workbowl as needed; transfer to a medium bowl. Add the bread, milk, ½ teaspoon salt, and ½ teaspoon pepper to the now-empty food processor and pulse until a paste forms, about eight 1-second pulses. Add the beef and pulse until the mixture is well combined, about six 1-second pulses.

2. Heat the oil in a large saucepan over medium-high heat until just smoking. Add the onion and mushrooms; cook, stirring frequently, until the vegetables are browned and

---

GETTING IT RIGHT: Keys to Great Flavor

Minced mushrooms browned in oil boost the sauce's meaty taste. A spoonful of tomato paste and a sprinkle of Parmesan cheese add complexity.

Mushrooms

Tomato Paste

Parmesan Cheese

dark bits form on the pan bottom, 6 to 12 minutes. Stir in the garlic, red pepper flakes, and tomato paste; cook until fragrant and the tomato paste starts to brown, about 1 minute. Add the ¼ cup reserved tomato liquid and 2 teaspoons of the fresh oregano (if using dried, add the full amount), scraping the bottom of the pan with a wooden spoon to loosen the browned bits. Add the meat mixture and cook, breaking the meat into small pieces with a wooden spoon, until no longer pink, 2 to 4 minutes, making sure that the meat does not brown.

3. Stir in the drained diced and crushed tomatoes and bring to a simmer; reduce the heat to low and gently simmer until the sauce has thickened and the flavors have blended, about 30 minutes. Stir in the cheese and the remaining 1 teaspoon fresh oregano; season with salt and pepper to taste.

SCIENCE DESK: Panade to the Rescue

A PASTE OF MILK AND BREAD, CALLED A PANADE, is responsible for keeping the ground beef in our meat sauce moist and tender. Because panades are typically used to help foods like meatballs and meat loaf hold their shape (and moisture), adding a panade to a meat sauce in which the beef is crumbled seemed like an odd idea. Wouldn't the mashed-up milk and bread just dissolve into the sauce? We were left scratching our heads when the panade worked.

Our science editor filled us in. The bread's starches absorb liquid from the milk to form a gel that coats and lubricates the protein molecules in the meat, much in the same way as fat, keeping them moist and preventing them from linking together to form a tough matrix. Mixing the beef and panade in a food processor helps to ensure that the starch is well dispersed so that all the meat reaps its benefits.

SHOPPING NOTES: Buying Ground Beef

Ground beef can be made from a variety of cuts, and fat levels vary from 70 to 95 percent lean. Our meat sauce recipe calls for any 85 percent lean ground beef other than ground round. But when a recipe doesn't specify, how do you know what to buy? Here's a guide:

Ground Chuck: Cut from the shoulder, ground chuck is distinguished by its rich, beefy flavor and tender texture.

Ground Sirloin: This cut from the cow's midsection near the hip offers good beefy flavor, but it can be on the dry side. Generally fairly lean.

Ground Beef: A mystery meat of sorts, ground beef can be any cut or combination of cuts, which means flavor and texture are rarely consistent.

Ground Round: Lean, tough, and often gristly, ground round comes from the rear upper leg and rump of the cow.

CREAMY TOMATO PASTA SAUCE

WHAT WE WANTED: A smooth, full-flavored tomato sauce enriched with, but not overwhelmed by, cream.

In the best examples of creamy tomato sauce, the acidity of fruity tomatoes is balanced with the unctuousness of rich dairy; the worst deliver instant heartburn and make you wish the two components had never met. What's the best way to merge these seemingly incompatible ingredients in a sauce that brings out the best in each?

This sauce appears in many forms. While digging through stacks of Italian cookbooks, we found everything from simple *salsa rosate,* which took just minutes and a single pot to prepare, to long-simmered, ragù-like sauces that required the better part of a day to pull together. We were disappointed when the recipe of one of our culinary heroes, Marcella Hazan, yielded a copper-colored slurry that tasted way too similar to canned tomato soup (all of the ingredients were simply boiled together and pureed). There were no winners among the lot, but there were plenty of thought-provoking methods and ingredients to test.

Traditional Italian sauces (as well as most Italian soups and stews) are built upon *soffrito,* a blend of aromatics, such as onion, carrot, celery, garlic, and parsley, stewed in lots of fat. For the richest-flavored sauce, we assumed that more was more and started with the full list of classic ingredients. As testing progressed, however, we couldn't shake the criticism that the sauce tasted too vegetal. Perhaps in this case, less was more. We cooked a batch of soffrito without celery, and tasters unanimously approved. Next we eliminated carrot, and the reaction was again positive. Left with just garlic and onion, we decided to omit long-cooked garlic in favor of a few quickly sautéed minced cloves, which packed a brighter, cleaner punch.

Our goal was a smooth sauce we could make year-round, so fresh tomatoes didn't make much sense. We turned to canned tomatoes. We tested our sauce with whole, diced, crushed, and pureed. Crushed was preferred for its bright flavor and smoothest texture, when pureed.

A simple sauce of onion, garlic, and crushed tomatoes didn't have the legs to stand up to heavy cream, no matter how long (or short) we simmered it. In light-tasting tomato sauces, we typically eschew tomato paste, but adding a bit here made sense. A tablespoon contributed depth, and a tablespoon more proved better yet. Simply stirring it into the bubbling sauce left the paste tasting raw and tinny, so we cooked it with the softened aromatics until it darkened to brick red.

But tasters demanded more tomato flavor. To develop deep flavor in tomato sauces and soups, the test kitchen has taken whole, drained canned tomatoes, dusted them with sugar, and then roasted them before combining them with the other ingredients. But when we tried adding tomatoes prepared with this technique, the sauce was too sweet, even when we omitted the sugar. Roasting also toughened the tomatoes' texture, which made the finished sauce decidedly pulpy.

For another of the test kitchen's pasta sauces, tomatoes are browned in a saucepan to generate a flavorful *fond,* which is deglazed and incorporated into the sauce. But when we tried this method with our working recipe, the fond had more undertones of caramel than tomato. There's a time and a place for the deep, caramel flavors that thorough browning can provide, but this wasn't it.

How else could we generate a bigger, brighter tomato flavor? After sifting through a list of options and testing the most promising, we landed on sun-dried tomatoes, whose sunny flavor enlivened the sauce and cut through the palate-deadening cream.

Between the tomato paste and the sun-dried tomatoes, however, the sauce's flavor had grown too sweet. A pinch of red pepper flakes helped rebalance things, and a stiff shot of wine—added prior to the crushed tomatoes and cooked down to evaporate the bitter alcohol—brought the sweetness under control and further intensified the sauce's flavor.

In our initial survey, we'd tried a recipe that included pancetta. Though the meat lent the sauce an undeniable body and depth, we had ruled it out as too assertive. If pancetta was too strong, we reasoned, perhaps milder prosciutto might work. We minced a few paper-thin slices and added them to the pan along with the onion. We're always mindful of the effect a bit of cured pork can have on a dish (all apologies to vegetarians), and this sauce was easily the best yet. The tomatoes tasted so full and the cream so deep, we might have stirred MSG into the pot.

We liked how the sun-dried tomatoes had softened and the sauce's flavors had unified after half an hour of slow simmering, but we wondered if perhaps the sauce tasted too homogeneous. When we make rich, meaty stews, we typically add a splash of wine to the finished dish to brighten the otherwise dark flavors. We thought it might work in this instance, too. It did—quite well. Then we decided to try adding a bit of raw crushed tomatoes at the last minute, too, a trick the test kitchen came up with in prior testing. Like the wine, the raw tomatoes contributed some needed acidity, and the combination of the two cut through the dairy and brought the sauce's ingredients into sharp relief.

From the start we had assumed that heavy cream was the best dairy product for the job, but a few of the recipes we found used clotted cream, pureed ricotta, or mascarpone cheese instead. We quickly ruled out the clotted cream (very, very odd here), and the ricotta came across as grainy, no matter how long we processed it. To our surprise, we quite liked the flavor of the mascarpone (and turned a blind eye to its unholy calorie count), but its ultra-thick texture turned the sauce gummy.

Heavy cream, then, contributed the clearest creamy flavor, but what was the best way to blend it with the tomato base? In some of the recipes we had tried the cream was reduced by half to enhance its flavor and silkiness, which we felt made the sauce too sweet. In other recipes the tomato base was blended with the cream and boiled until thick, which proved dangerous; the molten sauce splattered over the stovetop.

We thought the sauce tasted best and most balanced when we simply stirred the cream into the finished tomato mixture and brought it up to temperature before tossing it with the pasta. We found that half a cup was the ideal amount to make the sauce taste rich without overpowering the tomatoes.

Up to this point we had pureed each of the finished sauces to a velvety texture, thinking that smoothness was the best way to highlight creaminess. And our sauce did taste good when smooth, but it was one-dimensional. On a whim, we left a batch unpureed, and tasters loved the bits of chewy sun-dried tomatoes, soft minced onion, and pulpy crushed tomato that punctuated the otherwise silky consistency. This was finally it: a dynamic sauce in which tomatoes and cream boosted each other's flavors and packed enough complexity to keep us coming back for more.

Italians may adhere to an orthodoxy regarding pasta shapes and the sauces with which they should be served, but we're a bit more flexible. Ziti and penne worked well, as would any pasta shape that traps the sauce.

WHAT WE LEARNED: Readily available, crushed canned tomatoes trump canned whole and diced tomatoes—they're bright in flavor, easy to puree in the food processor, and contain just the right amount of juice. Cook a few tablespoons of tomato paste with some onion and garlic, and add sun-dried tomatoes, to deepen the flavor of the sauce. Add depth and tame some of the sauce's distracting sweetness with a pinch of red pepper flakes, a splash of wine, and a little minced prosciutto; add a bit of raw crushed tomatoes and another splash of wine before serving to bring the sauce's ingredients into sharp relief. As for the cream, traditional heavy cream can't be beat; add it to the just-finished sauce to enrich it without subduing the bright tomato flavor.

¼ cup plus 2 tablespoons dry white wine
2 cups plus 2 tablespoons crushed tomatoes
   (from one 28-ounce can)
1 pound pasta (see note)
½ cup heavy cream
   Ground black pepper
¼ cup chopped fresh basil leaves
   Grated Parmesan cheese, for serving

1. Melt the butter in a medium saucepan over medium heat. Add the prosciutto, onion, bay leaf, red pepper flakes, and ¼ teaspoon salt; cook, stirring occasionally, until the onion is very soft and beginning to turn light gold, 8 to 12 minutes. Increase the heat to medium-high, add the garlic, and cook until fragrant, about 30 seconds. Stir in the tomato paste and sun-dried tomatoes and cook, stirring constantly, until slightly darkened, 1 to 2 minutes. Add ¼ cup of the wine and cook, stirring frequently, until the liquid has evaporated, 1 to 2 minutes.

2. Add 2 cups of the crushed tomatoes and bring to a simmer. Reduce the heat to low, partially cover, and cook, stirring occasionally, until the sauce is thickened (a spoon should leave a trail when dragged through the sauce), 25 to 30 minutes.

3. Meanwhile, bring 4 quarts water to a boil. Add the pasta and 1 tablespoon salt and cook until al dente. Reserve ½ cup of the cooking water; drain the pasta and transfer it back to the cooking pot.

4. Remove the bay leaf from the sauce and discard. Stir the cream, remaining 2 tablespoons crushed tomatoes, and remaining 2 tablespoons wine into the sauce; season with salt and pepper to taste. Add the sauce to the cooked pasta, adjusting the consistency with up to ½ cup pasta cooking water. Stir in the basil and serve immediately, passing the Parmesan separately.

PASTA WITH CREAMY TOMATO SAUCE

serves 4

This sauce is best served with short pasta, such as ziti, penne, or fusilli.

3 tablespoons unsalted butter
1 ounce prosciutto, minced (about 2 tablespoons)
1 small onion, diced fine (about ¾ cup)
1 bay leaf
   Pinch red pepper flakes
   Salt
3 medium garlic cloves, minced or pressed
   through a garlic press (about 1 tablespoon)
2 tablespoons tomato paste
2 ounces oil-packed sun-dried tomatoes, drained,
   rinsed, patted dry, and chopped coarse
   (about 3 tablespoons)

GETTING IT RIGHT: Tomatoes Three Ways

Concentrated

Tomato paste packs enough punch to enliven flavor-deadening heavy cream.

Sun-Dried

With their dense, sweet-tart taste, sun-dried tomatoes round out the other flavors.

Crushed

Pulpy crushed tomatoes lend a bright taste and subtle texture.

TASTING LAB:
Supermarket Extra-Virgin Olive Oils

THE EXTRA-VIRGIN OLIVE OIL INDUSTRY IS A BOOMING business: The United States imported 261,000 metric tons of extra-virgin olive oil in 2006, up from 163,000 metric tons a decade ago. But given the cost—an average of $18.99 per liter for the oils in our lineup—should you just grab the cheapest or try for something better from a gourmet shop or online seller?

To find out if extra-virgin olive oils from the supermarket measure up, we chose 10 of the top-selling brands and conducted a blind tasting—first plain, and then warmed and tossed with pasta. (Because high heat destroys the distinctive fruity taste of extra-virgin olive oil, we reserve it for mixing into pasta dishes and vinaigrettes or drizzling on grilled steak and vegetables; for cooking, we turn to cheaper, lower-grade olive oil.)

Here's the not-so-great news: Our highest average scores barely reached five out of a possible 10 points. A few supermarket oils passed muster, but most ranged from plain Jane to distinctly unpleasant.

Extra-virgin is the highest grade of olive oil. At its best, it's simply fresh olive juice, extracted from any of hundreds of olive varieties that were picked at the grower's desired level of ripeness and pressed as soon as possible. To be designated "extra-virgin," the oil should meet certain standards set by the International Olive Council (IOC) in Madrid. It must be pressed—or, more commonly today, spun out using a centrifuge—without using heat or chemicals, which can extract more oil from the olives, but at the cost of flavor and quality. It must have less than 0.8 percent oleic acid, a measure of quality based on the level of free fatty acids, a product of deterioration. Finally, it can have absolutely no chemical or flavor defects, as determined by both laboratory tests and tasting experts.

These stringent olive oil standards sound good, but it's important to note: They don't apply in the United States. This country has never adopted the IOC standards, instead holding to unrelated grades of "fancy," "choice," "standard," and "substandard."

By now it's common knowledge that although the majority of mass-market olive oil manufacturers have Italian-sounding names, most do not sell Italian oils—Italy alone can't supply enough olives to meet demand. Italian companies buy olive oil from all over the Mediterranean, then ship it in-country for bottling and sell it as a "product

of Italy." At each company, experts blend these various oils to match the brand's characteristic flavor profile.

After our tasting, we had to wonder if the majority of olive oil destined for the American market isn't intentionally blended to be bland. (A number of experts we spoke to said yes; many European producers assume Americans want their olive oil to be as neutral as vegetable oil.) Worse, we wondered whether some of the oils that arrive here labeled "extra-virgin" are even extra-virgin at all.

Having read reports of fraudulent adulteration of mass-market olive oils with cheaper oils such as soybean or hazelnut, we sent our samples to an independent laboratory for analysis. All were confirmed to be made only from olives. But in the absence of any regulatory standards in the United States, that's all we were able to confirm. Companies importing olive oil are free to label their products "extra-virgin"—even if the same oils wouldn't qualify for that appellation in Europe, as many impassioned olive oil advocates believe is the case. Nancy Loseke, editor of *Fresh Press,* a newsletter devoted to olive oil, put it bluntly: "Americans mostly shop the world's olive oil dregs, the low-rung stuff."

Organizations such as the North American Olive Oil Association (NAOOA), which represents the interests of olive oil importers (including six out of the 10 we tasted), claim to provide oversight the government does not. According to president Bob Bauer, the NAOOA independently buys and tests the oils of member companies at a European laboratory with IOC certification for this testing, and he asserts that NAOOA members meet international standards. But in our own tasting, these assurances meant little. None of the manufacturers of the top three oils in our lineup were members. Furthermore, the NAOOA

currently tests only for the presence of chemicals and the percentage of oleic acid—not for flavor defects that are an equally important "sensory" part of the IOC standards.

And what about those flavor defects our tasters identified so readily? These included soapy, metallic, or chemical notes; dirty, rotten, or medicinal aspects. According to Alexandra Devarenne, a California-based olive oil consultant trained in sensory evaluation of olive oil according to IOC standards, many of these flaws are the result of delays between harvesting and pressing olives.

In addition, the oil can sometimes be a victim of poor storage. Olive oil has a shelf life of 12 to 18 months, but supermarkets frequently do not rotate their supply of olive oil accordingly. And although high-end oils usually indicate the harvest year, most mass-market brands do not, and lack sell-by dates on their labels; fewer than half the oils in our lineup had them.

Despite all we didn't like about most of the olive oils in our tasting, we did find two acceptable products. Price stood out: Our top picks were the two most expensive oils. In fact, our favorite cost almost $40 per liter, nearly twice the average price of the rest of the lineup, and as much as many high-end olive oils from gourmet stores. This front-runner was Lucini Italia Premium Select Extra Virgin Olive Oil, made (according to the manufacturer) from olives grown on Italian estates, handpicked, and pressed within 24 hours. It was closely followed by Colavita Extra Virgin Olive Oil, also described as being made exclusively from olives harvested and pressed in Italy.

But in the end, although these two oils were favored among the supermarket sampling, they were easily bested in a second blind tasting that included our favorite premium extra-virgin olive oil by Columela, which is made with a blend of olives grown in Spain; tasters found it offered exceptionally fruity and well-balanced flavor. At about $36 per liter, Columela is actually cheaper than Lucini, our top supermarket brand. This raises the question: Is the supermarket the best place to buy your extra-virgin olive oil? Unfortunately, we'd have to say no.

Rating Supermarket Extra-Virgin Olive Oils

TWENTY-ONE MEMBERS OF THE AMERICA'S TEST KITCHEN STAFF TASTED 10 BRANDS OF OLIVE OIL PLAIN AS WELL AS heated and tossed with pasta. We then tasted them plain a second time with our favorite high-end extra-virgin olive oil, Columela, which is available in better supermarkets and gourmet shops. Brands are listed in order of preference. Information about the national origin of the oils was provided by the manufacturers. See www.americastestkitchen.com for updates to this tasting.

HIGHLY RECOMMENDED
Columela Extra Virgin Olive Oil
$17.95 for 17 ounces ($36 per liter); Origin: Spain

Our favorite premium extra-virgin olive oil from a previous tasting, Columela took top honors for its fruity flavor and excellent balance.

RECOMMENDED
Lucini Italia Premium Select Extra Virgin Olive Oil
$19.99 for 500 ml ($39.98 per liter); Origin: Italy

Tasters noted this oil's flavor was "much deeper than the other samples," describing it as "fruity, with a slight peppery finish."

RECOMMENDED
Colavita Extra Virgin Olive Oil
$17.99 for 750 ml ($23.98 per liter); Origin: Italy

Virtually tied for second place, this oil was deemed "round and buttery," with a "light body" and flavor that was "briny and fruity."

RECOMMENDED WITH RESERVATIONS
Bertolli Extra Virgin Olive Oil
$12.49 for 750 ml ($16.65 per liter); Origin: Italy, Greece, Spain, and Tunisia

A clear step down from the top oils, tasters noted "overall mild" flavor with only a "hint of green olive."

RECOMMENDED WITH RESERVATIONS
Filippo Berio Extra Virgin Olive Oil
$10.99 for 750 ml ($14.65 per liter); Origin: Italy, Spain, Greece, and Tunisia

While some tasters found this oil "sweet" and "buttery," others complained that it had "zero olive flavor."

RECOMMENDED WITH RESERVATIONS
Goya Extra Virgin Olive Oil
$13.99 for 1 liter; Origin: Spain

The best comments tasters could muster were "mild" and "neutral." Some liked it on pasta, but complaints were myriad: "metallic," "soapy," and "briny."

RECOMMENDED WITH RESERVATIONS
Pompeian Extra Virgin Olive Oil
$9.99 for 473 ml ($21.12 per liter); Origin: Spain

Some tasters called this oil "mild" and "smooth," but others found it "thin, greasy" and "not very interesting." "Could be canola—it is so bland," mused one taster.

RECOMMENDED WITH RESERVATIONS
Botticelli Extra Virgin Olive Oil
$10.99 for 1 liter; Origin: Italy

A few tasters liked this "potent" oil, but others said they detected "mushroom," "rotten walnuts," and a quality that was "downright medicinal."

NOT RECOMMENDED
Carapelli Extra Virgin Olive Oil
$10.99 for 750 ml ($14.65 per liter); Origin: Italy, Greece, Spain, Tunisia, Turkey, Cyprus, Morocco, and Syria

"Nothing remarkable here—just greasy, no flavor," summarized one taster. "Where did the olive go?" said another.

NOT RECOMMENDED
Da Vinci Extra Virgin Olive Oil
$17.99 for 1 liter; Origin: Italy, Greece, Spain, Tunisia, and Turkey

Although this oil won top place in a previous tasting, because olive oil is an agricultural product, it can differ from year to year. This time, tasters found it "washed out and muted."

NOT RECOMMENDED
Star Extra Virgin Olive Oil
$11.99 for 750 ml ($15.99 per liter); Origin: Spain, Italy, Greece, and Tunisia

"Boring" and "not very complex," this oil came across as "plasticky and industrial; some hint of olives, but it fades quickly."

For moist and tender oven-baked fish with an extraordinarily crunchy crust, pre-toast homemade bread crumbs and cook the fish on a rack set over a baking sheet.

FISH MADE
easy

Fish doesn't often turn up in the weeknight repertoire, and that's too bad. When prepared well, fish is flavorful and satisfying. It's true that fish's delicate nature makes it prone to overcooking, but still, cooking fish isn't difficult. We chose two very different methods for cooking it—poaching and oven-frying—and aimed to devise foolproof recipes for each one.

Poaching, the slow simmering of fish in a flavorful liquid, provides a gentle heat environment that turns fish flesh moist and silky. Salmon is especially good poached, but most recipes are for poaching a whole side of salmon (for a crowd). We wanted to take this classic recipe down to size by using fillets. We also wanted to streamline the process, so that poached salmon could appear on the table any day of the week (not just Saturday) for a satisfying weeknight supper.

Frying fish isn't hard, but oh, is it messy. A bubbling pot of oil often translates to a splattered stovetop—and on a weeknight, fussy frying is a hassle. Thus, we turned to developing an easy oven-frying method for crispy fish fillets. In the past we've found oven-fried fish disappointing. The coating simply isn't crisp and the undersides of the fillets inevitably turn soggy. We aimed to develop a recipe for oven-baked fish with all the flavor and crunch of real batter-fried fish.

FLAVORFUL POACHED SALMON

WHAT WE WANTED: A silky-textured poached salmon complemented by a simple sauce that is rich enough to stand up to the fish—made without any fuss.

Poached salmon seems like the ideal stovetop recipe: It's fast, it requires just one pot, and there's no splattering oil to burn yourself on or strong odors to permeate the house. And, when done right, the fish has an irresistibly supple, velvety texture delicately accented by the flavors of the poaching liquid. Add a simple sauce, and the dish is even more flavorful. But when done wrong, which seems to be the usual case, the fish has a dry, chalky texture and washed-out taste that not even the richest sauce can redeem.

The classic method for poaching salmon is to gently simmer an entire side of fish in a highly flavored broth called a *court-bouillon*. The salmon is cooled and served cold, often as part of a buffet. But we weren't looking for a make-ahead method for cold salmon to serve a crowd. We wanted to produce perfectly cooked, individual portions of hot salmon and a sauce to go with them—all in under half an hour.

Our first objective was to achieve great texture and flavor in the salmon itself; after that we'd focus on the sauce. First consideration: the cooking liquid. A classic court-bouillon is made by filling a pot with water, wine, herbs, vegetables, and aromatics, then boiling it all very briefly (*court-bouillon* is French for "short-boiled stock"). After straining the solids, you're left with an intensely flavored liquid in which to poach your fish. The fish absorbs the broth's strong flavors, which helps compensate for all the salmon flavor that leaches out into the liquid.

This method certainly did produce flavorful results. However, there was just one annoying little problem: To cook dinner for four, we'd just prepped a slew of ingredients (onions, carrots, celery, leeks, parsley) and bought still others

(bay leaves, tomato paste, peppercorns, and white wine), only to dump them and the stock down the drain at the end. This waste isn't bothersome when you're preparing a side of fish to feed a group, but it's hardly worth it for a simple Tuesday night supper at home.

What if we used less liquid? At the very least, this would mean we'd have to buy and prep (and waste) fewer ingredients, plus using less liquid would likely mean less flavor leaching out of the salmon. We poached the salmon in just enough liquid to come one-half inch up the side of the fillets. Flavor-wise, this was our most successful attempt yet. In fact, the salmon retained so much of its own natural flavor that we wondered if we could cut back even more on the quantity of vegetables and aromatics we were using in the liquid. A couple of shallots, a few herbs, and some wine proved to be all we needed. But nailing the flavor issue brought another problem into sharp relief—dry texture.

Like all animal flesh, salmon has a certain temperature range at which it is ideal to be eaten. The proteins in salmon begin coagulating at around 120 degrees, transforming it from translucent to opaque. At around 135 degrees, the flesh is completely firm and will start to force moisture out from between its protein fibers. Any higher, and the salmon becomes dry as cardboard (like a well-done steak). We had been using an instant-read thermometer to ensure that the centers of our salmon fillets were exactly 125 degrees (medium) before removing them from the poaching liquid. But testing the temperature of various parts of the fillet showed that by the time the center was 125 degrees, most of the other thinner sections registered higher temperatures. We were concerned that the texture of these thinner areas would be dry, but found their higher fat content kept them moist (see "Benefits of Belly Fat," page 42).

At high cooking temperatures, the exterior of a piece of meat will cook much faster than the interior. This is great when pan-searing the skin of a salmon fillet or a beef steak, when you want a browned exterior and rare interior, but it's no good for poaching, where the goal is to have a piece evenly cooked all the way through. The most obvious solution was to lower the cooking temperature. For the next batch, we placed the salmon in the cold pan with poaching liquid, brought the liquid barely up to a simmer, reduced the heat to its lowest possible setting, and covered the pan until the salmon cooked through. Then we realized a new problem that we'd unwittingly introduced when we reduced the amount of cooking liquid: Since the salmon wasn't totally submerged in liquid, it relied on steam to deliver heat and flavor. At such a low temperature, even with a lid on, not enough steam was being created to efficiently cook the parts of the fish sticking out above the liquid. Was there a way to create more steam without increasing the temperature?

Thinking back to high school chemistry, we remembered that adding alcohol to water lowers its boiling temperature: The higher the concentration of alcohol, the more vapor will be produced as the liquid is heated. More vapor, in turn, means better heat transfer, which leads to faster cooking, even at temperatures below a simmer. We also knew that alcohol could increase the rate at which proteins denature. Therefore, if we used more alcohol in the cooking liquid, it would theoretically be able to cook the fish faster and at a lower temperature. We increased the ratio of wine to water, going from a few tablespoons of wine to ½ cup. Acid also helps fish protein denature (in addition to improving flavor), so we squeezed a little lemon juice into the liquid before adding the salmon. Our hopes were high as we opened the lid to a burst of steam and salmon that appeared perfectly cooked. Everything was fine until a fork got to the bottom of the fillet. Even though the top, sides, and center were now just right, the bottom, which had been in direct contact with the pan, was still overcooked.

We knew we weren't the first to have this problem—in fact, a solution already exists: a fish poacher. This specialized pan comes with a perforated insert that elevates the fish, allowing it to cook evenly on all sides. But we weren't about to go out and buy an expensive new pan for a technique that we'd use only a few times a year. Then we realized that we had the solution literally in our hands. Instead of squeezing lemon juice into the poaching liquid, we sliced the fruit into thin disks and lined the pan with them. By resting the salmon fillets on top of the lemon slices, we were able to insulate the fish from the pan bottom while simultaneously flavoring it. This time the salmon came out evenly cooked all the way through.

It was time to focus on the sauce. Ticking off the list of ingredients in our super-concentrated poaching liquid, we realized we had the foundation of a beurre blanc, so we didn't have to make a separate sauce. This classic French sauce is made by reducing wine flavored with vinegar, shallots, and herbs, and then finishing it with butter. We would need only to reduce the poaching liquid and whisk in the butter. But since a few tablespoons of butter per serving would push this dish out of the "everyday" category, we developed a vinaigrette-style variation in which we used olive oil instead of butter; tasters liked the oil version as much as the original.

This salmon-poaching method guarantees moist and delicately flavored fish and produces just the right amount of poaching liquid for a great-tasting sauce—all without boiling away any flavor or pouring ingredients down the drain.

WHAT WE LEARNED: To keep prep to a minimum and salmon flavor to a maximum, poach the salmon in very little liquid. For evenly cooked salmon fillets, heat the salmon and the liquid together until the liquid barely simmers, then reduce the heat to the lowest possible setting and cover the pan until the salmon is cooked. To ensure that enough steam is created to efficiently cook the parts of the fish above the liquid, add a good dose of wine (adding alcohol to water lowers its boiling point). Lastly, use the poaching liquid to make a beurre blanc–inspired vinaigrette.

POACHED SALMON WITH HERB AND CAPER VINAIGRETTE

serves 4

To ensure even-sized pieces of fish, we prefer to buy a whole center-cut fillet and cut it into four pieces. If a skinless whole fillet is unavailable, follow the recipe as directed with a skin-on fillet, adding 3 to 4 minutes to the cooking time in step 2. Remove the skin after cooking (see "Removing Skin from Salmon," page 43). This recipe will yield salmon fillets cooked to medium. If you prefer rare salmon (translucent in the center), reduce the cooking time by 2 minutes, or cook until the salmon registers 110 degrees in the thickest part.

2   lemons

2   tablespoons chopped fresh parsley leaves, stems reserved

2   tablespoons chopped fresh tarragon leaves, stems reserved

2   small shallots, minced (about 4 tablespoons)

½   cup dry white wine

½   cup water

1   skinless salmon fillet (1¾ to 2 pounds), about 1½ inches at thickest part, white membrane removed, fillet cut crosswise into 4 equal pieces (see note)

2   tablespoons capers, rinsed and roughly chopped

1   tablespoon honey

2   tablespoons extra-virgin olive oil
    Salt and ground black pepper

1. Cut the top and bottom off 1 lemon; cut the lemon into 8 to 10 ¼-inch-thick slices. Cut the remaining lemon into 8 wedges and set aside. Arrange the lemon slices in a single layer across the bottom of a 12-inch skillet. Scatter the herb stems and 2 tablespoons of the minced shallots evenly over the lemon slices. Add the wine and water.

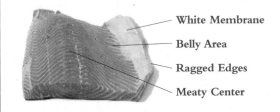

GETTING IT RIGHT:
Benefits of Belly Fat

A center-cut salmon fillet typically tapers down on one side to the fattier belly of the fish. The belly's fattiness helps keep this section of the fish moist, despite its thinner profile. The belly area is sometimes covered with a chewy white membrane, which should be trimmed away before cooking. We also like to neaten up any ragged edges that can dry out and fray during cooking.

— White Membrane
— Belly Area
— Ragged Edges
— Meaty Center

2. Place the salmon fillets in the skillet, skinned side down, on top of the lemon slices. Set the pan over high heat and bring the liquid to a simmer. Reduce the heat to low, cover, and cook until the sides are opaque but the center of the thickest part is still translucent (or until an instant-read thermometer inserted in the thickest part registers 125 degrees), 11 to 16 minutes. Remove the pan from the heat and, using a spatula, carefully transfer the salmon and lemon slices to a paper towel–lined plate. Tent loosely with foil.

3. Return the pan to high heat and simmer the cooking liquid until slightly thickened and reduced to 2 tablespoons, 4 to 5 minutes. Meanwhile, combine the remaining 2 tablespoons minced shallots, chopped herbs, capers, honey, and olive oil in a medium bowl. Strain the reduced cooking liquid through a fine-mesh strainer into the bowl with the herb-caper mixture, pressing on the solids to extract as much liquid as possible. Whisk to combine; season with salt and pepper to taste.

TECHNIQUE:

Removing Skin from Salmon

Our recipe specifies skinless salmon fillets. But if you can find only skin-on fillets, removing the skin is simple. Transfer the cooked fillet to a paper towel–lined plate and allow it to cool slightly. Gently slide a thin, wide spatula between the flesh and the skin and use the fingers of your free hand to help separate the skin. It should peel off easily and in one piece.

4. Season the salmon lightly with salt and pepper. Using a spatula, carefully lift and tilt the salmon fillets to remove the lemon slices. Place the salmon on a serving platter or individual plates and spoon the vinaigrette over the top. Serve, passing the reserved lemon wedges separately.

VARIATIONS

POACHED SALMON WITH BOURBON AND MAPLE

1	lemon
2	tablespoons bourbon or brandy
3	tablespoons maple syrup
2	tablespoons whole grain mustard
1	tablespoon cider vinegar
1	medium shallot, sliced thin (about 3 tablespoons)
¾	cup water
4	center-cut skinless salmon fillets, 6 to 8 ounces each
1	tablespoon unsalted butter
1	tablespoon chopped chives
	Salt and ground black pepper

1. Cut the top and bottom off the lemon; cut it into 8 to 10 ¼-inch-thick slices. Arrange the lemon slices in a single layer across the bottom of a 12-inch skillet. Whisk the bourbon, maple syrup, mustard, vinegar, and shallot together in a small bowl. Add the bourbon mixture and water to the skillet.

2. Place the salmon fillets in the skillet, skinned side down, on top of the lemon slices (to prevent the salmon from coming into direct contact with the bottom of the pan). Set the pan over high heat and bring the liquid to a simmer. Reduce the heat to low, cover, and cook until the center of the thickest part of the fillets is still translucent when cut into with a paring knife, 11 to 16 minutes (or until an instant-read thermometer inserted into the thickest part of the fillets registers 125 degrees). Remove the pan from the heat and, using a spatula, carefully transfer the salmon and lemon slices to a paper towel–lined plate. Tent loosely with foil.

3. Return the pan to high heat and simmer the cooking liquid until slightly thickened and reduced to 2 tablespoons, 4 to 5 minutes. Remove the pan from the heat; whisk in the butter and chives. Season with salt and pepper to taste.

4. Season the salmon lightly with salt and pepper. Using a spatula, carefully tilt the salmon fillets to remove the lemon slices. Place the salmon on a serving platter or individual plates; spoon the sauce over the top and serve.

POACHED SALMON WITH DILL AND SOUR CREAM SAUCE

Follow the recipe for Poached Salmon with Herb and Caper Vinaigrette through step 2, substituting 8 to 12 dill stems for the parsley and tarragon stems and omitting the capers, honey, and olive oil. Strain the cooking liquid through a fine-mesh strainer into a medium bowl; discard the solids. Return the strained liquid to the skillet; whisk in 1 table-spoon Dijon mustard and the remaining 2 tablespoons shallots. Simmer over high heat until slightly thickened

and reduced to 2 tablespoons, 4 to 5 minutes. Whisk in 2 tablespoons sour cream and the juice from 1 reserved lemon wedge; simmer for 1 minute. Remove from the heat; whisk in 2 tablespoons unsalted butter and 2 tablespoons minced fresh dill fronds. Season with salt and pepper to taste. Continue with the recipe from step 4, spooning the sauce over the salmon before serving.

GETTING IT RIGHT:
A Fish (Almost) out of Water

Standard Poach

The classic poaching method calls for submerging salmon completely in liquid in a deep pan, which causes flavor to leach out and leads to dry, flavorless fish.

Shallow Poach

In our method, small amounts of liquid allow the salmon to cook at a lower temperature, preserving flavor. Lemon slices under the fillets keep their bottoms from overcooking.

SUPER-CRISPY OVEN-FRIED FISH

WHAT WE WANTED: Moist, tender fish fillets surrounded by a golden brown, crunchy crust—all without the mess of stovetop frying.

When it comes to cooking fish in a flavorful coating, batter-fried is the gold standard. Done right, the fish is flaky and moist, encased in a crisp, delicate crust. But it's also a messy operation that splatters hot oil all over the stove and spreads fishy odors throughout the house. Most cooks forgo the grease and smells of stovetop frying for the far greater convenience of "oven-fried" fish. Here, the fillets are simply dipped in liquid, covered in bread crumbs, and baked in the oven.

The trouble is, most recipes for this dish are disappointing. The fish is often mushy and overcooked, and the bread-crumb coating ranges from thin and sandy to soggy and crumbly. Was it possible, we wondered, for tender and flavorful fillets baked in a crunchy crust to not merely play second fiddle to batter-fried fish, but stand out as worthy in their own right?

Our first task was to select the fish. We immediately ruled out dense kinds like swordfish from consideration, as their meaty texture wouldn't provide the contrast we wanted between crust and interior. Thin fillets like sole and flounder were also out; they would overcook well before the coating had a chance to brown and harden. The flaky flesh of cod or haddock (the traditional choices for fried fish) was our best bet.

As for the crumbs, we knew better than to even think of cutting corners with anything from a can or box. These stale-tasting products are the key culprits behind gritty, insubstantial coatings. But fresh crumbs made from sandwich bread also present problems: Even the thickest fish fillet will cook through too rapidly, leaving fresh crumbs undercooked and soft. And once the fish is out of the oven, any crumbs that manage to get crunchy quickly turn soggy and fail to adhere to the moist fish.

Why not start with something that was already dry and crisp? We went to our pantry and pulled out a few things that looked promising: saltine crackers, potato chips, and Melba toast. We pulsed each in the food processor and applied them to three different batches of fish, using a standard breading method: We dusted the fillets in flour, dipped them in a basic egg wash, then pressed on the crumbs. Our results were mixed. The saltines delivered a crust that was too soft. Although the chips created crusts with definite crunch, their distinctive flavors might limit our options for seasoning the fish. The neutral flavor of the Melba toast worked better, but it produced a crust so crunchy it bordered on tough.

The best option, it seemed, was to stick with fresh crumbs. We've had success toasting fresh crumbs before using them in breading for meat or chicken, and we followed suit. We tore white bread into pieces, which we pulsed in a food processor along with some melted butter. We then spread the buttery crumbs on a baking sheet and baked them in a 350-degree oven until they were a deep golden brown. We then pressed the crumbs firmly on a new batch of fillets. When we pulled the fillets out of the oven 20 minutes later, we could see that the breading on the top and sides of the fish was crispy, but the bottom crust remained soggy. We tried again with a new batch of larger, more coarsely processed crumbs. This helped, but it wasn't enough. Placing the fish on a wire rack set inside the baking sheet to allow air to circulate underneath was another step in the right direction, but we needed something more.

Moisture leaking out of the fish as it cooked was the source of the sogginess. What if we tried to remove some of this moisture before cooking? We'd already been patting the fish dry with paper towels before breading it, but a bit of extra salt might help pull out more excess moisture. We salted the fillets and left them to sit on a rack. Twenty minutes or so later, we blotted away the drops of water that had begun beading on the fish's surface. But our hopes were dashed when we took this batch of fish out of the oven: Not only were the bottom crusts still soggy, but the fish was way too salty.

Maybe the solution would be found not in the fish or the crumbs, but in the egg wash. What if we were to thicken it up, turning it into a kind of buffer zone between the moist fish and the dry bread crumbs? Casting back to deep-fried fish for inspiration, we added a few tablespoons of flour to our egg wash, thickening it to a viscous batter-like texture. We also remembered that in the past we've added mustard to egg wash to give it more sticking power. Mustard was too strong for the fish, but mayonnaise worked beautifully, adding richness and a welcome note of acidity. We covered

our fillets in a generous layer of this revamped wash before pressing on the bread crumbs. When this fish came out of the oven, we held our breath as we turned a few over to check their bottom crusts. Success! The crust was crisp and dry all the way around and firmly bonded to the fish.

Now that we'd achieved a crunchy crust, we could focus on finessing flavor. Up to this point we had seasoned the fish with nothing more than a little salt and pepper.

We mixed a range of different herb and aromatic combinations into the bread crumbs, including two of the most common additions to breading: garlic and thyme. In the end, tasters preferred the more subtle flavors of shallots and fresh parsley.

Now, what could we do to liven up the egg wash? Many deep-fried fish recipes call for a touch of paprika and cayenne pepper in their batter, and we found the same seasonings worked equally well in our wash. Still, the dish needed something more. We experimented with both Worcestershire and hot sauce, but neither did the trick. Horseradish adds a nice kick to cocktail sauce; would introducing a little bit into the coating have the same effect? We whisked a couple of teaspoons into the egg wash and found that most of the tasters couldn't even identify its flavor in the cooked fillets—just a new, fresh bite to the fish. As a final touch, we whipped up a quick tartar sauce with mayonnaise, capers, and a couple of tablespoons of sweet relish.

With or without the sauce, our moist, tender fillets in their crisp, flavorful crust could definitely hold their own as a lighter and far easier alternative to fried fish any day.

WHAT WE LEARNED: Use a thick and flaky fish like cod or haddock. To seal in moisture, dip the fish in an egg wash fortified with mayonnaise. Coat the fish with fresh bread crumbs made from sandwich bread, instead of stale store-bought crumbs. And pre-toast the bread crumbs until golden brown to get a crisp crust without overcooking the fish. To boost the flavor of the crust, add shallots and fresh parsley. For a crisp bottom crust, cook the fillets on a wire rack set inside a baking sheet to allow air to circulate underneath.

CRUNCHY OVEN-BAKED FISH

serves 4

To prevent overcooking, buy fish fillets that are at least 1 inch thick. The bread crumbs can be made up to 3 days in advance and stored at room temperature in a tightly sealed container (allow to cool fully before storing). Serve the dish with our Sweet and Tangy Tartar Sauce (recipe follows).

4	large slices high-quality white sandwich bread, torn into 1-inch pieces
2	tablespoons unsalted butter, melted Salt and ground black pepper
2	tablespoons minced fresh parsley leaves
1	small shallot, minced (about 2 tablespoons)
¼	cup plus 5 tablespoons unbleached all-purpose flour
2	large eggs
2	teaspoons prepared horseradish (optional)
3	tablespoons mayonnaise
½	teaspoon paprika
¼	teaspoon cayenne pepper (optional)
1¼	pounds cod, haddock, or other thick white fish fillet (1 to 1½ inches thick), cut into 4 pieces Lemon wedges

1. Adjust an oven rack to the middle position and heat the oven to 350 degrees. Pulse the bread, melted butter, ¼ teaspoon salt, and ¼ teaspoon black pepper in a food processor until the bread is coarsely ground, eight 1-second pulses (you should have about 3½ cups crumbs). Transfer to a rimmed baking sheet and bake until deep golden brown and dry, about 15 minutes, stirring twice during the baking time. Cool the crumbs to room temperature, about 10 minutes. Transfer the crumbs to a pie plate; toss with the parsley and shallot. Increase the oven temperature to 425 degrees.

2. Place ¼ cup of the flour in a second pie plate. In a third pie plate, whisk together the eggs, horseradish (if using), mayonnaise, paprika, cayenne (if using), and ¼ teaspoon

TECHNIQUE: Keys to a Crispy Crust

Soft, moist fish needs an extra-thick coating of bread crumbs to add flavor and crunch. Here's how we lay it on thick:

1. Pulse: Our fresh crumbs are processed very coarsely to maximize their crunch.

2. Toast: Prebaking the buttered crumbs ensures that they are brown and crisp by the time the fish is done.

3. Dip: A batter thickened with flour and mayonnaise prevents the toasted crumbs from turning soggy.

4. Coat: Pressing down gently on the crumbs helps to pack a thick layer on the fish.

5. Elevate: Elevating the fish on a wire rack set inside a baking sheet allows air to circulate underneath.

black pepper until combined; whisk in the remaining 5 tablespoons flour until smooth.

3. Spray a wire rack with vegetable oil spray and place in a rimmed baking sheet. Dry the fish thoroughly with paper towels and season with salt and pepper. Dredge 1 fillet in the flour; shake off the excess. Using tongs, coat with the egg mixture. Coat all sides of the fillet with the bread crumb mixture, pressing gently so that a thick layer of crumbs adheres to the fish. Transfer the breaded fish to the wire rack. Repeat with the remaining 3 fillets.

4. Bake the fish until an instant-read thermometer inserted into the center of the fillets registers 140 degrees, 18 to 25 minutes. Using a thin spatula, transfer the fillets to individual plates and serve immediately with lemon wedges.

SWEET AND TANGY TARTAR SAUCE

makes about 1 cup

This sauce can be refrigerated, tightly covered, for up to 1 week.

¾	cup mayonnaise
½	small shallot, minced (about 1 tablespoon)
2	tablespoons drained capers, minced
2	tablespoons sweet pickle relish
1½	teaspoons distilled white vinegar
½	teaspoon Worcestershire sauce
½	teaspoon ground black pepper

Mix all the ingredients together in a small bowl. Cover the bowl with plastic wrap and let the mixture rest to blend the flavors, about 15 minutes. Stir again before serving.

Rating Fish Spatulas

WE TESTED SIX SPATULAS, RATING THEM ON PERFORMANCE AND DESIGN. BRANDS ARE LISTED IN ORDER OF preference. See www.americastestkitchen.com for updates to this testing.

HIGHLY RECOMMENDED
Wüsthof Gourmet 7.5-Inch Slotted Turner/Fish Spatula
$29.95
Sturdy yet nimble, this arced blade sports a comfortable handle and is ideal for moving anything from fish fillets to vegetables and cookies.

RECOMMENDED
LamsonSharp Ebony 6-Inch Chef's Slotted Turner, Right Handed
$21.95
Just a notch below the Wüsthof for agility, this well-balanced turner would have been a contender for the top spot if its blade were slightly more curvaceous.

RECOMMENDED
Forschner 3 x 6-Inch Slotted Turner
$14.95
This spatula's thick poly grip and blunt design made fish-flipping a bit more challenging, but it fared well with potatoes and cookies.

RECOMMENDED WITH RESERVATIONS
Peltex Stainless Steel Spatula
$15.80
Fine for tasks that didn't involve a hot frying pan. When testers tried to turn over fish fillets with this skinny, short handle, their hands were just inches from the fire.

NOT RECOMMENDED
Kuhn Rikon Cook's 11-Inch Flexi Spatula
$15.95
An ironic name for such a rigid tool. Flexibility was at a minimum with this flat, stiff, all-metal tool that clanged every time it made contact with the pan.

NOT RECOMMENDED
OXO Good Grips Fish Turner
$11.99
Absurdly large for just about any task, this near 10-inch blade was almost as awkward to wield on a baking sheet as it was in a frying pan.

EQUIPMENT CORNER:
Fish Spatulas

FISH SPATULAS—ELONGATED VERSIONS OF THE standard pancake flipper—are designed expressly for shimmying underneath delicate fillets. And we've found no better tool for extracting sticky vegetables from a baking sheet or transferring fresh-baked pastries from oven to cooling rack.

That is, if you get your hands on a good one. A well-designed spatula combines ample strength for scraping up sticky food bits with enough pliability to sneak underneath delicate foods virtually unnoticed. Of the six blades we slipped under pan-fried fish fillets, glazed roasted sweet potato disks, and brittle butter cookies, two failed to pass muster. The OXO Good Grips Fish Turner ($11.99)

gawkily protruded almost 3 inches longer than most other models, making it nearly impossible to overturn one fish fillet without disturbing its neighbors. The uncomfortably stiff, flat, all-metal flipper from Kuhn Rikon ($15.95) needed a good, hard push to work its way under our caramelized potatoes—and even then it stuttered and lost one to the counter.

More agile blades ran a reasonable 6½ to 7 inches in length, sported a finely honed slant at their edges to dig nimbly under flaky fish, and curved gently upward at their tips to better cradle slippery foods. We didn't think the blunt and flimsy handles attached to the Forschner ($14.95) and Peltex ($15.80) blades, respectively, were deal-breakers, but it made us appreciate the ideal balance and control of the LamsonSharp ($21.95) and the sleek, supportive curl of our new favorite spatula from Wüsthof ($29.95).

Julia explains to Chris that for applesauce with the best flavor, don't peel the apples before cooking them—the skin deepens the apple taste. Once cooked, pass the applesauce through a food mill, which easily separates the skin from the fruit and makes for a smooth sauce.

THE CRUNCHIEST
pork chops ever

Most of us are familiar with the "shake-and-bake" style of seasoned coating mixes found at the supermarket. For years, moms (and kids) everywhere have been drawn in by that photo on the front of the box—the one showing a pork chop sliced open to reveal juicy meat covered by an impossibly crunchy bread crumb crust. But the truth is, those pork chops never taste as good as the picture looks. The coating can be dry, dusty, and bland, and it is far from thick—it's downright stingy. Our goals were twofold: Devise a method for baking a well-seasoned, juicy chop, and encase it in a thick, extraordinarily crunchy, flavorful crust that retains its crunch all around—even on the bottom, where most chops turn soggy.

Applesauce, paired with pork chops or simply eaten on its own, is always a treat. Most of us eat applesauce from the jar. But what about homemade? We set our sights on developing an applesauce that was worth making—so good and easy, it'll make you forget about the jarred stuff.

ULTRA-CRUNCHY BAKED PORK CHOPS

WHAT WE WANTED: Pork chops that are juicy and tender and covered with a well-seasoned, crunchy crust.

When done right, baked breaded pork chops are the ultimate comfort food: tender cutlets surrounded by a crunchy coating that crackles apart with each bite. But all too often, baked chops fall short of that ideal. Opt for the convenience of a shake-in-the-bag packaged product from the supermarket for your breading, and you wind up with a bland-tasting chop with a thin, sandy crust. Make your own breading with fresh crumbs, and the flaws are different—a soggy, patchy crust that won't stick to the meat. Our goal was clear: to cook a juicy, flavorful chop with a crisp, substantial crust that would stay on the meat from fork to mouth.

Our first task was choosing the best cut of meat. Though bone-in chops retain moisture better, we decided on a boneless cut for this dish, so we wouldn't have to bread the bone and there would be no distraction from the crunchy crust. This gave us two options: sirloin or center-cut. We settled on center-cut boneless loin chops, which were not only easier to find in the supermarket but also cooked more evenly.

Next we needed to determine the chop size. The ½-inch-thick chops generally used for pan-frying were too easily overwhelmed by the kind of crust we wanted, and the 1½-inch-thick chops usually reserved for barbecuing or stuffing proved to be too thick, giving us too much meat and not enough crust. Pork chops that fell in between—¾ to 1 inch thick—were the tasters' top choice.

The test kitchen's standard breading method (dusting with flour, dipping in beaten egg, and rolling in toasted bread crumbs) was sufficient as we figured out the best cooking technique. Simply baking the breaded chops on a baking sheet, the most obvious method and one used in many recipes, made the bottoms soggy. We tried breading just the top and sides, and although this quick fix worked, tasters felt cheated. What if we let air circulation keep the

bottom crumbs crisp? Placing the chops on a wire rack set inside the baking sheet definitely helped. Upping the oven temperature from 350 to 425 degrees helped even more. The coating crisped up more readily, and the excess moisture evaporated by the time the pork reached the requisite 150-degree serving temperature.

We had figured out the right chops to use and the proper way to cook them. Now we could concentrate on the breading. Tasters deemed panko too fine-textured and bland. Crushed Melba toast was crunchier but didn't stick together. Ultimately, tasters preferred the fresh flavor and slight sweetness of crumbs made from white sandwich bread. We tossed the fresh crumbs with a little salt, pepper, and oil, then spread them on a baking sheet and toasted them until they were golden brown. The resulting crust was decently crisp but still not as good as we knew it could be. What if we took a cue from the supermarket coating and toasted the crumbs to a deeper brown? Though boxed crumbs produce a crust that is thin and sandy, the processed coating does have one thing going for it: a true crispness that we'd yet to achieve. For the next test, we left the crumbs in the oven until they looked dangerously overtoasted and were pleasantly surprised that this worked—the breading didn't burn when baked again on the chops, and our crumb coating was now seriously crisp. To add even more flavor, we stirred in some minced garlic and shallot with the crumbs before they went into the oven and tossed in some grated Parmesan cheese and minced herbs after they cooled. These chops tasted great. Everything would be perfect if we could just ensure one thing: that the crumbs stuck onto the pork evenly, rather than peeling off in patches.

With crumbs as thick and coarse as these, we knew we'd need something with more holding power than a typical egg wash to glue them to the pork. We recalled a cookbook recipe that used mustard instead of eggs to stick crumbs on chops. A straight swap made the taste too intense, but keeping the eggs and adding a few tablespoons of Dijon mustard thickened the mixture nicely and brought just enough new flavor to the mix. But although the crumbs stuck onto the baked chops better than they had with a simple egg wash, a few areas still flaked off.

We then wondered what would happen if we got rid of the egg wash altogether and dipped the floured chops into a thick batter before breading them. It seems an odd suggestion. After all, batter is for fried food. Who ever heard of using it for baking? We did it anyway, using a basic fritto misto batter of flour, cornstarch, water, oil, and eggs as our base. Fully expecting this experiment to tank, we were surprised when the pork chops came out with a crust that was crunchier than before and stayed on like a protective sheath. This batter, though, requires resting and seemed too fussy for a weeknight dish. But what if we made a quick egg wash that was more like a batter?

We whisked enough flour into the egg and mustard mixture to give it the thick consistency of mayonnaise. After flouring the chops, we coated them evenly in the egg wash/batter hybrid, covered them in bread crumbs, and baked them again. Much better, but there was a soft, puffy layer directly beneath the crumbs. Replacing the whole eggs with egg whites, which have less fat but enough protein to lend sticking power, provided just the crisp, dry crust we were looking for. But even more impressive, the crumbs clung firmly to the meat, even during some heavy knife-and-fork action. This pork finally had some real chops.

WHAT WE LEARNED: Use center-cut boneless loin chops—they are easy to find and they cook more evenly—and brine them so they are moist and juicy. For the coating, use fresh bread crumbs, but toast them first for crispness, then doctor them with garlic, shallots, Parmesan cheese, and minced herbs for flavor. To form a strong adhering agent for the crumbs, make a quick batter-like mixture by whisking flour and mustard into egg whites. Place the breaded chops on a wire rack set inside a baking sheet to allow air to circulate completely around the chops, keeping the bottom crumbs crisp.

CRUNCHY BAKED PORK CHOPS

serves 4

This recipe was developed using natural pork, but enhanced pork (injected with a salt solution) will work as well. If using enhanced pork, eliminate the brining in step 1. The bread crumb mixture can be prepared through step 2 up to 3 days in advance. The breaded chops can be frozen for up to 1 week. They don't need to be thawed before baking; simply increase the cooking time in step 5 to 35 to 40 minutes.

Salt
4   boneless center-cut pork chops, 6 to 8 ounces each, ¾ to 1 inch thick, trimmed of excess fat (see note)
4   slices good-quality white sandwich bread, torn into 1-inch pieces
1   small shallot, minced (about 2 tablespoons)
3   medium garlic cloves, minced or pressed through a garlic press (about 1 tablespoon)
2   tablespoons vegetable oil
    Ground black pepper
2   tablespoons grated Parmesan cheese
½   teaspoon minced fresh thyme leaves
2   tablespoons minced fresh parsley leaves
¼   cup plus 6 tablespoons unbleached all-purpose flour
3   large egg whites
3   tablespoons Dijon mustard
    Lemon wedges

1. Adjust an oven rack to the middle position and heat the oven to 350 degrees. Dissolve ¼ cup salt in 1 quart water in a medium container or gallon-sized zipper-lock bag. Submerge the chops, cover the container with plastic wrap or seal the bag, and refrigerate for 30 minutes. Rinse the chops under cold water and dry thoroughly with paper towels.

2. Meanwhile, pulse the bread in a food processor until coarsely ground, about eight 1-second pulses (you should

1. Dip: A thick batter of flour, mustard, and egg whites grips the bread crumbs like glue.

2. Coat: Coating the chops with fresh, well-toasted bread crumbs results in a crust with flavor and crunch.

3. Elevate: Baking the chops on a rack set in a baking sheet allows greater air circulation and prevents the bottoms from turning soggy.

have about 3½ cups crumbs). Transfer the crumbs to a rimmed baking sheet and add the shallot, garlic, oil, ¼ teaspoon salt, and ¼ teaspoon pepper. Toss until the crumbs are evenly coated with the oil. Bake until deep golden brown and dry, about 15 minutes, stirring twice during the baking time. (Do not turn off the oven.) Cool to room temperature. Toss the crumbs with the Parmesan, thyme, and parsley.

3. Place ¼ cup of the flour in a pie plate. In a second pie plate, whisk the egg whites and mustard until combined; add the remaining 6 tablespoons flour and whisk until almost smooth, with pea-sized lumps remaining.

4. Increase the oven temperature to 425 degrees. Spray a wire rack with vegetable oil spray and place in a rimmed baking sheet. Season the chops with pepper. Dredge 1 pork chop in the flour; shake off the excess. Using tongs, coat with the egg mixture; let the excess drip off. Coat all sides of the chop with the bread crumb mixture, pressing gently so that a thick layer of crumbs adheres to the chop. Transfer the breaded chop to the wire rack. Repeat with the remaining 3 chops.

5. Bake until an instant-read thermometer inserted into the center of the chops registers 150 degrees, 17 to 25 minutes. Let rest on the rack for 5 minutes before serving with lemon wedges.

GETTING IT RIGHT: Coatings without the Crunch

Thin
This popular boxed mix gives chops an insubstantial, bland crust.

Patchy
The crust peels off chops dipped in a typical thin egg wash.

Crumbly
Fresh, untoasted crumbs have trouble sticking to the chop.

CRUNCHY BAKED PORK CHOPS WITH PROSCIUTTO AND ASIAGO CHEESE

Follow the recipe for Crunchy Baked Pork Chops through step 3, omitting the salt in the bread crumb mixture. Before breading, place a ⅛-inch-thick slice Asiago cheese (about ½ ounce) on top of each chop. Wrap each chop with 1 thin slice prosciutto, pressing on the prosciutto so that the cheese and meat adhere to each other. Proceed with the recipe from step 4, being careful when handling the chops so that the cheese and meat do not come apart during breading.

SCIENCE DESK: The 30-Minute Brine

YOU MIGHT BE TEMPTED TO SKIP THE BRINING STEP when preparing Crunchy Baked Pork Chops. Don't. Center-cut chops are quite lean, and left untreated they will be very dry and chewy, even when cooked to medium (an internal temperature of 150 degrees). The salt in the brine changes the structure of the muscle proteins and allows them to hold on to more moisture when exposed to heat. Tasters had no trouble picking out the chops that were brined versus chops that were untreated.

If you're accustomed to brining a turkey for the holidays, you might think you don't have time to brine pork chops for a weeknight recipe like this. But we found that making the brine super-concentrated (with ¼ cup of table salt dissolved in 1 quart water) gets the job done in just 30 minutes—the time it will take you to prepare the fresh bread crumb coating. And our potent brine fits, along with four chops, in a medium container or gallon-sized zipper-lock bag. No brining bucket needed.

One exception: If you've purchased enhanced chops injected with a salt solution, don't brine them. The injected solution will make the chops moist, even spongy, and brining will make the meat way too salty. We prefer the flavor of natural chops and find that 30 minutes in a strong brine makes them plenty juicy.

TASTING LAB: Dijon Mustards

TO BE LABELED DIJON, A MUSTARD MUST ADHERE TO the formula developed more than 150 years ago in Dijon, France. Finely ground brown or black mustard seeds are mixed with an acidic liquid (vinegar, wine, and/or grape must) and sparsely seasoned with salt and sometimes a hint of spice. Dijon should be smooth and have a clean, nose-tingling heat. To find out which Dijon mustard is best, we rounded up eight nationally available brands and tasted them plain and in a simple mustard vinaigrette. What did we find out?

Our tasters preferred spicier mustards. The three hottest mustards—Grey Poupon, Maille, and Roland—were our tasters' overall favorites. Interestingly, when we measured the pH level of each brand, this hot trio also proved to be the least acidic. (Note that a higher pH value equals lower acidity.) A peek inside the mustard-making process explains why. When mustard seeds are ground, an enzyme

Rating Dijon Mustards

TWENTY-TWO MEMBERS OF THE AMERICA'S TEST KITCHEN STAFF TASTED EIGHT BRANDS OF MUSTARD PLAIN (with pretzels on the side) and in a simple vinaigrette. Brands are listed in order of preference. See www.americastestkitchen.com for updates to this tasting.

HIGHLY RECOMMENDED
Grey Poupon Dijon Mustard

$3.79 for 10 ounces; pH: 3.64

This "potent," "bold" American-made mustard was deemed the hottest by tasters. It "gets you in the nose like a Dijon should." A "nice balance of sweet, tangy, and sharp" sealed the deal for one happy taster, who declared, "I want this on my ham and cheese sandwich."

HIGHLY RECOMMENDED
Maille Dijon Originale Traditional Dijon Mustard

$3.99 for 7.5 ounces; pH: 3.68

This French brand is made in Canada, where the bulk of the mustard seeds for the French mustard industry are grown. It had a "nice balance of heat and complexity," with tasters calling out "perfumey" flavors of "smoke," "butter," "fruit," and "pepper." It was the second-hottest mustard in our lineup.

HIGHLY RECOMMENDED
Roland Extra Strong Dijon Mustard

$4.79 for 13 ounces; pH: 3.80

This French mustard features a "sharp horse-radish bite" and "nasal heat" and was the third-hottest mustard overall. Tasters loved the "smoky," "oaky," and "meaty" flavors. "Surprising complexity."

RECOMMENDED
Jack Daniel's Stone Ground Dijon Mustard

$3.49 for 9 ounces; pH: 3.58

Tasters didn't detect much heat in this "mild and sweet" sample when tasting it plain, but its heat bloomed in the vinaigrette, where it was deemed "robust" and "salty" (it had the most salt of any sample).

RECOMMENDED WITH RESERVATIONS
Annie's Naturals Organic Dijon Mustard

$3.49 for 9 ounces; pH: 3.45

This sample's "warm spice flavor" hurt its overall scores: "weird sweet and spicy notes" was a common complaint. Tasters thought this mustard was too acidic, noting its "tart," "pickley" character.

RECOMMENDED WITH RESERVATIONS
French's Dijon Mustard

$2.99 for 9 ounces; pH: 3.47

"Highly acidic—almost tastes pickled," "way too much vinegar," and "overly tangy without balance" were common complaints. Still, some tasters thought it was passable, calling this supermarket standard "not remarkable, but not terrible" and "like ballpark mustard."

RECOMMENDED WITH RESERVATIONS
Westbrae Natural Dijon Style Mustard

$2.50 for 8 ounces; pH: 3.45

This mustard tied for the most acidic and had the least amount of salt, prompting tasters to describe it as "lacking depth," "with no interesting dance of flavors." A few did like its "mellow, building heat."

NOT RECOMMENDED
Plochman's Premium Dijon Mustard

$2.99 for 9 ounces; pH: 3.46

Tasters were disappointed that this "watery," "sour," "fruity and weak" sample had "no heat or complexity." "Sissy mustard" sums up its performance.

called myrosinase is released. The myrosinase activates the mustard's dormant heat-producing chemicals (called glucosinolates), but the addition of acid retards this reaction. So less acid produces a mustard with more heat-producing chemicals. These heat-producing chemicals, however, are volatile and will dissipate over time. For this reason, we recommend checking "use by" dates, buying fresher mustards when possible, and never storing Dijon for more than six months.

What other qualities mattered? The presence or absence of wine in these mustards did not impact results: Grey Poupon has it, but Maille and Roland do not. Country of origin didn't matter either, as Grey Poupon is made in the United States, Maille in Canada, and Roland in France. What was important was balance. Our tasters downgraded mustards that were too acidic, too salty, or muddied with other flavors.

EQUIPMENT CORNER:
Inexpensive Nonstick Skillets

WE'VE ALWAYS RECOMMENDED BUYING INEXPENSIVE nonstick skillets, because with regular use the nonstick coating inevitably scratches, chips off, or becomes ineffective. Why spend big bucks on a pan that will last only a year or two? We rounded up eight models priced under $60 and pitted them against our gold standard, the $135 nonstick skillet from All-Clad, to see how they measure up.

We evaluated the skillets through a series of tests with each pan: Sautéing onions and carrots, cooking thin fillets of sole, making omelets, and frying eggs (with no added fat). We found that they all did an acceptable job cooking and releasing these foods. There were noticeable differences in sauté speed, but most home cooks know if their cookware runs a bit fast or slow and adjust accordingly; we did not factor sauté speed into our scoring.

Next, we examined the size of each skillet. Each skillet measures 12 inches from lip to lip, but we found plenty of differences in the usable cooking space. The actual flat cooking surface ranged from 9 inches (in four pans) to 10½ inches (for the T-fal pan), which can make all the difference when you need room to sear an extra pork chop or piece of chicken. Volume capacity ranged from the WearEver pan's shade below 13 cups to the Circulon's 19-plus cups. Unless the pans were too heavy for some users (like the KitchenAid and Farberware models), we think bigger is better. Testers also preferred pans with flared sides (which made maneuvering food easier).

We also considered each skillet's handle. Our testers preferred handles made entirely of metal, which are securely riveted to the pan and can withstand higher temperatures in the oven. The Farberware, Rachael Ray, and Circulon handles consist of metal and heat-resistant silicone, but their heat resistance is limited to 400 degrees (per manufacturers' recommendations). A skillet handle should also be comfortable, sturdy, and balanced, and it should stay cool during cooking. Finally, all testers disliked the helper handles on the Cuisinart and KitchenAid skillets, which made the pans cumbersome to use on a stove filled with other pots and pans.

To gauge the skillets' durability, we cooked 12-egg frittatas while doing several things that manufacturers specifically forbid in each pan: broiling, cutting with a sharp knife, removing the slices with a metal pie server, and washing with an abrasive metal scrubber. Two pans, the Circulon and WearEver, made it through these tests with only minimal scratching, while the Cuisinart, Rachael Ray, and T-fal pans were quite beat up.

So what did we find? The $135 All-Clad is still the best pan out there, but some of the cheaper pans performed nearly as well. You can buy four of the solid WearEver pans (and get change back) for the cost of the All-Clad. The larger Circulon pan is a good choice for the strong-armed cook.

Rating Inexpensive Nonstick Skillets

WE TESTED EIGHT MODELS OF NONSTICK SKILLETS (ALL PRICED UNDER $60) ALONG WITH OUR TEST KITCHEN FAVORITE, the $135 All-Clad Skillet, by sautéing onions and carrots, cooking thin fillets of sole, making omelets, and frying eggs (with no added fat). In addition to performance, we rated the skillets on ease of use and durability. Brands are listed in order of preference. See www.americastestkitchen.com for updates to this testing.

RECOMMENDED
WearEver Premium Hard Anodized 12-Inch Nonstick Skillet
$28.03

This light pan was a breeze to maneuver and sautéed at a rapid pace. Testers "liked the feel" of the "comfortable" handle, which stayed cool on the stovetop. We wish the cooking surface and capacity were a tad larger.

RECOMMENDED
Circulon Elite Hard Anodized 12-Inch Nonstick Deep Skillet
$59.95

This "heavy" pan aced the durability test; the signature raised concentric ridges really do seem to improve longevity. One tester was especially impressed by the huge volume: "You could make stock in this." A few testers were put off by its straight sides, which made manipulating food a little tricky.

RECOMMENDED
Calphalon Simply Calphalon Nonstick 12-Inch Skillet
$54.95

This pan performed well, thanks in part to its light weight and the even, gentle slope of the sides. The "nicely angled" handle stayed cool, but many testers disliked the "awkward" molded ridge on the grip. This pan has a relatively small capacity.

RECOMMENDED
Cuisinart Chef's Classic Non-Stick Hard Anodized 12-Inch Skillet
$49.95

This heavy pan cooked well, and testers liked the nicely flared lip and overall shape. The handle stayed cool in the kitchen but was considered to be "too thin" for a perfect grip, and the helper handle was deemed "completely unnecessary."

RECOMMENDED
Farberware Millennium Soft Touch Stainless Steel 12-Inch Nonstick Skillet
$39.99

This "nicely shaped" pan felt "very sturdy" and sautéed very slowly. Some testers praised this pan as "heavy and big," but others thought it too "awkward," "too heavy," and "not well balanced." The handle was comfortable but "not balanced perfectly."

RECOMMENDED WITH RESERVATIONS
KitchenAid Gourmet Distinctions Stainless Steel 12-Inch Nonstick Skillet
$49.95

As the heaviest pan in our lineup, this drew mixed reviews. Some testers called it "beastly" and "ridiculously" heavy, but a few praised its "hefty" construction. The helper handle just "got in the way."

RECOMMENDED WITH RESERVATIONS
Rachael Ray Porcelain Enamel Nonstick 12-Inch French Skillet
$29.95

This "wok-like" pan has a "comfortable" metal and silicone handle—but the exposed metal closest to the pan got dangerously hot. The cooking surface became significantly scratched up during our abuse tests.

NOT RECOMMENDED
T-fal Solano Hard Enamel 12-Inch Sauté Pan
$24.99

"Bad ergonomics" and "handles awkwardly" were typical complaints from testers. We liked the large cooking surface, but this pan finished at the bottom for all our other criteria, and its screw-on plastic handle loosened considerably during testing.

SIMPLIFYING APPLESAUCE

WHAT WE WANTED: A thick, smooth sauce that showcases the flavor of the apples without too much sweetness or spice.

Choose the right apple and add nothing more than sugar and water—it's that simple. The joys of homemade applesauce are subtle but persuasive. Compared with its jarred counterpart, which tends to be sweet, bland, and runny, homemade is noticeably fresh, with a deep apple flavor and a thick, supple texture. And it's simple to make. In fact, if you have a food mill nearby, you don't even need to peel the apples. Still, applesauce doesn't always come out perfectly. Often the tart, sweet, fruity, floral nuances of fresh apple flavor are lost to a heavy hand with sweeteners and spices, so the sauce ends up tasting like a bad pie filling. The texture, too, can vary from dry and chunky to loose and thin.

To us, preserving the taste of fresh apples was paramount. We wanted a pure, deep apple flavor that was neutral enough to swing both ways, either savory or sweet. For texture, we wanted a sauce that was soft, smooth, and thick, almost like a pudding.

We kicked off this project with a massive tasting of 18 different apple varieties, each made into a simple applesauce. Following considerable post-tasting deliberation and discussion, we broke down the group into three categories: highly recommended, recommended, and not recommended for making sauce (see the chart on page 60).

The flavor of the apples, more than their texture or color, influenced our judgment. Each of the apples that we recommend highly for sauce has distinctive individual flavor characteristics, yet each earned praise for its balance of sweet and tart, which many tasters interpreted as depth of flavor. The standouts in this group were the Jonagold, which garnered comments such as "delicate, spicy, fruity, and peachy," and the Pink Lady, which was described as "spicy, perfumed, and balanced." Jonagold's victory is

good news for applesauce aficionados. According to a representative of the U.S. Apple Association, this variety is widely grown and readily available throughout the country during apple season. Pink Lady is included on the Apple Association's list of "up-and-coming" new varieties.

Apples that were not as well loved but still made acceptable sauce fell into the "recommended" category. The common thread among these varieties, including Golden Delicious, Rome, McIntosh, and Empire, was a milder flavor, with less dimension and depth than our absolute favorites. In short, these are fine choices in the absence of more interesting varieties. The apples in our "not recommended" category produced sauces that tasted either sour or flat.

We then decided to test combinations of apples. We were shocked when tasters flatlined in response to the first few blends. For instance, a McIntosh–Golden Delicious combination was judged to have a "muddy, indistinct" flavor. One taster thought that a mix of Cortland and Macoun tasted like jarred baby food. Based on the first few tests, tasters concluded that single-variety sauces had purer, stronger character. So rather than continue down this twisty path of combinations, we decided to leave well enough alone.

In the recipes we tested, debate raged as to whether the apples should be cooked with or without their peels, and test results tipped the scales in favor of including peels. Most tasters thought this sauce tasted more complex than the skinless sauce, which was judged simple and straightforward. Cooking the apples with their peels has both advantages—it saves time and effort—and disadvantages—a food mill is required for pureeing to separate the spent skins from the sauce. We opted in favor of the food mill because it is an easy, effective way to puree, and it produces a sauce with the smooth, thick, almost silky texture we considered ideal. We also tried running the apples through a food processor and blender, but these sauces were too runny, and the bits of skin left behind, though tiny, were unpleasant.

To determine how the apples should be prepared, we

Rating Apples for Applesauce

WE TESTED 18 APPLE VARIETIES FOR OUR APPLESAUCE RECIPE. APPLES ARE LISTED IN ORDER OF PREFERENCE.

HIGHLY RECOMMENDED

Jonagold
Fruity, spicy, honey-like, sweet/tart, balanced

Jonathan
Complex, tangy, interesting, well rounded

Pink Lady
Spicy, assertive, sweet/tart, perfumed, balanced

Macoun
Sweet/tart, deep, solid, round

RECOMMENDED

Golden Delicious: Sweet, solid, mainstream
Empire: Mild, buttery, strawberry-like tones
McIntosh: Refreshing, tart, watery, balanced
Rome: Beautiful color, mild, generic

NOT RECOMMENDED

Granny Smith: Mealy, mushy, tart
Braeburn: Odd, plasticky
Cortland: Mild, uninteresting, plasticky
Baldwin: Chalky, bland, little flavor
IdaRed: Dense, tart, vegetal
Northern Spy: Sour, sour, sour, flat
Stayman/Winesap: Gluey, sour, tart
Spartan: Gummy, mealy, dull
Honeycrisp: Shallow, sour, citrusy
Mutsu/Crispin: Floury, potatoey, sour

---

tried cooking apples that had been broken down into both neat 1½-inch slices and rough 1½-inch chunks. Both the slices and the chunks cooked at about the same rate and resulted in no flavor differences, so we took the easier route and went with the chunks. Though we had been cooking the apples in a Dutch oven on the stovetop, we tried microwaving them, as suggested in several recipes. These apples tasted steamed and bland, so we stuck to the stovetop. We found that covering the Dutch oven accelerated the cooking time by up to 10 minutes, reducing it to a total of roughly 15 minutes.

Some of our initial tests produced applesauce that was too dry for our tastes, making it clear that a little extra liquid was necessary. So we tested various amounts of plain water, apple juice, cider, and sparkling cider and found that we preferred water for its invisibility. One cup, added at the beginning of cooking, was just right.

We tried the three sweeteners that we came across most often in recipes: granulated sugar, brown sugar, and honey. Plain white sugar earned unanimous approval because, like the water, it did not compete with the flavor of the apples.

To decide how much sugar we wanted, we tried batches with 1 tablespoon and up to 6 for our 4 pounds of apples. Four tablespoons of sugar enhanced the apple flavor of the sauce without oversweetening it. A pinch of salt added at the outset of cooking heightened the flavor even further, but all of the usual blandishments, including cinnamon, cloves, ground ginger, nutmeg, allspice, and vanilla, competed with the apple flavor. As far as the master recipe was concerned, any seasonings other than sugar and salt were out.

This applesauce is about as pure and as streamlined as they come. It may take a little more time than opening a jar, but once you taste the difference, you'll be dusting off the food mill and buying extra bushels of Jonagolds this fall.

WHAT WE LEARNED: Choose the right apple—Jonagold, Jonathan, Pink Lady, and Macoun varieties all produce a sauce with a pleasing balance of tart and sweet. Don't peel the apples; cooking the skin with the fruit further boosts flavor. Pass the cooked apples through a food mill for a silky-smooth, thick texture. And season the sauce modestly, with just a little sugar and a pinch of salt.

SIMPLE APPLESAUCE

makes about 3½ cups

If you do not own a food mill or you prefer applesauce with a coarse texture, peel the apples before coring and cutting them, and, after cooking, mash them against the side of the pot with a wooden spoon or against the bottom of the pot with a potato masher. Applesauce made with out-of-season apples may be somewhat drier than sauce made with peak-season apples, so it's likely that in step 2 of the recipe you will need to add more water to adjust the texture. If you double the recipe, the apples will need 10 to 15 minutes of extra cooking time.

4	pounds apples (8 to 12 medium), preferably Jonagold, Pink Lady, Jonathan, or Macoun, unpeeled, cored, and cut into rough 1½-inch pieces
¼	cup sugar, plus more as needed
	Pinch salt
1	cup water, plus more as needed

1. Toss the apples, sugar, salt, and water in a large, heavy-bottomed nonreactive Dutch oven. Cover the pot and cook the apples over medium-high heat until they begin to break down, 15 to 20 minutes, checking and stirring occasionally with a wooden spoon to break up any large chunks.

2. Process the cooked apples through a food mill fitted with the medium disk. Season with extra sugar or add water to adjust the consistency as desired. Serve hot, warm, at room temperature, or chilled.

APPLESAUCE: Dressing It Up

Although we prefer our applesauce straight up, it takes well to a wide range of flavorings. We tested dozens of options and have listed our favorites below.

Butter: 2 tablespoons, unsalted—stir into finished sauce

Cinnamon: two 3-inch sticks—cook with apples and remove prior to pureeing; or ¼ teaspoon ground—stir into finished sauce

Clove: 4 pieces, whole—cook with apples and remove prior to pureeing

Cranberry: 1 cup, fresh or frozen—cook and puree with apples

Ginger: three ½-inch slices fresh ginger, smashed—cook with apples and remove prior to pureeing

Lemon: 1 teaspoon zest—cook and puree with apples; or 2 tablespoons juice—stir into finished sauce

Red Hot Candy: ⅔ cup—cook and puree with apples

Star Anise: 2 pieces, whole—cook with apples and remove prior to pureeing

Here, Becky prepares stuffed chicken breasts the French way, with a meat-based filling complemented by mushrooms, leeks, and herbs. The filling remains moist after cooking and adds rich flavor to every bite.

FOUR-STAR STUFFED
chicken breasts

CHAPTER 6

The next time you're planning a menu for company, choose chicken breasts. Easy to serve, chicken breasts require no last-minute fussing (or carving!). Boring, you say? We don't think so—especially when chicken breasts are given a stylish French makeover. The French skin and bone a whole chicken and stuff the breast with the leg meat. Once stuffed, the whole chicken is rewrapped in the skin. It sounds complicated—and it is. We aimed to apply this concept to chicken breasts—a whole lot simpler, but no less impressive. Our goals were to develop a flavorful, moist stuffing that didn't rely on chicken legs and we wanted to find a way to evenly distribute the stuffing so that each bite contained a flavor-packed forkful. And what about the stuffing method? We'd need to home in on just the right technique so these chicken breasts stayed sealed all the way through cooking.

What makes a company-worthy salad? For starters, don't begin with the same old lettuce; instead, choose spicy arugula. The challenge with arugula is finding other salad components (as well as a dressing) that will complement its peppery bite. And because we wanted these salads to be special enough for company, we'd be looking beyond our crisper drawer for worthy candidates.

IN THIS CHAPTER

THE RECIPES

Stuffed Chicken Breasts

Arugula Salad with Figs, Prosciutto, Walnuts, and Parmesan
Arugula Salad with Grapes, Fennel, Gorgonzola, and Pecans
Arugula Salad with Oranges, Feta, and Sugared Pistachios

EQUIPMENT CORNER

Meat Pounders

TASTING LAB

Black Peppercorns

FRENCH-STYLE STUFFED CHICKEN BREASTS

WHAT WE WANTED: An easier approach to the classic but complicated approach to stuffing chicken breasts.

Cheesy, bready stuffing is the first thing an American cook falls back on to fill chicken breasts. This approach is fine but ho-hum. The French, however, take the concept in a different direction: a stuffing of forcemeat made from the chicken itself. The idea derives from a classic preparation known as a *ballotine*. This complex method involves skinning and boning a whole chicken, stuffing the breasts with the leg meat, and wrapping them back up in the skin. The real deal is usually made only by professional chefs in four-star restaurants. Could we come up with a version that doesn't require a culinary degree to create?

Since we wanted to make things as simple as possible, boning a whole chicken was out of the question. We decided to start with boneless, skinless breasts, which meant we'd have to come up with a stuffing that didn't rely on the traditional dark meat. We tried eliminating the meat altogether and simply using vegetables as a base. The meatless stuffing of mushrooms accented by leeks and herbs tasted great, but as soon as we cut into the chicken, the filling fell out onto the board. We needed a binder. We tried a wide assortment, including cubed white bread, ricotta cheese, and cornbread. A few of these variations tasted fine, but they took us back to producing a more pedestrian style of stuffed chicken breast.

We thought of buying one extra chicken breast to use in the filling, but most supermarkets sell them in packages of two or four. What if we bought larger breasts and trimmed a little meat off each? The trimmings, used in conjunction with the mushroom and leek stuffing we'd already developed, might make a filling that was both tasty and cohesive.

We began with a new batch of breasts that weighed 8 ounces each. We trimmed 1½ ounces off each, pureed the trimmings to a fine paste in the food processor, then folded in the sautéed mushrooms and leeks. Success!

With just a small amount of meat as a binder, the filling firmed up enough to stay in place during cooking and stayed together even when we sliced the chicken into thin medallions.

We started off using the simple slit-and-tuck method of stuffing: cutting a pocket in the chicken, inserting the filling, and securing it with toothpicks. This technique, however, exposed the chicken's entire surface to the heat, which caused it to overcook and become dry and fibrous. The original ballotine method, in which the stuffing is spread over the pounded breast before being rolled up into a roulade, produced much better results. The chicken and stuffing were more uniformly distributed, allowing them to cook evenly and guaranteeing that each bite contained a mixture of both.

We were having difficulty pounding out the breasts to exactly the right thickness (they tended to tear apart or develop leaky holes) until we started butterflying, or opening the breasts up, before pounding. Now we could easily pound the breasts to a uniform ¼-inch thickness. But no matter how carefully we pounded the chicken, it inevitably came out unevenly shaped, making it difficult to roll into a neat roulade. There was an easy and elegant solution: Instead of trimming meat for the stuffing before pounding the chicken, we reversed the order. We first pounded the breasts, then trimmed them to form perfect, easy-to-roll rectangles, reserving the trimmings for the stuffing. Now all we had to do was spread the stuffing mixture on each breast, roll it up, and tie it with twine.

Now that we had a flavorful, cohesive stuffing and a good assembly method, we shifted our attention to cooking technique. A classic ballotine is generally cooked in one of two ways: roasting or poaching. Roasting nicely browns the exterior but can produce leathery results. Poaching, on the other hand, produces meat that's very tender and moist but also bland. What if we combined the high-heat browning of a hot skillet with a gentler cooking method to finish? A quick braise might do the trick.

For our next test, we browned the chicken on all sides, added chicken broth and wine to the pan, covered it, and brought it to a simmer. We'd unwittingly killed two birds with one stone: We had the most flavorful, evenly cooked chicken yet and also a braising liquid that could serve as a base for a pan sauce. When the chicken was cooked through, we removed it from the pan, stirred in some mustard, and reduced the contents of the pan to create a concentrated sauce. Chopped parsley and a little butter rounded out the flavors.

Sliced into thin medallions and drizzled with the pan sauce, our stuffed chicken breasts had all the hallmarks of the French original: moist chicken wrapped around a cohesive stuffing, all enhanced with an intense sauce. Even with shortcuts, it was definitely a meal worthy of four stars.

WHAT WE LEARNED: For even cooking—and to better distribute the filling—butterfly the chicken breasts, then pound them to ¼-inch thickness. Trim the extra chicken meat off the pounded chicken breasts to make perfectly symmetric rolls, and save the chicken trimmings to bind the leek and mushroom stuffing together. For the best flavor and texture, cook the chicken two ways: Brown it in a skillet to get a nice brown exterior, and then braise it for a moist interior. Lastly, use the braising liquid as a flavorful base for the sauce.

STUFFED CHICKEN BREASTS

serves 4 to 6

If your chicken breasts come with the tenderloins attached, pull them off and reserve them to make the puree in step 1. If necessary, trim these breasts to make uniform rectangles and to yield 1½ to 2 ounces total trimmings per breast. Because the stuffing contains raw chicken, it is important to check its temperature in step 5.

chicken

4   boneless, skinless chicken breasts (8 ounces each, see note)

stuffing

3   tablespoons vegetable oil
10   ounces white mushrooms, trimmed, wiped clean, and sliced thin
1   small leek, white part halved lengthwise, washed, and chopped (about 1 cup)
2   medium garlic cloves, minced or pressed through a garlic press (about 2 teaspoons)
½   teaspoon chopped fresh thyme leaves
1   tablespoon juice from 1 lemon
½   cup dry white wine
1   tablespoon chopped fresh parsley leaves
     Salt and ground black pepper
1   cup low-sodium chicken broth

sauce

1   teaspoon Dijon mustard
2   tablespoons unsalted butter

1. FOR THE CHICKEN: Use the tip of a sharp chef's knife to cut each breast horizontally, starting at the thinnest end and stopping the knife tip ½ inch away from the edge so that the halves remain attached. Open up the breasts to create 4 cutlets. Place 1 cutlet at a time in a heavy-duty zipper-lock bag and pound to ¼-inch thickness (the cutlet should measure about 8 by 6 inches). Trim about ½ inch

TECHNIQUE: The Secrets to Successful Stuffed Chicken Breasts

1. Butterfly: Slice each breast horizontally, stopping ½ inch from the edges so the halves remain attached.

2. Pound: Open up each breast, place it in a zipper-lock bag, and pound it to ¼-inch thickness.

3. Trim: Trim about ½ inch from the long side of each cutlet to form an 8 by 5-inch rectangle. Reserve the trimmings for the stuffing.

4. Spread: Spread the stuffing evenly over each cutlet, leaving a ¾-inch border along the short sides and a ¼-inch border along the long sides.

5. Roll: With the short side facing you, roll up each cutlet and secure it snugly with twine.

from the long sides of the cutlets (about 1½ to 2 ounces of meat per cutlet, or a total of ½ cup from all 4 cutlets) to form rectangles that measure about 8 by 5 inches. Process all the trimmings in a food processor until smooth, about 20 seconds. Transfer the puree to a medium bowl and set aside. (Do not wash the food processor bowl.)

TESTING NOTES: Filling Failure

The typical bread and cheese fillings for stuffed chicken breasts come with a host of problems.

Pasty and Dense
The bread stuffing in this breast was heavy and thick and failed to adhere to the chicken.

Overly Oozy
The ricotta filling in this slit-and-stuff breast oozed out while cooking, releasing curds of cheese.

2. FOR THE STUFFING: Heat 1 tablespoon of the oil in a 12-inch skillet over medium-high heat until shimmering. Add the mushrooms and cook, stirring occasionally, until all the moisture has evaporated and the mushrooms are golden brown, 8 to 11 minutes. Add 1 tablespoon more oil and the leek; continue to cook, stirring frequently, until softened, 2 to 4 minutes. Add the garlic and thyme and cook, stirring frequently, until fragrant, about 30 seconds. Add 1½ teaspoons of the lemon juice and cook until all the moisture has evaporated, about 30 seconds. Transfer the mixture to the bowl of the food processor. Return the pan to the heat; add the wine and scrape the pan bottom to loosen the browned bits. Transfer the wine to a small bowl and set aside. Rinse and dry the skillet.

3. Pulse the mushroom mixture in the food processor until roughly chopped, about five 1-second pulses. Transfer the mushroom mixture to the bowl with the pureed chicken. Add 1½ teaspoons of the parsley, ¾ teaspoon salt, and ½ teaspoon pepper. Using a rubber spatula, fold together the stuffing ingredients until well combined (you should have about 1½ cups stuffing).

4. TO ASSEMBLE AND COOK: With the thinnest ends of the cutlets pointing away from you, spread one-quarter of the stuffing evenly over each cutlet with a rubber spatula, leaving a ¾-inch border along the short sides of the cutlet and a ¼-inch border along the long sides. Roll each breast up as tightly as possible without squeezing out the filling and place seam side down. Evenly space three pieces of twine (each about 12 inches long) beneath each breast and tie, trimming any excess.

5. Season the chicken with salt and pepper. Heat the remaining tablespoon oil in the skillet over medium-high heat until just smoking. Add the chicken bundles and brown on 4 sides, about 2 minutes per side. Add the broth and reserved wine to the pan and bring to a boil. Reduce the heat to low, cover the pan, and cook until an instant-read thermometer registers 160 degrees when inserted into the thickest part of the chicken, 12 to 18 minutes. Transfer the chicken to a cutting board and tent loosely with foil.

6. FOR THE SAUCE AND TO SERVE: While the chicken rests, whisk the mustard into the cooking liquid. Increase the heat to high and simmer, scraping the pan bottom to loosen the browned bits, until dark brown and reduced to ½ cup, 7 to 10 minutes. Off the heat, whisk in the butter and the remaining 1½ teaspoons parsley and 1½ teaspoons lemon juice; season with salt and pepper to taste. Remove the twine and cut each chicken bundle on the bias into 6 medallions. Spoon the sauce over the chicken and serve.

EQUIPMENT CORNER: Meat Pounders

A GOOD MEAT POUNDER SHOULD PRODUCE THIN cutlets of uniform thickness with a low number of strokes—without leaving your arm fatigued. To find a favorite, we pounded out chicken breasts with five models of various weights and shapes. Testers grew impatient with tools that weighed less than a pound: They tapped rather than pounded. Also panned were disk-shaped models whose vertical handles required a stamping motion that felt unnatural.

Rating Meat Pounders

WE TESTED FIVE MODELS OF MEAT POUNDERS, USING them to pound chicken breasts into thin cutlets. We rated them on performance and ease of use (heavier-weight models required less work than lighter models). Brands are listed in order of preference. See www.americastestkitchen.com for updates to this testing.

HIGHLY RECOMMENDED
Norpro Chrome-Plated Cast-Iron Meat Pounder
$23.99
This moderately heavy mallet pounded chicken breasts into cutlets in 35 strokes and kept testers' arms comfortable with its well-balanced offset handle.

RECOMMENDED WITH RESERVATIONS
Wüsthof Meat Tenderizer/Pounder
$179.95
This most effective model flattened chicken breasts in just 15 strokes, but its nearly 2½-pound heft, awkward shape, and stratospheric price deterred most testers.

RECOMMENDED WITH RESERVATIONS
Jaccard Four-In-One Meat Mallet
$24.99
A soft grip, offset handle, and light weight made this pounder comfortable to use, but what it lacked in heft, we had to make up for in strokes. Plus, its textured face left marks on the meat.

NOT RECOMMENDED
MIU France Zinc Alloy Reversible Meat Tenderizer and Pounder
$20.99
Fitted with a vertical handle, this pounder's weight rested uncomfortably in the head of the mallet.

NOT RECOMMENDED
OXO Good Grips i-Series Meat Pounder
$16.99
Though equipped with the trademark soft grip, this pounder's vertical arm required an unnatural stamping motion. Sixty-two strokes later, we still had uneven paillards.

BETTER ARUGULA SALADS

WHAT WE WANTED: Truly outstanding arugula-based salads, featuring vinaigrettes and ingredients that can stand up to the spicy green.

Unlike everyday (read: bland) iceberg, romaine, or butter lettuce, spicy arugula is more than just a leafy backdrop for salad garnishes. Yet that complex, peppery flavor also makes arugula something of a challenge to pair with other ingredients. To figure out the best way to temper this assertive green, we headed to the test kitchen with a stack of representative recipes.

Combinations with harsh, one-dimensional flavor profiles (arugula, radishes, and lemon-buttermilk dressing, for example) were left mostly uneaten. Salads containing fruit and cheese, however, were devoured, the sweet and salty notes offering nice counterpoints to the sharp, peppery arugula. Tasters also liked salads with crunchy elements.

We started at square one: the vinaigrette. Many recipes rely on ingredients like mustard to help the emulsion along. Mustard was clearly wrong—too spicy to partner with peppery arugula—but what if we chose an emulsifier that contributed sweetness? We added a drizzle of honey to a basic vinaigrette, and this worked well. But we wanted something more. How about adding a spoonful of jam instead of honey? This idea hit the mark: The jam added just the right viscosity and fruity sweetness, pulling the flavors of the salad right in line.

To echo the flavor of the fruity vinaigrettes, we next experimented with adding winter fruits to the salad. After some trial and error, we settled on dried figs plumped with balsamic vinegar for one salad, fresh red grapes for another, and juicy orange sections for a third.

Now that we had the sweet and spicy/peppery bases adequately covered, choosing the salty and crunchy components was a snap. Cured meat and crumbled cheese offered stark but appealing salty contrast. Finally, slivers of raw fennel along with toasted nuts delivered just the right amount of crunch.

WHAT WE LEARNED: Pair salty ingredients, like cured meats and crumbled cheeses, with arugula. And add a spoonful of jam to the vinaigrette to help emulsify the dressing and provide a sweet contrast to arugula's peppery bite. For additional sweetness and textural contrast, add fruit to the salad—dried figs, grapes, and orange segments all work well. For a crunchy element, add toasted nuts or thinly sliced fennel to the mix.

ARUGULA SALAD WITH FIGS, PROSCIUTTO, WALNUTS, AND PARMESAN

serves 6

Although frying the prosciutto adds crisp texture to the salad, if you prefer, you can simply cut it into ribbons and use it as a garnish. Honey can be substituted for the jam in any of these salad recipes.

    4   tablespoons extra-virgin olive oil
    2   ounces thinly sliced prosciutto, cut into
         ¼-inch-wide ribbons
    1   tablespoon raspberry jam
    3   tablespoons balsamic vinegar
    ½   cup dried figs, stems removed, fruit chopped
         into ¼-inch pieces
    1   small shallot, minced very fine (1 tablespoon)
         Salt and ground black pepper
    5   ounces lightly packed baby arugula (8 cups)
    ½   cup chopped walnuts, toasted
    2   ounces Parmesan cheese, shaved into thin strips
         with a vegetable peeler

1. Heat 1 tablespoon of the oil in a 10-inch nonstick skillet over medium heat; add the prosciutto and fry until crisp, stirring frequently, about 7 minutes. Using a slotted spoon, transfer to a paper towel–lined plate and set aside to cool.

2. Whisk the jam and vinegar together in a medium microwave-safe bowl; stir in the figs. Cover with plastic wrap, cut several steam vents in the plastic, and microwave on high until the figs are plump, 30 seconds to 1 minute. Whisk in the remaining 3 tablespoons oil, shallot, ¼ teaspoon salt, and ⅛ teaspoon pepper; toss to combine. Let cool to room temperature.

3. Toss the arugula with the vinaigrette in a large bowl; season with salt and pepper to taste. Divide the salad among individual plates; top each with a portion of prosciutto, walnuts, and Parmesan. Serve immediately.

ARUGULA SALAD WITH GRAPES, FENNEL, GORGONZOLA, AND PECANS

serves 6

    4   teaspoons apricot jam
    3   tablespoons white wine vinegar
    3   tablespoons extra-virgin olive oil
    1   small shallot, minced very fine (1 tablespoon)
         Salt and ground black pepper
    ½   small fennel bulb, cored, trimmed of stalks, and
         sliced very thin (about 1 cup), fronds chopped
         coarse (about ¼ cup)
    5   ounces lightly packed baby arugula (8 cups)
    6   ounces red seedless grapes, halved lengthwise
         (about 1 cup)
    3   ounces Gorgonzola cheese, crumbled (¾ cup)
    ½   cup chopped pecans, toasted

Whisk together the jam, vinegar, oil, shallot, ¼ teaspoon salt, and ¼ teaspoon pepper in a large bowl. Toss the fennel bulb with the vinaigrette; let stand for 15 minutes. Add the fennel fronds, arugula, and grapes; toss and season with salt and pepper to taste. Divide the salad among individual plates; top each with a portion of Gorgonzola and pecans. Serve immediately.

ARUGULA SALAD WITH ORANGES, FETA, AND SUGARED PISTACHIOS

serves 6

The sugared pistachios can be made ahead and stored in an airtight container at room temperature for up to 5 days. You can substitute an equal amount of roughly chopped toasted pistachios.

sugared pistachios
    ½   cup whole shelled pistachios
    1   large egg white, lightly beaten
    ⅓   cup sugar

salad

        5   teaspoons orange marmalade
        2   tablespoons plus 2 teaspoons juice from
            1 lemon
        3   tablespoons extra-virgin olive oil
        1   small shallot, minced very fine (1 tablespoon)
        1   tablespoon minced fresh mint leaves
            Salt and ground black pepper
        5   ounces lightly packed baby arugula (8 cups)
        2   large oranges, peeled, cut into segments,
            segments halved and drained to remove
            excess juice
        3   ounces feta cheese, crumbled (¾ cup)

1. FOR THE SUGARED PISTACHIOS: Adjust an oven rack to the middle position and heat the oven to 325 degrees. Toss the pistachios with the egg white in a small bowl. Using a slotted spoon, transfer the nuts to an 8-inch square baking pan lined with parchment paper; discard the excess egg white. Add the sugar and stir until the nuts are completely coated. Bake, stirring the mixture every 5 to 10 minutes, until the coating turns nutty brown, 25 to 30 minutes. Transfer the nuts to a plate in a single layer to cool.

2. FOR THE SALAD: Whisk together the marmalade, lemon juice, oil, shallot, mint, ¼ teaspoon salt, and ⅛ teaspoon pepper in a large bowl. Add the arugula and oranges; toss and season with salt and pepper to taste. Divide the salad among individual plates; top each with a portion of feta and sugared pistachios. Serve immediately.

TASTING LAB: Black Peppercorns

WE TAKE BLACK PEPPER FOR GRANTED. BUT THIS pantry staple was once so deeply desired and valuable that the kingdoms of Europe launched voyages (including the one that led Columbus to America) to find better trade routes to India with an eye toward controlling the crop. In the Middle Ages, rent could be paid in peppercorns instead of cash. When the Visigoths held Rome ransom, they demanded gold, silver—and 3,000 pounds of peppercorns.

Beyond its heat and sharp bite, black pepper enhances our ability to taste food, stimulating our salivary glands so we experience flavors more fully. This effect comes only from freshly ground pepper. Once the peppercorn's hard black shell is cracked, its aroma starts to fade, and most of its flavor and scent disappear within a half hour. Not surprisingly, we have never found a preground pepper worth buying. In fact, replacing your pepper shaker with a good grinder is one of the simplest ways to enhance your cooking. But can choosing a fancy variety of peppercorn improve it even more?

Until recently, spice brands sold in supermarkets never specified the origin or variety of their peppercorns, as they simply bought the cheapest they could get. But specialty spice retailers offering multiple varieties bearing exotic names like Sarawak, Lampong, Malabar, and Tellicherry have raised consumer awareness; now two of the largest supermarket brands, McCormick and Spice Islands, have added "gourmet" Tellicherry peppercorns to their lines. Though Tellicherry is generally considered to be the world's finest pepper, all true peppercorns—black, green, and white—actually come from the same plant, *Piper nigrum*. Native to India, this flowering vine is now grown in many other tropical areas close to the equator, including Vietnam, Indonesia, Malaysia, Ecuador, Brazil, and Madagascar. It sprouts clusters of berries that are dried and treated to become peppercorns. Like grapes, coffee beans, and cacao beans, pepper's flavor depends on exactly where it is cultivated, when the berries are picked, and how they are processed. But all are defined by the heat-bearing compound piperine, which perks up our taste buds.

Most peppercorns are picked as soon as the immature little green berries appear on the vine, but Tellicherry (named after a port town in the state of Kerala on India's Malabar Coast) is left to ripen the longest, allowing its flavor to develop, becoming deeper and more complex, even a

little fruity—not just sharp, hot, and bright like peppercorns made from younger berries. But given that we generally use just a few grinds of pepper on our food, would we actually be able to detect such differences?

To find out, we sampled Tellicherry peppercorns from McCormick and Spice Islands along with six of the other most popular supermarket brands. Priced from about $1.35 to $2.22 per ounce, most of these brands did not specify variety. As we tasted each black pepper freshly ground with optional white rice, it was immediately clear there were significant differences among brands. Some were searingly hot, others mild; some one-dimensional, others complex. Only two peppers impressed our tasters enough to be recommended without reservations: McCormick Tellicherry and the organic, Indonesian-grown Lampong peppercorns from a lesser-known brand, Morton & Bassett. The most widely available peppercorns in the country, ordinary McCormick Whole Black Peppercorns, were not recommended at all, finishing dead last.

If the fancier supermarket peppercorns were good, would peppercorns from specialty merchants taste even better? Peppercorns are extremely light, so shipping is cheap. A few ounces last many months, and online prices are only a few dollars higher than supermarket prices. We decided to focus on Tellicherry peppercorns for their stellar reputation, choosing six mail-order brands to pit against our two supermarket winners. Once again, we tasted the freshly ground pepper plain or with rice.

Though tasters detected a range of flavor nuances from brand to brand, the final rankings among these peppercorns were close. We gave top marks to highly aromatic peppercorns with complex flavor and preferred moderate rather than strong heat, which tended to overpower any other taste. Our favorite peppercorn was the fresh, earthy, and only moderately hot Tellicherry sold by the Manhattan emporium Kalustyan's, available online ($6.99 plus shipping for 2.5 ounces). Coming in a close second, however, was one of the supermarket winners, Morton & Bassett Whole Black Peppercorns ($5.39 for 2 ounces). As with Kalustyan's Tellicherry, tasters praised this pepper for being spicy but not too hot, as well as fragrant and floral. Sampled against this steep competition, our other supermarket brand, McCormick Gourmet Collection Tellicherry Black Peppercorns ($4.99 for 1.87 ounces), was deemed "unremarkable."

So what would account for differences in the flavor and heat levels of the Tellicherry peppercorns, when all come from the same region? The most important factor probably has to do with differences in cultivars, or varieties, of the plant itself, which grows on plantations in the state of Kerala, an area about the size of the Netherlands. Though none of the spice companies we spoke to would share details of the processing methods used by their suppliers, these approaches can also influence taste—peppercorns can be picked by hand or by machine, dried in the sun or a kiln, even boiled. Storage also has an impact. Peppercorns subjected to too much heat or moisture grow musty-smelling mold and bacteria, all the while losing flavor. In fact, some peppercorns, including our winner from Kalustyan's, get a special cleaning in the United States before they go on sale, restoring freshness after months at sea.

Now that we had our winners, a question remained: Would a better pepper's complexity actually be evident if we just added the usual pinch or two in cooking? We chose two polar opposites—top-ranked Kalustyan's and the bottom-ranked McCormick Whole Black Peppercorns from our supermarket tasting—and sampled them in scrambled eggs and tomato soup. Interestingly, with pepper as a mere accent, the distinctions between these two very differently rated brands became hard to detect: Votes were split as to which tasted better. But what if peppercorns are one of the main attractions, as in steak au poivre, a steak thickly crusted with crushed peppercorns and pan-seared? We compared steaks made with Kalustyan's Tellicherry, Morton & Bassett's Lampong, and the McCormick Tellicherry. This time, the nuances of the peppercorns came through, and tasters echoed their original assessments. Kalustyan's impressed tasters most, Morton & Bassett came in right behind it, and the McCormick Tellicherry ranked a few steps down from those top two—just as it had in the plain tasting.

The verdict? In applications that call for a small dose, just about any pepper will be fine as long as it is freshly ground. But if you're cooking a peppery specialty or you like to grind fresh pepper over your food before eating, choosing a superior peppercorn can make a difference. Given that it costs only a few dollars more than supermarket pepper, we'll be filling the test kitchen's peppermills with Kalustyan's Tellicherry. If you can't be bothered to mail-order peppercorns, look for Morton & Bassett Organic Whole Black Peppercorns in the supermarket.

TESTING NOTES:
Praiseworthy Pepper (and Packaging)

While shopping for peppercorns, we kept running across purveyors praising Parameswaran's Special Wynad Estate Peppercorns ($30 for 200g/7 ounces), so we tried them. These organic, hand-picked black peppers weren't included in our mail-order lineup because they aren't Tellicherry; instead they are a blend of Karimunda and Panniyor varieties from India. However, the unusual mix was a big hit with our tasters, who praised its "rich," "beautiful floral fragrance," with a "ripe, flowery, lavender-like warmth" and flavor that is "earthy and smooth," with "moderate heat that builds gradually, not ferociously." Most importantly, it doesn't suffer the typical ills of transport, as the peppercorns are vacuum-packed right on the estate to preserve freshness and flavor. These peppers are pricey but still worth considering.

Rating Black Peppercorns

NINETEEN MEMBERS OF THE AMERICA'S TEST KITCHEN STAFF TASTED EIGHT SAMPLES OF FRESHLY GROUND WHOLE black peppercorns plain or with white rice. The samples included six mail-order Tellicherry peppercorns and two supermarket brands. The supermarket peppercorns were singled out as favorites in an earlier tasting of the eight top-selling brands, identified by research compiled by the Chicago-based research firm Information Resources, Inc. We were joined by chefs Ana Sortun of Oleana (author of *Spice: Flavors of the Eastern Mediterranean*) and Tony Maws of Craigie Street Bistrot; both restaurants are in Cambridge, Massachusetts. We rated the peppercorns on aroma, heat, complexity, and overall taste. Brands are listed in order of preference. See www.americastestkitchen.com for updates to this tasting.

RECOMMENDED
Kalustyan's Indian Tellicherry Peppercorn
$6.99 for a 2.5-ounce jar

With high marks for "enticing" aroma and complex flavor, with only "moderate" heat, tasters praised these peppercorns from the Manhattan emporium for a "beautiful scent," "like licorice, sweet and spicy," with "mild heat that gradually builds."

RECOMMENDED
Morton & Bassett Organic Whole Black Peppercorns
$5.39 for a 2-ounce jar

"Spicy but not hot," this organic Lampong pepper from Indonesia (sold by a San Francisco–based spice company) won our initial supermarket-brand tasting and was the only non-Tellicherry pepper to make it to our final lineup. It won praise for being "very fragrant and floral and piney, very spicy."

RECOMMENDED
Zingerman's Tellicherry Peppercorns
$8 for a 2.53-ounce jar

"This smells like green peppercorns, pungent, sharp, and hot," noted one taster of this pepper from a Michigan-based gourmet catalog and retailer; others described its "creeping heat and lovely floral undertones."

RECOMMENDED WITH RESERVATIONS
Vanns Spices Tellicherry Peppercorns
$3.77 for a 2.25-ounce jar

With a "bright, fresh scent" and a "mellow bite," this pepper from a Baltimore spice purveyor was described as "floral" and "fruity." Others less flatteringly mentioned "slightly pungent barnyard flavors."

RECOMMENDED WITH RESERVATIONS
McCormick Gourmet Collection Tellicherry Black Peppercorns
$4.99 for a 1.87-ounce jar

Several tasters remarked on this supermarket pepper's "very nice" "floral" aroma, with notes of "coffee grounds, clove, turpentine, pine" or "menthol," but they also noted that compared to other samples, it was "bland" and "flat."

RECOMMENDED WITH RESERVATIONS
Penzeys India Tellicherry Peppercorns
$3.49 for a 2.2-ounce jar

Tasters enjoyed this gourmet spice purveyor's offering for its "piney, rosemary scent" with "citrus" and "lavender" notes, but many complained of "a lot of burning heat" that was "not very pleasant."

RECOMMENDED WITH RESERVATIONS
The Spice House Tellicherry Black Peppercorns
$2.98 for a 2.5-ounce jar

With a "super-strong aroma," these peppercorns from the Chicago spice purveyor founded by a branch of the Penzey family also came across with a peppery intensity that "is really assertive—a smack-you-in-the-face kind of heat." But reactions were mixed: Several found it "slightly bitter" and "stale."

RECOMMENDED WITH RESERVATIONS
Dean & DeLuca Tellicherry Peppercorns
$5.75 for a 2-ounce tin

Tasters repeatedly noted this pepper's "mild aroma and flavor," described as "soft," "faint," and even "dull"—and "barely detectable heat." But overall: "Not great; smells better than it tastes."

EVEN LESS RECOMMENDED: We eliminated the following brands in a preliminary tasting of eight top-selling supermarket brands: Vigo Whole Black Peppercorns (also sold as Alessi), Badia Whole Black Pepper, Spice Islands Tellicherry Black Peppercorns, Tone's Whole Black Peppercorns (also sold as Durkee), Drogheria & Alimentari All Natural Black Pepper Corns, and plain McCormick Whole Black Peppercorns.

For a browned, crusty exterior, we sear our eye-round roast before transferring it to the oven, where it cooks low and slow. The result? Meat that is remarkably tender and juicy.

RESURRECTING
CHAPTER 7
the roast beef dinner

At one time, Sunday used to mean a hefty platter of roast beef with all the fixings. Sometimes the meat would be juicy and full of beefy flavor, but all too often it would be so dry that lots of gravy (or gulps of water) was required to get it down. Is there a way to guarantee the former? By most accounts, only if you're willing to spend money on prime rib. But such a pricey cut of meat makes little sense for Sunday dinner with the family. Therefore, we set out to find a way to transform a tough cut of beef into a juicy, succulent roast. We'd start by zeroing in on the right cut of beef—not all roasts are created equal; some roasts can be fatty and gristly, and some can be so oddly shaped that it's a battle to cook them evenly. Next, we'd determine what, if any, prep is required for the roast prior to cooking—keeping in mind that roast beef doesn't need much dressing up to really taste good. And finally, we'd test roasting methods to turn out a Sunday dinner main course so good, everyone would make it to dinner on time.

When we're served roast beef, there had better be mashed potatoes on the side. But do mashed potatoes need to be the same dish week after week? What about adding root vegetables to the mix? We've often come across recipes that suggest enriching mashed potatoes with carrots, parsnips, and the like. But the results are disappointing—sometimes astringent, sometimes overly sweet. Our goal, therefore, would be to develop a recipe for an earthy, flavorful mash that tasted balanced, not bitter.

INEXPENSIVE ROAST BEEF

WHAT WE WANTED: A method for transforming a bargain cut of beef into a juicy, flavorful roast.

For most families, Sunday roast beef isn't prime rib; it's a lesser cut that's sometimes good, sometimes not. The roasts we most remember from our childhood were tough and dried out and better suited for sandwiches the next day. But other times, the roast was beefy-tasting, tender, and juicy. It was so good that everyone asked for seconds. How can we guarantee the latter?

First we needed to zero in on the most promising beef. After a week in the kitchen testing a slew of low-cost cuts, we had a clear winner: the eye-round roast. Though less flavorful than fattier cuts from the shoulder (the chuck) and less tender than other meat from the back leg (the round), the eye roast had one key attribute the others lacked: a uniform shape from front to back. This was a roast that would not only cook evenly but look good on the plate as well.

Our next challenge was choosing between the two classic methods for roasting meat—high and fast or low and slow. We began with the more common high-heat approach, quickly searing the meat on the stovetop and then transferring it to a 450-degree oven for roasting. The technique works great with more upscale rib and loin cuts but showed its flaws with the leaner eye round, yielding meat that was overcooked and dried out.

But before heading down the low-temperature path, which normally involves roasting meat in an oven set between 250 and 325 degrees, we wanted to try something more extreme. To extract maximum tenderness from meat, the popular 1960s nutritionist Adelle Davis advocated cooking it at the temperature desired when it was done. For a roast to reach an end temperature of 130 degrees for medium-rare, this process could involve 20 to 30 hours of cooking. Davis's advice wasn't new. Benjamin Thompson, the 18th-century physicist who invented the roasting oven, observed that leaving meat to cook overnight in an oven heated by a dying fire resulted in exceptional tenderness.

Tossing aside practical considerations like food safety and the gas bill, we decided we had to replicate these two experts' findings. We set the one oven in the test kitchen capable of maintaining such a low temperature to 130 degrees and popped in an eye round. Twenty-four hours later, we pulled out a roast with juicy, meltingly tender meat. What special beef magic was going on here?

We remembered from prior test kitchen work on thick-cut steaks that beef contains enzymes that break down its connective tissues and act as natural tenderizers. These enzymes work faster as the temperature of the meat rises—but just until it reaches 122 degrees, at which point all action stops. Roasting the eye round in an oven set to 130 degrees allowed it to stay below 122 degrees far longer than when cooked in the typical low-temperature roasting range, transforming this lean, unassuming cut into something great.

But given that most ovens don't heat below 200 degrees—and that most home cooks don't want to run their ovens for a full day—how could we expect others to re-create our results? We would have to go as low as we could and see what happened. We settled on 225 degrees as the lowest starting point. We also decided we would brown the meat first to give it nice color and a crusty exterior. (Although tender, our 130-degree roast had an unappetizing gray exterior.) Searing would also help to ensure food safety, since bacteria on roasts are generally confined to the outside.

When we took the roast out of the oven, however, we were disappointed. It was tender, but nothing like the texture of the eye round cooked at 130 degrees. What could we do to keep the meat below 122 degrees longer? A new idea occurred to us: Why not shut off the oven just before the roast reached 122 degrees? As the oven cooled, the roast would continue to cook even more slowly.

Using a meat-probe thermometer to track the internal

temperature of the roast, we shut off the oven when the meat reached 115 degrees. Sure enough, the meat stayed below 122 degrees 30 minutes longer, allowing its enzymes to continue the work of tenderizing, before creeping to 130 degrees for medium-rare. Tasters were certainly happy with this roast. It was remarkably tender and juicy for a roast that cost so little.

With the tenderness problem solved, it was time to tackle taste. So far we'd simply sprinkled salt and pepper on the roast just before searing it. Perhaps the flavor would improve if the meat were salted overnight or even brined. Brining—normally reserved for less fatty pork and poultry—certainly pumped more water into the beef and made it very juicy, but it also made it taste bland, watery, and less beefy. Next we tried salting the meat for first four, then 12, and finally 24 hours. As might be expected, the roast benefited most from the longest salting. Because the process of osmosis causes salt to travel from areas of higher to areas of lower concentration, the full 24 hours gave it the most time to penetrate deep into the meat. There was another benefit: Salt, like the enzymes in meat, breaks down proteins to further improve texture.

At last we had tender, flavorful beef for a Sunday roast that even our grandparents would have been proud to serve. The leftovers—if there were any—would have no need for mayonnaise or mustard to taste good.

WHAT WE LEARNED: Choose an eye-round roast over some of the other inexpensive cuts—its consistent shape ensures even cooking and attractive slices. Cook the roast at a low temperature (225 degrees) and turn the oven off for the final 30 to 50 minutes to keep the roast's internal temperature below 122 degrees. When the roast is cooked this way, the enzymes in the meat, which act as natural tenderizers, have more time to work. Finally, to achieve an even more tender, juicy roast beef, salt the roast 24 hours in advance—this yields a meltingly tender texture and a roast that is seasoned throughout.

INEXPENSIVE ROAST BEEF

serves 6 to 8

We don't recommend cooking this roast past medium. Open the oven door as little as possible and remove the roast from the oven while taking its temperature. If the roast has not reached the desired temperature in the time specified in step 3, heat the oven to 225 degrees for 5 minutes, shut it off, and continue to cook the roast to the desired temperature. For a smaller (2½- to 3½-pound) roast, reduce the amounts of kosher salt to 3 teaspoons (1½ teaspoons table salt) and black pepper to 1½ teaspoons. For a 4½- to 6-pound roast, cut in half crosswise before cooking to create 2 smaller roasts. Slice the roast as thinly as possible and serve with Horseradish Cream Sauce, if desired (recipe follows).

1   boneless eye-round roast (3½ to 4½ pounds, see note)
4   teaspoons kosher salt or 2 teaspoons table salt (see note)
2   teaspoons plus 1 tablespoon vegetable oil
2   teaspoons ground black pepper (see note)

1. Sprinkle all sides of the roast evenly with the salt. Wrap with plastic wrap and refrigerate for 18 to 24 hours.

2. Adjust an oven rack to the middle position and heat the oven to 225 degrees. Pat the roast dry with paper towels; rub with 2 teaspoons of the oil and sprinkle all sides evenly with the pepper. Heat the remaining 1 tablespoon oil in a 12-inch skillet over medium-high heat until starting to smoke. Sear the roast until browned on all sides, 3 to 4 minutes per side. Transfer the roast to a wire rack set in a rimmed baking sheet. Roast until a meat-probe thermometer or instant-read thermometer inserted into the center of the roast registers 115 degrees for medium-rare, 1¼ to 1¾ hours, or 125 degrees for medium, 1¾ to 2¼ hours.

TECHNIQUE: The Transformation from Tough to Tender

Along with salting and searing, the key to our eye round's makeover into a tender, juicy roast is keeping its internal temperature below 122 degrees for as long as possible. Below 122 degrees, the meat's enzymes act as natural tenderizers.

 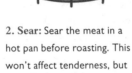 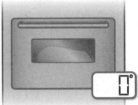

1. Salt: Salt the roast and allow it to rest for 18 to 24 hours. Salt breaks down proteins to improve the texture.

2. Sear: Sear the meat in a hot pan before roasting. This won't affect tenderness, but it will boost flavor.

3. Oven On: Cook the meat in an oven set to 225 degrees and open the door as infrequently as possible.

4. Oven Off: When the roast reaches 115 degrees, turn off the oven and continue to cook the roast as the oven cools.

GETTING IT RIGHT: Low-Cost Lineup

Not all bargain cuts have the potential to taste like a million bucks—or look like it when carved and served on a plate.

Our Favorite: Eye Round
($4.99 per pound)
We singled out this cut not only for its good flavor and relative tenderness but also for its uniform shape that guarantees even cooking and yields slices that look good on the plate.

Too Fatty: Chuck Eye
($3.99 per pound)
Though undeniably tender and flavorful, its fat and gristle make this meat better for stew and pot roast than roast beef.

Odd Shape: Top Round
($3.99 per pound)
A deli staple for sandwiches, this cut comes in irregular shapes that can cook unevenly.

Tough to Carve:
Bottom Round Rump
($4.29 per pound)
We ruled out this roast for being both tough and hard to carve against the grain.

3. Turn the oven off; leave the roast in the oven, without opening the door, until the meat-probe thermometer or instant-read thermometer inserted into the center of the roast registers 130 degrees for medium-rare or 140 degrees for medium, 30 to 50 minutes longer. Transfer the roast to a carving board and let rest for 15 minutes. Slice the meat crosswise as thinly as possible and serve.

HORSERADISH CREAM SAUCE

makes about I cup

½	cup heavy cream
½	cup prepared horseradish
1	teaspoon salt
⅛	teaspoon ground black pepper

Whisk the cream in a medium bowl until thickened but not yet holding soft peaks, 1 to 2 minutes. Gently fold in the horseradish, salt, and pepper. Transfer to a serving bowl and refrigerate at least 30 minutes or up to 1 hour before serving.

EQUIPMENT CORNER:
Meat-Probe Thermometers

REPEATEDLY OPENING THE OVEN DOOR TO MONITOR the internal temperature of a roast can throw cooking times off-kilter. One solution? Meat-probe thermometers. These remote devices transmit temperature from a long probe left in the meat and attached to a thin cord that snakes out of the oven to a digital console. But don't throw out your instant-read thermometer just yet. We tested 11 models—several by the same manufacturers—and not one was flawless. The ones that accurately measured temperature sported function buttons that were too slow or too hard to figure out. Others that were user-friendly were also unreliable.

The best of the bunch—an easy-to-use thermometer from ThermoWorks ($19)—was great when it worked but has probes that even its manufacturer admits are sometimes defective. Check the probe's accuracy by boiling water and taking a reading before trying it with a roast. If the probe doesn't read very close to 212 degrees, ask for a replacement.

Rating Meat-Probe Thermometers

WE RATED 11 MODELS OF MEAT-PROBE THERMOMETERS FOR ACCURACY AND EASE OF USE. BRANDS ARE LISTED IN order of preference. See www.americastestkitchen.com for updates to this testing.

RECOMMENDED WITH RESERVATIONS

ThermoWorks Original Cooking Thermometer/Timer

$19

This user-friendly model allows you to view both time and temperature simultaneously and is free of the annoying and unnecessary USDA-recommended presets for various types of meat that are all too common in other brands. The model lost points for having probes that are sometimes defective.

RECOMMENDED WITH RESERVATIONS

Polder Classic Cooking Thermometer/Timer

$24.99

The same thermometer as the ThermoWorks model, but its prettier facade wasn't worth the extra $6.

RECOMMENDED WITH RESERVATIONS

Maverick ET-8 Roast Alert Oven Roasting Thermometer

$25

Multifunction buttons, preprogrammed USDA meat settings, and an irritating alarm overcomplicate this otherwise acceptable tool.

RECOMMENDED WITH RESERVATIONS

Maverick ET-83 Dual Probe Roast Alert Thermometer

$29

Even more complicated to use than its sister model, but we like the added functionality of two probes.

NOT RECOMMENDED

Acu-Rite Programmable Digital Meat Thermometer

$29.95

Slow-functioning buttons and irritatingly loud beeps plagued this model. We also disliked not being able to view time and temperature readings simultaneously.

NOT RECOMMENDED

Taylor Commercial Remote Probe Digital Cooking Thermometer/Timer

$24.95

Near-perfect accuracy made this model a good bet (albeit hard to operate), until we noticed it went into power-save mode and didn't come back on to alert us when dinner was ready.

NOT RECOMMENDED

BonJour Compact Meat Thermometer

$21.95

Though this model was fairly easy to use, its readings were off by as much as 4 degrees, and we couldn't view time and temperature simultaneously.

NOT RECOMMENDED

CDN Touch Screen Probe Thermometer/Timer

$29.95

A huge display and clear buttons made this thermometer quite user-friendly, but the 28-inch cord was too short to reach our countertop.

NOT RECOMMENDED

Polder Preprogrammed Cooking Thermometer

$24.95

This tool was accurate to within 2 degrees, but its slow multifunction buttons and loud beeps were irritating. Above all, it lacked a timer.

NOT RECOMMENDED

CDN Combo Probe Thermometer, Timer & Clock

$23.95

Though this multifunction machine did it all—clock, thermometer, and timer (with seconds)—it randomly skipped numbers as we tried to preset the temperature.

NOT RECOMMENDED

CDN Programmable Probe Thermometer/Timer

$24.95

This model skipped numbers while we were presetting the temperature, and it was not intuitive to use.

MASHED POTATOES AND ROOT VEGETABLES

WHAT WE WANTED: A potato and root vegetable mash with a creamy consistency and a balanced flavor that highlights the natural earthiness of these humble root cellar favorites.

Because mashed potatoes are relatively simple, many cookbook authors suggest that introducing root vegetables to the mash requires little forethought. In fact, most of the cookbooks we consulted didn't even devote a complete recipe to the topic; they merely tacked footnotes onto mashed potato recipes: "Try boiling parsnips along with the potatoes" or "Substitute celery root for half of the potatoes." The idea of adding the earthy, intriguing flavor of carrots, parsnips, turnips, or celery root to plain mashed potatoes is certainly appealing, but most of the recipes we tried failed miserably.

The trouble is that root vegetables and potatoes (tubers) are quite different in three important ways. First, our preferred root vegetables contain more water (80 to 92 percent) than russet potatoes (about 79 percent), the test kitchen's first choice for mashing. Second, our root vegetables have less starch (between 0.2 and 6.2 percent) than potatoes (about 15 percent). Finally, many root vegetables are either noticeably sweet or slightly bitter—traits that can overwhelm mild potatoes. If you're not careful, these differences can add up to a watery, lean, or saccharine mash.

In early rounds of recipe testing, we'd concluded that the 1-to-1 (or greater) ratio of root vegetables to potatoes that the majority of cookbooks advocate was much too heavy on the vegetable side. We experimented with a 1-to-2 ratio, boiling 12 ounces of root vegetables and 24 ounces of russet potatoes together in the same pot, draining them, mashing them, and stirring in cream and melted butter, but the texture was still too thin. For optimal consistency, we had to go all the way down to a 1-to-3 ratio. But with only 8 ounces of root vegetables to 1½ pounds of potatoes, the distinctive flavor of the vegetables was barely recognizable.

If we wanted to maintain an agreeable texture, we had to find a way to make the most of a small amount of vegetables. Could we enhance their character by cooking them separately and bolstering their flavor? Three possibilities sprang to mind: microwaving the root vegetables in chicken broth, sautéing them in butter, and roasting them in the oven with a coating of olive oil. We cooked one batch of vegetables using each technique, then mashed them with boiled potatoes. All of the samples were more appealing than the one made with potatoes and vegetables boiled in the same pot, but the mashes made with sautéed vegetables outshone the others because of their nutty, buttery qualities.

So cooking the vegetables separately amplified their flavor, and our problem was solved. Or was it? We envisioned the hectic predinner rush that is typical of holiday celebrations. Boiling potatoes in one pot and sautéing vegetables in another might be beyond the pale for a straightforward side dish. Could we come up with a more convenient way? We remembered from past testing that we had slowly cooked sweet potatoes in a small amount of liquid in a tightly covered pot rather than boiling them. What if we incorporated this technique into our recipe by sautéing the root vegetables first, then adding raw potatoes and braising them?

We returned to the kitchen and quickly sautéed some parsnips in a generous amount (4 tablespoons) of butter. Next, we added peeled and sliced potatoes to the pot, along with ⅓ cup of water and a dash of salt. After 30 minutes of gentle cooking, the potatoes and parsnips were completely tender and all of the water had been absorbed. We did some quick mashing, then folded in warm cream and black pepper. The flavor was good, but not remarkable. On our next try, we cooked the vegetables longer, allowing the butter to brown and the vegetables to caramelize, which accented their unique flavors. The flavor was now spot-on: rich, earthy, and well balanced. Swapping chicken broth (preferred to vegetable broth) for the water allowed the potatoes to soak up even more savory notes. As for dairy options, tasters didn't deviate from the test kitchen's usual choice of half-and-half, preferring it to milk and cream. We let the potatoes drink up as much as they could, eventually settling on ¾ cup.

The flavor of our recipe was finally just right, but the texture had been thrown off in the meantime. When potatoes are boiled, some of their starch leaches out into the cooking water, never making it into the finished dish. With our unusual procedure, however, the starch could not escape and ended up being incorporated into the mash. The result was an overly starchy, almost gluey texture. Would switching to a lower-starch potato help? A batch made with Yukon Golds offered a modest improvement, but tasters still complained about excess starchiness. Thinking things over, we realized we needed to get rid of some starch before we cooked the potatoes. We rinsed some peeled, sliced potatoes in several changes of water (this took just a minute or two) and watched the cloudy, starch-filled rinsing liquid run down the drain. Once the potatoes were cooked and mashed, we knew that we'd found our solution—the starchiness was gone. Rinsing even made starchier russets an acceptable choice.

To finish the potatoes off, a sprinkling of fresh herbs was in order. The delicate onion flavor of minced chives offered a nice counterpoint to the earthy vegetables. At last, we had a standout recipe for mashed potatoes and root vegetables that was more than just an afterthought.

WHAT WE LEARNED: To achieve the proper balance of flavor in the mash, use a ratio of two-thirds potatoes to one-third root vegetables. Caramelize the root vegetables first in a little butter to bring out their natural earthy sweetness; this step also boosts the flavor of the overall dish. To make this a one-pot dish and for best flavor, don't boil the potatoes separately—simply cook them with the caramelized root vegetables in a little bit of broth. For the type of potato, choose Yukon Golds, whose flavor works well in this dish. And be sure to rinse them of excess starch after slicing; this keeps the mash from turning overly starchy.

MASHED POTATOES AND ROOT VEGETABLES

serves 4

Russet potatoes will yield a slightly fluffier, less creamy mash, but they can be used in place of the Yukon Gold potatoes if desired. Rinsing the potatoes in several changes of water reduces the amount of starch and prevents the mashed potatoes from becoming gluey. It is important to cut the potatoes and root vegetables into even-sized pieces so they cook at the same rate. This recipe can be doubled and cooked in a large Dutch oven. If doubling, increase the cooking time in step 2 to 40 minutes.

    4   tablespoons unsalted butter
    8   ounces carrots, parsnips, turnips, or celery root,
        peeled; carrots or parsnips cut into ¼-inch-thick
        half moons; turnips or celery root cut into
        ½-inch dice (about 1½ cups)
 1½   pounds Yukon Gold potatoes, peeled, quartered
        lengthwise, and cut crosswise into ¼-inch-thick
        slices; rinsed well in 3 or 4 changes of cold
        water and drained well (see note)
    ⅓   cup low-sodium chicken broth
        Salt
    ¾   cup half-and-half, warmed
    3   tablespoons minced fresh chives
        Ground black pepper

1. Melt the butter in a large saucepan over medium heat. When the foaming subsides, add the root vegetables and cook, stirring occasionally, until the butter is browned and the vegetables are dark brown and caramelized, 10 to 12 minutes. (If after 4 minutes the vegetables have not started to brown, increase the heat to medium-high.)

2. Add the potatoes, broth, and ¾ teaspoon salt and stir to combine. Cook, covered, over low heat (the broth should simmer gently; do not boil), stirring occasionally, until the potatoes fall apart easily when poked with a fork and all the

Parsnips

Divide the tapered end from the bulky top and halve the top end lengthwise. Remove the fibrous core by carefully cutting a V-shaped channel down the center.

Turnips

Using a chef's knife, trim the top and bottom, then use a vegetable peeler to remove the thin skin.

Celery Root

Using a chef's knife, trim the top and bottom so the vegetable rests flat on the work surface, then cut away the thick, knobby skin in wide swaths.

liquid has been absorbed, 25 to 30 minutes. (If the liquid does not gently simmer after a few minutes, increase the heat to medium-low.) Remove the pan from the heat; remove the lid and allow the steam to escape for 2 minutes.

3. Gently mash the potatoes and root vegetables in the saucepan with a potato masher (do not mash vigorously). Gently fold in the warm half-and-half and chives. Season with salt and pepper to taste; serve immediately.

VARIATIONS

MASHED POTATOES AND ROOT VEGETABLES WITH BACON AND THYME

This variation is particularly nice with turnips.

Cook 4 slices (about 4 ounces) bacon, cut into ½-inch pieces, in a large saucepan over medium heat until browned and crisp, about 8 minutes. Using a slotted spoon, transfer the bacon to a paper towel–lined plate; set aside. Remove all but 2 tablespoons bacon fat from the pan. Add 2 tablespoons butter to the pan and continue with the recipe for Mashed Potatoes and Root Vegetables, cooking the root vegetables in the bacon fat–butter mixture instead of the butter. Substitute 1 teaspoon minced fresh thyme leaves for the chives and fold the reserved bacon into the potatoes along with the thyme.

MASHED POTATOES AND ROOT VEGETABLES WITH PAPRIKA AND PARSLEY

This variation is particularly nice with carrots.

Toast 1½ teaspoons smoked or regular paprika in a small skillet over medium heat until fragrant, about 30 seconds. Follow the recipe for Mashed Potatoes and Root Vegetables, substituting parsley for the chives and folding the toasted paprika into the potatoes along with the parsley.

TECHNIQUE: Rinse Cycle

Rinsing peeled, sliced potatoes in several changes of water removes excess starch and prevents gumminess once the potatoes are cooked and mashed.

The busy back kitchen readies all the dishes that appear on-camera. And because timing is key, the cooks must carefully coordinate with one another to make sure dishes are ready on set when needed.

SOUTH-OF-THE-
CHAPTER 8
border suppers

We place *enchiladas verdes,* a Mexican restaurant classic, firmly in the comfort food category. Basically a casserole, enchiladas shouldn't be difficult to pull off, so why do they often turn out so poorly? For starters, the chicken can dry out and turn stringy, and a heavy hand with the cheese can turn the dish unappealingly rich. The sauce can be finicky, too. It should taste bright and zesty, but we've run into sauces that are bland and boring or harsh and unbalanced. Even worse, the sauce can be so thin and copious that the enchiladas bake up soggy instead of tender. We aimed to tackle all of these issues and more for enchiladas as good as those found in your favorite restaurant.

Most times we take our steak straight up, with a little salt and pepper. But sometimes we like to give steak a south-of-the-border spin. That's when we turn to steak tacos. Steak tacos shouldn't contain gobs of guacamole, cheese, and other fast-food fixings that obscure the flavor of the beef. On the contrary, authentic steak tacos are simply thinly sliced steak slipped into warm, soft corn tortillas, typically served with nothing more than a squeeze of lime and maybe some onion or cilantro. The steak for the tacos is usually grilled, giving the meat an appealing savory crust. But what if you want to enjoy steak tacos year-round? Is there a way to mimic the flavor of the grill indoors—one that would guarantee tender, juicy beef? And what's the best steak for tacos? Most recipes call for flank steak or skirt steak, but would another relatively inexpensive cut do just as well? We'd head into the test kitchen to find out.

IN THIS CHAPTER

THE RECIPES
Enchiladas Verdes

Steak Tacos
Sweet and Spicy Pickled Onions

EQUIPMENT CORNER
High-Heat Spatulas

TASTING LAB
Jarred Hot Salsas

ENCHILADAS VERDES

WHAT WE WANTED: Enchiladas verdes with tender chicken, the right amount of cheese, and a sauce packed with intense, green chile flavor.

In Mexico, enchiladas come in myriad forms. In this country, these stuffed and baked corn tortillas are defined almost exclusively by whether they're covered in a red sauce or a green one. Red sauces boast the deep, earthy flavor of dried red chiles, whereas green sauces feature the brighter taste of fresh green chiles and tomatillos, the tangy little tomato-like fruit that is common in authentic Mexican cooking. For us, enchiladas topped by green sauce—enchiladas verdes—are as perfect a comfort food as any we know, especially when they include moist, tender pieces of chicken. We love the way the fresh, citrusy flavors and coarse texture of the sauce contrast with the richness of chicken wrapped in soft corn tortillas and topped with melted cheese.

For the home cook, enchiladas verdes offer a distinct advantage over red-sauce versions: To preserve its vibrant flavors, the sauce is relatively quick-cooking. (A great red sauce, on the other hand, can take the better part of a day—no small matter when, in addition to making the sauce and filling, you've got to prep the tortillas and assemble the enchiladas themselves.) But although we've had memorable enchiladas verdes with chicken in restaurants, we've never had much success re-creating them at home. The sauce is often too watery and thin, the tortillas mushy, and the filling marred by bland, dried-out chicken overpowered by cheese. Armed with a stack of recipes, we headed into the test kitchen to figure out how to get this Mexican restaurant classic right.

Our first step was to nail down the sauce. We began our tests using broad, dark green poblano chiles. Poblanos have mild to moderate heat and a deep herbal flavor that is far more complex than the straightforward grassy taste of chiles such as jalapeños or serranos, making the poblano a popular choice for this kind of sauce. As for the tomatillos, we decided from the outset to use fresh instead of canned to ensure that as much of their tangy flavor as possible made it into the dish. (Luckily, the fruit is increasingly available fresh year-round in supermarkets across the country.) Next question: What was the best way to bring out the flavors of these two key ingredients?

In traditional recipes whole tomatillos and chiles are dry-roasted on the stovetop until soft and charred. This method, which employs a flat cast-iron vessel known as a *comal,* imparts smokiness and concentrates flavor, all the while wicking away excess moisture that makes for a watery sauce. The blackened skins on the tomatillos have good flavor, but the chile skins taste bitter and need to be removed. These ingredients are then ground up in a mortar and pestle to form a sauce. More modern recipes skip the comal for similarly fast, intense cooking techniques such as sautéing, high-heat oven-roasting, or broiling, and use a blender or food processor to create the sauce.

We quickly eliminated sautéing and oven-roasting from consideration; neither method added enough char to create the smokiness we were looking for. Broiling seemed much more promising, especially when we tossed everything with a little oil to promote the charring. The tomatillos did fine left whole on a baking sheet under the broiler, but we found that slicing the poblanos in half and placing them skin side up under the glowing broiler helped blacken them more evenly. One taste let us know that we'd hit the jackpot: Broiling tempered the tartness of the tomatillos and brought a near-sweet richness to the poblanos.

It was now time to work on the texture of the sauce. Whirring the tomatillos and chiles in the blender made it too smooth; a few pulses in the food processor better approximated the coarse, rustic texture produced by a mortar and pestle that our tasters preferred. But we weren't done yet. In our initial testing, tasters rejected sauces that were so thin and soupy that they turned the tortillas to mush. Our

sauce was now on the other end of the spectrum—overly thick and pulpy. We tried thinning it with a number of ingredients, including milk, sour cream, and chicken broth. Dairy in any form deadened the bright flavors, but just ¼ cup of chicken broth lent a subtle richness and thinned the sauce while maintaining its body. For finishing touches, we added a little raw garlic to enhance the roasted flavors and a teaspoon or so of sugar to deepen the sweetness of the tomatillos.

In our preliminary test, tasters preferred white meat over dark in the filling, as the mild-tasting breast complemented the flavor of the sauce rather than competing with it. But what was the best method for cooking the chicken? With an eye on keeping the recipe as streamlined as possible, we settled on the fastest, simplest approach: poaching. A brief poach in plain chicken broth wasn't enough; tasters found the meat, which we'd shredded and chopped into bite-sized pieces, too bland. Spiking the broth with sautéed onion, garlic, and cumin before adding the chicken did the trick, infusing the meat with deeper flavor. In addition, we now had a great-tasting broth we could use to thin the sauce; we reserved ¼ cup before discarding the rest.

In many enchilada recipes the filling is larded up with cheese, weighing down the dish. At first we planned to leave it out of the filling entirely, but tasters complained that the dish lacked richness, even with the traditional sprinkling of cheese on top. What if we added a moderate amount of cheese to the filling? We tried a few obvious types: pepper Jack; cheddar; and queso fresco, a salty, crumbly fresh cheese from Mexico resembling feta. Though queso fresco might have bested the others south of the border, it is not a melting cheese, and our tasters wanted gooeyness in their filling. Cheddar lost out to 1½ cups of shredded pepper Jack, a milder cheese that nonetheless added a spicy kick. To keep the richness of the cheese in check, we added a handful of chopped cilantro.

Traditionally, corn tortillas are dipped in hot oil to make them pliable and to keep them from breaking apart when rolled. We opted for the quicker, less messy method we've developed in the test kitchen: spraying the tortillas with vegetable oil and gently baking them for a few minutes. Once they were soft and warm, we took them out of the oven, put them on the countertop, and proceeded to assemble the enchiladas: distributing filling in each, rolling them up, and placing them in a baking dish before topping them with sauce and Jack cheese. Quickly baked until heated through, then served with thinly sliced scallion, radish slices, and a dollop of sour cream, our enchiladas verdes were as good as any we'd enjoyed in our favorite Mexican restaurants.

WHAT WE LEARNED: For richly flavored enchiladas verdes, choose poblano chiles, with their intricate herbal flavor, over the more one-dimensional jalapeño and serrano chiles. Use fresh, zesty tomatillos, but if you can't find them, canned are fine. Toss the chiles (cut in half) and tomatillos with a little olive oil and broil them briefly to concentrate their flavors and give them the smoky char so characteristic of this dish. To achieve the texture of a sauce made with the traditional mortar and pestle, pulse the poblanos and tomatillos in a food processor with a little of the flavorful poaching liquid left from the chicken. Rather than frying each tortilla in oil to make it malleable, spray the tortillas lightly with vegetable oil and bake them quickly. Use a light hand with the cheese (pepper Jack was favored for its meltability and slight tang) and use some inside the enchiladas with the rest dusted on top—this keeps the cheese in balance with the rest of the flavors in the dish.

ENCHILADAS VERDES

serves 4 to 6

You can substitute 3 (11-ounce) cans tomatillos, drained and rinsed, for the fresh ones in this recipe. Halve large tomatillos (more than 2 inches in diameter) and place them skin side up for broiling in step 2 to ensure even cooking and charring. If you can't find poblanos, substitute 4 large jalapeño chiles (with seeds and ribs removed). To increase the spiciness of the sauce, reserve some of the chiles' ribs and seeds and add them to the food processor in step 3.

enchiladas

4	teaspoons vegetable oil
1	medium onion, chopped medium (about 1 cup)
3	medium garlic cloves, minced or pressed through a garlic press (about 1 tablespoon)
½	teaspoon ground cumin
1½	cups low-sodium chicken broth
1	pound boneless, skinless chicken breasts (2 to 3 breasts), trimmed of excess fat
1½	pounds tomatillos (16 to 20 medium), husks and stems removed, rinsed well and dried (see note)
3	medium poblano chiles, halved lengthwise, stemmed, and seeded (see note)
1–2½	teaspoons sugar
	Salt
	Ground black pepper
½	cup coarsely chopped fresh cilantro leaves
8	ounces pepper Jack or Monterey Jack cheese, grated (2 cups)
12	(6-inch) corn tortillas

garnish

2	medium scallions, sliced thin, for garnish
	Thinly sliced radishes, for garnish
	Sour cream

TECHNIQUE: Making Enchiladas Verdes

1. Poach: Simmer the chicken breasts in a flavored broth.

2. Broil: Broil the fresh tomatillos and chiles in the oven to intensify their flavors.

3. Puree: Puree the roasted chiles and tomatillos with the poaching liquid.

4. Warm: Spray the tortillas with vegetable oil spray and briefly heat in the oven to soften.

5. Fill and Roll: Place the filling in the center of each tortilla and roll them up.

6. Assemble: Pour the sauce over the enchiladas and top with grated cheese.

1. Adjust the oven racks to the middle and highest positions and heat the broiler. Heat 2 teaspoons of the oil in a medium saucepan over medium heat until shimmering; add the onion and cook, stirring frequently, until golden, 6 to 8 minutes. Add 2 teaspoons of the garlic and the cumin; cook, stirring frequently, until fragrant, about 30 seconds. Decrease the heat to low and stir in the broth. Add the chicken, cover, and simmer until an instant-read thermometer inserted into the thickest part of the chicken registers 160 degrees, 15 to 20 minutes, flipping the chicken halfway through cooking. Transfer the chicken to a large bowl; place in the refrigerator to cool, about 20 minutes. Remove ¼ cup liquid from the saucepan and set aside; discard the remaining liquid.

2. Meanwhile, toss the tomatillos and poblanos with the remaining 2 teaspoons oil; arrange on a rimmed baking sheet lined with foil, with the poblanos skin side up. Broil until the vegetables blacken and start to soften, 5 to 10 minutes, rotating the pan halfway through cooking. Cool 10 minutes, then remove the skin from the poblanos (leave the tomatillo skins intact). Transfer the tomatillos and chiles to a food processor. Decrease the oven temperature to 350 degrees. Discard the foil from the baking sheet and set the baking sheet aside for warming the tortillas.

3. Add 1 teaspoon of the sugar, 1 teaspoon salt, the remaining teaspoon garlic, and the reserved ¼ cup cooking liquid to the food processor; pulse until the sauce is somewhat chunky, about eight 1-second pulses. Taste the sauce; season with salt and pepper and adjust tartness by stirring in the remaining sugar, ½ teaspoon at a time. Set the sauce aside (you should have about 3 cups).

4. When the chicken is cool, pull into shreds using your hands or 2 forks, then chop into small bite-sized pieces. Combine the chicken with the cilantro and 1½ cups of the cheese; season with salt.

5. Smear the bottom of a 13 by 9-inch baking dish with ¾ cup of the tomatillo sauce. Place the tortillas on 2 baking sheets. Spray both sides of the tortillas lightly with vegetable oil spray. Bake until the tortillas are soft and pliable, 2 to 4 minutes. Increase the oven temperature to 450 degrees. Place the warm tortillas on the countertop and spread ⅓ cup filling down the center of each tortilla. Roll each tortilla tightly and place in the baking dish, seam side down. Pour the remaining tomatillo sauce over the top of the enchiladas. Use the back of a spoon to spread the sauce so that it coats the top of each tortilla. Sprinkle with the remaining ½ cup cheese and cover the baking dish with foil.

6. Bake the enchiladas on the middle rack until heated through and the cheese is melted, 15 to 20 minutes. Uncover, sprinkle with the scallions, and serve immediately, passing the radishes and sour cream separately.

TASTING LAB: Jarred Hot Salsas

WE DON'T LIKE JARRED SALSA. YES, WE KNOW IT'S NOW America's favorite condiment, but previous taste tests have been disappointing. Almost no jarred salsas have reached "recommended" status, and none have come close to the allure of homemade fresh salsa. But our prior taste tests have focused on mild and medium varieties. Might jarred hot salsas be more interesting than their timid cousins?

To find out, we sampled nine national brands and were surprised that most tasters didn't need to quell the burn with cold milk or water as they nibbled. Only the Pace, Frontera Habanero, and Green Mountain Gringo salsas were considered sufficiently hot, and none were excessively incendiary.

These hot salsas were livelier and better than the mild salsas we've tasted in the past, with eight of the nine receiving passing grades. But even the best—Pace, Frontera, and Newman's Own—were merely good, not great, and didn't approach the quality of fresh salsa. Why? Good salsa relies on the interplay of fresh vegetable flavors and textures. Jarred salsas have the freshness and crispness cooked out of them.

Our first- and third-place salsas, Pace and Newman's Own, respectively, came closest to replicating the fresh flavors and colors of homemade salsa, in part because they had high percentages of tomatoes and vegetables: The test kitchen measured both at around 60 percent solid matter by weight. (By comparison, lowest-rated Chi-Chi's contains just 45 percent solids.) Second-place Frontera Habanero contains an average amount of solids (51 percent) but uses roasted tomatoes to produce a fiery salsa that our tasters appreciated for its complexity.

Our advice: If you're going to buy jarred salsa, go for the hot stuff.

Rating Jarred Hot Salsas

TWENTY-ONE MEMBERS OF THE AMERICA'S TEST KITCHEN STAFF TASTED NINE BRANDS OF JARRED HOT SALSA PLAIN (with chips on the side) and in a cheese quesadilla. Brands are listed in order of preference. See www.americastestkitchen.com for updates to this tasting.

RECOMMENDED
Pace Hot Chunky Salsa
$2.49 for 16 ounces

Most tasters were impressed by this spicy salsa's "bright tomato and chile" and "vegetal" flavors, as well as its "chunky," "crunchy" texture. There is a "quick hit of tomato flavor, then fire" from the big burn.

RECOMMENDED
Frontera Hot Habanero Salsa with Roasted Tomatoes and Cilantro
$4.69 for 16 ounces

The roasted tomatoes in this brand were clearly identifiable: "Smoky and complex, yet still has fresh zing," said one taster. "Exciting to eat," said another. This was also the hottest salsa in our tasting.

RECOMMENDED
Newman's Own All Natural Chunky Hot Salsa
$2.79 for 16 ounces

This salsa is seasoned with plenty of garlic, cilantro, and black pepper. One taster made note of an "herby flavor I like, but that isn't typical for salsa." "Could be hotter" was a common comment.

RECOMMENDED
Herdez Hot Salsa Casera
$3.49 for 16 ounces

This salsa was the saltiest of the lot—and tasters noticed, saying, "Less of a cooked taste, but too salty." Several tasters praised this brand, which had the shortest ingredient list in our lineup, as "fresh-tasting" and "clean and crisp."

RECOMMENDED WITH RESERVATIONS
Tostitos Hot Chunky Salsa
$2.99 for 15.5 ounces

This "basic and inoffensive," "ordinary" salsa had average scores for heat level, flavor, and texture.

RECOMMENDED WITH RESERVATIONS
Old El Paso Thick n'Chunky Hot Salsa
$2.79 for 16 ounces

Many tasters commented on the "cloyingly sweet" nature of this salsa. The "strong tomato flavor" comes from the wealth of tomato chunks—this salsa had more solids (65 percent) than any other in our test.

RECOMMENDED WITH RESERVATIONS
Emeril's Kicked Up Chunky Hot Salsa
$3.79 for 16 ounces

"Another bland, tomatoey salsa" that was "not very interesting" but had "decent flavor." "Not hot enough," said one uninspired taster; "tastes like canned tomato puree," said another.

RECOMMENDED WITH RESERVATIONS
Green Mountain Gringo Hot Salsa
$3.79 for 16 ounces

This brand received some very high marks but also some dreadfully low ones. One thing is not debatable—it has a "fierce," "lingering" heat. The only brand to include tomatillos, which might have polarized tasters.

NOT RECOMMENDED
Chi-Chi's Hot Fiesta Salsa
$2.79 for 16 ounces

"I wouldn't dip into this twice," said one wincing taster. Many detected "soapy," "musty," "funky," "sour," or "bitter" flavors. "Just all-around bad," and thin, too—this salsa had the lowest solid content of the brands tasted. "Tastes stale, but if you had beer and chips you might not notice," cracked another.

STEAK TACOS

WHAT WE WANTED: An indoor method for cooking taco-worthy, juicy steak with a grill-like caramelized crust.

Beef tacos made indoors are typically the pedestrian ground beef kind, stuffed into a crisp corn tortilla and loaded with cheese and shredded lettuce. More upscale steak tacos, modeled after authentic Mexican carne asada, are generally reserved for the grill. Here a thin cut of beef, typically skirt or flank steak, is marinated, then grilled, cut into pieces, and served in a soft corn tortilla with simple garnishes. Done properly, the meat has rich, grilled flavor and the tacos themselves are simple to throw together.

Given the choice, we almost always prefer the beefier (and let's face it—better) flavors of a steak taco over a ground beef one, but what about those times when cooking outdoors isn't possible? We wanted to develop a method for bringing steak tacos indoors that would yield meat as tender, juicy, and rich-tasting as the grilled kind. We also wanted the technique to have the same success rate as grilling, without some of the common problems of cooking indoors: weak burners, poor ventilation, or a tendency to turn down the heat too soon so that by the time a crust develops on the meat, the center is overcooked.

Our first task was to choose the right cut of meat. We decided from the outset to shy away from steaks like rib eye and top loin; though both are exceptionally beefy and tender, paying $15 to $20 for meat that you are just going to wrap up in a tortilla seemed a waste. Traditional Mexican recipes typically call for skirt or flank steak for taco meat, both of which come from the belly of the cow. We also wanted to try two other inexpensive cuts: blade steak, which comes from the shoulder, and steak tips (also called flap meat), from the hip of the animal. We pan-seared each type to determine which would work best. Tasters liked the well-marbled steak tips and skirt steak, but we found that availability of these cuts was spotty. The flavor of the blade

steak was great, but it contained too much internal gristle. Flank steak proved to be the best choice all around. It had a nice beefy flavor and, when sliced thinly against the grain, was very tender.

Unadorned, the flank steak was good, but we wondered if there was a technique we could employ to render the meat even juicier. Referring back to our testing for grilled flank steak a few years ago, we found that sprinkling the meat with a liberal dose of salt and allowing it to sit for an hour markedly boosted juiciness, similar to brining. We were able to reduce that time to just 30 minutes by poking holes into the steak with a fork, which allowed the salt to sink more quickly into the meat's interior.

Given that the grill was the inspiration for this recipe, we wanted to try to mimic the caramelized exterior and crisp, brittle edges of grilled meat as much as possible. We figured that the intense heat of the oven's broiler would most closely resemble that of a grill and decided to start there. But after several tests, we knew the oven would never work with a thin cut like flank steak. The broiler was able to brown the exterior of the meat, but this didn't occur until the ¾-inch steak was well-done and way too tough to be acceptable.

Pan-searing proved to be a much more promising method that allowed us to achieve some caramelization. But we wanted more. We tried increasing the surface area by laying the steak flat on the cutting board and slicing it in half, parallel to the board—a technique known as butterflying—but this was a tedious process that didn't yield significantly better results. Next we experimented with cutting the steak lengthwise with the grain into 4 long strips about 2½ inches wide and around 1 inch thick. The results were great. Because the strips were relatively thick, we could brown them on four sides instead of two, which gave us even more exposed edges that became crisp and super-flavorful. We had two more tricks up our sleeves to promote caramelization and boost flavor even further: We sprinkled the steak pieces with a little sugar before browning them,

and we upped the oil we were cooking them in from 2 teaspoons to 2 tablespoons. Thanks to the salting and to the fact that the meat was in the skillet for only a very short period, the steak never dried out.

With a successful cooking method squared away, we now looked at adding some other flavor dimensions to the steak. Reviewing our recipe, we thought to incorporate a wet rub or paste, provided it was removed before cooking so it wouldn't impede caramelization. After looking into traditional marinades, we settled on a combination of cilantro, scallions, garlic, and jalapeño. Processed into a pesto-like paste with some oil, this marinade added fresh flavors to the steak. And coupled with the salt, the oil-based marinade was pulled into the steak, flavoring it throughout. The marinade yielded one more benefit. Before we slathered the herb paste over the steak, we reserved 2 tablespoons that we mixed with some lime juice. After the steak rested and was sliced, we tossed it with this sauce, which not only improved the perceived juiciness of the steak, but also brightened the flavor and presentation considerably.

When it comes to garnishing steak tacos, simplicity is customary. We opted for raw onion, cilantro leaves, and lime wedges—all of which echoed the flavors in our marinade. Tasters also liked thinly sliced radishes and cucumbers for the contrast in texture they provided to the steak. Lastly, we experimented with making some quick-pickled vegetables, which we loosely based on *curtido* (a relish commonly served in Latin America). In the end, we settled on onions that were "pickled" in a sweet and sour mixture of sugar and red wine vinegar enlivened by a couple of jalapeños. Like the other garnishes, the pickled onions provided a crisp texture and bright flavor that accentuated the other flavors in the taco.

With our list of garnishes complete, we finally had a great-tasting alternative to the ubiquitous ground beef taco—one that could be made in the middle of winter and in no time at all.

WHAT WE LEARNED: For economy's sake (after all, these are tacos), choose a cut of meat with good beef flavor, a tender chew, and a reasonable price tag. Flank steak tops the list—reliable at the market, great flavor, and surprisingly tender when sliced thinly against the grain. To boost flavor and juiciness, poke the steak multiple times with a fork, then season with salt and let stand for 30 minutes before cooking. Use a cilantro-based marinade, along with the salt, for fresh, zesty flavor (and reserve a little of the marinade to toss with the sliced cooked steak). Scrape the marinade off the steak before cooking so that a nice, caramelized crust develops. Pan-sear the steak to attain a crust similar to that of grilled steak.

TECHNIQUE: Keys to Tender, Flavorful Beef

1. Cut the flank steak with the grain into 4 strips.

2. Poke both sides of the steak pieces 10 to 12 times with a fork.

3. Salt the meat and coat with the herb paste; let stand for at least 30 minutes.

4. Sear the steak pieces in 2 tablespoons vegetable oil.

5. Slice the steak thinly across the grain, for a more tender chew.

6. Toss the steak with the reserved herb paste and lime juice.

STEAK TACOS

serves 4 to 6

For a less spicy dish, remove some or all of the ribs and seeds from the jalapeños before chopping them for the marinade. In addition to the toppings suggested below, try serving the tacos with Sweet and Spicy Pickled Onions (recipe follows), thinly sliced radish or cucumber, or salsa.

marinade

- ½ cup packed fresh cilantro leaves
- 3 medium garlic cloves, roughly chopped
- 3 medium scallions, roughly chopped (about ⅓ cup)
- 1 medium jalapeño chile, stemmed and roughly chopped (see note)
- ½ teaspoon ground cumin
- ¼ cup vegetable oil
- 1 tablespoon juice from 1 lime

steak

- 1 flank steak (1½ to 1¾ pounds), trimmed of excess fat and cut lengthwise (with the grain) into 4 equal pieces
- 1 tablespoon kosher salt or 1½ teaspoons table salt
- ½ teaspoon sugar
- ½ teaspoon ground black pepper
- 2 tablespoons vegetable oil

tacos

- 12 (6-inch) corn tortillas, warmed (see page 95)
  Fresh cilantro leaves
  Minced white onion
  Lime wedges

1. FOR THE MARINADE: Pulse the cilantro, garlic, scallions, jalapeño, and cumin in a food processor until finely chopped, ten to twelve 1-second pulses, scraping down the sides of the work bowl as necessary. Add the oil and process until the mixture is smooth and resembles pesto, about 15 seconds, scraping down the sides as necessary. Transfer 2 tablespoons of the herb paste to a medium bowl; whisk in the lime juice and set aside.

2. FOR THE STEAK: Using a dinner fork, poke each piece of steak 10 to 12 times on each side. Place in a large baking dish; rub all sides of the steak pieces evenly with the salt and then coat with the remaining herb paste. Cover with plastic wrap and refrigerate at least 30 minutes or up to 1 hour.

3. Scrape the herb paste off the steak and sprinkle all sides of the pieces evenly with the sugar and black pepper. Heat the oil in a 12-inch heavy-bottomed nonstick skillet over medium-high heat until smoking. Place the steak in the skillet and cook until well browned, about 3 minutes. Flip the steak and sear until the second side is well browned, 2 to 3 minutes. Using tongs, stand each piece on a cut side and cook, turning as necessary, until all cut sides are well browned and the internal temperature registers 125 to 130 degrees on an instant-read thermometer, 2 to 7 minutes. Transfer the steak to a cutting board and let rest for 5 minutes.

4. FOR THE TACOS: Using a sharp chef's knife or carving knife, slice the steak pieces against the grain into ⅛-inch-thick pieces. Transfer the sliced steak to the bowl with the herb paste–lime juice mixture and toss to coat. Season with salt. Spoon a small amount of the sliced steak into the center of each warm tortilla and serve immediately, passing the toppings separately.

TECHNIQUE:
How to Warm Tortillas
Our preferred method for warming tortillas is to place each one over the medium flame of a gas burner until slightly charred, about 30 seconds per side. We also like toasting them in a dry skillet over medium-high heat until softened and speckled with brown spots, 20 to 30 seconds per side. You can also use the oven: Divide the tortillas into two stacks and wrap each stack in foil. Heat the tortillas on the middle rack of a 350-degree oven for 5 minutes. Keep

the warmed tortillas wrapped in foil or a kitchen towel until ready to use or they will dry out. (If your tortillas are very dry, pat each with a little water before warming.)

GETTING IT RIGHT:
Mimicking the Grill
We tried several different cooking methods to achieve our goal of well-caramelized steak. Only one proved successful.

Broiled = Tough
Broiling such a thin cut dried out the meat.

Pan-seared = Tender
Pan-searing produced a caramelized exterior and a tender, juicy interior.

SWEET AND SPICY PICKLED ONIONS

makes about 2 cups

The onions can be refrigerated, tightly covered, for up to 1 week.

1	medium red onion, halved and sliced thin (about 1½ cups)
1	cup red wine vinegar
⅓	cup sugar
2	jalapeño chiles, stemmed, seeded, and cut into thin rings
¼	teaspoon salt

Place the onions in a medium heat-resistant bowl. Bring the vinegar, sugar, jalapeños, and salt to a simmer in a small saucepan over medium-high heat, stirring occasionally, until the sugar dissolves. Pour the vinegar mixture over the onions, cover loosely, and let cool to room temperature, about 30 minutes. Once cool, drain and discard the liquid.

EQUIPMENT CORNER:
High-Heat Spatulas

HARDLY ANYONE SPENDS MORE THAN TWO MINUTES a year thinking about problems with their spatulas. With a tool that costs only a couple of bucks, why bother? But the fact is, every spatula has its issues. Old-fashioned rubber spatulas melt in high heat. Newfangled kinds made from silicone are heat-resistant and come in all sorts of new shapes and designs, but many seem more gimmicky than useful. Some are so stiff they can't fold egg whites. Others are so flexible they bend when confronted with thick cookie dough. And still others have handles that are such instruments of torture they must have been designed by Torquemada. Why can't manufacturers come to the rescue and design a better spatula?

In our quest to find one spatula that could do it all, we singled out 10 silicone contenders with features promising greater convenience, versatility, or comfort. All were dishwasher-safe and priced between $7 and $19. We put each one through a series of nine tests that included everything from delicate mixing to high-heat cooking and heavy-duty stirring—we even tried to stain, melt, and destroy them. After all, what good is a great spatula if it isn't going to last?

The business end of a spatula, the head, is its single most critical feature. In many ways the ideal material for the head is silicone, which is heat-resistant, inert (it doesn't release chemicals into the air or your food), and endlessly customizable. Manufacturers have added curves and swoops to serve any number of purposes, some of which became clear only as we worked with the spatulas. One model boasted a small rectangular "rest" that kept the head from touching the countertop when it was laid down and also sported a useful notch for swiping the rim of a jar or bowl. Tips could be pointed to get into pan corners or squared off to scrape the bottom of a saucepan clean—and sometimes both features could be found on the same spatula. Not all shapes worked.

As we assessed the range of design variations in our lineup, we discovered certain preferred characteristics. First was the character of the silicone. Our favorite spatulas had heads that were not only soft and flexible enough to sweep all traces of batter out of a mixing bowl but also stiff enough to remove sticky brown bits, or *fond,* from a skillet. We also decided that the top edge of the head had to be flat, fairly rigid, and squared off (in other words, not unlike the design of the traditional rubber spatula). Spatulas with pointed, floppy, or particularly curvy tips just made us work harder to scrape up food. The edge of the tip and sides also had to be thin enough to maneuver into hard-to-reach corners, rounded bowls, or the edges of a skillet.

We learned that the face of the spatula head should be as flat as possible, so it would scrape clean in one stroke against the rim of a pot or bowl. A number of models have a central ridge where the handle is attached, which left batter stuck on either side, requiring multiple swipes. Flat "cheeks" also came in handy for swirling and blending pan sauces or slipping under the delicate edge of an omelet.

With spatulas, handles are nearly as important as heads. They can help or hurt when you're stirring for an extended time or pushing against stiff dough. And after folding dozens and dozens of whipped egg whites into batter for angel food cake and stirring pot after pot of steaming-hot risotto, we concluded that we liked a long handle on our spatulas to keep our hands a safe distance from the food. But length alone wasn't enough—handles also had to be rigid enough to provide leverage. A few of our models had handles that literally flopped like a wet noodle just when you needed them to have a backbone. Try blending Parmesan into a finished risotto with a spatula that can barely push through the rice.

Comfort was equally important. One spatula cut into our fingers with its hard plastic edge, making it a little painful to push through cookie dough. Another sported such an extreme curve that it forced our wrists to twist unnaturally as we stirred our way around a pan sauce. Others felt comfortable and easy as we shifted hand positions for different tasks, turning the spatula horizontal to a pan to fold over an omelet or vertical to scrape down a mixing bowl, or providing a firm grip as we pushed through stiff cookie dough to mix in nuts and chocolate chips.

And though flat, Popsicle-stick-style handles are the classic choice in a rubber spatula, we broke with tradition by preferring rounded handles, whether smooth like a dowel or with indentations for the thumb. We also liked our spatula handle to be as heat-resistant as the head—one handle actually melted as it rested on the edge of a hot skillet. A few handles with metal inserts heated up, as did a metal logo placed on the grip of another.

What good is a spatula that has a great shape and comfy handle if it can't hold up for years of hard cooking in your kitchen? Or one that stains and smells like the last thing you cooked? We concocted a witches' brew of curry and tomato sauce—the worst offenders—and tossed in all the spatulas for an hour-long simmer. Then we ran them through a home-style dishwasher twice. The dark-colored spatulas came clean, but lighter models stained. Depending on the formulation of the silicone in each brand, some spatulas absorbed odors, and others didn't. (As we write, the scent of turmeric is wafting up from a few of these spatulas—not too appealing if the next thing we want to use them for is making cookies.)

Putting the claims of heat resistance to the test, we also tried to melt the spatulas in a cast-iron skillet by firmly pressing their tips against the bottom of a hot pan for two minutes (using a thermocouple to monitor temperature). None of the spatulas lost their shape or showed signs of disintegrating, but a few turned brown or lost color at the point of contact. None gave off fumes or odors.

After all the flipping, folding, scraping, and stirring was done, we declared a pair of winners. The Rubbermaid Professional 13½-Inch Heat Resistant Scraper ($18.99) is a workhorse with an extra-long handle and a generously sized head that resembles a bigger, better version of the brand's traditional rubber spatula. The Tovolo Silicone Spatula ($8.99) boasts a snazzy blue head and a brushed stainless steel handle that never got hot and proved remarkably comfortable to hold. Both designs feature heads large enough to move volumes of food, with tips rigid enough to lift fond from a skillet. Their handles were easy to manipulate at any angle and didn't dip our fingers in the food. Neither showed signs of melting or discoloring, even when we left them in a hot pan at higher-than-recommended temperatures. The Tovolo's good looks and nice price make it hard to resist, but, in the end, the larger overall size and sturdiness of the Rubbermaid won our highest accolades.

Rating High-Heat Spatulas

WE EVALUATED 10 SILICONE SPATULAS, ALL DISHWASHER-SAFE, RUNNING EACH THROUGH NINE TESTS, INCLUDING lifting omelets, scraping the bowl of a food processor, hand mixing nuts and other ingredients into stiff cookie dough, folding whipped egg whites into cake batter, making a pan sauce, and stirring risotto. We also simmered the spatulas in a pot of tomato-curry sauce for an hour to see if they would stain and absorb odors, and we ran them through the dishwasher twice to see if they would come through clean and odor-free. And we tested their heat-safe claims, trying to melt them in a cast-iron skillet as hot as we could get it—up to 674 degrees Fahrenheit. Brands are listed in order of preference. See www.americastestkitchen.com for updates to this testing.

HIGHLY RECOMMENDED
Rubbermaid Professional 13½-Inch Heat Resistant Scraper
$18.99

A practical, no-nonsense spatula that aced every cooking test, with a great balance of flexibility and firmness for both the head and the handle; however, the head did become slightly discolored by the turmeric in the curry test.

HIGHLY RECOMMENDED
Tovolo Silicone Spatula
$8.99

This sleek spatula passed every performance test, scraping, stirring, folding, and sautéing like a champ. It also withstood our attempts to stain and melt it. And at only $8.99 it's our "best buy."

RECOMMENDED
Le Creuset Super Spatula
$13.95

Perfect for scraping down a bowl, folding whipped egg whites into batter, or slipping under an omelet, this well-shaped spatula also offers good resistance when stirring. An overly soft tip and edge kept this spatula from a top spot.

RECOMMENDED
Trudeau Silicone Spatula, Orange, 12 Inch
$9.99

With a "huge," slightly stiff head and rigid handle, this solid spatula was ideal for stirring thick, resistant ingredients and moved great volumes with few strokes when folding in whipped egg whites.

RECOMMENDED
Mario Batali Silicone Risotto Spatula
$7.95

This spatula's fairly firm, bouncy, curved head did well scraping bowls clean, but the pointed, floppy tip got in the way more than it helped, even when making risotto (despite the spatula's name).

RECOMMENDED WITH RESERVATIONS
OXO Good Grips Medium Silicone Spatula
$7.99

A too-small head (and slightly too-short handle) took points off the score for this otherwise decent spatula. Stained and held curry odor, blackened slightly under high heat, but retained its shape and pliant texture.

RECOMMENDED WITH RESERVATIONS
Kuhn Rikon Bakers' Silicone Spatula
$6.95

This lightweight spatula did well scraping mixing bowls, sliding under an omelet, or scraping fond, but it was too wimpy to mix chocolate chips and nuts into stiff cookie dough.

NOT RECOMMENDED
SiliconeZone Large Folia Spatula
$13.95

This flat, paddle-like spatula would be much better without its extremely curved shape, which made testers complain about being forced into "unnatural" and fatiguing arm positions.

NOT RECOMMENDED
Zyliss Does-It-All Spatula
$7.99

The head of this spatula is well designed, but the handle is much too short. We had to reach into a saucepan of hot risotto to grab it and got batter on our hands while making angel food cake.

NOT RECOMMENDED
Chef'n Switchit Dual-Ended Long Spatula
$10.99

This "bendy, floppy-tipped" spatula was little better than a wet noodle when tackling food that offered the least bit of resistance, such as cookie dough or risotto. Partly reinforced with a too-short, enclosed steel strip, its too-skinny head couldn't scrape up fond and did poorly when folding whipped egg whites.

Enchiladas Verdes **page 88**

Hearty Tuscan Bean Stew **page 20**

Pizza Bianca **page 8**

Charcoal-Grilled Potatoes with Garlic and Rosemary **page 218**

Poached Salmon with Herb and Caper Vinaigrette **page 42**

Inexpensive Roast Beef **page 77**

Best Drop Biscuits **page 195**

Crunchy Oven-Baked Fish **page 47** with Sweet and Tangy Tartar Sauce **page 48**

Stir-Fried Beef with Snap Peas and Red Peppers **page 170**

Creamless Creamy Tomato Soup **page 5** with Croutons **page 5**

Charcoal-Grilled Rack of Lamb **page 236**

Beef and Vegetable Soup **page 16**

Pork Lo Mein **page 165**

Charcoal-Grilled Pork Loin with Apple-Cranberry Filling **page 223**

Arugula Salad with Grapes, Fennel, Gorgonzola, and Pecans **page 69**

113

French Onion Soup **page 121**

FRENCH CLASSICS
reimagined

We have to hand it to the French. Just when we thought we knew all there was to know about cooking a whole chicken (roast it, right?), we discovered a centuries-old French recipe for roasting chicken that had us scratching our heads, thinking, "Why didn't we think of that?" Case in point: roasting a whole chicken *en cocotte,* which means "in a pot." As the chicken roasts in the covered pot (typically a Dutch oven), it essentially steam-cooks, releasing juices that stay in the pot, contributing to exceptionally moist meat and a rich-tasting jus. Although this method doesn't yield crisp skin, it's a small price to pay for such succulent meat. Our goal, therefore, would be to perfect this French technique as well as determine what else should go into the pot. Could we add vegetables to make a meal, or herbs and seasonings to enrich the jus? We'd round up our Dutch ovens and a whole lot of chickens to find out.

Onion soup is another timeless French classic. Really good French onion soup boasts loads of sweet onions swimming in a rich broth, the whole covered with crusty bread and gooey cheese. What's not to like? In short, the time it takes to get this soup on the table. Good recipes take the better part of a day, and "quick" recipes disappoint with their weak-flavored broths masked by an overdose of cheese. Could we find some middle ground? Our goal was to find an uncomplicated method for preparing this rustic soup—one that didn't cut corners on flavor—for a cold-weather soup we could make any time the craving strikes.

FRENCH CHICKEN IN A POT

WHAT WE WANTED: A foolproof technique for the French method of cooking chicken *en cocotte*—a method that delivers unbelievably moist meat and deeply satisfying flavor.

French chicken in a pot, or *poulet en cocotte,* is a Parisian bistro specialty. The dish features a whole chicken baked with a smattering of root vegetables in a covered pot. It sports a pale, soft skin, in contrast to the crisp exterior of roasted poultry. But what makes this dish so special is its rich, soul-satisfying flavor and incredibly tender, juicy meat. Chicken as good as this makes us question the American obsession with crisp chicken skin. We're so bent on getting this one aspect right that we'll sacrifice what's really important—the meat. In the test kitchen we'd certainly be willing to give up a crisp exterior if it meant tender, succulent meat bursting with concentrated chicken flavor—thus, poulet en cocotte would be our next experiment.

The basic method for poulet en cocotte is simple: Place a seasoned chicken in a pot, scatter in a small handful of chopped vegetables, cover, and bake. Unlike braising, little to no liquid is added to the pot, resulting in a drier cooking environment. Many of the recipes we found called for auxiliary ingredients such as bacon, mushrooms, or tomatoes. But when we tried these extras, we found they served only to cover up the great chicken flavor, pure and simple. We would stick with the chunks of potatoes, onions, and carrots, as is traditional.

Though in most recipes we tried nothing was done to the chicken except to season it before placing it in the pot to bake, we decided extra measures were necessary. We tried basting the bird, but going to the oven every 20 minutes was a hassle that had little impact on the taste. Next we tried lightly browning the top and bottom of the chicken on the stovetop before baking. Now we were getting somewhere—the flavor was beginning to deepen. But how could we get

even more intense chicken flavor? In earlier tests we'd added a splash of wine or broth to the pot at the start of cooking. These versions resulted in meat that was very juicy, but the steamier environment created a washed-out flavor. What if we actually decreased the humidity inside the pot? Would that give us the results we were looking for?

Eager for answers, we prepped a new chicken and a batch of vegetables, drying each thoroughly with paper towels before adding them to the pot. This had little effect. And then it dawned on us that the vegetables were releasing liquid and making the pot too steamy. To create something close to a one-pot meal, we had been using more vegetables and in larger chunks than other recipes included. But we'd gladly sacrifice the veggies if it meant a bird with better flavor.

In our next go-round, we cooked a chicken by itself save for a little oil to prevent it from sticking. When we pulled the pot from the oven and removed the lid, a tiny puff of steam emerged—not the great whoosh that had been escaping from the tests with vegetables. This was a bird with great flavor that easily won over tasters. And with no vegetables to soak them up, the flavorful juices remained in the pot. After defatting the liquid, we had a simple, richly flavored jus to accompany our chicken—a huge bonus. Still, the bird was not perfect. Tasters complained that the breast meat was a tad tough and fibrous, and we had to agree. We wondered what a lower oven temperature would do.

Setting up a half-dozen chickens in pots, we tested a range of oven temperatures below 400 degrees. To account for pots with poorly fitting lids, we sealed each with foil before adding the top, ensuring that as much of the chicken juices as possible would stay inside. Temperatures from 300 to 375 degrees produced better results, but even lower temperatures—between 250 and 300 degrees—yielded chickens with incredibly tender breast meat. And although these birds took much longer than average to cook (about an hour and

a half—all walk-away time, mind you), tasters raved about the meat's rich, concentrated flavor, which was all thanks to the technique: slow-cooking the chicken in nothing more than its own juices.

The last cooking hurdle to clear was the matter of the dark meat not cooking quickly enough. By the time the breast meat was perfectly cooked to 160 degrees, the dark meat (which needs to be cooked to 175 degrees) still wasn't ready. Placing the oven rack on the lowest position, so it was closer to the heat source, combined with browning the dark meat for an extra minute or two, solved the problem.

With the cooking process under control, it was time to finesse the flavors. Two teaspoons of kosher salt were enough to season the chicken without making the jus too salty. And we discovered that we could get away with adding a small amount of potently flavored aromatic vegetables—chopped onion, celery, whole garlic cloves—to the pot. Lightly browning them along with the chicken helped wick away any excess moisture, and the caramelization added rich color and flavor to the jus. Stirring in a little fresh lemon juice to finish the jus brightened and balanced all of its flavors.

Our French Chicken in a Pot will never place first in a beauty contest, of course, if a browned roast bird is the standard. But its tender, juicy, intensely flavored meat is sure to be a winner every time.

WHAT WE LEARNED: Cook the chicken slowly in its own juices to keep the meat tender and moist. To ensure that as much of the chicken juices as possible stays inside the pot, seal it tightly with foil before adding the lid. Add a small amount of browned aromatic vegetables with the chicken to minimize humidity in the pot and keep the flavors from washing out. Then create a richly flavored jus by defatting the liquid left in the pot.

FRENCH CHICKEN IN A POT

serves 4

The cooking times in the recipe are for a 4½- to 5-pound bird. A 3½- to 4½-pound chicken will take about an hour to cook, and a 5- to 6-pound bird will take close to 2 hours. We developed this recipe to work with a 5- to 8-quart Dutch oven with a tight-fitting lid. If using a 5-quart pot, do not cook a chicken larger than 5 pounds. If using a kosher chicken, reduce the amount of kosher salt to 1 teaspoon (or ½ teaspoon table salt). If you choose not to serve the skin with the chicken, simply remove it before carving. The amount of jus will vary depending on the size of the chicken; season it with about ¼ teaspoon lemon juice for every ¼ cup.

1	whole roasting chicken (4½ to 5 pounds), giblets removed and discarded, wings tucked under back (see note)
2	teaspoons kosher salt or 1 teaspoon table salt
¼	teaspoon ground black pepper
1	tablespoon olive oil
1	small onion, chopped medium (about ½ cup)
1	small celery rib, chopped medium (about ¼ cup)
6	medium garlic cloves, peeled and trimmed
1	bay leaf
1	medium sprig fresh rosemary (optional)
½–1	teaspoon juice from 1 lemon

1. Adjust an oven rack to the lowest position and heat the oven to 250 degrees. Pat the chicken dry with paper towels and season with salt and pepper. Heat the oil in a large Dutch oven over medium heat until just smoking. Add the chicken breast side down; scatter the onion, celery, garlic, bay leaf, and rosemary (if using) around the chicken. Cook until the breast is lightly browned, about 5 minutes. Using a wooden spoon inserted into the cavity of the bird, flip the chicken breast side up and cook until the chicken and vegetables are well browned, 6 to 8 minutes. Remove the Dutch oven from the heat; place a large sheet of foil over the pot and cover tightly

GETTING IT RIGHT:
Dry Cooking versus Braising

French Chicken in a Pot shares some similarities with braised chicken—both are cooked in covered pots in low-temperature ovens to yield tender, flavorful meat. Unlike braising, however, where lots of liquid is added to the pot, our chicken is placed in a dry pot and left to cook in nothing more than the essence of its own juices.

Dry Environment
In a dry pot with no added liquid, juices that come out of the chicken go right back into it, undiluted by other flavors.

Wet Environment
The wet environment of a braise creates an ongoing exchange between the flavors of the chicken and those of other ingredients, such as wine, broth, and vegetables.

with the lid. Transfer the pot to the oven and cook until an instant-read thermometer registers 160 degrees when inserted in the thickest part of the breast and 175 degrees in the thickest part of the thigh, 80 to 110 minutes.

2. Transfer the chicken to a carving board, tent with foil, and allow to rest 20 minutes. Meanwhile, strain the chicken juices from the pot through a fine-mesh strainer into a fat separator, pressing on the solids to extract the liquid; discard the solids (you should have about ¾ cup juices). Allow the liquid to settle 5 minutes, then pour into a saucepan and set over low heat. Carve the chicken, adding any accumulated juices to the saucepan. Stir the lemon juice into the jus to taste (see note). Serve the chicken, passing the jus at the table.

TECHNIQUE: Moist Chicken with Concentrated Flavor

1. Brown: Sear the chicken on both sides to enhance flavor.

2. Seal: Cover the pot with foil before adding the lid to trap chicken juices inside.

3. Slow-Cook: Cook the chicken at 250 degrees for 80 to 110 minutes.

4. Rest: Transfer the chicken to a carving board to rest so juices can redistribute.

SHOPPING NOTES: Clay Cookers

CLAY COOKERS HAVE GARNERED FAME FOR COAXING remarkable flavor from few ingredients and minimal work. You simply soak the cooker in water for 15 minutes, add the raw ingredients, and place the covered pot in a cold oven. You then crank the heat up to at least 400 degrees. The steam released from the water-soaked clay and the gradual temperature increase should yield tender, juicy meat.

Can a clay cooker outperform a Dutch oven? To find out, we compared two batches of our French Chicken in a Pot, one cooked in a Dutch oven and the other adapted for a clay roaster. We preferred the Dutch oven method. Though both chickens cooked up equally moist and fall-apart tender, clay cookers are not stovetop-safe, so we needed to brown the chicken in a skillet before transferring it to the clay pot.

Clay cookers aren't stovetop-safe, so you'll need to brown the chicken separately.

FRENCH ONION SOUP

WHAT WE WANTED: A method for achieving extraordinarily deep flavor from humble onions—the star of this classic soup.

The ideal French onion soup combines a satisfying broth redolent of sweet caramelized onions with a slice of toasted baguette and melted cheese. But the reality is that most of the onion soup you find isn't very good. Once you manage to dig through the layer of congealed cheese to unearth a spoonful of broth, it just doesn't taste like onions. We discovered the source of these watery, weak broths when we looked up some recipes. One was particularly appalling, calling for a mere 7 ounces of onions to make soup for six! Even more disturbing were those recipes that advised sautéing the onions for only five or six minutes—not nearly enough time for them to caramelize.

The good news is that we really didn't need these lackluster recipes. We know of a terrific one introduced to the test kitchen by a visitor from France, Henri Pinon. Henri patiently cooked 3 pounds of onions in butter over very low heat until they were golden brown (this took about 90 minutes), then deglazed the pot with water. Nothing unusual there—deglazing is common in onion soup recipes. What followed, however, was something entirely new. Henri allowed the onions to recaramelize, and then he deglazed the pan again. And again. He repeated this process several more times over the course of another hour, finally finishing the soup by simmering the onions with water, white wine, and a sprig of thyme. He garnished the soup in the traditional way, with a slice of crusty toasted baguette and a very modest amount of shredded Gruyère, passing the crocks under the broiler to melt the cheese. How did it taste? Beyond compare—the broth was impossibly rich, with deep onion flavor that burst through the tanginess of the Gruyère and bread.

Having watched Henri make his soup, we couldn't wait to give the recipe a try. But before we started cooking, we thought about his technique. When onions caramelize, a complex series of chemical reactions takes place. Heat causes water molecules to separate from the onions' sugar molecules. As they cook, the dehydrated sugar molecules react with each other to form new molecules that produce new colors, flavors, and aromas. (This is the same series of reactions that occurs when granulated sugar is heated to make caramel.) Each time Henri deglazed the pan and allowed the onions to recaramelize, he was ratcheting up the flavor of the soup in a big way.

Back in the test kitchen with Henri's recipe in hand, we started cooking, and a long while later, the soup was on. It was as delicious as when Henri had made it, but after standing at the stove for more than two hours, who had the energy to enjoy it? Was there a way to borrow Henri's technique while cutting down on the active cooking time?

We cranked the heat from low to high to hurry the onions along, and our risk taking was rewarded with burnt onions. We needed steady heat that wouldn't cause scorching—the stovetop was concentrating too much heat at the bottom of the pot. Why not use the oven? We spread oiled sliced onions on a baking sheet and roasted them at 450 degrees. Instead of caramelizing, however, they simply dried out. Lower temperatures caused the onions to steam. Next, we cooked as many sliced onions as we could squeeze into a Dutch oven (4 pounds), with far more promising results—the onions cooked slowly and evenly, building flavor all the while. After some trial and error, we finally settled on a method by which we cooked the onions, covered, in a 400-degree oven for an hour, then continued cooking with the lid ajar for another hour and a half.

With our new hands-off method, the onions emerged from the oven golden, soft, and sweet, and a nice *fond* had begun to collect on the bottom of the pot. Even better, we'd had to tend to them only twice in 2½ hours. Next, we continued the caramelization process on the stovetop. Because of their head start in the oven, deglazing only three or four times was sufficient (the process still took nearly an hour—but this was far better than the two-plus hours Henri spent on his dozens of deglazings). Once the onions were as dark as possible, we poured in a few splashes of dry sherry, which tasters preferred to sweet sherry, white wine, Champagne, red wine, and vermouth.

Settling on a type of onion from standard supermarket varieties was a snap. We quickly dismissed red onions—they bled out to produce a dingy-looking soup. White onions were too mild, and Vidalia onions made the broth candy-sweet. Yellow onions, on the other hand, offered just the sweet and savory notes we were after.

Henri had used only water for his soup, but after making batches with water, chicken broth, and beef broth alone and in combination, we decided the soup was best with all three. The broths added complexity, and our goal was to build as many layers of flavor as possible.

At last, we could focus on the soup's crowning glory: bread and cheese. So as to not obscure the lovely broth, we dialed back the hefty amounts that have come to define the topping in this country. Toasting the bread before floating a slice on the soup warded off sogginess. As for the cheese, Emmenthaler and Swiss were fine, but we wanted to stick to tradition. A modest sprinkling of nutty Gruyère was a grand, gooey finish to a great soup.

WHAT WE LEARNED: For a rich broth, the onions must fully caramelize. First, cook them, covered, in a 400-degree oven, then deglaze them on the stovetop three or four times to ratchet up the intensity of their flavor. Combine yellow onions with water, chicken broth, and beef broth for maximum flavor. Toast the bread before setting it on top of the soup to ward off sogginess, and add only a modest sprinkling of nutty Gruyère so the broth isn't overpowered.

FRENCH ONION SOUP

serves 6

Sweet onions, such as Vidalia or Walla Walla, will make this dish overly sweet. Be patient when caramelizing the onions in step 2; the entire process takes 45 to 60 minutes. Use broiler-safe crocks and keep the rims of the bowls 4 to 5 inches from the heating element to obtain a proper gratinée of melted, bubbly cheese. If using ordinary soup bowls, sprinkle the toasted bread slices with Gruyère and return them to the broiler until the cheese melts, then float them on top of the soup. For the best flavor, make the soup a day or 2 in advance. Alternatively, the onions can be prepared through step 1, cooled in the pot, and refrigerated for up to 3 days before proceeding with the recipe.

soup

3	tablespoons unsalted butter, cut into 3 pieces
6	large yellow onions (about 4 pounds), halved and cut pole to pole into ¼-inch-thick slices (see note)
	Salt
2	cups water, plus extra for deglazing
½	cup dry sherry
4	cups low-sodium chicken broth
2	cups beef broth
6	sprigs fresh thyme, tied with kitchen twine
1	bay leaf
	Ground black pepper

cheese croutons

1	small baguette, cut on bias into ½-inch slices
8	ounces Gruyère cheese, shredded (about 2½ cups)

1. FOR THE SOUP: Adjust an oven rack to the lower-middle position and heat the oven to 400 degrees. Generously spray the inside of a large (at least 7-quart) heavy-bottomed Dutch oven with vegetable oil spray. Place the butter in the pot and add the onions and 1 teaspoon salt. Cook, covered,

1 hour (the onions will be moist and slightly reduced in volume). Remove the pot from the oven and stir the onions, scraping the bottom and sides of the pot. Return the pot to the oven with the lid slightly ajar and continue to cook until the onions are very soft and golden brown, 1½ to 1¾ hours longer, stirring the onions and scraping the bottom and sides of the pot after 1 hour.

2. Carefully remove the pot from the oven and place over medium-high heat. Using oven mitts to handle the pot, cook the onions, stirring frequently and scraping the bottom and sides of the pot, until the liquid evaporates and the onions brown, 15 to 20 minutes, reducing the heat to medium if the onions are browning too quickly. Continue to cook, stirring frequently, until the pot bottom is coated with a dark crust, 6 to 8 minutes, adjusting the heat as necessary. (Scrape any fond that collects on the spoon back into the onions.) Stir in ¼ cup water, scraping the pot bottom to loosen the crust, and cook until the water evaporates and the pot bottom has formed another dark crust, 6 to 8 minutes. Repeat the process of deglazing 2 or 3 more times, until the onions are very dark brown. Stir in the sherry and cook, stirring frequently, until the sherry evaporates, about 5 minutes.

3. Stir in the broths, 2 cups water, thyme, bay leaf, and ½ teaspoon salt, scraping up any final bits of browned crust on the bottom and sides of the pot. Increase the heat to high and bring to a simmer. Reduce the heat to low, cover, and simmer 30 minutes. Remove and discard the herbs, then season with salt and pepper to taste.

4. FOR THE CROUTONS: While the soup simmers, arrange the baguette slices in a single layer on a baking sheet and bake in a 400-degree oven until the bread is dry, crisp, and golden at the edges, about 10 minutes. Set aside.

5. TO SERVE: Adjust an oven rack 6 inches from the broiler element and heat the broiler. Set individual broiler-safe crocks on the baking sheet and fill each with about 1¾ cups soup. Top each bowl with 1 or 2 baguette slices (do not overlap the slices) and sprinkle evenly with the Gruyère. Broil until the cheese is melted and bubbly around the edges, 3 to 5 minutes. Let cool 5 minutes before serving.

TECHNIQUE: Golden Onions without the Fuss

Forget constant stirring on the stovetop. Cooking onions in the oven takes time but requires little attention.

1. Raw: The raw onions nearly fill a large Dutch oven.

2. After 1 Hour in the Oven: The onions are starting to wilt and release moisture.

3. After 2½ Hours in the Oven: The onions are golden, wilted, and significantly reduced in volume.

GETTING IT RIGHT: Triple Deglaze

Most recipes for French onion soup call for deglazing—loosening the flavorful dark brown crust, or fond, that forms on the bottom of the pot—only once, if at all. The secret to our recipe is to deglaze the pot at least three times.

VARIATION

QUICKER FRENCH ONION SOUP

This variation uses a microwave for the initial cooking of the onions, which dramatically reduces the cooking time. The soup's flavor, however, will not be quite as deep as with the stovetop method. If you don't have a microwave-safe bowl large enough to accommodate all of the onions, cook in a smaller bowl in 2 batches.

Follow the recipe for French Onion Soup, combining the onions and 1 teaspoon salt in a large microwave-safe bowl and covering with a large microwave-safe plate (the plate should completely cover the bowl and not rest on the onions). Microwave on high power for 20 to 25 minutes until the onions are soft and wilted, stirring halfway through cooking. (Use oven mitts to remove the bowl from the microwave, and remove the plate away from you to avoid a steam burn.) Drain the onions (about ½ cup liquid should drain off) and proceed with step 2, melting the butter in the Dutch oven before adding the wilted onions.

TASTING LAB: Gruyère Cheese

THOUGH ITS FAME DERIVES MAINLY FROM ITS USE IN fondue and French onion soup, Gruyère is also a table cheese revered for its creamy texture and savory flavor. Both Switzerland and France make authentic versions that are crafted from raw cow's milk and aged for the better part of a year in government-designated regions (the French cheese is called Gruyère de Comté).

Though labeled "Gruyère," domestic cheeses of this type bear little resemblance to the real thing. Made from pasteurized cow's milk, they are aged for fewer months and have a rubbery texture and bland flavor. In fact, in a blind taste test of eight brands, tasters overwhelmingly panned the two domestic versions, likening one (from Boar's Head) to "plastic."

Imported Gruyères, on the other hand, received raves. The top picks in the lineup were two reserve cheeses, aged 10 or more months to develop stronger flavor: the Emmi Le Gruyère Reserve and a Gruyère Salé from a Boston-area cheese shop.

Rating Gruyère Cheese

TEN MEMBERS OF THE AMERICA'S TEST KITCHEN STAFF TASTED EIGHT BRANDS OF GRUYÈRE CHEESE PLAIN AND MELTED on slices of baguette. Brands are listed in order of preference. See www.americastestkitchen.com for updates to this tasting.

RECOMMENDED
Emmi Le Gruyère Reserve
$12.99 per pound

"Grassy," "salty," and "nicely dry," the reserve version of this well-known Swiss brand won favor with most tasters, especially when melted.

RECOMMENDED
Gruyère Salé
$19.99 per pound

Many tasters picked this artisanal sample as their favorite for its "smooth" yet "assertive and nutty" flavor and slightly granular curd that melted nicely. A few tasters, however, found it overly mellow and "pedestrian."

RECOMMENDED
Gruyère Alpage
$24.95 per pound

By far the most exotic Gruyère in the pack, this cheese is crafted from raw milk cooked in large copper kettles over a wood fire to lend "pungent," "smoky" flavor, then aged for over a year. Detractors, however, found it "funky" and "overripe."

RECOMMENDED
French Gruyère de Comté
$12.98 per pound

Though a bit "sharper" and more "tannic" than some tasters preferred in a table cheese, this yellow-hued sample from France offered favorable "nuttiness" once melted on bread.

RECOMMENDED WITH RESERVATIONS
Swiss Rose Le Gruyère
$17.98 per pound

Though many tasters enjoyed this cheese eaten on its own, it was deemed "greasy," "rubbery," and "bland" in melted form.

RECOMMENDED WITH RESERVATIONS
Emmi Le Gruyère
$9.99 per pound

Although some tasters liked the milder flavor of this younger sibling of the Swiss reserve sample, others thought it resembled "plastic."

NOT RECOMMENDED
Grand Cru Gruyère
$13.98 per pound

Though this young domestic cheese melted nicely, tasters found it unanimously "boring." One taster summed it up: "No flavor, no crunch, no spark."

NOT RECOMMENDED
Boar's Head Gruyère Cheese
$13.98 per pound

Tasters panned this young Wisconsin-made brand for a taste more like "cheap supermarket cheese" than real Gruyère. Even melted on bread, the product exhibited "zero flavor."

EQUIPMENT CORNER: Mandolines

CHURNING OUT LARGE QUANTITIES OF IDENTICALLY sliced fruits and vegetables is a challenge for any cook wielding only a chef's knife. Even the most skilled might wish for a faster, more precise tool. There is such a device—the mandoline. An appliance more often found in classic French or Japanese restaurants than in the home, this countertop gadget resembles a horizontal grater. It has two working surfaces: a razor-sharp blade and an adjustable platform that creates a downward cutting angle. Once the desired thickness is set, slicing requires nothing more than running a piece of food against the blade.

Despite the mandoline's speed and precision, we've always been skeptical of kitchen gadgets that perform the same function as basic tools we already own. Like most specialty kitchen tools, these slicers vary dramatically in size, price, and design. Many eat up counter space, and the most expensive can cost well over $100. Some even felt dangerous. Was there a mandoline that truly belonged in a home kitchen? We rounded up 13 models—from a $7 plastic tool to a souped-up $380 appliance—to find out.

Mandolines come in two styles: Classic, French-inspired models feature a straight blade for basic slicing, as well as serrated and comb blades for fancier applications such as julienned matchsticks or waffle cuts; hand-held slicers offer only a straight slicing blade, usually fit flat in a utensil drawer, and cost less (many are plastic). Either type must be sharp enough to glide through firm produce such as potatoes without bumping or jerking and slice softer foods without snagging or mangling. Most important, all good mandolines must include extensive safety features.

Nearly all models handled firm food effortlessly; a few turned out slices of potato so clean they could be reassembled into a perfect whole. Softer produce was another

matter. We tried slicing ripe beefsteak tomatoes as thinly as possible, figuring a blade that could cope with something so squishy could handle anything. Tomato skins can snag on straight-bladed knives (we usually cut them with serrated knives), and we wondered if the same would hold true for mandolines. Minutes later, we had two piles: a pulverized crime scene of red juice, seeds, and skins and a towering stack of beautiful, intact tomato disks. The difference? All of the flawlessly performing mandolines had V-shaped or diagonally slanted blades, which, like the teeth on a serrated knife, cut the tough skin more readily than did a horizontal edge.

We put a premium on the safety features of these potentially dangerous tools. Most models include hand guards to shield fingers from sharp blades and the prongs that grip the food. The safest guards were broad and ran smoothly along the slicing track. Some, shaped like derby hats, had brims whose diameters stretched at least as wide as the slicing plane. These felt far safer than guards shaped like small plastic plates that fit in the palm of our hand.

The type of food prongs on the guards made a real difference, too. We came across three basic styles: short, blunt teeth that could only poke at hard or heavy vegetables like carrots or potatoes; sturdy skewer-like prongs of an inch or

more sheathed by retractable food pushers, which worked best for both gripping produce and keeping hands out of harm's way; and the spring-loaded prongs featured on the two most expensive slicers. The spring-loaded prongs were a disaster. The coils were supposed to create enough tension to hold the food firmly against the blade—theoretically saving the cook from pressing down while sliding the food along the slicing plane—but loading this device was not easy: The food went in, and the food sprang back out. Finally, as much as we thought we'd like models whose food grippers locked on tracks—several guards, representing each style, could slide onto the slicing plane to prevent slipping—this feature proved irritating when the produce was too bulky to fit underneath.

Nobody likes to have to pore over a user's manual, and more than one slicer came with cryptic instructions or sent testers through multiple steps just to change a blade. Testers awarded highest marks to models with precise, measurement-marked dials that let you set the thickness of the slice. Not only could these knobs adjust thickness; on some models they simultaneously rotated the right blade into position, eliminating contact with sharp blades.

By the time we finished our testing, it was clear that a mandoline would be a welcome addition to any kitchen, but shelling out big bucks for classic French and Japanese models bought no added safety or comfort, only baffling designs and flashy storage cases. After spending between $100 and $400, we shouldn't have had to cringe in fear while slicing. For a fraction of the price, you can do better—and we did. We found our winner in OXO's V-Blade Mandoline Slicer ($49.99). Testers proclaimed its V-shaped blade ideal for both firm and delicate produce. It felt safe and comfortable and came with a rimmed, long-pronged hand guard. Best of all, delicate julienne and waffle cuts were simple; with a quick blade swap and one turn of a knob, this slicer could multitask better than some of the priciest models.

GETTING IT RIGHT:
Anatomy of an Ideal Mandoline

Hand guard to shield fingers

Gripper prongs firmly grasp food

Storage for extra blades

Measurement-marked dial makes precision cuts easy

V-blade easily cuts through tough produce

Rating Mandolines

WE HAD BOTH NOVICE AND EXPERIENCED TESTERS TRY OUT 13 MANDOLINES SLICING RUSSET POTATOES AND BEEF-steak tomatoes and assessing the models on safety features and ease of use. Where applicable, we also tested julienne and crinkle- or waffle-cutting blades. Brands are listed in order of preference. See www.americastestkitchen.com for updates to this testing.

HIGHLY RECOMMENDED
OXO Good Grips V-Blade Mandoline Slicer
$49.99

A razor-sharp V-blade made short work of a variety of fruits and vegetables, and the wide, sturdy gripper guard felt exceptionally safe. Extra blades conveniently store beneath the frame.

HIGHLY RECOMMENDED
Kyocera Adjustable Ceramic Mandoline Slicer
$24.95

"It looks like a toy, but it works like crazy!" exclaimed one tester, who pledged to go out immediately and buy one. No julienne or waffle blades, but this slicer is razor-sharp and our "best buy."

HIGHLY RECOMMENDED
Joyce Chen Benriner Asian Mandoline Plus
$39.96

Some testers argued its julienne was the best, if you can brave the super-sharp blade with the dinky hand guard.

HIGHLY RECOMMENDED
OXO Mandoline Slicer
$69.99

A close relative of the winning slicer, this model was intuitive, simple, and an all-around solid performer. Would have been the winner, but its straight blade struggled to slice tomatoes.

RECOMMENDED
Borner V-Slicer Prima Stainless Steel Mandoline
$99.95

The V-blade made "beautiful, intact" tomato slices, as well as julienned carrots testers called so "professional" you could "make log cabins with them." But waste was considerable, especially with harder vegetables that the guard couldn't grip.

RECOMMENDED
Zyliss Easy Slice 2 Folding Mandoline
$34.99

The other model with a click-wheel to set slice thickness, this slicer would have shared user-friendliness points with the OXO had it not been for its "flimsy" plastic frame.

NOT RECOMMENDED
Shun Mandoline
$379.95

A colossal disappointment with an equally colossal price tag. Testers who were quick to compare this "beast" to a "deli machine on steroids" at first sight were shocked when the spring-loaded gripper "destroyed" tomatoes.

NOT RECOMMENDED
Bron Coucke Stainless Steel Super Pro Mandoline
$179.95

Everyone agreed that "after the setup, the results are pretty nice." Directions were "cryptic" and "confusing."

NOT RECOMMENDED
Microplane V-Slicer
$39.99

Some testers liked the thickness-adjusting wheel; others felt it brought fingers too close to the blade. Tomato slices were "translucent," but the heavy, juicy fruit was too weighty for the gripper.

NOT RECOMMENDED
De Buyer V-Pro Mandoline
$199.99

"Completely unintuitive," "uncomfortable," and "overbuilt," this brawny French model's only saving grace was its incredibly sharp V-blades.

EVEN LESS RECOMMENDED: The following were eliminated in preliminary tests after failing to slice potatoes and tomatoes acceptably: Kuhn Rikon Hand-Held Mandoline Slicer with Handguard ($24.95), Progressive International Multi-Slicer ($6.99), and KitchenAid Mandoline Slicer Set ($49.99).

No toothpicks are required to keep our Chicken Saltimbocca intact. Our secret? We sear the assembled chicken breasts prosciutto side down—this keeps the prosciutto perfectly adhered to the chicken.

BRINGING HOME
CHAPTER 10
Italian favorites

Chicken saltimbocca, a sautéed chicken cutlet pressed with prosciutto and sage, isn't your usual weeknight chicken. In fact, we'd bet you've only enjoyed this dish at an Italian restaurant—and often with veal in place of the chicken. But chicken makes sense for a weeknight meal, and who wouldn't welcome a new chicken dish into the usual repertoire? We found that in most home adaptations the chicken is smothered in breadings, stuffing, and cheese. This wouldn't do. We wanted a dish that celebrated the trio's appealing simplicity, and because we wanted this to be a weeknight meal, we didn't want to overcomplicate its preparation.

In the United States, tiramisù's unflagging popularity has driven it onto so many dessert menus (not just Italian) that we wouldn't be surprised if apple pie were nudged out as America's favorite dessert. It's a shame, then, that so few prepare this dessert right. We've come across tiramisù that's boozy, soggy, and, at times, dry. With just a few ingredients and no cooking required, tiramisù is essentially an icebox cake and shouldn't be complicated. We set out to create a tiramisù that boasted moist, not soggy, espresso-soaked ladyfingers sandwiched with creamy mascarpone filling. And we wanted this dessert to be a looker, too, so we aimed to ensure that the chilled slices could be cut into neat pieces for easy serving.

CHICKEN SALTIMBOCCA

WHAT WE WANTED: An uncomplicated approach to this classic Italian preparation, in which the chicken, prosciutto, and sage are combined in a balanced and flavorful way.

We can never find enough quick and easy chicken dishes for our weeknight repertoire. So when we came across a new chicken spin on an old Italian classic—veal saltimbocca—we were immediately intrigued. The traditional version has long been a standard menu item in the trattorias of Italy as well as Italian restaurants in this country. Made by sautéing veal cutlets with prosciutto and sage, this simple yet elegant dish promises, literally, to "jump in your mouth" with its distinctive blend of flavors.

But as happens all too often when cooks start to meddle with a perfectly good thing, most chicken adaptations we found took the dish too far from its roots, with the cutlet wrapped around stuffing or the addition of unnecessary breading or cheese. Others fiddled with the proportions, allowing a thick slab of prosciutto to share equal billing with the chicken and knock the balance of flavors out of whack. Perfecting chicken saltimbocca, then, would be a matter of avoiding the temptation to overcomplicate the dish with extraneous ingredients and figuring out how to give each of the three key elements—chicken, prosciutto, and sage—its due.

Though we generally prefer to make our own cutlets to ensure that pieces are of uniform size and shape, we decided to forgo butchering and buy commercially prepared cutlets to keep the process as streamlined as possible. We opted for mass-produced supermarket cutlets and trimmed their edges to remove any thin, tattered pieces.

Most of the simpler chicken saltimbocca recipes we came across followed the traditional practice of threading a toothpick through the prosciutto and a whole sage leaf to attach them to the cutlet, then dredging the entire package in flour before sautéing it on both sides. We found this method to be problematic. Flour got trapped in the small gaps where the ham bunched up around the toothpick, leaving sticky, uncooked spots. We wondered if we could skip the flouring and sauté the chicken and prosciutto without any coating. This worked fine for the ham, which crisped nicely without help from the flour. The chicken, on the other hand, browned unevenly and tended to stick to the pan. Surprisingly, flouring only the cutlet—before attaching the ham—proved to be the solution. And by sautéing the cutlet prosciutto side down first, we were able to keep the flour under the prosciutto from turning gummy.

With our flouring method under control, it was time to turn our attention to proportions. We liked high-end prosciutto for the rich flavor it added to the overall dish, but if the slice was too thick, its taste overwhelmed everything else and the ham had trouble staying put. If the slice was ultrathin, however, it fell apart too easily. The ideal slice was just thick enough to hold its shape—about the thickness of two or three sheets of paper. Though some recipes call for folding the slice to make it fit on the cutlet, this resulted in ham that was only partially crisped and overpowered the chicken with its flavor. We found trimming the ham to fit the cutlet in a single layer worked best on all counts.

Whereas the prosciutto needed to be tamed, the sage flavor needed a boost. In the traditional dish, each cutlet features a single sage leaf (fried in oil before being attached), so that the herbal flavor imparted is very subtle. Perhaps the sage of yore boasted far bigger leaves than are grown today, but this was one aspect of the original that we found lacking. Tethering additional leaves to the cutlet with the toothpick, however, was cumbersome and still resulted in adding flavor only to bites that actually contained sage.

We wanted a more even distribution of herbal flavor. Would infusing the cooking oil with sage be a way to diffuse—and heighten—its flavor? We tossed a handful of leaves into the cooking oil before sautéing the cutlets, removing the herbs before they burned. Tasters, however,

detected only a very slight flavor boost in the finished dish. The way to more intense and evenly distributed sage flavor turned out to be as simple as chopping the leaves and sprinkling them over the floured cutlet before adding the ham. The only thing missing was the pretty look of the whole sage leaf. Although not necessary, frying extra sage leaves to place on the cooked cutlets is an elegant finishing touch.

The only aspect of the dish we had not yet examined was the toothpick. After skewering prosciutto to 150 cutlets in the course of our testing, we wondered what would happen if we just omitted the toothpick? After flouring the cutlet, sprinkling it with sage, and placing the prosciutto on top, we carefully lifted the bundle and placed it as we had been doing, prosciutto side down, in the hot oil. Once the bottom edges of the chicken had browned, we flipped the cutlet, revealing ham that seemed almost hermetically sealed to the chicken. A quick pan sauce made from vermouth, lemon juice, butter, and parsley was all we needed to accentuate the perfect balance of flavors. We now had a quick Italian food fix with all the jumping in our mouths, not the kitchen.

WHAT WE LEARNED: To keep preparation to a minimum, choose chicken cutlets and trim them of any ragged edges to ensure even cooking. Coat just the chicken breast (instead of the prosciutto and sage as is traditionally done) in flour to avoid gluey, uneven pockets of flour. Sear the chicken, prosciutto side down first to ensure that the prosciutto stays adhered to the chicken; this step also eliminates the need for the typical cumbersome toothpick. For sage flavor in every bite, sprinkle minced sage over the floured cutlets before covering with prosciutto. And for a pretty presentation, place a fried sage leaf on each cutlet before serving.

CHICKEN SALTIMBOCCA

serves 4

Buy cutlets that are approximately 5 to 6 inches long. If the tip is too thin, trim back 1 to 2 inches to make the cutlet of uniform thickness. If cutlets are unavailable, you can make your own with 4 (8-ounce) boneless, skinless chicken breasts (see page 133). Although whole sage leaves make a beautiful presentation, they are optional and can be left out of step 3. Make sure to buy prosciutto that is thinly sliced, not shaved; also avoid slices that are too thick, as they won't stick to the chicken.

½	cup unbleached all-purpose flour
	Ground black pepper
8	thin boneless, skinless chicken cutlets (about 2 pounds), trimmed of ragged edges as necessary (see note)
1	tablespoon minced fresh sage leaves, plus 8 large leaves (optional)
8	thin slices prosciutto, cut into 5- to 6-inch-long pieces to match chicken (about 3 ounces, see note)
4	tablespoons olive oil
1¼	cups dry vermouth or white wine
2	teaspoons juice from 1 lemon
4	tablespoons unsalted butter, cut into 4 pieces and chilled
1	tablespoon minced fresh parsley leaves
	Salt

1. Adjust an oven rack to the middle position and heat the oven to 200 degrees. Combine the flour and 1 teaspoon pepper in a shallow dish.

2. Pat the cutlets dry with paper towels. Dredge the chicken in the flour, shaking off any excess. Lay the cutlets flat and sprinkle evenly with the minced sage. Place 1 prosciutto slice on top of each cutlet, pressing lightly to adhere; set aside.

Saltimbocca Gone Wrong

As we discovered, many saltimbocca recipes include extraneous elements when switching from veal to chicken, ruining the simplicity of the dish.

Chock Too Full

Stuffing the cutlet with extra ingredients, such as spinach, dilutes the impact of the other flavors.

Breaded and Bland

Breading requires additional prep time and means that the flavorful pan sauce is out.

Cheesy and Greasy

Cheese adds unnecessary richness that masks the more subtle flavors of sage and wine.

3. Heat 2 tablespoons of the oil in a 12-inch skillet over medium-high heat until beginning to shimmer. Add the sage leaves (if using) and cook until the leaves begin to change color and are fragrant, about 15 to 20 seconds. Using a slotted spoon, remove the sage to a paper towel–lined plate; reserve. Add half of the cutlets to the pan, prosciutto side down, and cook until light golden brown, 2 to 3 minutes. Flip and cook on the other side until light golden brown, about 2 minutes more. Transfer to a wire rack set on a rimmed baking sheet and keep warm in the oven. Repeat with the remaining 2 tablespoons oil and the remaining cutlets, then transfer to the oven to keep warm while preparing the sauce.

4. Pour off the excess fat from the skillet. Stir in the vermouth, scraping up any browned bits, and simmer until reduced to about ⅓ cup, 5 to 7 minutes. Stir in the lemon juice. Turn the heat to low and whisk in the butter, 1 tablespoon at a time. Off the heat, stir in the parsley and season with salt and pepper to taste. Remove the chicken from the oven and place it on a platter. Spoon the sauce over the cutlets before serving, and place one fried sage leaf (if using) on top of each cutlet.

TECHNIQUE: Saltimbocca Made Simple

1. Flour Chicken Only: No need to flour the prosciutto before sautéing, just the chicken.

2. Spread Sage Flavor: Sprinkling the cutlets with sage and topping them with prosciutto distributes flavor evenly.

3. Forget the Toothpick: Searing the cutlets prosciutto side down first helps the ham stick.

4. Make Sauce: Stir the vermouth into the pan, reduce, and finish with the butter. Spoon the sauce over the cutlets.

TECHNIQUE: Cutting Your Own Cutlets

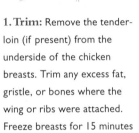

1. Trim: Remove the tenderloin (if present) from the underside of the chicken breasts. Trim any excess fat, gristle, or bones where the wing or ribs were attached. Freeze breasts for 15 minutes until firm but not fully frozen.

2. Slice: Place the chicken breast smooth side up on the work surface. Place one hand on top of the breast and, with a sharp chef's knife held parallel to the work surface, carefully slice through the middle of the breast horizontally to yield two ¼- to ½-inch-thick pieces.

TASTING LAB: Prosciutto

AMERICANS HAVE LONG LOOKED TO ITALY FOR THE BEST prosciutto. After all, Italy invented the method used to produce this salt-cured and air-dried ham. So when we heard about a new prosciutto on the market crafted not in Italy but in Iowa, we were more than curious.

Tasted side by side with prosciutto di Parma and prosciutto San Daniele, both of which are crafted under the strict specifications of two Protected Designations of Origin (PDO), the newcomer from Iowa, La Quercia Prosciutto Americano, was the hands-down winner. As for the other domestic brand we tasted, generic prosciutto sliced at the supermarket deli counter was cheap but not worth buying.

Rating Prosciutto

TEN MEMBERS OF THE AMERICA'S TEST KITCHEN STAFF tasted four brands of prosciutto plain and cooked in our chicken saltimbocca recipe. Brands are listed in order of preference. See www.americastestkitchen.com for updates to this tasting.

HIGHLY RECOMMENDED
La Quercia Prosciutto Americano
$18.99 per pound
Tasters marveled at the "deep," "earthy" flavor, "creamy" texture, and "melt-in-your-mouth," "porky yumminess" of this prosciutto produced on a relatively small scale in Iowa. Once available only by mail, this prosciutto is now available at the deli counter at Whole Foods supermarkets.

RECOMMENDED
Prosciutto di Parma
$18.99 per pound
This "lovely," "meaty and rich" Italian staple garnered much praise. Its "nutty undertones" come from the whey of the Parmiggiano-Reggiano cheese that producers add to their pigs' diet.

RECOMMENDED
Prosciutto San Daniele
$14.98 per pound
"Sweeter" and more "mellow" than the Parma pig, this Italian ham with "good, clean flavor" was the favorite among tasters who preferred a slightly milder sample.

NOT RECOMMENDED
Generic Domestic Prosciutto
$9.99 per pound
"Baloney," wrote one taster in reference to this domestic ham's claim to be prosciutto. (We purchased this non-branded prosciutto at the supermarket deli counter.) Some noted a resemblance to "bad pastrami." Others found it just plain "horrible."

TIRAMISÙ

WHAT WE WANTED: A streamlined approach to tiramisù—one that highlights the luxurious combination of flavors and textures that have made this Italian dessert so popular.

L ike balsamic vinegar and polenta, tiramisù was virtually unheard of in the United States until about 20 years ago. Now it's everywhere from pizza parlors to chain restaurants. Unlike many other Italian recipes, tiramisù hasn't been bastardized, but that's not to say it's generally well made. Despite tiramisù's simplicity (it requires just a handful of ingredients and no cooking), there is a lot that can go wrong. If it's soggy or parched, ponderously dense, sickly sweet, or fiery with alcohol, it's not worth the caloric cost.

The word *tiramisù* means "pick me up," a reference to the invigorating qualities of the dish's espresso, sugar, and alcohol. It's not an old-world dessert, but rather a 20th-century restaurant creation. Store-bought ladyfingers (spongecake-like cookies) are dipped into alcohol-spiked espresso and then layered into a dish along with buttery mascarpone (a thick cream) that has been enriched with sugar and eggs. The dish is dusted with cocoa or sprinkled with chocolate and served chilled.

A good tiramisù is a seamless union of flavors and textures—it's difficult to tell where cookie ends and cream begins, where bitter espresso gives over to the bite of alcohol, and whether *unctuous* or *uplifting* is the better adjective to describe it. Rather than lament all the unworthy tiramisùs out there, we decided to make a batch . . . or two . . . or 40 . . . to get to the bottom of a good one.

We sorted through the dozens of recipes we had gathered. The most complicated ones involved making a *zabaglione,* a frothy custard, as the base of the mascarpone filling. This required a double boiler, vigilance, and a lot of whisking. We made six recipes and determined that a zabaglione base was not worth the trouble.

As such, the mechanics of making the mascarpone filling became quite simple: We combined raw egg yolks and sugar, mixed in the spirits, and finished with the mascarpone. Our early tests taught us that a 13 by 9-inch dish was the right size and that the pound of mascarpone called for in most recipes was inadequate—the ladyfinger-to-cream ratio was off, and the tiramisù was slight in stature. Another ½ pound made the filling generous but not fulsome.

With too few yolks, the filling wasn't as rich as tasters liked, a problem that plagued several of the recipes we initially tested. Six yolks made the filling silky and suave, with a round, rich flavor. (For those wary of desserts made with raw eggs, we also created a slightly more involved variation in which the yolks are cooked.)

Next, we tested different amounts of sugar and decided that ⅔ cup provided the perfect amount of sweetness. We also added an ingredient—salt—that isn't found in most tiramisù recipes. (We saw only one that calls for salt, and it was just a pinch.) Salt greatly heightened all the flavors and made the most remarkable difference.

Tiramisù recipes fall into three camps: those that call for the addition of whipped egg whites to the filling, those that call for the addition of whipped cream, and those that call for neither. Without whipped whites or whipped cream, the filling was too heavy. Whipped egg whites watered down the flavor of the filling and made it too airy. Whipped cream lightened the texture without affecting the mascarpone's delicate flavor. We found that ¾ cup of cream (half the amount in many other recipes) was sufficient.

To make tiramisù, ladyfingers are dipped into espresso spiked with alcohol so that the rather dry, bland cookies are moistened and flavored. Brewed espresso is not practical for many home cooks, so we tried three things in its stead: strong coffee made from espresso-roast beans, espresso made from instant espresso granules, and a rather wicked potion made by dissolving instant espresso in strong brewed coffee. Though it wasn't palatable straight from a cup, this last concoction tasted best in tiramisù.

Tiramisù recipes don't bother to give detailed instructions about how to dip the ladyfingers, but we found that the dipping or soaking technique greatly affects the outcome. A quick in-and-out dip wasn't adequate for moistening the cookies, and the result was a dry tiramisù. Fully submerging or otherwise saturating the ladyfingers yielded a wet, squishy tiramisù. Eventually, we found a method that worked reliably. One at a time, we dropped each ladyfinger into the liquid so that it floated on the surface, then without

further ado we rolled it over to moisten the other side.

The only thing left to determine was the best spirit with which to spike the filling and the coffee soaking mixture. Marsala gave the tiramisù a syrupy, citrusy overtone without appreciable alcohol character. Brandy gave it a lightly fruity flavor and good kick. Dark rum, with its caramel notes, complemented the rich, deep, toasty qualities of the coffee; it was the undisputed favorite. We started with a modest 4 tablespoons (divided between the filling and the coffee), but that was far too weak. We ratcheted up the rum several times before hitting the ideal amount—9 tablespoons.

Our tiramisù was assembled like any other. We arranged half of the dipped ladyfingers in the dish and covered them with half of the mascarpone. We followed the lead of others and dusted the mascarpone with cocoa. The layering was repeated, and cocoa finished the tiramisù. (A sprinkling of grated chocolate was a nice addition.) The last detail: Tiramisù requires at least six hours in the fridge for the flavors and textures to meld.

Simple to prepare but grand enough to serve the most discerning *famiglia,* this tiramisù is an ideal holiday dessert. This pick-me-up is no longer a letdown—it's worth every creamy, coffee-flavored, rum-spiked calorie.

WHAT WE LEARNED: Instead of hauling out a double boiler to make a fussy *zabaglione*-based filling, simply whip egg yolks, sugar, salt, rum (our preferred spirit), and mascarpone together. Salt is not traditional, but it heightens the filling's subtle flavors. And to lighten the filling, choose whipped cream instead of egg whites. For the coffee soaking mixture, combine strong brewed coffee and espresso powder (along with more rum). To moisten the ladyfingers so that they are neither too dry nor too saturated, drop them one at a time into the spiked coffee mixture and, once they are moistened, roll them over to moisten the other side (about 2 to 3 seconds per ladyfinger). For best flavor and texture, allow the tiramisù to chill in the refrigerator for at least six hours.

TIRAMISÙ

serves 10 to 12

Brandy and even whiskey can stand in for the dark rum. The test kitchen prefers a tiramisù with a pronounced rum flavor; for a less potent rum flavor, halve the amount of rum added to the coffee mixture in step 1. Do not allow the mascarpone to warm to room temperature before using it; it has a tendency to break if allowed to do so.

2½	cups strong brewed coffee, room temperature
1½	tablespoons instant espresso granules
9	tablespoons dark rum (see note)
6	large egg yolks
⅔	cup sugar
¼	teaspoon salt
1½	pounds mascarpone
¾	cup heavy cream, chilled
14	ounces (42 to 60, depending on size) dried ladyfingers
3½	tablespoons cocoa, preferably Dutch-processed
¼	cup grated semisweet or bittersweet chocolate (optional)

1. Stir together the coffee, espresso, and 5 tablespoons of the rum in a wide bowl or baking dish until the espresso dissolves; set aside.

2. In the bowl of a standing mixer fitted with the whisk attachment, beat the yolks at low speed until just combined. Add the sugar and salt and beat at medium-high speed until pale yellow, 1½ to 2 minutes, scraping down the sides of the bowl with a rubber spatula once or twice. Add the remaining 4 tablespoons rum and beat at medium speed until just combined, 20 to 30 seconds; scrape the bowl. Add the mascarpone and beat at medium speed until no lumps remain, 30 to 45 seconds, scraping down the sides of the bowl once or twice. Transfer the mixture to a large bowl and set aside.

3. In the now-empty mixer bowl (no need to clean the bowl), beat the cream at medium speed until frothy, 1 to 1½ minutes. Increase the speed to high and continue to beat until the cream holds stiff peaks, 1 to 1½ minutes longer. Using a rubber spatula, fold one-third of the whipped cream into the mascarpone mixture to lighten, then gently fold in the remaining whipped cream until no white streaks remain. Set the mascarpone mixture aside.

4. Working one at a time, drop half of the ladyfingers into the coffee mixture, roll, remove, and transfer to a 13 by 9-inch glass or ceramic baking dish. (Do not submerge the ladyfingers in the coffee mixture; the entire process should take no longer than 2 to 3 seconds for each cookie.) Arrange the soaked cookies in a single layer in the baking dish, breaking or trimming the ladyfingers as needed to fit neatly into the dish.

5. Spread half of the mascarpone mixture over the ladyfingers; use a rubber spatula to spread the mixture to the sides and into the corners of the dish and smooth the surface. Place 2 tablespoons of the cocoa in a fine-mesh strainer and dust the cocoa over the mascarpone.

6. Repeat the dipping and arrangement of the ladyfingers; spread the remaining mascarpone mixture over the ladyfingers and dust with the remaining 1½ tablespoons cocoa. Wipe the edges of the dish with a dry paper towel. Cover

with plastic wrap and refrigerate for 6 to 24 hours. Sprinkle with the grated chocolate, if using; cut into pieces and serve chilled.

TECHNIQUE: Dip, Don't Submerge

Both of the ladyfingers below were in the coffee mixture for the same amount of time, but different soaking techniques yielded very different results.

Perfectly Soaked

This ladyfinger was dropped into the coffee mixture, rolled, and removed within 2 to 3 seconds. The coffee mixture has not completely saturated this cookie.

Oversoaked

This ladyfinger was fully submerged in the coffee mixture for 2 to 3 seconds. The coffee mixture has penetrated all the way to the center of the cookie.

TECHNIQUE: Assembling Tiramisù

1. Arrange the soaked ladyfingers snugly in a single layer in a baking dish.

2. Spread half of the mascarpone mixture over the ladyfingers.

3. Dust cocoa over the mascarpone mixture. Repeat the layering.

TIRAMISÙ WITH COOKED EGGS

This recipe involves cooking the yolks in a double boiler, which requires a little more effort and makes for a slightly thicker mascarpone filling, but the results are just as good as with our traditional method. You will need an additional ⅓ cup heavy cream.

Follow the recipe for Tiramisù through step 1. In step 2, add ⅓ cup cream to the yolks after the sugar and salt; do not whisk in the rum. Set the bowl with the yolks over a medium saucepan containing 1 inch gently simmering water; cook, constantly scraping along the bottom and sides of the bowl with a heatproof rubber spatula, until the mixture coats the back of a spoon and registers 160 degrees on an instant-read thermometer, 4 to 7 minutes. Remove from the heat and stir vigorously to cool slightly, then set aside to cool to room temperature, about 15 minutes. Whisk in the remaining 4 tablespoons rum until combined. Transfer the bowl to a standing mixer fitted with the whisk attachment, add the mascarpone, and beat at medium speed until no lumps remain, 30 to 45 seconds. Transfer the mixture to a large bowl and set aside. Continue with the recipe from step 3, using the full amount of cream specified (¾ cup).

GETTING IT RIGHT:
Is Mascarpone a Must?

Mascarpone is a rich cream thickened by acidification. In our tiramisù research, we came across suggestions for substitutes if mascarpone isn't available. Cream cheese was the base for all substitutions. To it, we added sour cream, heavy cream, pureed ricotta cheese, and softened butter in every combination and quantity. Unfortunately, every substitute made for a dastardly dessert. The lesson: There is no substitute for mascarpone.

EQUIPMENT CORNER:
Refrigerator Thermometers

HEAVY COOKING AROUND THE HOLIDAYS MEANS constantly opening your refrigerator and freezer, which causes temperatures to fluctuate. To monitor the safety of our cold storage, we use refrigerator and freezer thermometers. But is one model really superior to another? We chilled six brands (plus a digital thermocouple, which recorded our control temperature) to find out. All six offered wide temperature ranges (the lowest from -40 degrees to the highest at 86 degrees) and gave accurate readings, proof that shelling out more than $5 to $7 is unnecessary for simply reading the temperature. Spending up to $20, however, will buy you space-saving convenience and a few bells and whistles. Analog models from CDN ($5.95) and Taylor ($6.99) mounted on door shelves, but the CDN was a struggle to clip on. The Polder ($4.99) lost points because it had to sit on or hang from a shelf, taking up precious space, and was

Rating Refrigerator Thermometers

WE TESTED SIX BRANDS OF REFRIGERATOR THERMOMETERS, RATING THEM ON ACCURACY AND EASE OF USE. BRANDS are listed in order of preference. See www.americastestkitchen.com for updates to this testing.

HIGHLY RECOMMENDED

Maverick Cold-Chek Digital Refrigerator/Freezer Thermometer

$19.99

This product costs four times as much as the cheapest model we tested, but testers thought its clear digital display and simultaneous freezer/refrigerator readings were worth the extra dough.

RECOMMENDED

OXO Good Grips Refrigerator/Freezer Thermometer

$12.99

The best analog model, this thermometer conveniently suctioned to the wall and sported a large, easy-to-read display.

RECOMMENDED

ThermoWorks Ice-Box Food Storage Temp Alert

$19

Half of the display registers the refrigerator temperature while the other half registers the room temperature; this latter feature seemed unnecessary, but testers liked the optional beeping alert for when temperatures climbed out of the safety zone.

RECOMMENDED

Taylor Classic Freezer-Refrigerator Thermometer

$6.99

A basic model, this "best buy" thermometer hangs on the door or stands on the shelf and illustrates food safety zones along the temperature meter.

RECOMMENDED WITH RESERVATIONS

Polder Refrigerator and Freezer Thermometer

$4.99

The cheapest model with the widest temperature range, this model would have been a good option if it didn't sit in the way of the food.

RECOMMENDED WITH RESERVATIONS

CDN ProAccurate Professional Refrigerator/Freezer Thermometer

$5.95

Similar in shape to the Taylor model, this one lost points for being nearly impossible to fasten to the refrigerator door.

easily knocked over. The best analog model was by OXO ($12.99). It suctioned securely to the wall and sported an adjustable, easy-to-read display.

A step up were digital, wall-mounting models from ThermoWorks ($19) and Maverick ($19.99). In addition to exact readings and ultra-clear displays, both also offered alerts—the former beeps; the latter lights up automatically—when temperatures rise into danger zones (above 40 degrees for the refrigerator, above 0 degrees for the freezer). But the Maverick Cold-Chek Digital Refrigerator/Freezer Thermometer, which has a probe on a 75-inch wire that can easily reach a top, bottom, or side-by-side freezer, has earned a permanent spot in our cold storage for displaying simultaneous fridge and freezer readings. It's our new favorite.

Here, Julia separates the eggs for Meringue Cookies. Then she'll whip the whites to soft peaks before adding sugar and cornstarch—cornstarch helps stabilize the meringue without turning it overly sweet.

FRENCH COUNTRY cooking

CHAPTER 11

We love a good beef stew—whether it's an American-style stew rich with chunks of beef, potatoes, and carrots or French-style beef burgundy, in which the gravy is imbued with the sophisticated flavors of red wine and dainty pearl onions and mushrooms. Daube Provençal, another French-style stew, is lesser known but just as intriguing. Hailing from southern France, the stew boasts the region's celebrated flavors of olives, garlic, wine, herbs, tomatoes, oranges, and anchovies. You might think the combination a strange one, but when properly done, this stew has a deeply complex, zesty flavor. The challenge of this dish lies in getting these assertive flavors in balance; too often one flavor (such as oranges or olives) can dominate the whole. In addition to balanced flavor, we wanted the stew to be accessible to the American home cook. So, we'd be taking a hard look at the traditional methods and ingredients used to produce this beloved French classic.

Following a company-worthy main course like Daube Provençal, it's tempting to serve an over-the-top dessert like a decadent chocolate mousse. But actually something lighter, like meringue cookies, fits the bill perfectly, balancing the deep richness of the stew. With just two primary ingredients, eggs whites and sugar, you'd think they would be a cinch to make. But meringues can turn weepy, gritty, or saccharine. Our challenge would be to develop a foolproof recipe for meringues that turned out terrific cookies every time—so that when you're aiming to impress, you can do so with confidence.

DAUBE PROVENÇAL

WHAT WE WANTED: A rich beef stew that marries the bold flavors from the south of France in a unified stew for the American home kitchen.

Daube Provençal, also known as daube Niçoise, has all the elements of the best French fare: tender pieces of beef, luxurious sauce, and complex flavors. Those flavors come from local ingredients, including olives, olive oil, garlic, wine, herbs, oranges, tomatoes, mushrooms, and anchovies.

But few of these ingredients made it into the large stack of "authentic" recipes we uncovered in our research. When tested, many of these recipes were one-note wonders—beef stew with olives or beef stew with oranges. One exception to this early testing was a recipe from Julia Child, which included most of the flavors we wanted. Although not without problems, her version inspired us to follow suit and led to our main challenge with this recipe: We would have to find a way to turn these strong, independent flavors of Provence into a robust but cohesive stew.

Over the years the test kitchen has developed countless beef stews as well as a reliable set of techniques to turn tough beef into tender stew: Brown the beef (to ensure the richest, meatiest flavor); add the aromatic vegetables; sprinkle some flour in the pan (to thicken the braising liquid); deglaze with the predominant cooking liquid; add the meat back to the pot; and, finally, cover and cook in a low to medium oven until tender. Our choice of meat for stew is cut from the chuck, or shoulder, which is notoriously tough (the meat softens nicely during long, slow cooking) but also flavorful. Of the various cuts of chuck, we found that the chuck-eye roast offered the best flavor and texture.

Most beef stews have a personality-defining ingredient, like the wine in beef Burgundy or the beer in carbonnade. In contrast, daube Provençal relies on a complex blend of ingredients, which we methodically began to test. Tasters loved the earthiness of dried cèpes (the mushroom known

more commonly by its Italian name, porcini). Niçoise olives lent a briny and authentic local flavor, and tomatoes brought brightness and texture. Orange peel contributed a subtle floral element, and herbs, particularly thyme and bay, are a natural addition to anything from Provence.

Our tasters weren't enthusiastic about every authentic ingredient we tried. When we added anchovies, some tasters claimed that these pungent fish have no place in beef stew. Funny that no one noticed the two fillets that were already part of our working recipe. When we omitted the anchovies entirely, tasters claimed the stew lacked depth of flavor. Over the next couple of days, we quietly added back the anchovies one at a time and stopped at three fillets, at which point tasters praised the rich, earthy flavors of the dish and noticed a complexity that had been missing without them. (They never knew the secret!)

Pig's trotters, a standard ingredient in many older recipes, contribute body to the sauce in the form of gelatin and flavor from the pork meat and fat. But the protests against a foot in the stew were too much, and this time we caved in. As a compromise, we substituted salt pork, a salt-cured cut from the pig's belly, and adjusted the amount of salt in the stew to accommodate it. Several tasters still protested the extra fat on principle, but a side-by-side comparison made it clear that salt pork, like anchovies, added a richness of flavor that was unmistakably absent when it was not included. In any case, the salt pork was added in a single piece that we removed and discarded just before serving, once the pork had given up its flavor to the stew.

We had been following the French technique of adding a small amount of flour in the form of a roux, a butter and flour thickener, but up to this point we weren't satisfied with the consistency of the sauce. The butter sometimes ended up floating to the top of the stew, making it look greasy, and the sauce was still too thin. We returned to our established technique and omitted the step of making a roux. Instead, we sprinkled flour into the pot to cook out with the vegetables and tomato paste. We also increased the amount of flour to ⅓ cup, which is a little more than most recipes contain. The result was immediately noticeable. The extra flour created a braising liquid that thickened to the consistency of a luxurious sauce.

What started as a key ingredient in daube Provençal, the red wine, had now been relegated to a mere afterthought, barely discernible amid the other ingredients. Our recipe contained a half bottle. Could we add more? Conservatively, we began adding more wine, careful not to sacrifice the integrity of the other flavors. In the end, we discovered that this stew was bold enough to accommodate an entire bottle—at least in theory. The wine tasted a bit raw. So we put the stew back into the oven for additional 15-minute increments until the total cooking time approached three hours. The resulting sauce was gorgeous, with rich, round flavors and a velvety texture.

What was good for the sauce wasn't so good for the meat. We had been cutting the chuck roast into 1-inch cubes, a standard size for beef stew. But with the longer cooking time, the meat was drying out and losing its distinct character. By cutting the chuck roast into 2-inch pieces, we were able to keep our longer braising time and create a truly complex sauce. The beef was now tender and flavorful, and the larger pieces added to the rustic quality of this dish.

WHAT WE LEARNED: Choose chuck-eye roast for great beefy flavor and tender texture. For a stew rich with the bold flavors of Provence, include the region's hallmark ingredients: porcini mushrooms, tomatoes, niçoise olives, orange zest, anchovies, thyme, and bay leaves. But skip one traditional ingredient—pig's trotters—and use salt pork in its place. Easy-to-find salt pork creates the same body, complexity, and viscosity that pig's trotters provide. Don't be shy with the wine—a full bottle of Cabernet Sauvignon balances the richness of the dish. But to mellow the wine's alcohol bite, cook the stew longer than usual (2½ to 3 hours). And to compensate for the longer cooking time, cut the beef into large, 2-inch pieces, so they don't dry out.

DAUBE PROVENÇAL

serves 4 to 6

Serve this French beef stew with egg noodles or boiled potatoes. If niçoise olives are not available, kalamata olives, though not authentic, can be substituted. Cabernet Sauvignon is our favorite wine for this recipe, but Côtes du Rhône and Zinfandel also work. Our favorite cut of beef for this recipe is chuck-eye roast, but any boneless roast from the chuck will work. Because the tomatoes are added just before serving, it is preferable to use canned whole tomatoes and dice them yourself—uncooked, they are more tender than canned diced tomatoes. Once the salt pork, thyme, and bay leaves are removed in step 4, the daube can be cooled and refrigerated in an airtight container for up to 4 days. Before reheating, skim the hardened fat from the surface, then continue with the recipe.

¾ ounce dried porcini mushrooms, rinsed well
1 boneless beef chuck-eye roast (about 3½ pounds), trimmed of excess fat and cut into 2-inch chunks (see note)
1½ teaspoons salt
1 teaspoon ground black pepper
4 tablespoons olive oil
5 ounces salt pork, rind removed
4 large carrots, peeled and cut into 1-inch rounds (about 2 cups)
2 medium onions, halved and cut into ⅛-inch-thick slices (about 4 cups)
4 medium garlic cloves, sliced thin
2 tablespoons tomato paste
⅓ cup unbleached all-purpose flour
1 (750-ml) bottle bold red wine (see note)
1 cup low-sodium chicken broth
1 cup water
4 strips zest from 1 orange, each strip about 3 inches long, removed with a vegetable peeler, cleaned of white pith, and cut lengthwise into thin strips
1 cup pitted niçoise olives, drained well (see note)

3   anchovy fillets, minced (about 1 teaspoon)
5   sprigs fresh thyme, tied together with kitchen twine
2   bay leaves
1   (14.5-ounce) can whole tomatoes, drained and cut into ½-inch dice
2   tablespoons minced fresh parsley leaves

1. Cover the mushrooms with 1 cup hot tap water in a small microwave-safe bowl; cover with plastic wrap, cut several steam vents in the plastic with a paring knife, and microwave on high power for 30 seconds. Let stand until the mushrooms soften, about 5 minutes. Lift the mushrooms from the liquid with a fork and chop into ½-inch pieces (you should have about 4 tablespoons). Strain the liquid through a fine-mesh strainer lined with a paper towel into a medium bowl. Set the mushrooms and liquid aside.

2. Adjust an oven rack to the lower-middle position and heat the oven to 325 degrees. Dry the beef thoroughly with paper towels, then season with the salt and pepper. Heat 2 tablespoons of the oil in a large heavy-bottomed Dutch oven over medium-high heat until shimmering but not smoking; add half of the beef. Cook without moving the pieces until well browned, about 2 minutes on each side, for a total of 8 to 10 minutes, reducing the heat if the fat begins to smoke. Transfer the meat to a medium bowl. Repeat with the remaining 2 tablespoons oil and the remaining meat.

3. Reduce the heat to medium and add the salt pork, carrots, onions, garlic, and tomato paste to the now-empty pot; cook, stirring occasionally, until light brown, about 2 minutes. Stir in the flour and cook, stirring constantly, about 1 minute. Slowly add the wine, gently scraping the pan bottom to loosen the browned bits. Add the broth, water, beef, and any juices in the bowl. Increase the heat to medium-high and bring to a full simmer. Add the mushrooms and their liquid, orange zest, ½ cup of the olives, anchovies,

thyme, and bay leaves, distributing evenly and arranging the beef so it is completely covered by the liquid; cover partially and place in the oven. Cook until a fork inserted in the beef meets little resistance (the meat should not be falling apart), 2½ to 3 hours.

4. Discard the salt pork, thyme, and bay leaves. Add the tomatoes and the remaining ½ cup olives; warm over medium-high heat until heated through, about 1 minute. Cover the pot and allow the stew to settle, about 5 minutes. Using a spoon, skim the excess fat from the surface of the stew. Stir in the parsley and serve.

SCIENCE DESK:
Why "Simmer" in the Oven?

LIKE MANY OF THE BEEF STEWS TESTED IN OUR KITCHEN, our Daube Provençal is cooked in the oven. Why do we prefer this method to a stovetop simmer? To test this, we cooked one daube in a 350-degree oven and simmered the other one on the stove. Both stews produced moist, tender meat in 2½ hours, but the consistencies of the braising liquids differed dramatically. The stovetop stew produced a thin sauce more like soup, whereas the oven-braised daube yielded a silky and luxurious sauce.

Why so different? At moderate temperatures, the flour in a braising liquid gradually absorbs water, thus thickening the sauce. If the liquid gets too hot, however, the starch breaks down and loses its thickening properties, resulting in a thinner sauce. Because stovetop cooking heats from the bottom only, the flour closest to the heat source loses its thickening ability.

Daubes were traditionally cooked in a covered urn-shaped pot (called a *daubière*). The pot was placed in the fireplace—away from direct flame—on a bed of hot embers, with more embers piled into the indentations in the lid. The result? Even heat from above and below that gently simmered the stew. So oven braising is not only more effective than stovetop simmering, it's also more authentic.

On the Stove
Concentrated heat from below thwarts flour's thickening properties.

In the Oven
Evenly distributed heat allows starches to work their magic.

MERINGUE COOKIES

WHAT WE WANTED: Sweet, delicate meringue cookies with a crisp exterior that melt in your mouth.

A classic meringue cookie consists of just two ingredients—egg whites and sugar—whipped together, then baked. If all goes right, the cookie that emerges from the oven is glossy and white, with a shatteringly crisp texture that dissolves instantly in your mouth. But when things go wrong, you wind up with meringues as dense as Styrofoam or weepy, gritty, and cloyingly sweet. How can a cookie with so few ingredients produce such unreliable results?

Almost every meringue recipe we found fell into one of two categories: French meringue, in which egg whites are whipped with sugar, and fussier Italian meringue that calls for pouring hot sugar syrup into the whites as they are being beaten. The Italian meringue produced cookies that were dense and candy-like, so we decided to go with the French version. Though the French method was the simpler of the two, these meringues proved just as finicky. Add sugar too soon, and the meringue doesn't fully expand, resulting in flat, dense cookies. Add sugar too late, and you get a meringue that is voluminous when raw but weepy and gritty when cooked. Why such different results? It turns out that with egg whites, it's all about timing.

As an egg white is beaten, its proteins unfold and cross-link to create a network of bonds that reinforce the air bubbles produced in a sea of water (egg whites are composed mainly of water). Early in the process, the proteins have not completely unfurled and linked together, so the bubbles can't hold a firm shape. Sugar added at this stage will grab water molecules from the egg whites, lending stability to the bubbles. Sugar, however, interferes with the ability of proteins to cross-link; if it's added too early, fewer proteins will bond and trap air, resulting in a meringue that is less voluminous.

If, on the other hand, you continue to beat the whites without adding sugar, more air bubbles will form, more proteins will bond to reinforce them, and the meringue will puff up and take on the firm texture of shaving cream. Sugar added after this stage has been reached will have less water to dissolve in, giving the finished meringues a gritty texture and a tendency to weep out drops of sugar syrup during baking.

So the key is to add sugar only when the whites have been whipped enough to gain some volume but still have enough free water left in them for the sugar to dissolve completely. After some experimentation, we discovered that the best time to add sugar is just before the soft peak stage, when the meringue is very frothy and bubbly but not quite firm enough to hold a peak. Adding the sugar in a slow stream down the side of the bowl of a running standing mixer helped distribute the sugar more evenly, which created a smoother meringue.

Many recipes call for adding an acid such as cream of tartar before whipping the whites. In theory, acid helps the egg proteins unwind faster and bond more efficiently. But we got the best results when we left the acid out. Without acid, the whites formed peaks more slowly, giving us a wider time frame in which to add the sugar, leading to a more stable meringue.

Now that we had a smooth and stable meringue, we were ready to shape it into cookies and bake. We figured the simplest approach would be to scoop a small amount of meringue with a spoon and use a second spoon to drop the dollop onto a baking sheet. After much effort, however, we ended up with two baking sheets of misshapen blobs that didn't bake properly. Some came out browned and crumbly; others were wet in the center. To guarantee uniform shape and proper cooking, we would have to pipe them. A pastry bag produced perfectly shaped meringues, and a zipper-lock bag with a corner cut off worked nearly as well.

Traditionally, meringues are baked at a very low temperature and then left in the turned-off oven, sometimes

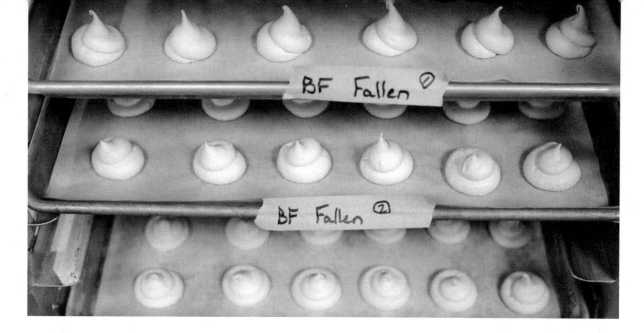

for as long as overnight. The idea is to completely dry out the cookies while allowing them to remain snow-white. We tried baking at temperatures as low as 175 degrees, but our ovens had trouble maintaining this temperature, leading to inconsistent results. An hour in a 225-degree oven followed by another hour in the turned-off oven produced perfectly cooked meringues every time.

It was time to shift our attention to flavor. There was one common complaint about every cookie we'd made so far: They were too sweet. Our working recipe used 1 cup of sugar for four egg whites (the lowest amount we could find in any recipe). Could we cut back the amount of sugar to ¾ cup with no adverse effects? We made up a new batch of meringues with less sugar, and everything was fine until we put them into the oven. Then disaster struck. The meringues, which up to now had been holding their shape perfectly, started collapsing and shrinking. Why would reducing the amount of sugar suddenly ruin our cookies?

It turns out that beyond its stabilizing role in the mixing bowl, sugar also plays a stabilizing role in the oven. Without sufficient sugar, the meringues lose moisture too rapidly as they bake, causing them to collapse. In order to solve this problem, we needed to find something with the hygroscopic (water-clinging) property of sugar, but without the sweetness. Our first thought was to swap some of the sugar for corn syrup, which is made from glucose and is about 75 percent as sweet as the sucrose in table sugar. This trick works—as long as you don't mind brown meringues.

We had forgotten that corn syrup browns much more easily than regular sugar, and our meringues emerged from the oven a light amber color instead of the pure white we wanted. We decided to try another corn product that is also hygroscopic and would add no sweetness to the meringues: cornstarch. Moderation was key; too much cornstarch, and tasters complained the cookies left a starchy aftertaste. With 2 teaspoons of cornstarch and ¾ cup of sugar, complaints disappeared.

All that remained to complete our cookies were a little vanilla and a pinch of salt (both found in many recipes that our tasters liked). As a final measure, we developed a few flavor variations with chocolate, citrus, and nuts. Plain or flavored, we finally had snow-white meringues that were light and crisp, with just the right amount of sweetness.

WHAT WE LEARNED: With just two main ingredients, sugar and egg whites, timing is key with meringue. Follow the classic French method (whipping egg whites with sugar) instead of the more difficult Italian method (whipping egg whites with a hot sugar syrup), not only for ease, but also for lighter, crisper cookies. Add the sugar to the egg whites just before they reach soft peaks to ensure a stable meringue with a smooth, not gritty, texture. To achieve the right level of sweetness without being cloying, use less sugar than most recipes include. But because sugar is necessary for stabilizing the meringue, replace the lost sugar with cornstarch (also a stabilizer).

MERINGUE COOKIES

makes 48 small cookies

Meringues may be a little soft immediately after being removed from the oven but will stiffen as they cool. To minimize stickiness on humid or rainy days, allow the meringues to cool in a turned-off oven for an additional hour (for a total of 2) without opening the door, then transfer them immediately to airtight containers and seal. Cooled cookies can be kept in an airtight container for up to 2 weeks.

- ¾ cup (5¼ ounces) sugar
- 2 teaspoons cornstarch
- 4 large egg whites
- ¾ teaspoon vanilla extract
- ⅛ teaspoon salt

1. Adjust two oven racks to the upper-middle and lower-middle positions and heat the oven to 225 degrees. Line 2 baking sheets with parchment paper. Combine the sugar and cornstarch in a small bowl.

2. In the bowl of a standing mixer fitted with the whisk attachment, beat the egg whites, vanilla, and salt together at high speed until very soft peaks start to form (peaks should slowly lose their shape when the whisk is removed), 30 to 45 seconds. With the mixer running at medium speed, slowly add the sugar mixture in a steady stream down the side of the mixer bowl (the process should take about 30 seconds). Stop the mixer and scrape down the sides and bottom of the bowl with a rubber spatula. Return the mixer to high speed and beat until glossy, stiff peaks have formed, 30 to 45 seconds.

3. Working quickly, place the meringue in a pastry bag fitted with a ½-inch plain tip or a large zipper-lock bag with ½ inch of the corner cut off. Pipe meringues into 1¼-inch-wide mounds about 1 inch high on the baking sheets, 6 rows of 4 meringues on each sheet. Bake for 1 hour, rotating the pans front to back and top to bottom halfway through baking. Turn off the oven and allow the meringues to cool in

the oven for at least 1 hour. Remove the meringues from the oven and let cool to room temperature before serving, about 10 minutes.

VARIATIONS
CHOCOLATE MERINGUE COOKIES

Follow the recipe for Meringue Cookies, gently folding 2 ounces finely chopped bittersweet chocolate into the meringue mixture at the end of step 2.

TOASTED ALMOND MERINGUE COOKIES

Follow the recipe for Meringue Cookies, substituting ½ teaspoon almond extract for the vanilla extract. In step 3, sprinkle the meringues with ⅓ cup coarsely chopped toasted almonds and 1 teaspoon coarse sea salt, such as Maldon (optional), before baking.

ORANGE MERINGUE COOKIES

Follow the recipe for Meringue Cookies, stirring 1 teaspoon finely grated zest from 1 orange into the sugar mixture in step 1.

SCIENCE DESK:
Twin Stabilizers—Sugar and Cornstarch

We wanted meringue cookies that were less sweet than the traditional kind, but when we cut back on the sugar, our cookies collapsed in the oven. What was going on? In their raw state, the tiny bubbles that form a meringue get their structure from two things: the cross-linking of egg white proteins and the surface tension of water. As a meringue bakes, its moisture slowly evaporates, weakening its structure. At the same time, the egg white protein ovalbumin is becoming stronger, providing additional structure for the foam. Because sugar has a tendency to hold on to water molecules, if there is not enough in the meringue, the water evaporates too quickly, causing the cookies to collapse before the ovalbumin has time to strengthen. We found that cornstarch, which shares the water-clinging property of sugar, could perform the same role in our recipe, allowing us to cut back on sweetness without compromising structure.

Sugar Withdrawal

Removing too much sugar causes meringues to collapse in the oven.

Fortified Foam

Replacing a little of the sugar with cornstarch helps meringues keep their shape while baking.

EQUIPMENT CORNER: Pastry Bags

Plain canvas may be traditional for a pastry bag, but it doesn't make the best one. Pastry chefs can make decorative work like piping perfect meringues or buttercream rosettes look easy. But as we piped out meringues with five different sacks, we found that the bag itself can make a difference. We preferred larger models of about 18 inches, which give you enough length to grip and twist the top. Instead of the traditional canvas, we liked materials such as plastic and coated canvas, which are easier to clean. Finding the apertures of our bags sometimes too large or too small to work with tips bought separately, we learned that pastry bags have larger openings for handling jobs such as meringues or mashed potatoes, whereas decorating bags' smaller openings fit the tiny piping tips for fine scrollwork and writing. If your pastry-tip set didn't come with a coupler to help adapt tips to your bag, you can buy one at any kitchen store.

Once fitted with the right size tip, each bag piped both heavy frosting and ethereal meringue equally well. Cut-to-fit disposable plastic bags from Thermohauser ($17.98 for 100) made for mess-free cleanup, but we ultimately preferred the more durable, reusable Ateco 18-Inch Plastic-Coated Pastry Bag ($4.45).

Rating Pastry Bags

WE LOADED UP FIVE PASTRY BAGS WITH MERINGUE, as well as thick frosting, to test each model. Performance and ease of use (as well as ease of cleanup), were all factors. Brands are listed in order of preference. See www.americastestkitchen.com for updates to this testing.

HIGHLY RECOMMENDED

Ateco 18-Inch Plastic-Coated Pastry Bag

$4.45

The diameter of this bag's opening—just over ½ inch—accommodates a wide range of tip sizes. Plus the plastic-coated canvas combines the best of a durable material with a slick, easy-cleaning interior.

RECOMMENDED

Thermohauser Thermo-Disposable 18-Inch Pastry Bags

$17.98 for 100 bags

Not quite as sturdy as canvas or nylon, but plenty strong enough for pastry work. The cut-to-fit option takes the guesswork out of which tips will fit, and disposable bags make for easy (albeit wasteful) cleanup.

RECOMMENDED WITH RESERVATIONS

Wilton 18-Inch Featherweight Decorating Bag

$8.99

This sturdy, lightweight, and easy-to-clean polyester bag would have been great were it not for its prohibitively small opening (less than ½ inch in diameter), which failed to fit a widemouthed tip.

RECOMMENDED WITH RESERVATIONS

Ateco 18-Inch Wunderbag

$11.99

Virtually the same as the Wilton bag, save for sturdier material (polyurethane-coated cotton felt), a loop for hanging, and a few extra dollars in cost. Its less than ½-inch aperture was also too small.

NOT RECOMMENDED

Ateco 18-Inch Canvas Pastry Bag

$4.75

Here we found the opposite problem: The tip hole ran a full inch wide and failed to hold the smallest metal point. Moreover, plain canvas felt stiff, and it retained odors and stayed damp after an overnight dry.

Latino-Style Chicken and Rice (Arroz con Pollo) boasts meaty chicken thighs and tender rice seasoned with tomato sauce, garlic, onions, peppers, and olives. The test kitchen streamlines its typical hours-long preparation—without sacrificing flavor.

DINNER WITH A
CHAPTER 12 Spanish accent

Spanish cuisine is anything but bland. Take Sizzling

Garlic Shrimp. This appetizer is a tapas bar classic and usually arrives at

the table with a bit of drama—served in a shallow earthenware casserole,

the tiny shrimp sizzle in a pool of briny olive oil perfumed with lots of

garlic. In the best versions of this dish, the shrimp and garlic share equal

billing; the shrimp should be tender and juicy, and the garlic should have

a deep, rounded flavor. But coordinating the cooking of the two can

take some finesse. Our challenge would be to achieve tender, not rub-

bery, shrimp in the time it takes to fully infuse them with garlic flavor.

Finding the right balance of garlic flavor is key, too—we wanted the

garlic to be deep and assertive, but not harsh.

In contrast to a restaurant classic like sizzling garlic shrimp, *arroz*

con pollo (Latino chicken and rice) couldn't be homier. Moist chicken

and tender rice mingle with sweet peppers, onions, and herbs to make

a satisfying one-dish meal. But preparing this dish can take the better

part of a day. We aimed to streamline its preparation without robbing

the dish of its deep, hearty flavor. And we'd need to take special care to

ensure that the chicken cooked up tender, not tough—a pitfall of some

versions of arroz con pollo. The rice can be tricky, too; achieving evenly

cooked (not mushy or crunchy!) rice would be another challenge. In

the end, we wanted a fast, flavorful weeknight meal that would rival the

traditional long-cooked version.

IN THIS CHAPTER

THE RECIPES
Sizzling Garlic Shrimp

Latino-Style Chicken and Rice
Latino-Style Chicken and Rice
    with Bacon and Roasted Red
    Peppers
Latino-Style Chicken and Rice
    with Ham, Peas, and Orange

EQUIPMENT CORNER
Crazy Kitchen Gadgets

SCIENCE DESK
Marinade Superheroes

SIZZLING GARLIC SHRIMP

WHAT WE WANTED: A superlative version of the traditional tapas bar classic—tender, juicy shrimp in garlicky olive oil.

If there is one thing that can catch your attention in a Spanish tapas restaurant, it's the heady aroma wafting up from a dish of *gambas al ajillo*—little shrimp sizzling in a pool of olive oil and garlic. One bite will confirm that the garlic shares equal billing with the shrimp; when properly prepared, the shrimp are wonderfully sweet and tender and infused with deep garlic flavor. The key to achieving this flavor is the oil. A large quantity is heated along with sliced garlic, Spanish chiles, and bay leaves in a *cazuela* (an earthenware ramekin) until shimmering. A handful of small shrimp is added, heated until just barely cooked through, and served directly out of the cooking vessel. The dish is always accompanied by crusty bread to soak up all the leftover garlic- and shrimp-flavored oil.

As perfect as the dish is, it needs some adjustments to work as an appetizer served at home. At a tapas restaurant, where your table is overflowing with other dishes, it's easy to be content with a few small shrimp. Back at home, where most cooks are going to prepare only a single appetizer, the dish needs to be more substantial, meaning either bigger shrimp or more small ones. Tasters in the test kitchen preferred bigger shrimp, and we settled on a pound of large shrimp as the ideal portion size for six people. But now that we were playing around with the size and quantity of shrimp, what would that mean for the rest of the dish?

Traditional recipes for gambas al ajillo call for completely submerging the shrimp in oil, where they can be heated very evenly and gently at a low temperature. Short of accidentally bringing the oil up to deep-fry temperatures, the shrimp are almost impossible to overcook. But to fully submerge the pound of large shrimp we wanted to use, we'd need nearly 2 cups of oil—far more than six people could ever finish. We wouldn't have to serve all that oil, of course,

but why waste it? We wanted to find a way to reduce the amount (about half a cup was a reasonable quantity for six people) but still maintain the juiciness and garlic flavor that are the hallmarks of this dish.

With less oil, we figured using the smallest pan into which we could fit the shrimp would be more effective, since a smaller pan size meant deeper oil. In an 8-inch saucepan, the oil came only ½ inch up the side, covering about half of the shrimp. The results? Overcooked shrimp on the bottom and raw shrimp on top. Even with almost constant stirring and tossing, we couldn't get the shrimp to cook as evenly as if they were completely submerged in oil.

We sat down and went back to thinking about cooking basics. In order to keep shrimp juicy and tender, it is important to not overcook them. Our shrimp were partially overcooking because they were heating unevenly. They were heating unevenly because they were arranged in the pan in layers—some shrimp were closer to the heat source than others. We switched out the 8-inch pot for a 12-inch skillet. In the wider pan, the oil provided only a thin coating beneath the shrimp, but at least we could fit them in a single layer.

The new single-layer method meant that we would have to turn the shrimp halfway through cooking. With this many shrimp in the pan, we were afraid that turning them with tongs would take too long; by the time we turned the last shrimp, the first ones would be overcooked. Keeping the heat at medium-low gave us plenty of time to turn each shrimp individually, so we managed to cook them as evenly and gently as if they had been completely submerged in oil. We now had tender shrimp, but the other key characteristic of the dish was missing: great garlic flavor.

With only a thin layer of oil in the pan, the shrimp were not absorbing enough garlic flavor. We increased the amount of garlic from four thinly sliced cloves to eight, which provided the right proportion of shrimp to garlic, but the slices were still acting more like a garnish than a fully integrated

part of the dish. More sliced garlic would just give us more garnish; we had to find a different way to get more garlic flavor into the shrimp.

We knew that allicin, the chemical responsible for garlic's flavor, is highly soluble in oil—which meant we could use the oil as a vehicle to deliver more flavor to the dish. Allicin is not formed until the garlic's cells are ruptured, so we smashed four garlic cloves before heating them in a fresh batch of olive oil. We allowed them to brown and impart a sweet roasted flavor to the oil, discarded the smashed cloves, and then added the shrimp. But to our frustration, despite the supercharged garlic base with its new type of garlic character, the shrimp were better but still not great.

We realized that the only way to get more garlic flavor into the shrimp was through a marinade. We minced two garlic cloves and combined them with 2 tablespoons of oil. Knowing that salt would draw flavorful juices out of the garlic through osmosis, we added a teaspoonful to the marinade. After 30 minutes, we cooked the marinated shrimp and sliced garlic in the oil in which we had previously browned the smashed cloves. We waited with bated breath while our tasters bit into the shrimp. The dish was a resounding success.

Finally, we had juicy shrimp that were deeply flavored with garlic in a robust and complex sauce. By adding the garlic to the pan in three forms and at three different stages (minced raw garlic to provide pungency in the marinade, crushed and browned garlic to infuse sweetness into the oil, and slow-cooked sliced garlic to add mild garlic flavor), we were able to coax three distinct flavors from the versatile bulb. Not only did the olive oil evenly coat each shrimp with garlic flavor, it also provided protection for the garlic (see "Marinade Superheroes," page 155).

The traditional additions of bay leaf and red chile (see "Choosing the Right Chile," page 154) were deemed essential to the recipe. Heating the aromatics in the pan along with the sliced garlic allowed them to flavor the oil, giving the finished dish a sweet, herbal aroma. Most recipes also call for a splash of dry sherry or brandy, but we found that sherry vinegar and chopped parsley were better suited to rounding out the flavors; they provided a jolt of brightness that cut through the richness of the olive oil.

As a finishing touch, we realized we could recapture some of the restaurant spirit by transferring the dish to a small cast-iron skillet that we'd heated on the stove. Placed on a trivet on the table, the shrimp and garlic continued to sizzle until our eager tasters downed the last one.

WHAT WE LEARNED: Use a skillet to cook the shrimp at a low temperature in a single layer. Only a minimal amount of oil is needed to reach halfway up the side of each shrimp—the gentle heat will prevent the shrimp from overcooking when they are turned to cook on the second side. For intense garlic flavor, add garlic in three ways: minced in a marinade, smashed and browned in the oil before the shrimp are added, and sliced and cooked in the oil with the shrimp. Finish with the traditional flavorings of bay leaf, red chile—and use sherry vinegar in place of sherry wine to round out the flavors.

Authentic Choice

The slightly sweet cascabel chile is the traditional choice for gambas al ajillo.

Best Substitute

The New Mexico chile (aka California chile, chile Colorado, or dried Anaheim chile) is far more widely available and has the same bright freshness as the cascabel.

Last Resort

You won't have any trouble finding paprika, but its slightly stale flavor cannot compare with the complex taste of whole dried chiles.

SIZZLING GARLIC SHRIMP

serves 6 as an appetizer

Serve the shrimp with crusty bread for dipping in the richly flavored olive oil. The dish can be served directly from the skillet (make sure to use a trivet) or, for a sizzling effect, transferred to an 8-inch cast-iron skillet that's been heated for 2 minutes over medium-high heat. We prefer the slightly sweet flavor of dried chiles in this recipe, but ¼ teaspoon sweet paprika can be substituted.

   14   medium garlic cloves, peeled
   1   pound large shrimp (31 to 40 per pound), peeled, deveined, and tails removed
   8   tablespoons olive oil
   ½   teaspoon salt
   1   bay leaf
   1   (2-inch) piece mild dried chile, such as New Mexico, roughly broken, seeds included (see note)
   1½   teaspoons sherry vinegar
   1   tablespoon chopped fresh parsley leaves

1. Mince 2 garlic cloves with a chef's knife or garlic press. Toss the minced garlic with the shrimp, 2 tablespoons of the olive oil, and salt in a medium bowl. Let the shrimp marinate at room temperature for 30 minutes.

2. Meanwhile, using the flat side of a chef's knife, smash 4 garlic cloves. Heat the smashed garlic with the remaining 6 tablespoons olive oil in a 12-inch skillet over medium-low heat, stirring occasionally, until the garlic is light golden brown, 4 to 7 minutes. Remove the pan from the heat and allow the oil to cool to room temperature. Using a slotted spoon, remove the smashed garlic from the skillet and discard.

3. Thinly slice the remaining 8 cloves garlic. Return the skillet to low heat and add the sliced garlic, bay leaf, and chile. Cook, stirring occasionally, until the garlic is tender but not browned, 4 to 7 minutes. (If the garlic has not begun to sizzle after 3 minutes, increase the heat to medium-low.) Increase the heat to medium-low; add the shrimp with the marinade to the pan in a single layer. Cook the shrimp, undisturbed, until the oil starts to gently bubble,

TECHNIQUE:

Garlic Flavor Three Ways

We imparted garlic flavor to the shrimp in three different ways for three different effects, resulting in a dish with multilayered garlic complexity.

Raw = Pungent
The minced garlic in the marinade gets cooked briefly with the shrimp, maintaining a hint of raw-garlic pungency.

Browned = Sweet
Gently browning smashed whole garlic cloves infuses the olive oil with a sweet roasted-garlic flavor.

Poached = Mellow
Sliced garlic cooked gently in low-temperature olive oil loses its harsh flavor, becoming soft and mellow.

SCIENCE DESK: Marinade Superheroes

WE FOUND THAT OMITTING EITHER THE OIL OR THE salt from our marinade significantly reduced garlic flavor in the cooked shrimp. Why? Oil protects and stabilizes allicin, the compound in garlic that is responsible for its characteristic flavor. Allicin is produced when garlic is cut or crushed, and it quickly degrades into less flavorful compounds when exposed to air. Once in oil, however, the allicin dissolves and is protected from air. With this protection in place, it can move into the shrimp. There's one more advantage to oil—it coats the shrimp and delivers flavor evenly, not just in areas directly in contact with the minced garlic. Salt contributes to the process by speeding things up. Salt draws water containing allicin out of the garlic at a faster rate than allicin would migrate on its own.

**Oil + Salt + Garlic + Shrimp =
Complete Flavor Distribution**

Oil protects garlic flavor, and salt speeds up the marinating time.

about 2 minutes. Using tongs, flip the shrimp and continue to cook until almost cooked through, about 2 minutes longer. Increase the heat to high and add the sherry vinegar and parsley. Cook, stirring constantly, until the shrimp are cooked through and the oil is bubbling vigorously, 15 to 20 seconds. Serve immediately.

LATINO-STYLE CHICKEN AND RICE (ARROZ CON POLLO)

WHAT WE WANTED: A flavorful one-dish chicken and rice dinner that won't take all day to prepare.

T he bold-flavored cousin of American-style chicken and rice, *arroz con pollo* (literally, "rice with chicken") is Latino comfort food at its most basic—moist, tender chicken nestled in rice rich with peppers, onions, herbs, and deep chicken flavor.

Like most staples, however, arroz con pollo runs the gamut from the incredible to the merely edible, depending on how much time and effort you're willing to spend. The traditional method is to stew marinated chicken slowly with aromatic herbs and vegetables, creating a rich broth in which the rice is cooked once the chicken is fall-off-the-bone tender—terrific, yes, but also time-consuming. Quick versions allow you to speed things up by cooking the rice and chicken (often boneless) separately, then combining them just before serving. The trade-off is rice that's devoid of chicken flavor. Our goal was to split the difference: to streamline the more time-consuming, traditional recipes for arroz con pollo without sacrificing great taste.

If we wanted chicken-infused rice, it was clear the chicken and the rice would have to spend some time together. But how long was long enough?

A few of the "quick" recipes we found called for simmering the chicken and rice together and chopping the chicken into small pieces that would be done in sync with the rice—in about half an hour. The timing was right, but the results were not. The white meat and dark meat cooked unevenly, the skin was flabby, and, after 30 minutes, the flavor infusion was minimal. Worse, the hacked-up chicken, replete with jagged bones, was wholly unappealing.

Regrouping, we decided to start with a traditional recipe and adjust things from there. We began by sautéing a mixture of chopped onions and green peppers (called a sofrito). Once the vegetables softened, we added the chicken

and a few cups of water, turned the burner to low, and let the chicken poach for an hour. After removing the chicken, we added the rice to the pot, and, 30 minutes later, the rice had absorbed every drop of the rich broth the chicken had left behind. We added the chicken back to rewarm for 10 minutes, then lifted the lid. Now this was chicken-infused rice!

Unfortunately, it was also a two-hour project—and we hadn't even factored in the traditional marinade yet. What's more, although the dark meat was moist and tender, the leaner white meat was in bad shape. In a vivid flashback to our childhood, we recalled fighting with our cousins at the dinner table over the thighs and the drumsticks. (The dry, stringy white meat had to be drenched in the wet beans served on the side.) Opting for all thighs meant uniform cooking times, shopping convenience (one big "value" pack), and the best chance for peace at the dinner table.

A new problem emerged: Thighs are laden with fat, and this made the dish greasy. Removing the skin helped, but the meat near the surface dried out and the flavor suffered. The answer was to trim away any visible pockets of waxy yellow fat and most of the skin, leaving just enough to protect the meat. We also replaced most of the water we were adding with an equal amount of store-bought chicken broth, which made up for lost chicken flavor. After stewing for almost an hour, the skin was pretty flabby, so we removed it while the rice finished cooking. To make the chicken even more appealing, we removed the meat from the bones.

The two traditional rice choices for arroz con pollo are long-grain and medium-grain. Both were fine, but tasters preferred the creamier texture of medium-grain rice. But medium-grain rice was not without its problems. The grains had a tendency to split and release too much starch, making the overall texture of the dish pasty. Giving the rice a stir partway through cooking helped keep any one layer from overcooking, as did removing the pot from the direct heat of the stovetop to the diffuse heat of the oven.

Traditionally, arroz con pollo has an orange hue that comes from infusing oil with achiote, a tropical seed also used for coloring cheddar cheese. Achiote is hard to find, so we experimented with substitutions. Turmeric and saffron looked right but tasted wrong. (Achiote has no distinct flavor.) The solution was adding 8 ounces of canned tomato sauce along with the broth.

A common method for infusing this dish with Latino flavors is to marinate the chicken for a few hours or even overnight. Instead, we tried a quick, 15-minute marinade with garlic, oregano, and white vinegar. Then later, after we pulled the meat off the bone, we tossed the chicken with olive oil, vinegar, and cilantro. Capers, red pepper flakes, pimientos, and briny olives rounded out the flavors.

All of our efforts at streamlining this dish had brought the cooking time down to 90 minutes—a far cry from the half-day affair we'd faced at the start. But was this the best we could do? To shave off still more time, we tried adding the rice to the pot when the chicken still had half an hour to go. The chicken was fine, but the rice near the chicken pieces cooked unevenly. The solution to this problem was easy: Instead of giving the rice only one stir during cooking, we gave it a second stir to redistribute the ingredients. Now both the rice and the chicken were perfectly cooked in just over an hour. We finally had a rich, flavorful dish that tasted authentic, and we didn't have to wait for the weekend to enjoy it.

WHAT WE LEARNED: Use meaty chicken thighs for best flavor. Cut away most of the skin and fat from the thighs, leaving just enough to cover the meat and keep it moist. For maximum flavor, marinate the chicken before cooking, and for a further flavor boost, toss it with olive oil, vinegar, and cilantro after cooking. Poach the thighs in a broth seasoned with chopped onions and green peppers. Add the rice before the chicken is done, and move the pot from the direct heat of the stovetop to the diffuse heat of the oven to cook it evenly. Instead of hard-to-find achiote, use canned tomato sauce to give the dish its traditional orange hue.

LATINO-STYLE CHICKEN AND RICE

serves 4 to 6

To keep the dish from becoming greasy, it is important to remove excess fat from the chicken thighs and trim the skin. To use long-grain rice instead of medium-grain, increase the amount of water to ¾ cup in step 2.

6	medium garlic cloves, minced or pressed through a garlic press (about 2 tablespoons)
	Salt
½	teaspoon dried oregano
1	tablespoon plus 2 teaspoons distilled white vinegar
	Ground black pepper
8	bone-in, skin-on chicken thighs (3½ to 4 pounds), trimmed of excess skin and fat
2	tablespoons olive oil
1	medium onion, chopped fine (about 1 cup)
1	small green pepper, stemmed, seeded, and chopped fine (about ¾ cup)
¼	teaspoon red pepper flakes
¼	cup minced fresh cilantro leaves
1	(8-ounce) can tomato sauce
1¾	cups low-sodium chicken broth
¼	cup water, plus more if needed (see note)
3	cups medium-grain rice (see note)
½	cup green manzanilla olives, pitted and halved
1	tablespoon capers
½	cup jarred pimientos, cut into 2 by ¼-inch strips
	Lemon wedges, for serving

1. Adjust an oven rack to the middle position and heat the oven to 350 degrees. Place the garlic and 1 teaspoon salt in a large bowl; using a rubber spatula, mix to make a smooth paste. Add the oregano, 1 tablespoon of the vinegar, and ½ teaspoon black pepper to the garlic-salt mixture; stir to combine. Place the chicken in the bowl with the marinade. Coat the chicken pieces evenly with the marinade; set aside for 15 minutes.

2. Heat 1 tablespoon of the oil in a Dutch oven over medium heat until shimmering. Add the onion, green pepper, and pepper flakes; cook, stirring occasionally, until the vegetables begin to soften, 4 to 8 minutes. Add 2 tablespoons of the cilantro; stir to combine. Push the vegetables to the sides of the pot and increase the heat to medium-high. Add the chicken to the clearing in the center of the pot, skin side down, in an even layer. Cook, without moving the chicken, until the outer layer of the meat becomes opaque, 2 to 4 minutes. (If the chicken begins to brown, reduce the heat to medium.) Using tongs, flip the chicken and cook on the second side until opaque, 2 to 4 minutes more. Add the tomato sauce, broth, and water; stir to combine. Bring to a simmer; cover, reduce the heat to medium-low, and simmer for 20 minutes.

3. Add the rice, olives, capers, and ¾ teaspoon salt; stir well. Bring to a simmer, cover, and place the pot in the oven. After 10 minutes, remove the pot from the oven and stir the chicken and rice once from the bottom up. Return the pot to the oven. After another 10 minutes, stir once more, adding another ¼ cup water if the rice appears dry and the

bottom of the pot is beginning to burn. Cover and return the pot to the oven; cook until the rice has absorbed all the liquid and is tender but still holds its shape and the temperature of the chicken registers 175 degrees on an instant-read thermometer, about 10 minutes longer.

4. Using tongs, remove the chicken from the pot; replace the lid and set the pot aside. Remove and discard the chicken skin; using 2 spoons, pull the meat off the bones into large chunks. Using your fingers, remove the remaining fat and any dark veins from the chicken pieces. Place the chicken in a large bowl and toss with the remaining 1 tablespoon oil, remaining 2 teaspoons vinegar, remaining 2 tablespoons cilantro, and pimientos; season with salt and pepper to taste. Place the chicken on top of the rice, cover, and let stand until warmed through, about 5 minutes. Serve, passing the lemon wedges separately.

LATINO-STYLE CHICKEN AND RICE WITH BACON AND ROASTED RED PEPPERS

Bacon adds a welcome layer of richness, and red peppers bring subtle sweet flavor and color to this variation.

1. Follow the recipe for Latino-Style Chicken and Rice through step 1, substituting 2 teaspoons sweet paprika for the oregano and sherry vinegar for the white vinegar.

2. Fry 4 strips bacon, cut into ½-inch pieces, in a Dutch oven over medium heat until crisp, 6 to 8 minutes. Using a slotted spoon, transfer the bacon to a paper towel–lined plate; pour off all but 1 tablespoon bacon fat. Continue with step 2, substituting 1 small red pepper, finely chopped, and 1 medium carrot, finely chopped, for the green pepper and sautéing the vegetables in the bacon fat.

3. Continue with the recipe, substituting ¼ cup minced fresh parsley leaves for the cilantro, omitting the olives and capers, and substituting ½ cup roasted red peppers, cut into 2 by ¼-inch strips, for the pimientos. Garnish the chicken and rice with the reserved bacon before serving.

LATINO-STYLE CHICKEN AND RICE WITH HAM, PEAS, AND ORANGE

Ham gives this variation further richness, and orange zest and juice provide a bright accent. To use long-grain rice, increase the amount of water to ¾ cup and the salt added in step 3 to 1 teaspoon.

1. Follow the recipe for Latino-Style Chicken and Rice through step 1, substituting 1 tablespoon ground cumin for the oregano.

2. Continue with step 2, adding 8 ounces ham steak or Canadian bacon, cut into ½-inch pieces (about 1½ cups), with the onion, green pepper, and pepper flakes.

3. Continue with step 3, adding 3 strips zest from 1 orange, removed with a vegetable peeler, each strip about 3 inches long, with the rice, olives, capers, and salt. Add 1 cup frozen peas to the pot with ¼ cup water, if necessary, after stirring the contents of the pot the second time.

4. In step 4, add 3 tablespoons juice from 1 orange to the bowl with the olive oil, vinegar, cilantro, and pimientos.

TECHNIQUE: Maximum Flavor in Minimum Time

Here's how we shaved time without sacrificing taste.

Marinate
Briefly marinating the chicken in garlic, vinegar, and herbs gave us a quick infusion of Latino flavors.

Enrich
Stewing the chicken in store-bought chicken broth instead of water upped the chicken flavor.

Double Up
Adding the rice to the pot when the chicken was partially cooked saved us another half an hour.

Marinate Again
Tossing the chicken with a second marinade (after cooking) gave it the flavor boost it needed.

EQUIPMENT CORNER:
Crazy Kitchen Gadgets

ADMIT IT. YOU'VE FOUND YOURSELF (MORE THAN ONCE), flipping through a cookware catalog or glued to the television watching an infomercial, fascinated by the promises of a crazy kitchen gadget. "Does it really work?" you wonder. We've been there, too, so we rounded up seven are-they-too-good-to-be-true kitchen gadgets and headed into the test kitchen to see if those promises are empty—or not. See www.americastestkitchen.com for updates to this testing.

UNIVERSAL KNIFE BLOCKS

Do "universal" knife blocks hold knives of every shape, size, and make? We tested three models. The VivaTerra Bamboo Box Knife Holder ($89) is a simple wooden box of tightly packed bamboo skewers meant to cradle the knives. It holds knives at an awkward 90-degree angle, and when you pull them out, unattached skewers pop up, too. It's also flimsily constructed: Three of the four we ordered arrived broken. A bit better, the Bisbell Magnabloc ($143.50) is a magnetized wooden block that grips up to 10 knives (but not ceramic ones) along its surface. Unfortunately, its grasp is almost too strong: Knives release only with a vigorous tug that makes the tall, narrow structure wobble. The best (and cheapest) of the lot, the oak-framed Igo Home Kapoosh Universal Knife Block ($29.99), comfortably shelters up to 10 tools in its dishwasher-safe nest of spaghetti-like plastic rods, and the sturdy box's opening is at an accessible angle. Though we wish it were deeper—handles of blades over 8 inches stuck out—it makes a practical home for most knives.

The **Igo Home Kapoosh Universal Knife Block** contains thousands of fine plastic rods that easily accommodate up to 10 knives and tools.

MINI ADJUST-A-CUP

For measuring sticky ingredients such as honey or peanut butter, we have always liked the KitchenArt Adjust-A-Cup measure. Available in 1- and 2-cup capacities, this plunger-fitted tube forces the food out of the cup with a slow, steady push of the sliding base. Now, a new Mini Adjust-A-Cup ($2.99) is ideal for measuring just a few teaspoons, tablespoons, milliliters, or ounces. It works with the ease of its larger counterpart and, at just under three inches tall, stores handily in a drawer.

Our favorite measuring tool for sticky, gooey ingredients, the **Adjust-A-Cup,** now has a shorter sibling for smaller amounts.

THREE-BLADE PEELER

Different peelers suit different requirements: Straight, traditional peelers work best for cucumbers and potatoes; serrated peelers make quick work of tender tomato and peach skins; julienne peelers turn out fine matchsticks for stir-fries and salads. A new gadget, the Prepara Trio Tri-Blade Peeler ($14.95), claims to do it all. Similar to a multicolor pen, this three-in-one peeler stores two blades in its grip-covered shaft while the third pops up for use. Switching blades is as simple as a click of the release button and a turn of the wheel on the base of the handle. We found each blade performed well on a range of produce and, thankfully, the blade cartridge is dishwasher-safe. A great option for those looking to save drawer space.

The **Prepara Trio Tri-Blade Peeler** frees up drawer space by combining three peelers in one.

PIE GATE

Leftover pie doesn't last long, but when there is some to spare, a Pie Gate ($6.95) from Progressive International promises to keep the filling intact. This plastic tool, which looks like two wings attached to a central hinge, adjusts to fit any angle—and most pie plates. Its flexible silicone edges do the job of neatly and tightly sealing in leaky fillings. The device can also double as a dam for cut rounds of creamy, oozy cheeses such as Brie or Camembert.

Runny pie fillings and oozy cheeses stay intact with the **Progressive International Pie Gate.**

BAKER'S EDGE BAKING PAN

This redesign of a conventional 13 by 9-inch baking pan features nothing more than three internal walls that extend across the pan. Could they really eliminate the problem of undercooked middles and burnt edges when baking brownies, bar cookies, and even lasagna? When we tested this pan in our kitchen, we were pleased to discover that the answer is yes. The heavy-gauge cast-aluminum pan evenly distributed heat while cooking, and because the Baker's Edge ($34.95) has six more baking surfaces than ordinary pans, it gave each serving of our brownies at least two chewy edges (a great thing if you like edge pieces). And when we made lasagna, we discovered another advantage of the interior walls—they kept the layers from sliding apart, making for easy serving. The only disadvantage when making lasagna: You must cut the noodles to fit the pan.

The interior walls of the **Baker's Edge Baking Pan** eliminate the problems of undercooked middles and burnt edges in brownies and lasagna.

UNICORN MINIMILL

The maker of the test kitchen's top-rated Unicorn Magnum Plus and Unicorn Magnum Pepper Mills has fashioned an elf-like mill fit for a slender pocket or purse. Filling the tablespoon-capacity Unicorn Minimill ($17.50) demands nimble fingers; twisting a coin in the head's built-in slot loosens the lid easily enough, but it takes a few practice rounds (and a few peppercorns lost to the floor) to master the tasks of steadying the shaft-like base with your forefinger while pouring in the peppercorns and then affixing the crown. Once assembled, however, the mill supplies enough perfectly ground pepper (coarse, medium, or fine) for many meals.

If you want a less expensive option and don't mind the small size, the **Unicorn Minimill** pepper grinder gets the job done just fine.

ONION GOGGLES

Chopping and dicing our way through 30 pounds of onions per week in the test kitchen, we're always interested in new methods of eye defense. Although they certainly look a bit goofy, the RSVP International Onion Goggles ($19.99) do help maintain focus on the onions—yellow, Vidalia, red, or otherwise—rather than the tissue box. We found that they block irritating fumes better than sunglasses, and the foam padding around the antifog lenses is a more comfortable alternative to swim goggles. Available in white or black with lime green trim.

RSVP International Onion Goggles protect your eyes when you're chopping onions.

Chris explains that the wide surface area of a nonstick skillet is preferred to the limited space afforded by the curved shape of a wok.

SKILLET vs. WOK TEST

SKILLET

WOK

AVERAGE TEMPERATURE

600
500
400
300
200
100

2 3 4 5 6 7 8
TIME (MINUTES)

0 1 2 3 4 5 6 7 8
TIME (MINUTES)

America's

LET'S DO Chinese

We love the convenience of Chinese takeout, but all too often we find that convenience comes at a price—namely, the quality of the food. We knew we could do a better job, so we turned our attention to two of our favorite Chinese dishes—pork lo mein and beef stir-fries—and set out to create foolproof versions of each one.

Pork lo mein, soft egg noodles tossed with smoky barbecued pork and pungent Chinese vegetables, is a seductive combination of flavors and textures. But the barbecued pork, *char siu,* takes most of the day to cook. We'd need to find a quicker-cooking cut for our lo mein, but we wanted it to have the same rich, caramelized flavor as real char siu. And though this dish is typically made with a modest amount of meat and vegetables (the noodles are the star of the dish), could we increase their presence for a heartier meal? These were just a few of the questions we hoped to answer.

What's the secret to a really great beef stir-fry—one with juicy, seared beef, crisp, tender vegetables, and a lively sauce that pulls it all together? We'd start by determining the right cut of beef for stir-frying; some cuts are better than others. And the vegetables? Not all vegetables hold up in a stir-fry, so we'd need to narrow down our choices. Finally, we wanted brightly flavored sauce and plenty of it for serving our meat and vegetables over steamed rice. In short, we hoped our efforts would result in a tasty meal, far better than we could get through picking up the phone.

IN THIS CHAPTER

THE RECIPES

Pork Lo Mein

Teriyaki Stir-Fried Beef with Green Beans and Shiitakes
Stir-Fried Beef with Snap Peas and Red Peppers
Tangerine Stir-Fried Beef with Onions and Snow Peas
Stir-Fried Red Curry Beef with Eggplant

EQUIPMENT CORNER

Rice Cookers

SCIENCE DESK

Skillet vs. Wok

PORK LO MEIN

WHAT WE WANTED: A winning version of this takeout classic, with fresh noodles, smoky barbecued pork, and crisp-tender Chinese vegetables.

Pork lo mein is like shrimp fried rice: Order it from your typical takeout joint, and the dish invariably disappoints with greasy flavors and sodden vegetables. A few years back, we revamped fried rice with our own lighter, fresher renditions. That got us wondering: Could we do the same with pork lo mein? We wanted a dish representative of the best any good Chinese home cook could turn out: chewy noodles tossed in a salty-sweet sauce and accented with bits of smoky *char siu* (barbecued pork) and still-crisp Chinese cabbage.

Our first task was to find a suitable replacement for the char siu. This Cantonese specialty takes the better part of a day to roast, and although enterprising cooks might attempt it themselves, it's more the province of restaurants and professional kitchens. A trip to Boston's Chinatown for some char siu wouldn't be out of the question on some occasions, but we wanted a dish we could whip up anytime with ingredients from home. We would already be stir-frying the vegetables. As part of our makeover, why not stir-fry the pork as well?

But what cut would work best? We considered pork tenderloin, which we've used with great success in stir-fries. The only problem is that tenderloin, though tender, can be a little bland—worlds apart from the richly flavored, well-marbled pork shoulder traditional to char siu. Pork shoulder itself was out—it requires hours of cooking to become fall-apart tender. Pork belly is popular in Chinese cooking, but this fat-streaked meat from the underside of the pig is also the cut of choice for most bacon made in this country, and we could only find it smoked or cured. The most sensible option was country-style pork ribs. Though fatty, these meaty ribs from the upper side of the rib cage have the same rich flavor of pork shoulder, and they're naturally tender.

Following the protocol for char siu, we knew we wanted to marinate the pork before cooking. To avoid a dish that was overly greasy, we first trimmed the ribs of surface fat and cut them into thin strips that would allow the marinade to penetrate more efficiently. We then soaked the meat in a classic Chinese marinade of hoisin sauce, oyster sauce, soy sauce, toasted sesame oil, and five-spice powder, an aromatic blend of cinnamon, star anise, and other spices. After 20 minutes we removed the pork from the liquid and seared it quickly over high heat in a cast-iron skillet. (Because more of its surface is in contact with the burner, a large skillet provides more sizzle and sear than a wok, whose conical bottom was not designed for a Western stovetop.) One bite and we knew we had hit on a very good thing our first try. The meat cooked up tender and juicy on the inside with a crisp caramelized exterior. We took the flavor one step further by adding a few drops of liquid smoke for a little of that slow-roasted flavor we love so much in char siu.

Pork issues settled, we were ready to tackle the noodles. *Lo mein* literally translates to "tossed noodles," referring to the way the strands, made from wheat and egg and resembling thick spaghetti, are tossed in sauce. Traditionally the dish calls for fresh noodles, as these absorb the flavors of the sauce better than dried kinds. We tried a variety of fresh Chinese egg noodles, but only the ones labeled "lo mein" from the Asian grocery near our offices boasted the good wheaty taste and firm texture we were after. These came in a loose tangle packaged in a simple plastic bag. Disappointingly, the more readily available fresh "Chinese-style" egg noodles from the supermarket, sold in vacuum-packed containers in the produce aisle, had a pasty texture and an inferior taste that sent us seeking a better alternative. Back in the test kitchen, we scanned the shelves of our pantry and landed on a box of dried linguine. Despite its flat shape, these long Italian strands are similar in width to lo mein. Cooked to al dente, they worked beautifully, having the same firm chewiness of the fresh Chinese noodles.

In restaurants, for expediency's sake, the noodles are typically cooked well ahead of serving, rinsed in cold water, and then slathered in oil to keep them from clumping together as they wait to be added to the stir-fry. This not only makes the noodles excessively oily, but it also prevents the sauce from clinging to them. Home cooking offered an advantage in this area—we could simply boil the noodles before tossing them with the sauce in the pan, avoiding the need for extra oil.

All that was left was to figure out the vegetables and the sauce. We opted for traditional choices—cabbage, scallions, and shiitake mushrooms—stir-frying them in batches in a little vegetable oil with garlic and fresh ginger after cooking the meat. As for the sauce, our tasters decided the same mixture we had been using for the meat marinade would serve just fine as a base, with a little chicken broth and a teaspoon of cornstarch added for body. The final step: tossing the stir-fried meat and vegetables with the drained noodles in the pot we'd just used for boiling them, with a little chili sauce for some added kick.

Traditionally, noodles are the star of lo mein; the meat and vegetables serve as little more than garnishes. To meet the demands of our American tasters, we increased the amount of pork from 4 ounces to a pound and upped the vegetable amounts by several cups. The net effect was a richer yet fresher-tasting dish—a far cry from takeout.

WHAT WE LEARNED: Country-style pork ribs are naturally tender, but trim the excess fat to avoid a greasy dish. Cut the ribs into thin strips so the marinade—made with hoisin sauce, oyster sauce, soy sauce, toasted sesame oil, five-spice powder, and a few drops of liquid smoke for that famous slow-roasted flavor—can penetrate more efficiently. For a caramelized, crisp exterior, sear the pork quickly over high heat in a cast-iron skillet, which provides great sizzle and sear. And if fresh Chinese noodles aren't available, dried linguine works well as a substitute, offering both good wheaty taste and chewy texture.

PORK LO MEIN

serves 4

Use a cast-iron skillet for this recipe if you have one—it will help create the best sear on the pork. When shopping for Chinese rice wine, look for one that is amber in color; if not available, sherry may be used as a substitute. If no hoisin sauce is available, substitute 1 tablespoon sugar. If boneless pork ribs are unavailable, substitute 1½ pounds bone-in country-style ribs, followed by the next-best option, pork tenderloin. Liquid smoke provides a flavor reminiscent of the Chinese barbecued pork traditional to this dish. It is important to cook the noodles at the last minute to avoid clumping.

- 3 tablespoons soy sauce
- 2 tablespoons oyster sauce
- 2 tablespoons hoisin sauce (see note)
- 1 tablespoon toasted sesame oil
- ¼ teaspoon five-spice powder
- 1 pound boneless country-style pork ribs, trimmed of surface fat and excess gristle, sliced crosswise into ⅛-inch pieces (see note)
- ¼ teaspoon liquid smoke (optional, see note)
- ½ cup low-sodium chicken broth
- 1 teaspoon cornstarch
- 2 medium garlic cloves, minced or pressed through a garlic press (about 2 teaspoons)
- 2 teaspoons grated fresh ginger
- 4½ teaspoons vegetable oil
- 4 tablespoons Chinese rice cooking wine (Shao-Xing) or dry sherry (see note)
- 8 ounces shiitake mushrooms, stems trimmed, caps cut in halves or thirds (about 3 cups)
- 2 bunches scallions, whites thinly sliced and greens cut into 1-inch pieces (about 2 cups)
- 1 small head Napa cabbage, halved and sliced crosswise into ½-inch strips (about 4 cups)
- 12 ounces fresh Chinese noodles or 8 ounces dried linguine
- 1 tablespoon Asian chili-garlic sauce

1. Bring 6 quarts water to a boil in a Dutch oven over high heat.

2. Whisk the soy sauce, oyster sauce, hoisin sauce, sesame oil, and five-spice powder together in a medium bowl. Place 3 tablespoons of the soy sauce mixture in a large zipper-lock bag; add the pork and liquid smoke, if using. Toss to combine; press out as much air as possible and seal the bag. Marinate in the refrigerator for at least 15 minutes or up to 1 hour. Whisk the broth and cornstarch into the remaining soy sauce mixture in a medium bowl. In a separate bowl, mix the garlic and ginger with ½ teaspoon of the vegetable oil; set aside.

3. Heat 1 teaspoon of the vegetable oil in a 12-inch non-stick skillet (or cast-iron skillet) over high heat until just smoking. Add half of the pork in a single layer, breaking up the clumps with a wooden spoon. Cook without stirring for 1 minute. Continue to cook, stirring occasionally, until browned, 2 to 3 minutes. Add 2 tablespoons of the wine to the skillet; cook, stirring constantly, until the liquid is reduced and the pork is well coated, 30 to 60 seconds. Transfer the pork to a medium bowl and repeat with the remaining pork, 1 teaspoon more oil, and the remaining 2 tablespoons wine. Wipe the skillet clean with paper towels.

4. Return the skillet to high heat, add 1 teaspoon more vegetable oil, and heat until just smoking. Add the mushrooms and cook, stirring occasionally, until light golden brown, 4 to 6 minutes. Add the scallions and continue to cook, stirring occasionally, until the scallions are wilted, 2 to 3 minutes longer; transfer the vegetables to the bowl with the pork.

5. Add the remaining 1 teaspoon vegetable oil and cabbage to the now-empty skillet; cook, stirring occasionally, until spotty brown, 3 to 5 minutes. Clear the center of the skillet; add the garlic-ginger mixture and cook, mashing the mixture with a spoon, until fragrant, about 30 seconds. Stir the garlic mixture into the cabbage; return the pork-vegetable mixture and the chicken broth–soy sauce mixture to the skillet. Simmer until thickened and the ingredients are well incorporated, 1 to 2 minutes. Remove the skillet from the heat.

6. While the cabbage is cooking, stir the noodles into the boiling water. Cook, stirring constantly, until the noodles are tender, 3 to 4 minutes for fresh Chinese noodles or 10 minutes for dried linguine. Drain the noodles and transfer back to the Dutch oven; add the cooked stir-fry mixture and chili-garlic sauce, tossing the noodles constantly, until the sauce coats the noodles. Serve immediately.

SCIENCE DESK: Skillet vs. Wok

WE HAVE ALWAYS PREFERRED A SKILLET TO A WOK IN our stir-fry recipes. Its flat-bottom design allows more of its surface area to come in direct contact with the flat burner of a Western stove, delivering more heat over more of its parts than a wok—and enabling it to remain hot even after food is added.

To quantify their differences, we heated oil in a wok and a heavy 12-inch skillet over high heat on gas burners. Once the oil was smoking (at around 415 degrees), we added stir-fry ingredients to each pan. The wok's temperature plummeted dramatically, to 220 degrees at its center, rising only another 50 degrees over the course of cooking. The skillet's temperature dipped to 345 degrees, then recovered quickly, continuing to rise to almost 500 degrees. This higher heat translated to better browning and more flavor.

Flat-Bottom Benefits

The flat bottom of a 12-inch skillet is better suited to a flat burner, maintaining heat (and even continuing to rise) after food is added.

Conical Compromise

The conical bottom of a traditional wok was designed for a pit-style stove. On a flat Western burner, it heats inefficiently, dropping its temperature when food is added.

BEEF AND VEGETABLE STIR-FRIES

WHAT WE WANTED: A technique that would yield consistent stir-fries with crisp-tender vegetables and juicy meat, in a lively sauce.

The Chinese invented stir-frying as a means to conserve energy—the theory being the hotter the pan (or wok), the faster the cooking and the less energy used. To make the most of the heat being used, stir-fry recipes call for cooking in stages—items that take the longest to cook go into the pan first, followed by the other ingredients in sequence until the last garnish is tossed in and the dish is served. The Chinese have had thousands of years to perfect this process; who were we to argue with the nuts and bolts? We set out to adapt this method of cooking to our home kitchens.

Stir-frying requires blazing heat to cook food quickly. In kitchen tests on several stoves, we found that the bottom of a traditional round wok reached an average of 564 degrees (a temperature sufficient to brown meat and vegetables), but when we moved the thermometer halfway up the side of the wok, we saw that the temperature dropped more than 100 degrees. At the top edge of the wok, the temperature averaged just 336 degrees—perfect for steaming beef but useless for searing it.

For years the test kitchen has advocated using a large nonstick pan for stir-fries. Because the pan is basically flat, its usable cooking surface is much larger than a wok's. In our tests we found that the temperature was remarkably consistent—it averaged 560 degrees in the center of the pan, 555 degrees halfway between the center and the edge of the pan, and 554 degrees at the edge of the cooking surface. So a nonstick skillet is a must, but be sure the pan is large. Pan sizes are measured across the top. We prefer a pan that measures at least 12 inches.

Next, we turned to the protein element of our stir-fry—beef. Because beef takes longer to cook than the other elements in the stir-fry, it goes into the pan first. Unlike Americans, who make meat the centerpiece of the meal, the Chinese incorporate meat into their diets in a less expensive and decidedly more healthful manner, by using meat (and other proteins such as fish and tofu) as a team player alongside vegetables. As for cut, flank steak is the obvious choice, but we also like sirloin tip steaks and blade steaks. You will need to remove excess fat and gristle from blade steaks, so start with 1 pound to compensate for trimmings. To make slicing easier, freeze the meat for 20 to 30 minutes. It's also important to cut across the grain so the meat won't be

tough. Cutting the meat into small pieces gives the illusion of more meat in the stir-fry, and it also provides more surface area for absorbing flavors and browning.

After cutting the meat, we like to marinate it. A 10-minute soy marinade adds flavor and helps the meat retain moisture. (The soy acts like a brine.) Drain the meat before searing to remove excess liquid. Don't be tempted to hurry the cooking of the stir-fry along by dumping all the meat into the pan at once; it's important to cook it in batches. You want the meat to brown, so give it some space. Once all the meat is browned, empty the pan and you're ready to turn to slower-cooking vegetables, so they'll get a head start on softer, quicker-cooking vegetables. Again, if you added all the vegetables at once, some would get soggy and over-cooked by the time others finished cooking.

Add aromatics like garlic and ginger last. Adding them late in the game lessens the likelihood that they'll burn—plus adding them toward the end of cooking helps preserve their flavor. We also like to add a little oil to the aromatics before they hit the pan. This further ensures that the aromatics won't burn once they hit the hot pan.

Stir-frying isn't difficult, but by following a few simple steps and by having patience, you'll be well on your way to turning out great stir-fries every time.

WHAT WE LEARNED: A large nonstick pan is essential for stir-fries; its usable cooking surface is much greater than that of a wok, and the temperature remains consistent throughout the pan. Pick the right cut of beef—flank steak is terrific, but sirloin tip steaks and blade steaks are also good choices—and marinate it for flavor and to prevent it from drying out in the pan. Allow plenty of room for the meat to brown properly, adding it in batches if necessary. Add the vegetables in batches, too—longer-cooking vegetables (such as onions) first, then softer, quicker-cooking vegetables (such as green beans). Mix a little oil with the aromatics so they don't scorch in the pan, and add them to the pan late in the cooking process to further ensure they don't burn—and to preserve their flavor.

TERIYAKI STIR-FRIED BEEF WITH GREEN BEANS AND SHIITAKES

serves 4

You can substitute 1 tablespoon white wine or sake mixed with 1 teaspoon sugar for the mirin.

    4   tablespoons soy sauce
    1   teaspoon plus 2 tablespoons sugar
   12   ounces flank steak, cut into 2-inch-wide
        strips with grain, then sliced across grain into
        ⅛-inch-thick slices
    ½   cup low-sodium chicken broth
    1   tablespoon mirin (see note)
    ¼   teaspoon red pepper flakes
    1   teaspoon cornstarch
    3   medium garlic cloves, minced or pressed
        through a garlic press (about 1 tablespoon)
    1   tablespoon minced fresh ginger
    2   tablespoons vegetable oil
    8   ounces shiitake mushrooms, wiped clean,
        stemmed, and cut into 1-inch pieces
   12   ounces green beans, ends trimmed and halved
    ¼   cup water
    3   scallions, cut into 1½-inch pieces, white and
        light green pieces quartered lengthwise

1. Combine 2 tablespoons of the soy sauce and 1 teaspoon of the sugar in a medium bowl. Add the beef, toss well, and marinate for at least 10 minutes or up to 1 hour, stirring once. Meanwhile, whisk the remaining 2 tablespoons soy sauce, remaining 2 tablespoons sugar, broth, mirin, pepper flakes, and cornstarch in a medium bowl. Combine the garlic, ginger, and 1 teaspoon of the oil in a small bowl.

2. Drain the beef and discard the liquid. Heat 1 teaspoon more oil in a 12-inch nonstick skillet over high heat until just smoking. Add half of the beef in a single layer, breaking up any clumps. Cook, without stirring, for 1 minute, then

stir and cook until browned, 1 to 2 minutes. Transfer the beef to a clean bowl. Heat 1 teaspoon more oil in the skillet and repeat with the remaining beef. Rinse the skillet and dry with paper towels.

3. Add the remaining 1 tablespoon oil to the now-empty skillet and heat until just smoking. Add the mushrooms and cook until beginning to brown, about 2 minutes. Add the green beans and cook, stirring frequently, until spotty brown, 3 to 4 minutes. Add the water and cover the pan; continue to cook until the green beans are crisp-tender, 2 to 3 minutes longer. Uncover the skillet and push the vegetables to the sides to clear the center; add the garlic-ginger mixture to the clearing and cook, mashing with a spatula, until fragrant, 15 to 20 seconds. Stir to combine the garlic-ginger mixture with the vegetables. Return the beef and any juices to the skillet, add the scallions, and stir to combine. Whisk

the sauce to recombine, then add to the skillet; cook, stirring constantly, until thickened, about 30 seconds. Serve.

VARIATIONS

STIR-FRIED BEEF WITH SNAP PEAS AND RED PEPPERS

The flavors in this variation are enriched by the oyster sauce and sherry in the sauce.

- 2   tablespoons soy sauce
- 1   teaspoon plus 1 tablespoon sugar
- 12 ounces flank steak, cut into 2-inch-wide strips with grain, then sliced across grain into ⅛-inch-thick slices
- 2   tablespoons dry sherry
- ½   cup low-sodium chicken broth
- ¼   cup oyster sauce

1 teaspoon cornstarch
3 medium garlic cloves, minced or pressed through a garlic press (about 1 tablespoon)
1 tablespoon minced fresh ginger
2 tablespoons vegetable oil
12 ounces sugar snap peas, ends trimmed and strings removed (about 4 cups)
1 medium red bell pepper, seeded and cut into ¼-inch slices
2 tablespoons water

1. Combine the soy sauce and 1 teaspoon of the sugar in a medium bowl. Add the beef, toss well, and marinate for at least 10 minutes or up to 1 hour, stirring once. Meanwhile, whisk the remaining 1 tablespoon sugar, sherry, broth, oyster sauce, and cornstarch in a medium bowl. Combine the garlic, ginger, and 1 teaspoon of the oil in a small bowl.

2. Drain the beef and discard the liquid. Heat 1 teaspoon more oil in a 12-inch nonstick skillet over high heat until just smoking. Add half of the beef in a single layer, breaking up any clumps. Cook, without stirring, for 1 minute, then stir and cook until browned, 1 to 2 minutes. Transfer the beef to a clean bowl. Heat 1 teaspoon more oil in the skillet and repeat with the remaining beef. Rinse the skillet and dry with paper towels.

3. Add the remaining 1 tablespoon oil to the now-empty skillet and heat until just smoking. Add the snap peas and bell pepper; cook, stirring frequently, until the vegetables begin to brown, 3 to 5 minutes. Add the water and continue to cook until the vegetables are crisp-tender, 1 to 2 minutes longer. Push the vegetables to the sides of the skillet; add the garlic-ginger mixture to the clearing and cook, mashing with a spatula, until fragrant, 15 to 20 seconds. Stir to combine the garlic-ginger mixture with the vegetables. Return the beef and any juices to the skillet and stir to combine. Whisk the sauce to recombine, then add to the skillet; cook, stirring constantly, until thickened, about 30 seconds. Serve.

TANGERINE STIR-FRIED BEEF WITH ONIONS AND SNOW PEAS

Two to 3 oranges can be substituted for the tangerines. If available, substitute 1 teaspoon toasted and ground Sichuan peppercorns for the red pepper flakes.

4 tablespoons soy sauce
1 teaspoon plus 1 tablespoon light brown sugar
12 ounces flank steak, cut into 2-inch-wide strips with grain, then sliced across grain into ⅛-inch-thick slices
¾ cup juice plus 1 teaspoon grated zest from 3 to 4 tangerines (see note)
1 teaspoon sesame oil
1 teaspoon cornstarch
3 medium garlic cloves, minced or pressed through a garlic press (about 1 tablespoon)
1 tablespoon minced fresh ginger

TECHNIQUE:
Browning Meat for Stir-Fries

Problem: Cooking the meat in one large batch causes it to steam in its own liquid. The meat will be chewy, dry, and gray.

Solution: Cooking the meat in two smaller batches allows it to brown quickly without drying out or becoming tough.

1	tablespoon Chinese black bean sauce
¼–½	teaspoon red pepper flakes (see note)
2	tablespoons vegetable oil
1	large onion, halved and cut into ½-inch wedges
10	ounces snow peas, ends trimmed and strings removed (about 4 cups)
2	tablespoons water

1. Combine 2 tablespoons of the soy sauce and 1 teaspoon of the sugar in a medium bowl. Add the beef, toss well, and marinate for at least 10 minutes or up to 1 hour, stirring once. Meanwhile, whisk the remaining 2 tablespoons soy sauce, remaining 1 tablespoon sugar, tangerine juice, sesame oil, and cornstarch in a medium bowl. Combine the tangerine zest, garlic, ginger, black bean sauce, pepper flakes, and 1 teaspoon of the vegetable oil in a small bowl.

2. Drain the beef and discard the liquid. Heat 1 teaspoon more vegetable oil in a 12-inch nonstick skillet over high heat until just smoking. Add half of the beef in a single layer, breaking up any clumps. Cook, without stirring, for 1 minute, then stir and cook until browned, 1 to 2 minutes. Transfer the beef to a clean bowl. Heat 1 teaspoon more vegetable oil in the skillet and repeat with the remaining beef. Rinse the skillet and dry with paper towels.

3. Add the remaining 1 tablespoon vegetable oil to the now-empty skillet and heat until just smoking. Add the onion and cook, stirring frequently, until beginning to brown, 3 to 5 minutes. Add the snow peas and continue to cook until spotty brown, about 2 minutes longer. Add the water and cook until the vegetables are crisp-tender, about 1 minute. Push the vegetables to the sides of the skillet; add the zest-garlic mixture to the clearing and cook, mashing with a spatula, until fragrant, 15 to 20 seconds. Stir to combine the zest-garlic mixture with the vegetables.

Return the beef and any juices to the skillet and stir to combine. Whisk the sauce to recombine, then add to the skillet; cook, stirring constantly, until thickened, about 30 seconds. Serve.

STIR-FRIED RED CURRY BEEF WITH EGGPLANT

Lime and coconut milk work well here, creating a tangy, sweet environment for the beef. Serve with basmati rice.

2	tablespoons soy sauce
2	tablespoons plus 1 teaspoon light brown sugar
12	ounces flank steak, cut into 2-inch-wide strips with grain, then sliced across grain into ⅛-inch-thick slices
1	tablespoon juice from 1 lime
½	cup low-sodium chicken broth
3	tablespoons coconut milk
1	tablespoon fish sauce
1	teaspoon cornstarch
3	medium cloves garlic, minced or pressed through a garlic press (about 1 tablespoon)
1½	teaspoons red curry paste
2	tablespoons vegetable oil
1	medium eggplant (1 pound), peeled and cut into ¾-inch cubes (about 6 cups)
2	cups packed fresh basil leaves Lime wedges, for serving (optional)

1. Combine the soy sauce and 1 teaspoon of the sugar in a medium bowl. Add the beef, toss well, and marinate for at least 10 minutes or up to 1 hour, stirring once. Meanwhile, whisk the remaining 2 tablespoons sugar, lime juice, chicken broth, coconut milk, fish sauce, and cornstarch in a medium bowl. Combine the garlic, curry paste, and 1 teaspoon of the oil in a small bowl.

2. Drain the beef and discard the liquid. Heat 1 teaspoon more oil in a 12-inch nonstick skillet over high heat until just smoking. Add half of the beef to the skillet in a single layer, breaking up any clumps. Cook, without stirring, for 1 minute, then stir and continue to cook until browned, 1 to 2 minutes. Transfer the beef to a clean bowl. Heat 1 teaspoon more oil in the skillet and repeat with the remaining beef. Rinse the skillet and dry with paper towels.

3. Add the remaining 1 tablespoon oil to the now-empty skillet and heat until just smoking. Add the eggplant and cook, stirring frequently, until browned and no longer spongy, 5 to 7 minutes. Push the eggplant to the sides of the skillet; add the garlic-curry mixture to the clearing and cook, mashing with a spatula, until fragrant, 15 to 20 seconds. Stir to combine the garlic-curry mixture with the eggplant. Return the beef and any accumulated juices to the skillet and stir to combine. Whisk the sauce to recombine, then add to the skillet along with the basil leaves; cook, stirring constantly, until the sauce is thickened and evenly distributed, about 30 seconds. Serve, passing the lime wedges separately, if using.

EQUIPMENT CORNER: Rice Cookers

ACHIEVING PERFECT RICE IS SURPRISINGLY CHALLENGing even for an accomplished cook. The same cooking technique that delivers excellent long-grain white rice needs adjusting to produce perfect brown or sushi rice. Enter rice cookers, which promise to produce well-cooked rice every time and to keep it warm until ready to serve. But with rice cookers priced from $15 to $830, we wondered: Just what features do you really need, and how much do you need to pay?

All rice cookers work on the same principle. The cooker brings water to a boil (212 degrees). When the rice

has absorbed all the water, the temperature inside the cooker begins to rise. A built-in thermostat detects this temperature rise and turns the machine off or down to a keep-warm setting for four to 13 hours. Rice cookers vary, however, by programming ability and machine structure.

All rice cookers call for different water amounts for different basic rice types (long-grain, brown, and sushi), but programmable models have a computer chip that further tweaks the machine's temperature and finish time to allow for preferences such as softer texture or moister grains, or to adjust to highly specialized rice types. These more expensive machines also have an ability to program a cooking start time. Regardless of whether they are programmable, though, all of the rice cookers from the big three manufacturers (Zojirushi, Sanyo, and Panasonic) are constructed as one-piece models, with tightly closing lids and steam caps and dew collectors to trap excess water. Nonprogrammable models from other manufacturers are often two-piece

models, a simple pot with a glass lid that has a hole through which steam escapes.

We chose both programmable and nonprogrammable versions from Zojirushi, Sanyo, and Panasonic as well as two-piece models from Rival and Breville. Prices ranged from $15 to $180; all of the rice cookers came with nonstick pots and keep-warm functions (in our opinion, mandatory features).

One other word about purchasing: In the rice cooker world, a cup is not a full measuring cup. Rice cookers use plastic cups that hold about ¾ cup of raw rice, and these are the cups referred to on the packages and in the instruction manuals. A "6-cup rice cooker" cooks up to 4½ standard cups of raw rice, making about 10 cups of cooked rice (a rice-cooker "cup" of rice makes about 2¼ standard cups of cooked rice). Cookers labeled as within the 5- to 6-cup range are the biggest sellers, since they can handle a small amount for 2 to 3 people, but still make 5 ample servings. Buyers beware, though; some manufacturers do not follow this naming protocol. We ordered Rival's "6-cup rice cooker," expecting the same size machine as the others, but the "6 cups" referred to cooked rice, so the cooker was half the size of the others.

Unless you're very particular about your rice texture, cook highly specialized rice types, or want to preset your rice cooker in the morning, we recommend buying a basic Sanyo or Zojirushi electric rice cooker. For a reasonable price, they delivered consistently good white, brown, and sushi rice, and the keep-warm option delivered well-cooked rice even after more than two hours.

A final note: Each rice cooker came with a small plastic paddle for stirring and serving the rice. The paddles for the Zojirushi and Sanyo models have a textured surface (with small bumps) that proved to be very effective in dislodging the rice—especially sticky sushi rice—and were very easy to wash. We recommend these paddles even if you prefer to cook rice in a saucepan. You can buy a textured paddle at www.fantes.com for $2.79, item #42011.

Rating Rice Cookers

WE TESTED EIGHT RICE COOKERS, RATING THEM ON THE QUALITY OF RICE COOKED (RICES INCLUDED WHITE RICE, brown rice, and sushi rice), efficiency, ease of use, and special features. Please note that capacity refers to a standard cup measurement of raw rice. Brands are listed in order of preference. See www.americastestkitchen.com for updates to this testing.

RECOMMENDED
Sanyo Electric Rice Cooker & Steamer, Model ECJ-N55W, 5½ cups
$54.95; Capacity: 4⅛ cups

The Sanyo excelled with all three types of rice, especially the brown rice, and it was our second-lowest-priced model. Two minor complaints: After two hours in the keep-warm stage the rice became a bit dry, and the indicator lights were hard to read in a bright kitchen.

RECOMMENDED
Zojirushi Electric Rice Cooker/Warmer, Model NS-PC10, 5 cup
$79.99; Capacity: 3¾ cups

The Zojirushi also excelled at cooking all three types of rice, and the keep-warm function performed well. However, unlike all the other brands, Zojirushi did not provide steamer baskets with their cookers.

RECOMMENDED
Zojirushi Neuro Fuzzy Rice Cooker and Warmer, Model NS-ZCC10, 5½ cup
$179.99; Capacity: 4⅛ cups

The Fuzzy produced excellent rice, though the 1-cup test produced slightly softer rice than the 3-cup. Like all of the computerized versions, a menu option (rather than an on/off lever) allows you to fine-tune the machine for a variety of rice types and textures—but at the price of a lengthy cooking time.

RECOMMENDED
Sanyo Micro-Computerized Rice Cooker/Warmer, Model ECJ-D55S, 5½ cup
$114.94; Capacity: 4⅛ cups

Similar to the Zojirushi, the Sanyo offers two extra features: a countdown clock to keep you informed of when the rice should be done and a steamer basket. Some slight inconsistency in grain texture in the brown rice test.

RECOMMENDED
Panasonic Rice Cooker/Steamer, Model SR-TMB10, 5½ cup
$75.83; Capacity: 4⅛ cups

The rice (both white and brown) made in this cooker was softer in texture than the rice cooked in the others—it lacked the slight bite we prefer. We also found the inside lid somewhat hard to clean.

RECOMMENDED
Panasonic Electronic Rice Cooker/Warmer with Advanced Fuzzy Logic Technology, Model SR-NA10, 5½ cup
$104.63; Capacity: 4⅛ cups

We had problems with the brown rice in this model. On one attempt the rice was finished in over 2 hours, but it was still mushy and lacked a nutty flavor. The white and sushi rice, however, were well cooked.

RECOMMENDED WITH RESERVATIONS
Breville Gourmet Rice Duo Cooker, Model BRC350XL, 10 cup
$59.95; Capacity: 7½ cups

This model cooked the rice a bit unevenly; it was the only cooker that created a brown layer on the bottom. But the primary problem was its ability to keep the rice warm. The rice lost temperature fast and hardened into a block.

NOT RECOMMENDED
Rival Rice Cooker, Model RC61, 6 cup
$14.99; Capacity: 2½ cups

This cooker had a serious consistency issue. In the same batch of white rice some of the grains were cooked well, but others were blown out. And the cooker had worse problems with brown rice; some grains were blown out, and some were undercooked.

Chris watches as Becky carefully cuts a pocket in the turkey's breast meat to hold herb paste. In addition, she'll rub paste over the breast, thigh, and drumstick meat. The result? Roast turkey that's rich with vibrant herb flavor.

ONE GREAT Thanksgiving

We can't imagine that anyone would be disappointed with a traditional roasted turkey on Thanksgiving. After all, there's something to be said for tradition. But what if the annual roast turkey were tweaked a bit with the fresh flavor of herbs? That's a change we'd welcome. In most recipes we've come across, the turkey cavity is stuffed with a handful of herbs, or chopped herbs and butter are rubbed under the turkey skin. And the results? Barely noticeable flavor. We didn't want a turkey with superficial herb flavor—we wanted one in which every forkful of meat is infused with the bright, fresh flavor of herbs, and we'd roast as many turkeys as it took to get there.

One Thanksgiving tradition we'd never mess with is mashed potatoes. But is there an easier way to produce them? For mashed spuds with deep potato flavor, we boil them in their jackets. But peeling hot potatoes is an onerous task—not to mention the burnt fingers that are often the result from this last-minute step. Our goal was to rethink our method and come up with an easier alternative that didn't sacrifice scorched fingers for great mashed potatoes.

HERBED ROAST TURKEY

WHAT WE WANTED: A fresher alternative to the usual holiday bird—moist roast turkey packed with bright herb flavor.

This Thanksgiving, we decided to forgo the safe and reliable (aka boring) plain roasted bird for something riskier but potentially more flavorful and exciting: an herbed roast turkey. Now, let it be said that in prior years we have tried merely throwing a bunch of herbs into the cavity or rubbing the outside of the bird with a savory paste. The results were, at best, no better than the usual roasted bird and, at worst, just downright weird or blotched in appearance. We didn't want merely to flirt with the idea of great herb flavor; we wanted it in each and every bite.

At the outset, we knew we would stick to several of our established turkey-roasting procedures: brining the turkey, roasting it starting breast side down, and flipping it over to finish breast side up. (This technique, our testing has shown, is the one sure way to keep the white meat from overcooking before the rest of the bird is done.) Also, we weren't exactly starting our quest for intense herb flavor at square one. Recently, the test kitchen developed a recipe that calls for applying a spice rub onto the skin, directly onto the flesh (under the skin), and onto the walls of the cavity. We knew that this three-pronged approach could provide worlds more herb flavor than simply garnishing the cavity with a sprig or two of unprocessed herbage, and it was a fine starting point. But to get the herbal intensity we were after—powerful, aromatic flavor that permeated well beyond the meat's surface—more hard-core measures were called for: We would have to go in deep.

As we gathered an arsenal of excavation tools that might come in handy during our journey to the center of the bird, an idea hit. Was there a way to reach the turkey's depths without actually piercing the flesh? After all, brining had proved an effective method for infusing salt and moisture. Could we use this less invasive procedure to, well, kill two birds

with one stone? Temporarily pushing aside our collection of knives, shears, and syringes, we set about creating an herb-infused brine. We boiled some fresh herbs in water, strained out the solids, stirred in the salt, then "herb-brined" the turkey for six hours. But the experiment was a bust; the fresh herbs contributed hardly any additional flavor. Interestingly, we did get powerful results when we repeated the experiment using dried herbs—too powerful. This time the meat had an overwhelming, perfumed flavor that tasters found more "pickled" than herb-infused. Brining good, pickling bad; we had to come up with a powerful herb infusion method, but one that we could control.

Taking a step back, we experimented with a poke-and-fill approach. We carefully made multiple incisions

throughout the breast and thigh meat and spooned the herb paste into the slots. Instead of a beautiful Thanksgiving dinner centerpiece, however, we got a turkey with puncture wounds oozing green stuff. (Too bad Halloween had already come and gone.) But what if the points of insertion were not as large and ghastly? Reaching for a solid food injector, we pumped the paste into several key spots throughout the meat. Although more attractive than our previous, slasher-film-ready turkey, this version left us with the same condensed blobs of overwhelmingly strong, raw-tasting herbs. What's more, the deeper layers of meat were still lacking in noticeable herb flavor.

Thus began our attempts at full-frontal bird surgery. To get a thin, even layer of herb paste within the meat, we butterflied each side of the breast, applied the paste to both flaps, then sutured the sides back up using skewers. Finally, we were on the right track! Like a coffee cake with a nice swirl of streusel in the center, this turkey's meat boasted an attractive layer of herbs in every slice, yet still had enough "unherbed" portions to provide welcome contrast. On the downside, the procedure was labor-intensive, and the bird was difficult to flip (the skewers got caught in the roasting rack). Was there a less invasive (and less tacky-looking) way to achieve similar results?

Racking our brains for ideas, we borrowed a technique the test kitchen had developed for stuffing a thick-cut pork chop. Using a paring knife, we made a 1½-inch vertical slit in the breast meat and created an expansive pocket by sweeping the blade back and forth, being careful not to increase the size of the original slit on the surface. This newly created void covered an interior surface area nearly as large as the one in the butterflied breasts. Into this space we rubbed a small amount of herb paste (too much, and the herbs began to taste raw and strangely medicinal). This method yielded flavor that was just as good as that of the butterflied version. Who would have thought that treating a turkey like a pork chop was the secret to true herb flavor?

Now that we'd upped the three-pronged method we'd started with to a four-pronged affair, we realized that rearranging the order of our herbal assaults made sense. We began by applying the paste underneath the skin (directly onto the flesh), then inside the newly created pockets (reversing these two steps caused the skin at the incision site to widen and tear), inside the cavity, and, finally, over the skin.

Until now our herb paste had been a combination of parsley, sage, rosemary, and thyme. It was time to focus on its details. When used alone in large quantities, strong herbs such as piney rosemary and minty sage were overpowering and needed to be balanced with the softer flavors of lemony thyme and fresh, grassy parsley. As a general rule, the more pungent the herb, the less we used in the blend (less sage than thyme, and even less rosemary than sage). Alliums—minced shallot and garlic—boosted the savory, aromatic qualities of the mixture, and a minimal amount of lemon zest contributed a fresh, bright note. (Too much, however, left tasters complaining of artificial, "Pledge-like" off-notes.)

In terms of paste construction, some fat was necessary, but too much thwarted the crisping of the skin. Although melted butter tasted great, it also tended to congeal on the cold surface of the turkey. Olive oil and a small amount of Dijon mustard, on the other hand, smoothed the mixture out into a fairly emulsified, easily spreadable paste.

Once our herb-swathed turkey was roasted to perfection, allowed to rest, and carved up, we watched as tasters marveled over its fancy appearance and deep, fragrant aroma. Plain Jane no more, this tasty bird would liven up any holiday table.

WHAT WE LEARNED: For serious herb flavor, the usual tactics—rubbing an herb paste on the skin, underneath the skin, and in the cavity of the bird—are a good start, but they're not enough. To get maximum herb flavor in every bite, create large pockets in the meat to hold a small amount of herb paste. Combine parsley, thyme, sage, and rosemary for the right balance of herb flavor, and add a little oil and Dijon mustard to turn the herbs into a flavorful, spreadable paste.

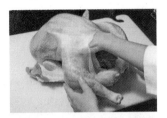

1. Carefully separate the skin from the meat on the breast, thigh, and drumstick areas.

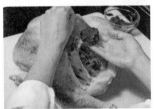

2. Rub the herb paste under the skin and directly onto the flesh, distributing it evenly.

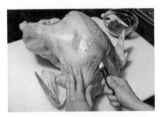

3. Make a 1½-inch slit in each breast. Swing a knife tip through the breast to create a large pocket.

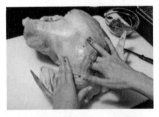

4. Place a thin layer of paste inside each pocket.

5. Rub the remaining paste inside the turkey cavity and on the skin.

HERBED ROAST TURKEY

serves 10 to 12

Note that kosher salt measures differently from table salt, and brands of kosher salt also measure differently from each other. If roasting an 18- to 22-pound bird, double all of the ingredients for the herb paste except the black pepper; apply 2 tablespoons paste under the skin on each side of the turkey, 1½ tablespoons paste in each breast pocket, 2 tablespoons inside the cavity, and the remaining paste on the turkey skin. Roast breast side down at 425 degrees for 1 hour, then reduce the oven temperature to 325 degrees, rotate the turkey breast side up, and continue to roast for about 2 hours. Let rest 35 to 40 minutes before carving.

If roasting a 14- to 18-pound bird, increase the amount all of the ingredients for the herb paste (except the black pepper) by 50 percent; follow the instructions below for applying the paste under the skin, in the breast pockets, and in the cavity; use the remaining paste on the skin. Increase the second half of the roasting time (breast side up) to 1 hour, 15 minutes.

If you have the time and the refrigerator space, air-drying produces extremely crisp skin and is worth the effort. After brining, rinsing, and patting the turkey dry, place the turkey breast side up on a flat wire rack set over a rimmed baking sheet and refrigerate, uncovered, 8 to 24 hours. Proceed with the recipe. Serve with Easy Turkey Gravy (recipe follows), if desired.

turkey and brine

2 cups table salt, 2½ cups Morton Kosher Salt, or 4 cups Diamond Crystal Kosher Salt (see note)

1 (12- to 14-pound) turkey, rinsed thoroughly, giblets and neck reserved for gravy (if making), tailpiece removed

herb paste

1¼ cups roughly chopped fresh parsley leaves

4 teaspoons minced fresh thyme leaves

2 teaspoons roughly chopped fresh sage leaves

1½ teaspoons minced fresh rosemary leaves

1 medium shallot, minced (about 3 tablespoons)

2 medium garlic cloves, minced or pressed through a garlic press (about 2 teaspoons)

¾ teaspoon grated zest from 1 lemon

¾ teaspoon table salt

1 teaspoon ground black pepper

1 teaspoon Dijon mustard

¼ cup olive oil

1. FOR THE TURKEY AND BRINE: Dissolve the salt in 2 gallons cold water in a large stockpot or clean bucket. Add the turkey and refrigerate 4 to 6 hours.

2. Remove the turkey from the brine and rinse under cool running water. Pat dry inside and out with paper towels. Place the turkey breast side up on a flat wire rack set over a rimmed baking sheet or roasting pan and refrigerate, uncovered, for 30 minutes. (Alternatively, air-dry the turkey; see note.)

3. FOR THE HERB PASTE: Pulse the parsley, thyme, sage, rosemary, shallot, garlic, lemon zest, salt, and pepper in a food processor until the consistency of coarse paste, ten 2-second pulses. Add the mustard and olive oil; continue to pulse until the mixture forms a smooth paste, ten to twelve 2-second pulses; scrape the sides of the processor bowl with a rubber spatula after 5 pulses. Transfer the mixture to a small bowl.

4. TO PREPARE THE TURKEY: Adjust an oven rack to the lowest position and heat the oven to 400 degrees. Line a large V-rack with heavy-duty foil and use a paring knife or skewer to poke 20 to 30 holes in the foil; set the V-rack in a large roasting pan. Remove the turkey from the refrigerator and wipe away any water collected in the baking sheet; set the turkey breast side up on the baking sheet.

5. Using your hands, carefully loosen the skin from the meat of the breasts, thighs, and drumsticks. Using your fingers or a spoon, slip 1½ tablespoons of the paste under the breast skin

---

TECHNIQUE: Carving the Breast

The wings and legs on our Herbed Roast Turkey can be carved just as they would be on any other turkey, but the breast, which is stuffed with herb paste, needs some special attention. Here's how to ensure that every slice has a nice swirl of herbs.

  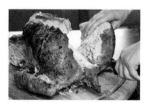 

1. With wings facing toward you, cut along both sides of the breastbone, slicing from the tip of the breastbone to the cutting board.

2. Gently pull each breast half away to expose the wishbone. Then, pull and remove the wishbone.

3. Using the knife tip, cut along the rib cage to remove the breast completely.

4. Place the entire breast half on a cutting board and cut on the bias into thin slices. Repeat step 3 on the other side.

on each side of the turkey. Using your fingers, distribute the paste under the skin over the breast, thigh, and drumstick meat.

6. Using a sharp paring knife, cut a 1½-inch vertical slit into the thickest part of each side of the breast. Starting from the top of the incision, swing the knife tip down to create a 4- to 5-inch pocket within the flesh. Place 1 tablespoon more paste in the pocket of each side of the breast; using your fingers, rub the paste in a thin, even layer.

7. Rub 1 tablespoon more paste inside the turkey cavity. Rotate the turkey breast side down; apply half the remaining herb paste to the turkey skin; flip the turkey breast side up and apply the remaining herb paste to the skin, pressing and patting to make the paste adhere; reapply the herb paste that falls onto the baking sheet. Tuck the wings behind the

back and tuck the tips of the drumsticks into the skin at the tail to secure.

8. TO ROAST THE TURKEY: Place the turkey breast side down on the prepared V-rack in the roasting pan. Roast 45 minutes.

9. Remove the roasting pan with the turkey from the oven (close the oven door to retain the oven heat). Using clean potholders (or a wad of paper towels), rotate the turkey breast side up. Continue to roast until the thickest part of the breast registers 165 degrees and the thickest part of the thigh registers 170 to 175 degrees on an instant-read thermometer, 50 to 60 minutes longer. (Confirm the temperature by inserting the thermometer in both sides of the bird.) Transfer the turkey to a carving board; let rest 30 minutes. Carve the turkey and serve.

EASY GRAVY

makes about 2 cups

Adding roasted turkey drippings will enhance the gravy's flavor. Using a food processor to chop the vegetables is not only easier, but it actually helps to release their moisture so they brown more quickly. Adding drippings from the roasted turkey will enhance the flavor of the gravy.

1 small carrot, peeled and chopped coarse
1 small celery rib, chopped coarse
1 small onion, chopped coarse
3 tablespoons unsalted butter
¼ cup unbleached all-purpose flour
2 cups low-sodium chicken broth
2 cups low-sodium beef broth
1 bay leaf
2 sprigs fresh thyme
5 whole black peppercorns
  Defatted pan drippings from Herbed Roast
  Turkey (see note); optional
  Salt and ground black pepper

1. Pulse the carrot into ¼-inch pieces in a food processor, about 5 pulses. Add the celery and onion and continue to pulse until all of the vegetables are finely chopped, 5 pulses.

2. Melt the butter in a large saucepan over medium-high heat. Add the vegetables and cook, stirring often, until softened and well browned, about 7 minutes. Reduce the heat to medium, stir in the flour, and cook, stirring constantly, until well browned, about 5 minutes.

3. Gradually whisk in the broths until smooth. Bring to a boil, skimming any foam that rises to the surface. Add the bay leaf, thyme, and peppercorns. Reduce the heat to medium-low and simmer, stirring occasionally, until the gravy is thickened and measures about 3 cups, 20 to 25 minutes. Stir in any juices from the roasted meat (if using) and continue to simmer the gravy as needed to re-thicken.

4. Strain the gravy through a fine-mesh strainer into a serving pitcher, pressing on the solids to extract as much liquid as possible; discard the solids. Season the gravy with salt and pepper to taste and cover to keep warm until needed. Serve hot.

TESTING NOTES:
Imparting Herb Flavor

We stopped at (almost) nothing to pack our roast turkey with herb flavor. Here are two of our more unorthodox, and less successful, attempts.

More Ooze than Aahs
Multiple incisions stuffed with herb paste looked like puncture wounds oozing green stuff.

Post-Op Complications
Intricate surgery gave us the flavor we wanted, but certainly not the right look. And the procedure was truly unwieldy.

FLUFFY MASHED POTATOES

WHAT WE WANTED: Creamy, fluffy mashed potatoes, full of earthy potato flavor, without the cumbersome, last-minute step of peeling hot spuds.

Our favorite mashed potato recipe calls for boiling whole potatoes in their jackets, then peeling and mashing them right before serving. Keeping the skins on during cooking yields the best potato flavor, but the method itself isn't all that convenient. After boiling the potatoes for 30 minutes, there you are, right before dinner, burning your fingers on hot skins. We decided it was time to revisit this recipe to come up with something that allowed a little more of the prep work to be done in advance.

Ask people their favorite way to make mashed potatoes, and most will say the same thing: They peel the skins, chop the spuds, then throw them into a pot of cold water to boil. We like cooking the potatoes in their jackets because it keeps the earthy potato flavor from leaching out into the water, and also because we find it yields the creamiest texture. The skins prevent the starch granules in the potato cells from absorbing too much water and bursting like overfilled water balloons when mashed, spilling their sticky, gluey contents into the mix. But to meet our goal of cutting back on last-minute prep, clearly the skins would have to go before cooking. Waterlogged starch granules, then, were a given. Was there a way to prevent at least some of them from bursting?

One way is to use a ricer, rather than a potato masher, to finish the dish. Potatoes pass through the sieve-like hopper of this tool only once, avoiding the repeated abuse of mashing. (Pounding already-mashed portions over and over greatly increases the chance of bursting starch granules.) Ricing aside, what else could we do?

We tried a lot of unlikely techniques, most of which yielded poor results. One bright light during this early testing was a recipe in Jeffrey Steingarten's book *The Man Who*

Ate Everything that employed a technique invented by the instant-mashed-potato industry. Steingarten partially cooks the spuds in simmering water, drains and rinses them under cool water, and sets them aside for half an hour. Once fully cooled, the potatoes are cooked again and mashed. Cooling the potatoes partway through cooking causes the sticky gel in the starch granules to crystallize and become resistant to dissolving in water or milk (even if the cell walls surrounding them subsequently rupture), leading to fluffier potatoes. The only problem: This meant cooking potatoes for over an hour in numerous changes of hot and cold water. This was not the "advance prep" we had in mind.

Another method, recommended on the Web site of the Idaho Potato Board, was simpler and equally intriguing. To avoid gluey mashed potatoes, the site suggests a two-step cooking process of starting the potatoes in actively boiling water (rather than the traditional cold water) and then immediately reducing the temperature to keep the water at a bare simmer. After 20 minutes, you crank up the heat and boil the spuds until soft. The idea is to keep the pectin that glues individual potato cells together (and helps keep water out) from degrading too quickly. At temperatures below the boiling point, the pectin won't dissolve and can continue to act as a barrier to water.

Tasted side by side with conventional one-step potatoes started in cold water, the two-step spuds were definitely lighter. But they still tasted thinner and more watery than the potatoes cooked with their jackets on. To get both fluffy consistency and great flavor, we were going to have to keep excess water from getting into the starch granules in the first place. Why not just forget simmering and boiling and go with a method that would expose the potatoes to little or no water?

Baking the potatoes was out—it would take too long (plus, if we cooked potatoes with their skins on, we were back where we started). Microwaving produced a starchy, pasty mash. Steaming was our best bet.

We fashioned a steamer by placing a colander in a Dutch oven, then brought a few inches of water to a boil. We peeled, cut, and rinsed the spuds (to remove any surface starch) and dropped them into the colander. About 20 minutes later, the potatoes were soft and ready for mashing. They were also covered in a sticky substance that we knew to be free amylose, the very thing that turns potatoes gluey (see "Rinsing Is Key," page 186). We tried rinsing the potatoes before ricing to get rid of the amylose, but some of the potato flavor washed away as well, resulting in a mash that was as bland as the two-step potatoes. And the potatoes were now cold. Would rinsing the potatoes earlier in the process, before they got fully cooked, bring us better results?

We put a new batch of spuds into the steamer. Peeking after 10 minutes, we saw they were already covered in gluey amylose. We took the colander out of the pot, rinsed the hot potatoes under cold water for a couple of minutes, then returned them to the pot of still-boiling water to finish cooking. When riced, these potatoes were wonderfully light and fluffy and had the best flavor yet.

Ideally, this recipe should work with a wide range of potatoes: russets, Yukon Golds, red potatoes, and white potatoes. But due to their low starch content, the red potatoes were a bust, tasting bland and uninspiring no matter how much butter was added to the mix. The other potatoes worked fine, but tasters liked the deeper flavor of the Yukon Golds best.

With our cooking method solved and the type of potato chosen, we were ready to tackle the butter and mashing liquid. Up to this point we had been using a stick of butter and a cup of cream. We had been getting complaints all along that the potatoes tasted a little rich—surprising, since these are the very proportions we have loved for so long for mashed potatoes. Could it be that our cooking method was creating so much rich potato flavor on its own that less butter or cream was now necessary? As it turned out—yes. Just 4 tablespoons of butter yielded the right amount of richness. As for liquid, our potatoes needed less than the full cup of cream. Two-thirds of a cup created the right consistency but still left the potatoes too heavy. In head-to-head tests, our tasters actually preferred whole milk to cream or half-and-half.

We now had a fluffy, smooth mash with robust, earthy potato flavor. And we were able to get it on the table without once burning our fingers on hot skins.

WHAT WE LEARNED: Cooking potatoes in their skins preserves their earthy flavor and keeps the starch granules from absorbing too much water, thereby preventing gluey mashed potatoes. But peeling hot potatoes is a hassle. To get creamy, flavorful mashed potatoes without this last-minute inconvenience, peel the potatoes and steam them instead of boiling them in water. When they are cooked partway, rinse them under cold water to rid them of free amylose, the substance that results in gluey mashed potatoes, and return them to the steamer to finish cooking. Because potatoes cooked this way are so full of rich potato flavor, use less butter and whole milk, instead of cream, to finish them.

1. Washing off excess starch from cut potatoes is the first step in preventing dense mashed potatoes.

2. Cooking the potatoes over simmering water maintains flavor and cuts down on burst starches.

3. Rinsing the potatoes half-way through cooking washes away any sticky starches that do burst.

4. Pushing the potatoes through a ricer is another way to prevent the swollen starch granules from bursting.

FLUFFY MASHED POTATOES

serves 4

This recipe works best with either a metal colander that sits easily in a Dutch oven or a large pasta pot with a steamer insert. To prevent excess evaporation, it is important for the lid to fit as snugly as possible over the colander or steamer. For the lightest, fluffiest texture, use a ricer. A food mill is the next best alternative. Russets and white potatoes will work in this recipe, but avoid red-skinned potatoes.

> 2 pounds Yukon Gold potatoes (4 to 6 medium), peeled, cut into 1-inch chunks, rinsed well, and drained (see note)
>
> 4 tablespoons unsalted butter, melted
> Salt
>
> ⅔ cup whole milk, warm
> Ground black pepper

1. Place a metal colander or steamer insert in a large pot or Dutch oven. Add enough water to barely reach the bottom of the colander. Turn the heat to high and bring the water to a boil. Add the potatoes, cover, and reduce the heat to medium-high. Cook the potatoes for 10 minutes. Transfer the colander to the sink and rinse the potatoes under cold water until no longer hot, 1 to 2 minutes. Return the colander and potatoes to the pot, cover, and continue to cook until the potatoes are soft and the tip of a paring knife inserted into the potatoes meets no resistance, 10 to 15 minutes longer. Pour off the water from the pot.

2. Set a ricer or food mill over the now-empty pot. Working in batches, transfer the potatoes to the hopper of the ricer or food mill and process, removing any potatoes stuck to the bottom. Using a rubber spatula, stir in the melted butter and ½ teaspoon salt until incorporated. Stir in the warm milk until incorporated. Season with salt and pepper to taste and serve immediately.

SCIENCE DESK: Rinsing Is Key

WE FOUND THAT RINSING STEAMED POTATOES HALFWAY through cooking produced mashed potatoes with a particularly light and fluffy texture and rich potato flavor. What was going on? Potatoes contain two starches, including one called amylose. If these starch granules absorb too much water during cooking, they will eventually burst, spilling a sticky gel that turns potatoes gluey. Because steaming exposes the potatoes to less water, it reduces the chance that these granules will burst. Some granules will inevitably burst anyway, but rinsing midway through cooking helps remove some of this escaped amylose, resulting in potatoes with a lighter, silkier texture.

Uncooked Starch Granules **Granules Swell with Water** **Swollen Granules Burst**

EQUIPMENT CORNER: Potato Ricers

FOR SILKY-SMOOTH MASHED POTATOES, THE BEST TOOL is a potato ricer—a device that resembles an oversized garlic press. Cooked spuds are loaded into a hopper and squeezed (or "riced") through a sieve-like disk: brilliant, but not complicated. How much difference could there really be from model to model? We pressed our way through six ricers to find out.

Most models riced potatoes acceptably. Beyond that, testers appreciated large hoppers—both of our recommended models hold at least 1¼ cups of sliced potatoes—as well as interchangeable fine and coarse disks; sturdy, ergonomic handles that don't require brute force to squeeze; and a pot extension grip to hold the ricer steady.

Rating Potato Ricers

WE PRESSED OUR WAY THROUGH SIX RICERS TO FIND THE BEST, RATING THEM ON PERFORMANCE AND EASE of use. Brands are listed in order of preference. See www.americastestkitchen.com for updates to this testing.

HIGHLY RECOMMENDED
RSVP International Classic Kitchen Basics Potato Ricer
$11.99
The only plastic model in the mix, this easy-squeezing ricer features a large hopper, interchangeable disks that produce a range of fine to coarse textures, a pot extension grip, and comfortable handles.

RECOMMENDED
Bethany Housewares Heavy-Duty Potato Ricer
$16.99
The hopper of this typical food-service model sports two walls of holes for efficient ricing, but offers no pot grip and is a bit stiff to open.

RECOMMENDED WITH RESERVATIONS
Cuisipro Stainless Steel Potato Ricer
$29.95
On the small side, Cuisipro's hopper holds barely 1 cup of potatoes. Plus, a good portion of those spuds squirted over the top of the mashing plate rather than through the holes.

RECOMMENDED WITH RESERVATIONS
OXO Good Grips Potato Ricer
$20
OXO's trademark rubber grips line the handle of this short (under 1-foot-long) ricer, but they offer little in the way of comfort when it comes to squeezing spuds through its small hopper.

RECOMMENDED WITH RESERVATIONS
MIU France Stainless Steel Potato Presser
$23.07
Relatively good capacity (1¼ cups) and interchangeable disks made this stainless model seem like a decent contender . . . until we loaded up a hopper and tried to squeeze—a near-impossible task.

RECOMMENDED WITH RESERVATIONS
RSVP Endurance Jumbo Stainless Steel Potato Ricer
$24.49
This jumbo model offers a good pot grip and the largest hopper of all, holding nearly 2 cups of potatoes, but squeezing the sharp metal handles left gouges on our hands.

How do we produce a spiral-cut ham that warms through but stays moist and juicy? We soak the ham in hot water prior to cooking and then bake it in an oven bag—both steps prevent the ham from drying out in the oven.

HOLIDAY HAM
CHAPTER 15
and biscuits

For some, Christmas and Easter mean a big, rosy ham at the center of the holiday table. Its salty meat complemented by a sweet glaze is as good fresh out of the oven as it is in leftover form, sliced into sandwiches. But how can something seemingly so simple—just heat and serve—sometimes turn out so dry and jerky-like? Does the type of ham make a difference? Should you use an oven bag? What about the glaze? How do you make one that's sweet but not saccharine? These are just a few of the questions we set out to address in our quest for a top-notch glazed ham—one that is always moist and tender.

Biscuits are a must alongside ham, especially if you're from the South. No-fuss drop biscuits, where the batter is simply scooped right onto the baking sheet, are a welcome departure from fussier rolled and cut biscuits. The only problem is that most recipes are stingy with the butter, which results in a leaner flavor. And the mixing method—adding melted butter (or oil) to the flour mixture—results in a texture that could use some improvement. We like the biscuits' craggy crust, but its interior can sometimes be dry or gummy. We set out to revamp this humble biscuit into one that would be holiday-worthy, but still easy to prepare—a no-fuss biscuit that's rich with buttery flavor and boasts a light and fluffy texture.

GLAZED HOLIDAY HAM

WHAT WE WANTED: A foolproof recipe for spiral-sliced ham, brushed with a not-too-sweet glaze that complements—not overwhelms—the meat.

Isn't cooking a ham remarkably simple? You just throw it in the oven, slather on some glaze, and wait. But this approach can often yield inferior results—dried-out, leathery meat that tastes like salty jerky with a sticky, saccharine exterior. Ideally, ham is moist and tender and the glaze complements but doesn't overwhelm the meat. We've cooked hundreds of hams in the test kitchen over the years and have had our share of disasters. We decided to reexamine this topic to learn what really works—and what doesn't.

In most supermarkets, cured hams come in five forms: boneless, semiboneless, bone-in, whole, and half. Each of these types is available unsliced or presliced (often labeled "spiral-sliced"). After cooking up each in the test kitchen, we clearly favored bone-in hams that had been spiral-sliced, since they offered the best flavor with the least amount of postcooking carving. As a rule of thumb, you should allow about ½ pound of ham per person. This takes into consideration any weight lost during cooking as well as the weight of the bone. Unless you are feeding a very large crowd, we recommend a half ham.

With all hams, it is important to read the label. Typically, supermarket hams are wet-cured, a process that involves soaking the ham in brine. During this process, the ham will absorb water and gain weight. Not surprisingly, we found hams that gained the least water weight (labeled "ham with natural juices") taste the best. Avoid hams with labels that read "ham with water added" or "ham and water products."

Whole ham is the entire leg of the animal. Half hams are available in two distinct cuts: shank end (the bottom part of the leg) and sirloin end (the portion of the leg closer to the rump). If labeling is unclear, it's easy to identify half hams by their shape—shank hams have a pointed end much smaller than the larger end, whereas the sirloin (or butt) end is rounded. In the past, we have recommended the shank end for ease of carving, since the bone is relatively straight compared with the odder-shaped bones in the sirloin end. However, in our most recent round of tastings, we found the sirloin end to be meatier and less fatty. If you're up for a slightly more challenging carving job, the larger sirloin end will not disappoint.

There is nothing you have to do to serve a cured and cooked ham other than cut it off the bone. When ham is the centerpiece of a holiday dinner, however, most people prefer to have it served warm, and often with a glaze. After roasting many hams to temperatures ranging from 100 to 160 degrees, we found the ideal temperature to be between 110 and 120 degrees. This was enough to take the chill off the meat without drying it out. Cooking the ham to a higher internal temperature (as many sources suggest) guarantees dry meat.

Most recipes specify cooking the ham at 350 degrees, so by the time the center finally comes up to temperature, the exterior is parched. We roast ham in a 250-degree oven, which lessens the temperature differential between the exterior and the interior. Also, rather than starting with an ice-cold ham, we found that we could cut oven time (and thus drying) by leaving the ham at room temperature for 90 minutes prior to cooking. But could we do even better? Soaking the ham in warm water for 90 minutes raises the temperature considerably and cuts oven time by a full hour. Finally, we've discovered that roasting the ham in an oven bag reduces roasting time even further. (The bag speeds cooking by providing insulation.) Compared with a cold ham shoved into a 350-degree oven, a 10-pound ham cooked by our method loses 50 percent less moisture.

We've found that oven bags produce the moistest ham in the least amount of time. If unavailable, aluminum foil will work, but you will have to add three to four minutes of cooking time per pound of meat (between 21 and 40 minutes for a 7- to 10-pound ham). Remember, less oven time means a moister ham.

Almost all spiral hams come with a packet of premixed glaze and instructions to brush it on the ham while it's cooking. Glaze is a good idea, but the stuff in the packets tastes awful. Take 10 minutes to make your own glaze. Since we cook ham inside an oven bag, we needed to figure out a new approach to glazing. Once the internal temperature of the ham reaches 100 degrees, cut open the bag and increase the oven temperature to 350 degrees. Apply the glaze and bake the ham for 10 minutes. Remove the ham from the oven, apply more glaze, and then make a quick sauce with the remaining glaze and the drippings in the oven bag.

We've found that a 15-minute rest allows the internal temperature to increase by 5 to 15 degrees, which allows us to bake the ham less in order to reach the ideal serving temperature of 110 to 120 degrees. (Cover the ham with foil as it rests.)

WHAT WE LEARNED: Choose a bone-in, spiral-sliced ham for superior flavor and easy carving. Soak the ham in hot water prior to cooking and roast it in an oven bag to reduce the cooking time dramatically (which helps prevent the ham from drying out). Roast the ham until it reaches 110 to 120 degrees to ensure that it will be sufficiently warmed through and moist. Toss the packet of glaze packaged with the ham and instead make your own. Apply a fruit-based glaze (in stages) for modest, rounded sweetness that complements the ham's salty, rich flavor. And for further flavor and moistness, mix some of the reserved glaze with the pan drippings for a quick sauce to serve at the table.

GLAZED SPIRAL-SLICED HAM
serves 12 to 14, with leftovers

You can bypass the 90-minute soaking time, but the heating time will increase to 18 to 20 minutes per pound for a cold ham. If there is a tear or hole in the ham's inner covering, wrap it in several layers of plastic wrap before soaking it in hot water. Instead of using the plastic oven bag, the ham may be placed cut side down in the roasting pan and covered tightly with foil, but you will need to add 3 to 4 minutes per pound to the heating time. If using an oven bag, be sure to cut slits in the bag so it does not burst.

1   (7- to 10-pound) spiral-sliced bone-in half ham
1   large plastic oven bag (see note)
1   recipe glaze (recipes follow)

1. Leaving the ham's inner plastic or foil covering intact, place the ham in a large container and cover with hot tap water; set aside for 45 minutes. Drain and cover again with hot tap water; set aside for another 45 minutes.

2. Adjust an oven rack to the lowest position and heat the oven to 250 degrees. Unwrap the ham; remove and discard the plastic disk covering the bone. Place the ham in the oven bag. Gather the top of the bag tightly so the bag fits snugly around the ham, tie the bag, and trim the excess plastic. Set the ham cut side down in a large roasting pan and cut 4 slits in the top of the bag with a paring knife.

3. Bake the ham until the center registers 100 degrees on an instant-read thermometer, 1 to 1½ hours (about 10 minutes per pound).

4. Remove the ham from the oven and increase the oven temperature to 350 degrees. Cut open the oven bag and roll back the sides to expose the ham. Brush the ham with one-third of the glaze and return to the oven until the glaze

Sirloin End
The meatier option, but the bones make it harder to carve.

Shank End
Easy to carve, but not quite as meaty.

TECHNIQUE: How to Keep a Ham Moist

A big ham can take hours to heat through in the oven, by which time the meat becomes very dry. We found two tricks for reducing oven time and increasing moisture retention.

Soaking
Placing the wrapped ham in warm water for 90 minutes raises its internal temperature and decreases the cooking time by over an hour.

Wrapping
Cooking the ham in an oven bag reduces the oven time by another half hour or so.

becomes sticky, about 10 minutes (if the glaze is too thick to brush, return it to the heat to loosen).

5. Remove the ham from the oven, transfer to a cutting board, and brush the entire ham with another third of the glaze. Let the ham rest, loosely tented with foil, for 15 minutes. While the ham rests, heat the remaining third of the glaze with 4 to 6 tablespoons of the ham juices until it forms a thick but fluid sauce. Carve and serve the ham, passing the sauce at the table.

MAPLE-ORANGE GLAZE
makes 1 cup, enough to glaze 1 ham

¾	cup maple syrup
½	cup orange marmalade
2	tablespoons unsalted butter
1	tablespoon Dijon mustard
1	teaspoon ground black pepper
¼	teaspoon ground cinnamon

Combine all the ingredients in a small saucepan. Cook over medium heat, stirring occasionally, until the mixture is thick, syrupy, and reduced to 1 cup, 5 to 10 minutes; set aside.

CHERRY-PORT GLAZE
makes 1 cup, enough to glaze 1 ham

½	cup ruby port
½	cup cherry preserves
1	cup packed dark brown sugar
1	teaspoon ground black pepper

Simmer the port in a small saucepan over medium heat until reduced to 2 tablespoons, about 5 minutes. Add the remaining ingredients and cook, stirring occasionally, until the sugar dissolves and the mixture is thick, syrupy, and reduced to 1 cup, 5 to 10 minutes; set aside.

BEST DROP BISCUITS

WHAT WE WANTED: A simple, no-fuss drop biscuit that's as buttery and satisfying as its fussier rolled biscuit counterpart.

Of the countless styles of biscuit out there, our favorite is the simple but often forgotten drop biscuit. This rustic biscuit offers a unique duality of textures: a crisp and craggy golden brown exterior full of hills and valleys and a tender, fluffy interior. It's the savory, stand-alone cousin of shortcake or cobbler topping. Unlike fairly pale, flat-topped, uniformly tender baking-powder biscuits that are split in half and buttered, drop biscuits are meant to be broken apart and eaten as is, piece by buttery piece.

Both types of biscuit use the same handful of ingredients and are quick to prepare, but drop biscuits don't rely on any of the finicky steps rolled biscuits require to get them just right. There's no need to cut super-cold butter into the dry ingredients. Kneading and rolling are not necessary, so you don't have to worry about overworking the dough. And there's no fussy biscuit cutter or rerolling of the scraps. Drop biscuits barely require a recipe. Flour, leavener, and salt are combined in a bowl; the wet ingredients (milk or buttermilk and either melted butter or vegetable oil) are stirred together in a measuring cup; the wet ingredients are stirred into the dry ingredients; and the resulting batter (which is wetter than traditional biscuit dough) is scooped up and dropped onto a baking sheet.

We headed into the test kitchen to try a sampling of drop biscuit recipes. The techniques were as simple as we'd expected, but the texture of the biscuits often fell short, and the flavor was uninspiring. If they weren't dense, gummy, and doughy, our test biscuits were lean and dry. The generous amounts of leavener in most recipes gave the biscuits a bitter, metallic flavor. But the recipes that called for less than 1 tablespoon of baking powder produced biscuits that were heavy and squat. Evidently, you need a lot of leavener to compensate for the lack of cold chunks of butter that produce steam and assist with the rise in classic rolled biscuits.

Still, we had made some progress during this first round of testing. Oil-based biscuits were easy to work with but lacked the most important element: buttery flavor. So butter was a must. We'd also come to some conclusions about the flour.

Some rolled biscuits use softer, low-protein Southern brands of flour or a mixture of cake and all-purpose flours to achieve a light, cottony-soft texture, but neither of these improved the texture of the drop biscuits. Instead, because the dough isn't kneaded—and therefore not much gluten development occurs—these softer flours made the biscuits too delicate and unable to form a substantial crust. We stuck with regular all-purpose flour, which provided the structure the drop biscuits needed.

Our working recipe contained 2 cups of flour, 1 tablespoon of baking powder, ¾ teaspoon of salt, ¾ cup of milk, and 6 tablespoons of melted butter. Once the wet and dry ingredients were just combined, we used a ¼-cup dry measure to scoop the batter onto a parchment-lined baking sheet and baked the biscuits in a 475-degree oven. Although the results were definitely better than for some of the recipes we'd tried early on, these biscuits were still far from perfect: They weren't quite buttery enough and they still tasted of leavener.

Increasing the amount of butter to 8 tablespoons answered our tasters' demand for deeper butter flavor, but something was still missing. Since milk didn't seem to be adding much flavor, we were tempted to try other dairy products in its place. Yogurt provided a tangy complexity, but at the price of unwanted gumminess. Sour cream made the biscuits way too rich. Buttermilk offered the best of both worlds: biscuits that had a rich, buttery tang and were also texturally appealing—crisper on the exterior and fluffier on the interior. Increasing the amount of buttermilk to a full cup amplified these effects.

Although one might think that more liquid would make the biscuits heavier and less crisp, just the opposite was happening. Discussions with several scientists cleared up the confusion. The more liquid we added to the dough, the more steam was created in the hot oven. This steam acts as a powerful leavener, which, in conjunction with the chemical leaveners, lightens the texture of the biscuits. And just as water sprayed on rustic bread dough helps crisp its crust, the additional steam was making the exterior of our biscuits seriously craggy, almost crunchy.

Switching to buttermilk meant that baking soda (not just baking powder) was now an option, as the soda would react with the acid in the buttermilk. After trying various combinations of baking soda and baking powder, we settled on what ended up being a fairly standard ratio for traditional rolled buttermilk biscuits: 2 teaspoons of baking powder to ½ teaspoon of baking soda. We knew we'd succeeded when the biscuits rose properly and we could no longer taste any metallic bitterness. As an added bonus, the baking soda aided browning, giving the biscuits a darker, more attractive crust. A mere teaspoon of sugar brought all the flavors into balance without making the biscuits sweet.

There was just one aspect of our recipe that continued to bother us: the need to get the temperatures of the buttermilk and melted butter just right. For a quick and simple recipe, having to wait for two things to happen—for the buttermilk to come to room temperature and for the melted butter to cool—in order for them to emulsify properly seemed like a hassle. But whenever we were impatient and tried to get away with combining the melted butter with straight-from-the-refrigerator buttermilk, the butter would start to form clumps. No matter how hard we whisked the mixture, the bits of butter would stubbornly remain.

In most cases, lumpy buttermilk is considered a mistake, but we wondered what would happen if we actually tried to use this mixture. Maybe the effects wouldn't be too noticeable. To find out, we made one batch of biscuits with a completely smooth buttermilk mixture and another with lumpy buttermilk. Compared side by side, the biscuits made with the lumpy buttermilk rose slightly higher and had a more distinct textural contrast between interior and exterior than did the batch made with the smooth buttermilk mixture.

A "mistake" turned out to be the final secret to our recipe. The lumps of butter turned to steam in the oven and helped create more rise. The clumpy buttermilk seemed to mimic the positive effects of making biscuits the old-fashioned way—with bits of cold butter left in the dough—but this method was better on two counts: It was more reliable and less messy. The only hard part was having the patience to wait for the biscuits to cool down before grabbing one to eat.

WHAT WE LEARNED: Choose butter (over oil) for the best flavor. The duo of baking soda and baking powder encourages a high rise, all-purpose flour provides the right structure, and a full cup of buttermilk gives the biscuits an ideal texture—crisp on the outside and fluffy on the inside (the liquid creates steam, which helps the biscuits rise). Add buttermilk straight from the fridge to the melted butter (rather than waiting for it to come to room temperature); the mixture will be lumpy, but the lumps mimic the effect of bits of cold butter used in old-fashioned rolled biscuits. These lumps help create more steam, which results in a high rise and superior texture.

BEST DROP BISCUITS

makes 12 biscuits

If buttermilk isn't available, powdered buttermilk added according to package instructions or clabbered milk can be used instead. To make clabbered milk, mix 1 cup milk with 1 tablespoon lemon juice and let stand 10 minutes. A ¼-cup (#16) portion scoop can be used to portion the batter. To refresh day-old biscuits, heat them in a 300-degree oven for 10 minutes.

2 cups (10 ounces) unbleached all-purpose flour
2 teaspoons baking powder
½ teaspoon baking soda
1 teaspoon sugar
¾ teaspoon salt
1 cup cold buttermilk (see note)
8 tablespoons unsalted butter, melted and cooled slightly (about 5 minutes), plus 2 tablespoons melted butter for brushing the biscuits

1. Adjust an oven rack to the middle position and heat the oven to 475 degrees. Line a large, rimmed baking sheet with parchment paper. Whisk together the flour, baking powder, baking soda, sugar, and salt in a large bowl. Combine the buttermilk and 8 tablespoons of the melted butter in a medium bowl, stirring until the butter forms small clumps.

2. Add the buttermilk mixture to the dry ingredients and stir with a rubber spatula until just incorporated and the batter pulls away from the sides of the bowl. Using a greased ¼-cup dry measure, scoop a level amount of batter and drop onto the prepared baking sheet (the biscuits should measure about 2¼ inches in diameter and 1¼ inches high). Repeat with the remaining batter, spacing the biscuits about 1½ inches apart. Bake until the tops are golden brown and crisp, 12 to 14 minutes.

TECHNIQUE: Scoop, Drop, and Bake
A greased ¼-cup measure is a great tool for scooping dough onto a parchment-lined baking sheet.

3. Brush the biscuit tops with the remaining 2 tablespoons melted butter. Transfer to a wire rack and let cool 5 minutes before serving.

VARIATIONS

BLACK PEPPER AND BACON DROP BISCUITS

Cut 6 strips bacon in half lengthwise and then crosswise into ¼-inch pieces; fry in a 10-inch nonstick skillet over medium heat until crisp, 5 to 7 minutes. Using a slotted spoon, transfer the bacon to a paper towel–lined plate and cool to room temperature. Follow the recipe for Best Drop Biscuits, adding the crisp bacon and 1 teaspoon coarsely ground black pepper to the flour mixture in step 1.

CHEDDAR AND SCALLION DROP BISCUITS

Follow the recipe for Best Drop Biscuits, adding ½ cup (2 ounces) shredded cheddar cheese and ¼ cup thinly sliced scallions to the flour mixture in step 1.

ROSEMARY AND PARMESAN DROP BISCUITS

Follow the recipe for Best Drop Biscuits, adding ¾ cup (1½ ounces) grated Parmesan cheese and ½ teaspoon finely minced fresh rosemary leaves to the flour mixture in step 1.

Rating Orange Marmalade

TWENTY MEMBERS OF THE AMERICA'S TEST KITCHEN STAFF TASTED EIGHT BRANDS OF ORANGE MARMALADE PLAIN and with dry toast. Brands are listed in order of preference. See www.americastestkitchen.com for updates to this tasting.

RECOMMENDED
Trappist Seville Orange Marmalade
$3.79 for 12 ounces

This brand earned many points for its natural orange flavor and was also the favorite of our tasters who liked a solid level of sweetness as well as a moderate amount of tartness, which they defined as grapefruit-level. Tasters also liked the balance of rind to jelly as well as the marmalade's consistency—it was praised as an excellent spreading marmalade.

RECOMMENDED
Hero Swiss Marmalade
$3.39 for 12 ounces

This brand had the "truest" and strongest orange flavor of our samples. Many testers also relished the Hero's bracing bitterness, praising it for being straightforward in flavor. The rind was appreciated for its nice chew and zesty flavor. Some tasters did complain that the jelly was a little runny, making it a bit problematic to spread.

RECOMMENDED
Smucker's Sweet Orange Marmalade
$2.19 for 12 ounces

Tasters who like sweet marmalade enjoyed the Smucker's floral orange flavor and noted that the rind wasn't bitter at all, tasting like candied orange (Smucker's does not use Seville oranges). Others, however, thought the sweetness was cloying. Its relish-like texture was perfect for spreading on toast.

RECOMMENDED WITH RESERVATIONS
Crosse & Blackwell Orange Marmalade
$3.69 for 12 ounces

Tasters liked the texture and flavor of the rind (this brand specified Seville oranges), but many were not complimentary of the jelly component, which was considered too clear and light, "like apple jelly with orange peels in it."

RECOMMENDED WITH RESERVATIONS
Chivers Olde English Orange Marmalade
$4.59 for 12 ounces

Both Chivers and Dundee (see below) were distinguishable from the other samples due to dark color and large, chewy pieces of rind. Some tasters liked the caramelized flavor and found the rind very tasty, with full citrus flavor, but many others thought the spread tasted burnt, with an alcohol residue that masked the orange flavor. Its thickness also made the marmalade difficult to spread.

RECOMMENDED WITH RESERVATIONS
Dundee Orange Marmalade
$6.99 for 16 ounces

The Dundee earned comments similar to the Chivers. Tasters were split as to whether the caramel flavor prevented the spread from being too candy-like (a good thing) or gave it a sour taste. Tasters also picked up an alcohol flavor; those who liked it compared the flavor to brandy. It was also difficult to spread on toast.

NOT RECOMMENDED
Smucker's Sugar Free Orange Marmalade
$2.79 for 12.75 ounces

Smucker's uses Splenda for its sugar-free marmalade, but it didn't fool the tasters. The spread was criticized for tasting fake, being overly sweet, and having a texture reminiscent of Jell-O—tasters compared it to an orange Creamsicle or chewy orange soda.

NOT RECOMMENDED
Bonne Maman Orange Marmalade
$3.39 for 13 ounces

Tasters gave the Bonne Maman poor ratings because of minimal orange flavor, uninteresting texture (runny consistency), and a flat overall taste. Tasters also found a strange, chemical aftertaste, with one comparing it to an "orange-scented house cleaner."

TASTING LAB: Orange Marmalade

ORANGE MARMALADE IS A FRUIT PRESERVE THAT includes pieces of rind in the jelly base. Because of the sour tang derived from both the rind and the flesh of the Seville oranges customarily used as the base fruit, good orange marmalade should have a complexity and depth not associated with sweeter jams and jellies.

We rounded up eight readily available orange marmalades to see if we could find that agreeable complexity in marmalade sold at supermarket prices. Tasters sampled each marmalade straight and with pieces of dry toast. When the results were tallied, we found both consensus and division. Those earning a "recommended" rating had the strongest natural orange flavor, those given a "recommended with reservations" rating had some, and those ranked "not recommended" had only a chemical orange taste.

But within our recommended group, our tasters disagreed about the level of sourness that defined the best marmalade. Some celebrated a strong, sour bite, finding this tartness accented the orange flavor. Others, however, found that the same sourness overwhelmed the orange flavor. Another segment wanted a balance between these two elements. In the end, we found three brands to recommend—one for each flavor profile.

Our top-rated brand, Trappist Seville Orange Marmalade, uses Seville orange rind, but its first ingredient is sugar, earning it a middle-of-the-road sweet/tart profile. Our second-rated brand, Hero Swiss Marmalade, had the highest degree of bitterness—it was the only brand that listed oranges rather than sugar as its first ingredient. Those who loved it claimed its "true orange flavor" made their "taste buds jump"; those who didn't like it complained of a "bitter, pithy aftertaste." Our third recommended brand, Smucker's Sweet Orange Marmalade, was favored by those who wanted a "good floral/orange element" without any pithy/bitter distraction.

Our suggestion? If you like an orange marmalade with intense orange flavor and significant tartness, look for one that lists oranges as its first ingredient (before any sugar component). For a more balanced tart/sugary taste in a marmalade that also features good orange flavor, sugar may be listed first as an ingredient, but the label should at least specify Seville or bitter oranges. For a sweet version without any bitterness, Smucker's Sweet Orange Marmalade (not the sugar-free) is widely available.

EQUIPMENT CORNER: Cutting Boards

BUYING A CUTTING BOARD STARTS WITH DECIDING on its material. Until recently there were just two good options: wood and plastic. Wood boards appeal to cooks who love how they feel and don't mind that they need to be hand-washed. Fans of plastic rate a dishwasher-safe, maintenance-free board over everything else—even if it means a surface that will never feel as cushiony as wood. Recently, eco-friendly bamboo boards claiming to match and even surpass the benefits of wood have appeared in kitchenware stores everywhere. Alongside them are lightweight composite boards, fashioned from laminated wood fiber, which look like wood but clean up like plastic. Do these newcomers offer anything better than the old standbys?

To find out, we gathered a lineup of boards made from all four materials (plus a glass board; we haven't liked glass in the past, but we know many people do). We whacked at them with a cleaver, subjected them to hundreds of cuts with a new, factory-sharpened knife, and repeatedly knocked them off the countertop. When we were done, we chopped chipotle chiles in brick-red adobo sauce to see how easily they would clean up. Our ultimate goal was to find the ideal surface: soft enough to keep your knife and hands in good shape but sturdy enough to take on any cutting job without undue damage.

At the outset, we were impressed by what many consider the king of cutting boards: a 10-pound maple butcher block from John Boos. Heavy and solid (with a $75 price tag to match), this board's end-grain wood took cleaver strikes and repetitive cuts without showing any damage to its surface or the knife. But the board's virtues were also its undoing: Its heft made it uncomfortable to set up, wash, and put away. And despite being oiled, it split along a glue line after routine use. We preferred a lighter yet still substantial maple board from J. K. Adams, which had a convenient size—roomy but not unwieldy or heavy—felt great under the knife, and took all the abuse we could dish out.

In the plastic category, two didn't measure up—a folding board that proved more gimmicky than useful, and a plain plastic board that was too slick, making the knife, food, and board itself skid around as we worked. This board's soft surface also became deeply stained and cut up. But the Architec Gripper board we've loved in the past remains highly recommended for its durable surface and rubber feet, thermally bonded to the plastic, which keeps it rock-solid on the counter. Any stains on this board were blasted clean in the dishwasher, but we weren't influenced by its sanitized appearance. Our lab tests have shown that, contrary to popular belief, bacteria don't wash off plastic boards any more easily than they do off wood ones (see "Bacteria on Board").

We were most skeptical about the wood-composite boards. The Epicurean model immediately lived down to our low expectations, making a nasty clack under the knife and giving off sawdust under repeated cuts.

Bamboo boards are lightweight and attractive, but we wondered about their endurance. This material is often misunderstood to be a type of hardwood; it's actually a kind of grass.

The butcher-block-style Totally Bamboo Congo board turned out to be a pleasant surprise. In test after test, it matched the outstanding comfort and ease of cutting of a classic maple butcher block—and it was so impervious to abuse that it looked new after hundreds of cuts. Like wood, this board can't go into the dishwasher and would benefit from occasional oiling, but we were more than willing to trade those inconveniences for its superior feel. An unexpected bonus: Lab tests confirmed bamboo has natural antimicrobial properties that help kill bacteria even before you wash it.

But not all bamboo boards are created equal. The other bamboo boards' surfaces were not as durable or forgiving as the Congo's, due in part to their construction and possibly also to the age of the bamboo at harvest—the younger it is, the softer the cane and the cheaper the board.

In the final analysis, our top-rated boards cut across material distinctions, displaying similar features of comfort, durability, and solid construction. If you're willing to wash by hand and do occasional maintenance to keep your board in peak form, the top-performing Totally Bamboo Congo board and J. K. Adams's Takes Two maple board are good choices. If the dishwasher is the only way you'll go, we recommend the plastic Architec Gripper Nonslip board.

SCIENCE DESK: Bacteria on Board

IN 2004 WE ASKED AN INDEPENDENT LABORATORY to compare wood and plastic cutting boards to see which harbors more harmful bacteria. The answer? There's no difference—both are equally safe as long as you scrub them in hot, soapy water. We repeated the tests on bamboo and composite boards, which are new to the market since we conducted the earlier tests. Just as with wood and plastic, if you wash these boards with soap and water, the bacteria will die. Interestingly, even before being washed, the bamboo board's natural antimicrobial properties helped kill off much of the bacteria. You shouldn't skip washing bamboo—but it's nice to have a built-in head start.

Rating Cutting Boards

WE TESTED 12 CUTTING BOARDS BY EVALUATING THEIR DESIGN, DURABILITY, WEAR ON A CHEF'S KNIFE, AND SUITABILITY for a variety of kitchen tasks. Brands are listed in order of preference. See www.americastestkitchen.com for updates to this testing.

HIGHLY RECOMMENDED
Totally Bamboo Congo
$39.99; butcher-block-style bamboo

This board has the solid and cushy surface of a wooden butcher block, but it's lightweight, with nicely rounded edges that are easy to grasp. A perfect score in every test.

HIGHLY RECOMMENDED
J. K. Adams Takes Two
$22; hard rock sugar maple

This classic plank board is solid but light enough to be convenient for frequent use. The knife felt cushioned during use and the board showed few cut marks. The chipotle stain hung on.

HIGHLY RECOMMENDED
Architec Gripper Nonslip
$14.99; polypropylene (plastic)

The nonslip "gripper" underside keeps the board extremely stable but makes it one-sided. A pleasant cutting surface, but it slightly dulled a new knife.

RECOMMENDED
Totally Bamboo Kauai
$28; vertical-grain bamboo (narrow strips)

This pretty board was easy to handle, felt solid and well cushioned under the knife, and was tough enough to handle the cleaver. The surface became deeply incised in one area, but it didn't stain.

RECOMMENDED
John Boos Chopping Block
$74.95; northern hard rock maple

This deluxe cutting board is mighty heavy to hoist around the kitchen. It feels great under the knife; it definitely needs oiling and careful drying to keep its good looks and avoid splitting, as our first sample did.

RECOMMENDED
TruBamboo Palm Beach
$39.99; flat-grain bamboo (inch-wide planks)

This board did the job but was unremarkable. Its surface showed faint cuts and became increasingly fuzzy, with tiny raised fibers, as we used and cleaned it.

RECOMMENDED WITH RESERVATIONS
The Cutting Board Company
$11.35; polypropylene (plastic)

The surface was too slick when new—an onion skidded as we cut. The cleaver made deep cuts and raised ridges on the surface. This board slipped around if we didn't use a mat underneath, and it stained deeply.

RECOMMENDED WITH RESERVATIONS
Epicurean Cutting Surfaces, Kitchen Series
$24.95; wood-laminate composite

This hard board clacked loudly under the knife, and the surface gave off sawdust after repeated cuts. The board smells like a wet dog when washed (it's the glue).

RECOMMENDED WITH RESERVATIONS
Architec Gripper Bamboo
$14.99; vertical-grain bamboo

Four rubber feet trapped wetness and gave the board a hollow feel. It is more difficult to cut across the planks than along them. The surface showed every cut, and stains hung on.

NOT RECOMMENDED
OXO Good Grips Folding Utility
$24.99; polypropylene (plastic)

The rubbery surface of the board felt pleasant, but the center-fold ridge got in the way of cutting. The board ripped in two at the fold when swept off the countertop.

NOT RECOMMENDED
Architec Gripperwood
$24.99; beechwood with rubber gripper feet

The wood felt lightweight but cheap; it made a hollow sound when the knife struck. The soft surface was heavily damaged, giving off $1/8$ teaspoon of sawdust as we cut. The board split in two when swept off the countertop.

NOT RECOMMENDED
Pyrex Glass
$17.99; tempered glass

This glass board clacked with every cut and dulled a new knife after 10 cuts. It didn't break (even when knocked off the countertop and whacked with a cleaver), but it's horrible as a cutting board.

Flare-ups can sometimes occur on the grill no matter how careful you are to prevent them. Here, while cooking Grilled Bone-In Chicken Breasts, Bridget grabs her spray bottle, filled with water, to douse a pesky flare-up.

WEEKNIGHT
CHAPTER 16 summer supper

The grill adds incomparable flavor to anything cooked on it. And for chicken breasts, grilling can be truly extraordinary. The mild-flavored meat becomes infused with the smoky flavor from the grill, the chicken taking on an entirely new character. We like grilling bone-in breasts with the skin on for better flavor and juicy meat, but there are issues. Chicken is delicate and the intense heat of the grill can be harsh, drying the meat out. And the skin is tricky, too—blackened skin and the other extreme, flabby skin, are a couple of pitfalls we've faced. So we fired up the grill to see just how we could ensure grilled chicken that had it all—crisp, golden skin and juicy, tender meat, rich with the smoky flavor of the grill.

Tomato salads are a natural in summertime. And bite-sized cherry tomatoes are perfect in salad. The problem is that they're awfully juicy. This may sound like a good thing, but once the tomatoes are cut, they release a sea of watery liquid that dilutes the salad's flavor. We'd need to find a way to handle the excess juice for a tomato salad that delivers sweet tomato flavor in every bite.

IN THIS CHAPTER

THE RECIPES

Charcoal-Grilled Bone-In Chicken Breasts
Gas-Grilled Bone-In Chicken Breasts
Orange-Chipotle Glaze
Curry-Yogurt Glaze
Soy-Ginger Glaze

Greek Cherry Tomato Salad
Cherry Tomato Salad with Basil and Fresh Mozzarella
Cherry Tomato Salad with Tarragon and Blue Cheese
Cherry Tomato and Watermelon Salad
Cherry Tomato Salad with Mango and Lime Curry Vinaigrette

EQUIPMENT CORNER

Solar Cookers

GRILLED BONE-IN CHICKEN

WHAT WE WANTED: Grilled chicken that has it all—moist meat, beautifully browned skin, and a smoky, grilled flavor that screams summer.

There's a lot to admire about a perfectly grilled chicken breast. Cooked bone-in with the skin on for extra flavor and juiciness, the smoke-infused meat should be tender and succulent and the skin golden and crisp. But don't let the everyday nature of this grill favorite fool you: This dish isn't that easy to get right. Burnt, limp skin and sooty, parched meat are too often the reality.

Part of the problem is the inherent difficulty of cooking lean, delicate breast meat over the grill's dry, intense heat. The even bigger issue is that grilling, by its very nature, is an inexact cooking medium. To help inject as much precision as possible into the process, every detail counts, from how much charcoal you use, to the arrangement of the coals, to where you place the meat. But most grilled chicken recipes forgo a well-thought-out approach and focus more on marinades, sauces, and glazes—all good ways to cover up tasteless scorched meat, if you ask us. We have nothing against a grilled chicken breast embellished by a sauce, but we want the meat underneath it to be perfect.

Before even striking a match to the charcoal, we knew we would need to brine our chicken breasts for an hour or so before grilling. This would help ensure juicy, seasoned meat throughout and leave us free to focus solely on the grilling technique.

Many recipes recommend grilling chicken over a blazing single-level fire where the coals are spread evenly in the grill. In the test kitchen we've learned this approach doesn't work. Fat eventually starts dripping onto the coals, and before you know it, you have an inferno on your hands. The only way to keep things under control is to move the chicken on and off the grill, drying out the meat and charring more skin every step of the way. Building what we call a modified two-level fire was a more promising technique.

Here, all the coals are pushed to one side of the grill to create a hot area and a cooler area. Food placed on the cooler side can cook gently through indirect heat with the cover on, with no risk of flare-ups.

We put the indirect-heat technique to the test, carefully arranging the breasts in a tidy row with the thicker sides facing the fire to promote even cooking. Tasters praised the chicken for its "grilled" flavor and minimal char—an encouraging step in the right direction. However, the method was far from perfect. Even though we used breasts of equal size and weight, each cooked at a different rate—some took 20 minutes, others as long as 40. Because a grill's heat is always in flux, with cool and hot spots throughout its interior, we knew we'd never get all the chicken breasts to cook at exactly the same rate no matter what we did. But we wanted them to at least cook at a similar rate.

The key would be to minimize temperature fluctuation as best we could. It occurred to us that we could try a trick we sometimes use when barbecuing a large cut of meat—covering it with a piece of foil before closing the lid. The foil creates a sort of oven within an oven, trapping a layer of heat against the meat that maintains a consistent temperature. We prepped the grill by lighting a full chimney's worth of charcoal (about 100 briquettes). When the coals were glowing, we once again arranged a modified two-level fire and replaced the cooking grate to heat it up. After scraping and greasing the grate, we placed the chicken breasts on the grill's cooler half, skin side down (to better render the fat), and laid a large sheet of foil over them. Thirty minutes later, all six of our chicken breasts were either ready or very close to ready to come off the grill. Our timing issues solved, we now had meat that was uniformly tender and juicy, with good grilled flavor. We also had a new problem: skin that was too flabby.

Our only choice was to start the breasts over the coals. Risking flare-ups, we tried lightly browning all sides of the chicken on the grill's hot side, keeping it there for a total

of less than 10 minutes before moving it to the cooler side. This short exposure to direct heat helped crisp the skin and kept flare-ups to a minimum. But the results didn't fully satisfy our tasters. We couldn't keep the breasts over the coals any longer at the beginning of grilling or we'd be back where we started, but what about at the end of cooking? We took out a new batch of breasts, started them on the hot side, moved them to the cooler side until they were 90 percent done, then put them back on the hot side to finish cooking. This three-step dance was a success. Because the coals had cooled down and the chicken had rendered most of its fat, the skin gently crisped and turned golden, unhindered by any violent flare-ups.

To accommodate tasters who love a glaze with their grilled chicken, we developed a few variations. But even with such embellishment, there was no question that our tender, juicy chicken, with its crisp golden skin, was the true star.

WHAT WE LEARNED: Brine the chicken prior to grilling to ensure juicy, flavorful meat. Use a modified two-level fire (with all the coals banked to one side) to create hotter and cooler parts of the grill, allowing the chicken to brown over high heat and finish cooking through over lower heat. Cover the chicken loosely with foil when it's on the cooler side of the grill to help minimize temperature fluctuations. And just before the chicken is done, move it back to the hot side of the grill to crisp up the skin.

CHARCOAL-GRILLED BONE-IN CHICKEN BREASTS

serves 6

Note that kosher salt measures differently from table salt, and brands of kosher salt also measure differently from each other. To help ensure that each breast finishes cooking at approximately the same time, buy pieces of similar size. Barbecue sauce can replace the optional glaze in step 4.

⅓   cup table salt, ⅓ cup plus 2 tablespoons Morton Kosher Salt, or ⅔ cup Diamond Crystal Kosher Salt (see note)
6   bone-in, skin-on chicken breast halves (about 12 ounces each), ribs removed, trimmed of excess fat and skin (see note)
     Ground black pepper
     Vegetable oil for the cooking grate
1   recipe glaze (recipes follow; optional; see note)

1. Dissolve the salt in 2 quarts cold water in a large container. Submerge the chicken, cover with plastic wrap, and refrigerate 1 hour. Rinse the chicken under cold water and dry thoroughly with paper towels. Season the chicken with pepper.

2. Meanwhile, light a large chimney starter filled with charcoal (6 quarts, or about 100 briquettes) and allow to burn until the coals are fully ignited and partially covered with a thin layer of ash, about 20 minutes. Build a modified two-level fire by arranging all the coals over one half of the grill, leaving the other half empty. Position the cooking grate over the coals, cover the grill, and let the cooking grate heat up, about 5 minutes. Scrape the cooking grate clean with a grill brush. Dip a wad of paper towels in the oil; holding the wad with tongs, wipe the cooking grate. The grill is ready when the side with the coals is medium-hot (you can hold your hand 5 inches above the cooking grate for 3 to 4 seconds).

3. Cook the chicken on all sides over the hotter part of the grill until the skin is lightly browned and the meat has faint grill marks, 6 to 8 minutes. (If constant flare-ups occur, slide the chicken to the cooler side of the grill and mist the fire with water from a spray bottle.) Move the chicken, skin side down, to the cooler side of the grill, with the thicker sides of the breasts facing the coals. Cover loosely with aluminum foil, cover the grill, and continue to cook until an instant-read thermometer inserted into the thickest part of the breast registers 150 degrees, 15 to 25 minutes longer.

4. Brush the bone side of the chicken with glaze (if using). Move the chicken, bone side down, to the hotter side of the grill and cook until browned, 4 to 6 minutes. Brush the skin side of the chicken with glaze; turn the chicken over

and continue to cook until browned and an instant-read thermometer inserted into the thickest part of the breast registers 160 degrees, 2 to 3 minutes longer. Transfer the chicken to a plate and let rest, tented with foil, 5 minutes. Serve, passing the remaining glaze separately.

VARIATION

GAS-GRILLED BONE-IN CHICKEN BREASTS

Follow the recipe for Charcoal-Grilled Bone-In Chicken Breasts through step 1. Turn all the burners to high and heat the grill with the lid down until very hot, about 15 minutes. Follow the instructions for cleaning and oiling the cooking grate in step 2. Leave the primary burner on high and turn off the other burner(s). Proceed with the recipe from step 3, increasing the browning time in step 3 to 10 to 14 minutes.

TECHNIQUE: Great Grilled Bone-In Chicken Breasts

 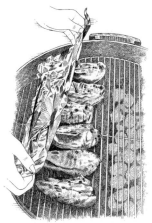 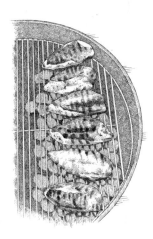

1. Start on the Hot Side: Cook the chicken on all sides over the hotter part of the grill until lightly browned.

2. Move to the Cool Side: Move the chicken, skin side down, to the grill's cooler half, with the thicker sides facing the coals. Cover with foil.

3. Finish on the Hot Side: To finish, return the chicken to the hotter side of the grill and cook on both sides until the skin is brown and crisp.

ORANGE-CHIPOTLE GLAZE

makes about ¾ cup

- ⅔ cup juice plus 1 teaspoon grated zest from 2 oranges
- 1 small shallot, minced (about 1 tablespoon)
- 1–2 chipotle chiles in adobo sauce, minced (1 to 2 tablespoons)
- 2 teaspoons minced fresh thyme leaves
- 1 tablespoon light molasses
- ¾ teaspoon cornstarch
  Salt

Combine the juice, zest, shallot, chipotle, and thyme in a small saucepan, then whisk in the molasses and cornstarch. Simmer the mixture over medium heat until thickened, about 5 minutes. Season with salt to taste. Reserve half of the glaze for serving and use the other half for brushing on the chicken in step 4.

CURRY-YOGURT GLAZE

makes about 1 cup

- ¾ cup plain yogurt
- 2 medium garlic cloves, minced or pressed through a garlic press (about 2 teaspoons)
- 2 teaspoons grated fresh ginger
- 2 teaspoons minced fresh cilantro leaves
- ½ teaspoon grated zest from 1 lemon
- 1½ teaspoons curry powder
- ½ teaspoon sugar
  Salt and ground black pepper

Whisk the ingredients together in a small bowl; season with salt and pepper to taste. Reserve half of the glaze for serving and use the other half for brushing on the chicken in step 4.

SOY-GINGER GLAZE

makes about 1 cup

Reduce the amount of salt in the brine to ¼ cup when using this glaze.

- ⅓ cup water
- ¼ cup soy sauce
- 2 tablespoons mirin
- 1 tablespoon grated fresh ginger
- 2 medium garlic cloves, minced or pressed through a garlic press (about 2 teaspoons)
- 3 tablespoons sugar
- ¾ teaspoon cornstarch
- 2 small scallions, minced

Combine the water, soy sauce, mirin, ginger, and garlic in a small saucepan, then whisk in the sugar and cornstarch. Simmer the mixture over medium heat until thickened, about 5 minutes; stir in the scallions. Reserve half of the glaze for serving and use the other half for brushing on the chicken in step 4.

EQUIPMENT CORNER: Solar Cookers

COOKING IN THE SUN HAS A LONG HISTORY. THE contemporary impetus for using solar cookers is largely economic and environmental. Solar cookers don't require any fuel, they don't create smoke pollution, and they use minimal water—all factors that make them attractive for use in developing regions around the world. Over 100,000 are reportedly used in India and China. Most solar cookers are produced by nonprofit organizations; profits from cookers sold in the United States or Europe subsidize cookers shipped elsewhere. In the United States, sales are geared to several audiences: those who advocate environmentally sound practices, people in sunny climates who want a fuel-efficient way to cook that doesn't heat up the kitchen, outdoor enthusiasts who like their portability, and food hobbyists who enjoy experimental cooking. But how well do they really work? Could anything simply left in a pot or box to cook in the sun actually taste good? And are solar cookers more than just a toy for a food hobbyist?

Over several weeks, we tested (and retested) a variety of food, including rice, whole chickens, broccoli, marinated pork, roasted garlic, potatoes, and chocolate chip cookies. Our conclusions? What the cookers cooked well, they cooked very well, especially food that appreciated long, slow cooking and could generate sufficient internal moisture to stay moist and tender, like the whole chicken, baked potatoes, garlic, and marinated pork. But time-sensitive and/or drier food presented a challenge, especially since the cookers proved very sensitive to temperature fluctuation, either from being opened to check the food's progress or from passing clouds. The cookies were the only time-sensitive food we liked, largely because we could check on their progress without opening the ovens (we could see through the covers). But despite checking frequently, we never got the rice right—we couldn't catch it before it was blown out and starchy—nor the broccoli, which turned army green and smelled skunky by the time it was tender.

The bottom line? Solar cookers are surprisingly good at cooking certain things, but overall they're unreliable. They won't replace our indoor ovens or our charcoal grills anytime soon. When someone figures out how to store and better control the energy the ovens capture from the sun, they'll become a lot more useful.

CHERRY TOMATO SALADS

WHAT WE WANTED: A method for transforming juicy, sweet cherry tomatoes into an intensely flavored, not water-logged, salad.

Cherry tomatoes are often considered a supporting player in salad. But when summertime cherry tomatoes are especially sweet and juicy, they are more than worthy of taking center stage. We knew from experience, however, that we couldn't merely slice them in half, toss them with vinaigrette, and call it a salad. Like bigger, meatier beefsteak and plum varieties, cherry tomatoes exude lots of liquid when cut, quickly turning a salad into soup.

In the test kitchen we often slice larger tomatoes, sprinkle them with salt, and allow them to drain to remove liquid and concentrate flavors. Following suit, we tossed 2 pints of halved cherry tomatoes with ¼ teaspoon of salt (plus a pinch of sugar to accentuate sweetness) and let them drain in a colander. After 30 minutes only a paltry 2 tablespoons of liquid had leached out. What if we exposed even more of the tomatoes' surface area to salt? We tried again with a fresh batch of tomatoes, cutting each one along the equator and then in half again. Progress: The salted, quartered tomatoes netted ¼ cup of liquid. But even this wasn't enough to prevent the salad from turning soggy when we tossed the tomatoes with oil and vinegar.

Some tomato salad recipes call for removing the watery seed pockets of the tomatoes, thus eliminating a major source of liquid. We weren't about to cut open 40 or so cherry tomatoes and painstakingly push out the jelly and seeds with our thumbs; we needed a more efficient method. That's when we thought of a salad spinner. The centrifugal force of the whirling bowl spins water off lettuce and herbs. Why wouldn't it have the same effect on tomatoes? It did—spinning salted and drained tomatoes resulted in the release of ½ cup of liquid.

Our tomatoes were no longer liquidy, but when we tossed them with dressing, we noticed they tasted a little dull. This was not too surprising, as the jelly is the most flavorful part of the tomato and we had stripped it away. If we added the jelly to the oil and vinegar we were already using to dress the tomatoes, we'd be putting the liquid we'd taken such pains to remove right back in. But how about reducing the jelly to concentrate its flavor? We strained the seeds from the jelly and then boiled it in a small saucepan with a chopped shallot and balsamic vinegar. After cooling the mixture and combining it with olive oil, we tossed it with the cherry tomatoes. This time we nailed it—every bite of the salad delivered sweet tomato flavor.

WHAT WE LEARNED: To prevent a soggy, watery salad, quarter the tomatoes, salt them, and then spin them in a salad spinner to remove as much of the jelly and seeds as possible. Reduce the jelly to concentrate its flavor, and add it to the oil and vinegar to create a dressing that brings the tomato flavor to the forefront.

GREEK CHERRY TOMATO SALAD

serves 4 to 6

If in-season cherry tomatoes are unavailable, substitute vine-ripened cherry tomatoes or grape tomatoes from the supermarket. Cut grape tomatoes in half along the equator (rather than quartering them). If you don't have a salad spinner, after the salted tomatoes have stood for 30 minutes, wrap the bowl tightly with plastic wrap and gently shake to remove seeds and excess liquid. Strain the liquid and proceed with the recipe as directed. The amount of liquid given off by the tomatoes will depend on their ripeness. If you have less than ½ cup juice after spinning, proceed with the recipe using the entire amount of juice and reduce it to 3 tablespoons as directed (the cooking time will be shorter).

2	pints ripe cherry tomatoes, quartered (about 4 cups; see note)
	Salt
½	teaspoon sugar
2	medium garlic cloves, minced or pressed through a garlic press (about 2 teaspoons)
½	teaspoon dried oregano
1	medium shallot, minced (about 3 tablespoons)
1	tablespoon red wine vinegar
2	tablespoons extra-virgin olive oil
	Ground black pepper
1	small cucumber, peeled, seeded, and cut into ½-inch dice
½	cup chopped pitted kalamata olives
4	ounces feta cheese, crumbled (about 1 cup)
3	tablespoons chopped fresh parsley leaves

1. Toss the tomatoes, ¼ teaspoon salt, and sugar in a medium bowl; let stand for 30 minutes. Transfer the tomatoes to a salad spinner and spin until the seeds and excess liquid have been removed, 45 to 60 seconds, stirring to redistribute the tomatoes several times during spinning.

Return the tomatoes to the bowl and set aside. Strain the tomato liquid through a fine-mesh strainer into a liquid measuring cup, pressing on the solids to extract as much liquid as possible.

2. Bring ½ cup of the tomato liquid (discard any extra), garlic, oregano, shallot, and vinegar to a simmer in a small saucepan over medium heat. Simmer until reduced to 3 tablespoons, 6 to 8 minutes. Transfer the mixture to a small bowl and cool to room temperature, about 5 minutes. Whisk in the oil and pepper to taste until combined. Taste and season with up to ⅛ teaspoon salt and set the dressing aside.

3. Add the cucumber, olives, feta, dressing, and parsley to the bowl with the tomatoes; toss gently and serve.

VARIATIONS

CHERRY TOMATO SALAD WITH BASIL AND FRESH MOZZARELLA

Follow the recipe for Greek Cherry Tomato Salad, substituting balsamic vinegar for the red wine vinegar and omitting the garlic and oregano in step 2. Substitute 1½ cups lightly packed fresh basil leaves, roughly torn, and 8 ounces fresh mozzarella cheese, cut into ½-inch cubes and patted dry with paper towels, for the cucumber, olives, feta, and parsley in step 3.

CHERRY TOMATO SALAD WITH TARRAGON AND BLUE CHEESE

Follow the recipe for Greek Cherry Tomato Salad, substituting cider vinegar for the red wine vinegar, omitting the garlic and oregano, and adding 2 teaspoons Dijon mustard and 4 teaspoons honey to the tomato liquid in step 2. Substitute ½ cup roughly chopped toasted pecans, 2 ounces blue cheese, crumbled, and 1½ tablespoons chopped fresh tarragon leaves for the cucumber, olives, feta, and parsley in step 3.

CHERRY TOMATO AND WATERMELON SALAD

Sweet watermelon and salty feta taste surprisingly well together.

Follow the recipe for Greek Cherry Tomato Salad, substituting white wine vinegar for the red wine vinegar and omitting the garlic and oregano in step 2. Substitute 1 cup watermelon, cut into ½-inch cubes, for the cucumber and olives and 3 tablespoons roughly chopped fresh mint leaves for the parsley in step 3.

CHERRY TOMATO SALAD WITH MANGO AND LIME CURRY VINAIGRETTE

Follow the recipe for Greek Cherry Tomato Salad, substituting 4 teaspoons lime juice for the red wine vinegar, omitting the garlic and oregano, and adding ¼ teaspoon curry powder in step 2. Substitute 1 mango, pitted and cut into ½-inch dice (about 1½ cups), ½ cup toasted slivered almonds, and 3 tablespoons chopped fresh cilantro leaves for the cucumber, olives, feta, and parsley in step 3.

TECHNIQUE: Avoiding Waterlogged Cherry Tomato Salad

1. Spin: Spinning the quartered tomatoes in a salad spinner removes excess liquid that can make salad watery.

2. Reduce: Simmering the strained tomato liquid creates a concentrated tomato base for the vinaigrette.

To find out if mail-order steaks are worth the hefty price tag, we grilled five prime, dry-aged porterhouses, plus a choice-grade porterhouse from the supermarket, and tasted them side-by-side. See page 216 to learn how each brand fared.

BACKYARD STEAK
CHAPTER 17
and potatoes

Steak and potatoes makes a satisfying meal year-round. And in the summer months, steak—hot off the grill with a savory crust and juicy meat—can't be beat. Many recipes call for marinating steak in Italian-style salad dressing to impart flavor quickly. The only problem is that the vinegar in the dressing—an acid—turns the meat mushy. We wanted to find a better way to flavor steak, one that would give the meat great flavor (in short order), yet still preserve its meaty chew.

If you're dressing up steak on the grill, why not give potatoes their due as well? We grill our potatoes, halved and slipped onto skewers, for perfectly cooked, creamy spuds with a crusty exterior. These potatoes are great plain, but adding seasonings, such as garlic and rosemary, would make them even better. But what's the best way to infuse the potatoes with these flavors? And would we have to revisit the test kitchen's method for grilling potatoes to do so? These are just a couple of the questions we hoped to answer.

GRILLED FLANK STEAK

WHAT WE WANTED: A great marinated grilled steak—one that is imbued with the lively flavors of the marinade but still retains its beefy chew.

America's love affair with flank steak marinated in a bottle of Italian-style salad dressing is both indisputable and curious. The flavor is often complex—or at least interesting—but the texture suffers terribly, the exterior turning mushy rather than tender. The culprit? It's the acid in the vinegar that ruins the texture and also turns the meat gray. (Yogurt, wine, and fruit juice can produce similarly distressing results.) The good news is that marinades do succeed in flavoring meat, even without the acid. So how could we develop a fresh, Mediterranean-style marinade that really boosts flavor without transforming this rough-and-ready piece of grilled meat into backyard baby food?

Before tackling the marinade, we first came up to speed on the cooking method. Prior work in the test kitchen gave us an excellent road map: Use a two-level fire, which lets you move the thin part of the steak to the cooler side of the grill once it is done and gives the thicker part more cooking time over higher heat. Cook the steak only to medium-rare to keep it from getting tough, and remember that carryover heat will continue to cook the meat once it comes off the grill. Let the steak rest for five to 10 minutes before slicing. (This reduces the loss of juices.)

Because fat carries flavor so well, we knew oil would be a key ingredient in our marinade. Without any vinegar or other acid, we also figured that our marinade would be more paste than liquid. Starting with those assumptions, we set out to determine the best method of infusing oil with standard Mediterranean flavors from ingredients such as garlic and rosemary. Our working recipe contained 6 tablespoons of olive oil and 1 tablespoon each of garlic and rosemary.

We were pretty sure that heat would intensify the flavors, so we tested two marinades—one made with raw garlic and rosemary, the other a heat infusion we made by briefly cooking the garlic and rosemary in the oil. After trying the grilled steaks, tasters thought that the heat did improve the flavor, but only slightly. Increasing the amounts of garlic and rosemary—to 2 tablespoons each—was far more effective. Adding shallots also improved our marinade paste.

We had been mincing the piles of garlic, rosemary, and shallots by hand and then stirring them together with the oil. To save time, we wondered if we could just throw everything into the blender. Unfortunately, the blender failed to mince things finely enough; the rough bits just didn't contribute as much flavor as the fine mince. In the end, we chose to mince the garlic, rosemary, and shallots with a knife and then combine them with the oil in the blender. When rubbed into the meat, this extremely fine, well-blended paste flavored the steak in just one hour.

Two minor tests and one failure followed. First, we pricked the flank steak with a fork before rubbing on the paste, and this did boost the flavor. Second, we tried grilling the steak with the paste on (we had been wiping it off before cooking), and this turned out a blotchy, burnt-tasting piece of meat. Removing the paste just prior to grilling was clearly the way to go.

Our recipe was good at this point, but we wanted to take a detour and explore the effects that salting might have on the meat. In prior test kitchen work on steak tips, we had marinated the beef in a mixture of oil and soy sauce. The salt in the soy sauce in effect "brines" the meat, adding moisture and seeming to tenderize it. Of course, soy sauce isn't right in a Mediterranean paste. Could we get the benefits of salt without the soy?

We tried adding salt to the marinade, but the salt wouldn't dissolve in the oil. What if we just salted the meat, then rubbed on the paste? Sure enough, this technique made for a beefier flavor and an improved texture. Kosher salt, with its large crystals, was easier to apply than table salt and won a place in our recipe.

For a final series of tests, we developed two additional marinade recipes, one with sesame oil, ginger, scallions, and garlic and the other a spicier version with chipotle and jalapeño chiles and garlic. Now we were done—or at least we thought so. One colleague suggested that we try marinating the meat the night before. Sliced and served, this steak was potently flavored, but so was the one-hour version. The good news is that the marinade can be made and applied to the steak well before you cook it, if you prefer, so you don't need to set aside an hour of marinating time before getting dinner on the table.

WHAT WE LEARNED: Omit any acid (such as vinegar, wine, and yogurt) from the marinade, because it will turn the texture of the meat mushy. Instead, rely on an oil-based paste-like marinade, enriched with such bold aromatics as garlic, rosemary, and shallots. Mince the aromatics, then emulsify them in a blender with the oil for best distribution of flavor. For marinated steak with optimal flavor, prick the meat before applying the paste—it will penetrate the meat more effectively. And salting the meat, prior to adding the marinade paste, highlights the steak's beefy flavor and helps preserve its meaty texture. Be sure to scrape off the marinade paste prior to grilling; otherwise the exterior of the meat will char.

CHARCOAL-GRILLED MARINATED FLANK STEAK

serves 4 to 6

Flank steaks smaller or larger than 2 pounds can be used, but adjust the amount of salt and pepper accordingly. We prefer flank steak cooked rare or medium-rare. If the steak is to retain its juices, it must be allowed to rest before being sliced.

1   whole flank steak (about 2 pounds), patted dry with paper towels
2   teaspoons kosher salt
1   recipe wet paste marinade (recipes follow)
¼   teaspoon ground black pepper
    Vegetable oil for cooking grate

1. Place the steak on a rimmed baking sheet or in a large baking dish. Using a dinner fork, prick the steak about 20 times on each side. Rub both sides of the steak evenly with the salt, and then with the paste. Cover with plastic wrap and refrigerate at least 1 hour or up to 24 hours.

2. Light a large chimney starter filled with charcoal (6 quarts, or about 100 briquettes) and allow to burn until the coals are fully ignited and partially covered with a thin layer of ash, about 20 minutes. Empty the coals into

1. Our novel "marinating" technique starts with pricking the steak with a fork to speed flavor absorption.

2. Next, kosher salt is rubbed into the meat, followed by a garlic-herb wet paste.

3. After an hour, the paste and salt are wiped off so the steak will brown nicely on the grill.

the grill; build a two-level fire by arranging two-thirds of the coals over half of the grill and arranging the remaining coals in a single layer over the other half. Position the cooking grate over the coals, cover the grill, and heat the grate for 5 minutes; scrape the cooking grate clean with a grill brush. The grill is ready when the coals are hot (you can hold your hand 5 inches above the grate for just 2 seconds). Dip a wad of paper towels in the oil; holding the wad with tongs, wipe the cooking grate.

3. Using paper towels, wipe the paste off the steak; season both sides with the pepper. Grill the steak directly over the coals until well browned, 4 to 6 minutes. Using tongs, flip the steak; grill until the second side is well browned, 3 to 4 minutes. Using a paring knife, make a small cut into

the thickest part of the meat; if the meat is slightly less done than desired, transfer the steak to a cutting board (the meat will continue to cook as it rests). If the steak is significantly underdone, position so that the thinner side is over the cool side of the grill and the thicker side is over the hot side; continue to cook until the thickest part is slightly less done than desired, then transfer the steak to a cutting board.

4. Loosely tent the steak with foil; let rest 5 to 10 minutes. Using a sharp chef's knife or carving knife, slice the steak about ¼ inch thick against the grain and on the bias. Serve immediately.

VARIATION
GAS-GRILLED MARINATED FLANK STEAK
Follow the recipe for Charcoal-Grilled Marinated Flank Steak through step 1. Turn all the burners to high and heat the grill until very hot, about 15 minutes. Use a grill brush to scrape the cooking grate clean; oil the cooking grate. Proceed with the recipe from step 3, cooking with the cover down. If the meat is significantly underdone when tested with a paring knife, turn off one burner and position the steak so that the thinner side is over the cool part of the grill and the thicker side is over the hot part of the grill.

TESTING NOTES:
Marinating No-No
A bottle of Italian dressing is a quick route to flavoring flank steak, but our tests convinced us that one of its primary ingredients—the vinegar—turns the meat mushy and gray.

GARLIC-SHALLOT-ROSEMARY WET PASTE MARINADE

makes enough for 1 flank steak

- 6 tablespoons olive oil
- 6 medium garlic cloves, minced or pressed through a garlic press (2 tablespoons)
- 1 medium shallot, minced (about 3 tablespoons)
- 2 tablespoons minced fresh rosemary leaves

Puree all of the ingredients in a blender until smooth, scraping down the sides of the blender jar as needed.

GARLIC-GINGER-SESAME WET PASTE MARINADE

makes enough for 1 flank steak

- 4 tablespoons toasted sesame oil
- 2 tablespoons vegetable oil
- 3 tablespoons minced fresh ginger
- 2 medium scallions, minced (about 3 tablespoons)
- 3 medium garlic cloves, minced or pressed through a garlic press (1 tablespoon)

Puree all of the ingredients in a blender until smooth, scraping down the sides of the blender jar as needed.

GARLIC-CHILE WET PASTE MARINADE

makes enough for 1 flank steak

This paste marinade makes for a smoky-spicy steak.

- 6 tablespoons corn or vegetable oil
- 6 medium garlic cloves, minced or pressed through a garlic press (2 tablespoons)
- 2 medium scallions, minced (about 3 tablespoons)

- 1 medium chipotle chile in adobo sauce, minced (about 1 tablespoon)
- 1 medium jalapeño chile, minced (about 1 tablespoon)

Puree all of the ingredients in a blender until smooth, scraping down the sides of the blender jar as needed.

TASTING LAB:
Mail-Order Porterhouse Steaks

FANCY MAIL-ORDER PORTERHOUSE STEAKS CAN cost 10 times as much as steaks from the supermarket. Are they worth the premium cost? We grilled five prime, dry-aged porterhouses, plus a choice-grade porterhouse from the grocery store, to find out.

Except for the Peter Luger USDA Prime Dry-Aged Porterhouse (about $44 per pound), tasters found the mail-order steaks far superior to the supermarket meat ($12.99 per pound). But the most expensive beef wasn't necessarily the best. Highest marks went to test kitchen favorite Brandt Beef USDA Dry-Aged Prime Porterhouse (nearly $50 per pound), a bargain compared to the priciest sample in the lineup—Lobel's Dry-Aged American Wagyu Porterhouse Steak (about $130 per pound).

Rating Mail-Order Porterhouse Steaks

TEN MEMBERS OF THE AMERICA'S TEST KITCHEN STAFF TASTED FIVE MAIL-ORDER PORTERHOUSE STEAKS ALONG WITH a steak from the supermarket. Steaks were grilled and seasoned with salt and pepper. Brands are listed in order of preference. See www.americastestkitchen.com for updates to this tasting.

HIGHLY RECOMMENDED
Brandt Beef USDA Dry-Aged Prime Porterhouse Steak
$46.66 per pound, plus shipping
A sky-high price tag buys "rich, buttery, smooth" texture and "fresh, complex beef flavor."

RECOMMENDED
Lobel's Dry-Aged American Wagyu Porterhouse Steak
$130.98 per pound, plus shipping
Not the same caliber as the true steakhouse Wagyu (Japanese-bred cows known for marbled meat) but with a "distinct, nutty-cheesy flavor."

RECOMMENDED
Lobel's Natural Prime Dry-Aged Porterhouse Steak
$69.98 per pound, plus shipping
This "nearly perfect" steak boasted "pronounced beef flavor."

RECOMMENDED
Allen Brothers Dry-Aged Prime Porterhouse
$47.98 per pound, plus shipping
Tasters found this steak "well-marbled," "beefy, tender, and juicy."

RECOMMENDED WITH RESERVATIONS
Supermarket Choice Porterhouse Steak
$12.99 per pound
Sampled on its own, the "mild" flavor and "tender but unremarkable" texture of this steak might have passed for higher quality, but it paled in comparison to the dry-aged mail-order beef.

NOT RECOMMENDED
Peter Luger USDA Prime Dry-Aged Porterhouse
$43.41 per pound, including shipping
This "ultra-thick" steak offered "bland beef flavor" and "dry, stringy" texture.

GRILLED POTATOES

WHAT WE WANTED: Tender grilled potatoes infused with the smoky flavor of the grill and enlivened with the bold flavors of garlic and rosemary.

The test kitchen's established technique for grilling potatoes needs no improvement: Halve and skewer small red potatoes, parboil them, brush them with olive oil, and then quickly place them on the hot grill. This method yields perfectly cooked potatoes—charred (not burnt) exteriors, smooth and creamy interiors, and plenty of smoky flavor—and the skewers hold them together, allowing for hassle-free transfer from pot to grill to serving platter.

Seeing as there are no finer complements for potatoes than garlic and rosemary, we decided to see if we could incorporate this combination into our recipe. Coating the potatoes with oil, garlic, and rosemary prior to grilling seemed too easy, and it was: The garlic burned and became bitter, and the rosemary charred. We tried tossing the potatoes in the oil after they came off the grill, but the raw garlic was too harsh. Tasters winced.

Clearly, this was going to take some experimenting. One of our first ideas was to add crushed garlic cloves and rosemary sprigs to the water in which the potatoes were parboiled, hoping the potatoes would drink up their flavors. Hardly.

Switching gears, we decided to precook the skewered potatoes in the microwave. We brushed the potatoes with oil to prevent sticking, seasoned them with salt, microwaved them, and threw them on the grill. Although their texture was firmer and their skins saltier than when parboiled, the interiors remained unseasoned. Piercing each potato prior to microwaving encouraged the salt on the skin to migrate to the inside.

Now all we needed was to find a bold way to deliver the garlic and rosemary flavors. We slowly cooked nine cloves of garlic and 1 teaspoon of rosemary in ¼ cup of oil, then brushed the potatoes with this mixture prior to microwaving. But we didn't stop there. We brushed them with the infused oil again before grilling, and we tossed the potatoes with the garlic-and-rosemary oil yet again before serving. This repeated contact resulted in the potent flavor we were searching for.

WHAT WE LEARNED: Make a garlic- and rosemary-infused olive oil—simply cook garlic cloves, fresh rosemary, and olive oil together in a skillet. Then, to load the potatoes with the oil's flavor, take a three-pronged approach. First, brush the skewered potatoes with the flavored olive oil prior to parcooking in the microwaving—and prick the potatoes all over to allow for easier penetration. Then brush them again before grilling. And finally, toss the potatoes in the flavored oil just before serving.

CHARCOAL-GRILLED POTATOES
WITH GARLIC AND ROSEMARY

serves 4

This recipe allows you to grill an entrée while the hot coals burn down in step 1. Once that item is done, start grilling the potatoes. This recipe works best with small potatoes that are about 1½ inches in diameter. If using medium potatoes, 2 to 3 inches in diameter, cut them into quarters. If the potatoes are larger than 3 inches in diameter, cut each potato into eighths. Since the potatoes are cooked in the microwave, use wooden skewers.

	Vegetable oil for cooking grate
4	tablespoons olive oil
9	medium garlic cloves, minced or pressed through a garlic press (about 3 tablespoons)
1	teaspoon chopped fresh rosemary leaves
	Kosher salt
2	pounds small Red Bliss potatoes (about 18), scrubbed, halved, and skewered according to photo on page 219 (see note)
	Ground black pepper
	13 by 9-inch disposable foil roasting pan
2	tablespoons chopped fresh chives

1. Light a large chimney starter filled with charcoal (6 quarts, or about 100 briquettes) and allow to burn until the coals are fully ignited and covered with a thin layer of ash, about 20 minutes. Empty the coals into the grill; build a two-level fire by arranging two-thirds of the coals over half of the grill and arranging the remaining coals in a single layer over the other half. Position the cooking grate over the coals, cover the grill, and heat the grate until hot, about 5 minutes; scrape the cooking grate clean with a grill brush. Remove the lid and let the coals burn until the fire on the

hotter part of the grill is medium (you can hold your hand 5 inches above the grate for 5 to 6 seconds), about 10 minutes. Dip a wad of paper towels in vegetable oil; holding the wad with tongs, wipe the cooking grate.

2. Meanwhile, heat the olive oil, garlic, rosemary, and ½ teaspoon salt in a small skillet over medium heat until sizzling, about 3 minutes. Reduce the heat to medium-low and continue to cook until the garlic is light blond, about 3 minutes. Pour the mixture through a fine-mesh strainer into a small bowl; press on the solids. Measure 1 tablespoon of the solids and 1 tablespoon of the oil into a large bowl and set aside. Discard the remaining solids but reserve the remaining oil.

3. Place the skewered potatoes in a single layer on a large microwave-safe plate and poke each potato several times with a skewer. Brush with 1 tablespoon of the strained oil and season liberally with salt. Microwave on high power until the potatoes offer slight resistance when pierced with the tip of a paring knife, about 8 minutes, turning them halfway through the cooking time. Transfer the potatoes to a baking sheet coated with 1 tablespoon of the strained oil. Brush with the remaining 1 tablespoon strained oil; season with salt and pepper to taste.

4. Place the potatoes on the hotter side of the grill. Cook, turning once, until grill marks appear, about 4 minutes. Move the potatoes to the cooler side of the grill; cover with the disposable pan and continue to cook until a paring knife slips in and out of the potatoes easily, 5 to 8 minutes longer. Remove the potatoes from the skewers and transfer to the bowl with the reserved garlic-oil mixture; add the chives and toss until thoroughly coated. Serve immediately.

VARIATION

GAS-GRILLED POTATOES WITH GARLIC AND ROSEMARY

Follow the recipe for Grilled Potatoes with Garlic and Rosemary, skipping step 1. Turn all the burners to high, cover, and heat the grill until very hot, about 15 minutes. Use a grill brush to scrape the cooking grate clean; oil the cooking grate. Proceed with the recipe from step 2, leaving the primary burner on high and reducing the other burner(s) to medium. Grill the potatoes, omitting the disposable pan, with the lid down.

TECHNIQUE:
Skewering Potatoes for the Grill

Place a potato half cut side down on the work surface and pierce through the center with a skewer. Repeat, holding the already-skewered potatoes for better leverage.

Here, Bridget brushes a pork loin with a tangy apple and cranberry glaze that underscores the fruity flavors of the apple-cranberry filling. For best results, she waits until the pork is almost cooked through before applying the glaze— otherwise the sugars will burn over the heat of the grill.

PORK ON
CHAPTER 18
the grill

Instead of roasting pork loin indoors, take it out to the grill, where a hot, smoky fire adds another flavor dimension to the meat. We usually advocate brining the meat to preserve its juicy character. But is there an alternative to brining, one that would add both moisture and substantial flavor? Stuffing the roast comes to mind. We envisioned a swirl of moist, well-seasoned stuffing distributed evenly throughout the meat so every bite would be full of flavor—but we'd have several challenges ahead of us. What should we look for when choosing a pork loin for stuffing? What stuffing flavors would best complement the meat? And what's the best method for stuffing the roast, so the filling would stay put and not leak out all over the grill? Finally, how could we ensure a roast with evenly cooked meat and an exterior with a savory, not tough or charred, crust? Discover the secrets to great grilled stuffed roast pork as the test kitchen moves outdoors.

Cooks can never have enough fast, flavorful side dishes in their repertoire. The test kitchen has always found sautéed crinkly spinach to be handy since it cooks in a flash. But the prep required—thoroughly washing the spinach leaves (which are often quite sandy) and then taking the time to stem each leaf—does slow things down. What about baby spinach, for which a quick rinse is all that's required? In the past, we've reserved baby spinach for salads since its tender leaves turn watery in a hot skillet. Could we find a way to get rid of the water for a worthwhile side dish with great flavor? We were ready to find out.

GRILLED STUFFED PORK LOIN

WHAT WE WANTED: A grilled pork loin made juicy and flavorful through careful cooking and a moist, well-seasoned stuffing.

We are fond of the meaty texture and moderate price of pork loin, but we're annoyed by its tendency toward dryness. Most grilled pork loin recipes try to compensate with some combination of brining (soaking the meat in a salt and sugar solution prior to cooking), rubs, sauces, or condiments, but we were intrigued by something a little different: a stuffing. In theory, a rich filling could keep the loin moist and add aesthetic appeal to the otherwise plain-Jane cut of meat.

In the test kitchen we typically favor the blade-end pork roast for grilling because of its abundant fat. However, this asset became a liability when we tried to stuff one. As soon as we split it open, the meat fell apart into a lumpy mess of muscle, sinew, and fat. A center-cut loin roast proved the better choice because this solid muscle cut cleanly, but its leanness worried us.

We explored a variety of approaches to the stuffing, including recipes based on cheeses, cured meats, bread crumbs, and herbs. Most of the fillings oozed free of the roast, turned mushy, or were bland, but a chutney-like blend of dried fruits, spices, sugar, and vinegar caught our attention. Its flavor was unbalanced and its texture was dusty from dried spices, but the fruit's dense, chewy consistency and deep flavor were well suited to the pork, and the stuffing stayed put.

After testing various combinations of dried fruits, our tasters proclaimed apples and cranberries the perfect pairing. We poached the fruit in a blend of apple cider and apple cider vinegar until tender, then added cayenne pepper, allspice, and grated fresh ginger. Brown sugar trumped white sugar and honey, and sliced shallot and mustard seeds added just the right zip to both the fruit and the pork. We strained off the excess poaching liquid to prevent the filling from being too wet, then ground the mixture to a coarse paste in the food processor.

How, exactly, do you stuff a pork loin? One popular method involves slicing the meat into a broad sheet onto which the filling is spread before the pork is rolled up tightly, like a jellyroll. Butchers call this a roll cut, and it sounds easy enough, but we found the knife work tricky. Our early attempts looked amateurish, so we rethought the approach. We regarded the loin as more square than cylindrical and saw that just three or four straight, short cuts, like a triple butterfly (see the illustrations on page 224), could produce the same results. Gentle persuasion with a meat pounder evened out any nicks and unevenness to give us a long, flat sheet that was easy to fill and roll up. Snugly tying up the rolled roast ensured a compact shape that cooked evenly and sliced easily.

To this point, we'd yet to try brining the roast. We hoped the filling would make brining redundant, and tests proved this to be the case. In fact, a stuffed and brined roast was, if possible, too moist. Turns out we'd made an unexpected scientific discovery, one our science editor confirmed. His analysis: Because the meat was sliced so thin (just ½ inch thick), the acids in the filling were denaturing the proteins in the meat and helping them hold on to moisture. The effects of acids on meat are limited to the area near the surface, so they don't usually do much for a thick pork loin. However, in this recipe, the entire roast was "surface," so we were essentially marinating the meat from the inside out.

To coax even more flavor out of the roast, most recipes tell you to sear the meat before or after cooking it, but our attempts to sear this leaner cut of pork left us with a tough exterior. We tried a variety of spice rubs but found them overpowering. A liberal coating of salt and pepper was more than sufficient.

Finally, we remembered a glazed pork recipe we had previously developed, in which the meat is rolled in the glaze after roasting. Didn't we have leftover liquid from

preparing the filling? We reduced the sticky-sweet, spiced blend of sugar, cider, and vinegar down to a thick, spreadable consistency and lacquered the loin during its last few minutes on the grill. The mahogany glaze not only improved the look of the roast, it also sharpened the flavor of the pork and filling alike.

WHAT WE LEARNED: Choose a center-cut loin roast—it's easier to stuff than other pork roasts. But make sure that the shape of the roast is short and wide. This shape is best for making the four straight, short cuts that open the loin into a long, flat sheet for easiest filling and rolling. Choose a filling that won't turn mushy, bland, or soggy during cooking; a dried fruit filling (apples and cranberries) fits the bill. Poach the fruit in a blend of apple cider, apple cider vinegar, and spices; this step gives the filling an intensified flavor (to perk up the mild-flavored pork) and a thick, chewy consistency (to stay put inside the meat). Follow the test kitchen's method for grilling large cuts of meat—grill-roast the pork loin. Grill-roasting (cooking with the lid down at a moderate temperature) mimics the steady heat of the oven. Flip the roast once during grill-roasting, and for a beautifully burnished finish, reduce the poaching liquid left over from preparing the stuffing into a glaze to brush over the pork toward the end of grilling.

CHARCOAL-GRILLED PORK LOIN WITH APPLE-CRANBERRY FILLING

serves 6

This recipe is best prepared with a loin that is 7 to 8 inches long and 4 to 5 inches wide. To make cutting the pork easier, freeze it for 30 minutes. If mustard seeds are unavailable, stir an equal amount of whole grain mustard into the filling after the apples have been processed. Use more or less cayenne, depending on how spicy you'd like the stuffing. The pork loin can be stuffed and tied a day ahead of time, but don't season the exterior until you are ready to grill.

filling

1	cup apple cider
½	cup cider vinegar
¾	cup packed light brown sugar
1	large shallot, halved lengthwise and sliced thin crosswise (about ¼ cup)
1½	cups (4 ounces) packed dried apples
½	cup (2½ ounces) packed dried cranberries
1	tablespoon grated fresh ginger
1	tablespoon yellow mustard seeds (see note)
½	teaspoon ground allspice
⅛–¼	teaspoon cayenne pepper (see note)

pork

2	(3-inch) wood chunks
1	boneless center-cut pork loin roast, 2½ pounds (see note)
	Kosher salt and ground black pepper
	Vegetable oil for cooking grate

1. FOR THE FILLING: Bring all of the ingredients to a simmer in a medium saucepan over medium-high heat. Cover, reduce the heat to low, and cook until the apples are very soft, about 20 minutes. Push the mixture through a fine-mesh strainer set over a bowl to extract as much liquid as possible. Return the liquid to the saucepan and simmer over medium-high heat until reduced to ⅓ cup, about 5

TECHNIQUE: How to Stuff a Pork Loin

1. Position the roast fat side up. Insert a knife ½ inch from the bottom of the roast and cut horizontally, stopping ½ inch before the edge. Open up this flap.

2. Cut through the thicker half of the roast about ½ inch from the bottom, stopping about ½ inch before the edge. Open up this flap.

3. Repeat until the pork loin is an even ½-inch thickness throughout. If uneven, cover with plastic wrap and use a meat pounder to even out.

4. With the long side of the meat facing you, season the meat and spread the filling, leaving a ½-inch border on all sides.

5. Starting from the short side, roll the pork loin tightly.

6. Tie the roast with twine at 1-inch intervals.

minutes; reserve the glaze. Meanwhile, pulse the apple mixture in a food processor until uniformly coarsely chopped, about fifteen 1-second pulses. Transfer the filling to a bowl and refrigerate while preparing the pork.

2. FOR THE PORK: Soak the wood chunks in water for 1 hour. Meanwhile, following illustrations 1 through 3 above, cut the meat to an even ½-inch thickness. Season inside liberally with salt and spread the apple filling in an even layer, leaving a ½-inch border (illustration 4). Roll tightly and tie with twine at 1-inch intervals (illustrations 5 and 6). Season the exterior liberally with salt and pepper.

3. Light a large chimney starter filled with 5 quarts of charcoal (about 85 briquettes) and allow to burn until the coals

are fully ignited and covered with a thin layer of ash, about 20 minutes. Build a modified two-level fire by arranging the coals to cover one half of the grill. Drain the wood chunks and place on the coals. Open the bottom vent fully. Position the cooking grate over the coals, cover the grill, and heat the grate until hot, about 5 minutes; scrape the cooking grate clean with a grill brush. Lightly dip a wad of paper towels in the oil; holding the wad with tongs, wipe the cooking grate.

4. Place the roast, fat side up, on the cooking grate over the cool side of the grill. Cover the grill and position the vent, halfway open, over the roast to draw the smoke through the grill. Grill-roast until an instant-read thermometer inserted into the thickest part of the roast registers 130 to 135 degrees, 55 to 70 minutes, flipping the roast once halfway

through the cooking time. Brush the roast with half of the reserved glaze; flip and brush with the remaining glaze. (You may need to reheat the glaze briefly to make it spreadable.) Continue to cook until the glaze is glossy and sticky, about 5 minutes longer.

5. Transfer the roast to a cutting board, loosely tent with foil, and let rest for 15 minutes. (The internal temperature should rise to about 145 degrees.) Cut into ½-inch-thick slices, removing the twine as you cut. Serve immediately.

VARIATION

GAS-GRILLED PORK LOIN WITH APPLE-CRANBERRY FILLING

Follow the recipe for Charcoal-Grilled Pork Loin with Apple-Cranberry Filling through step 2, substituting 2 cups wood chips for the chunks and soaking them for 30 minutes. Drain the chips and place in a small disposable foil pan. About 20 minutes before grilling, place the pan with the chips on the primary burner (the burner that will remain on during cooking); position the cooking grate over the burners. Turn all the burners to high and heat with the lid down for 15 minutes. Scrape and oil the cooking grate. Leave the primary burner on high and turn off the other burner(s). Place the roast, fat side up, on the side opposite the primary burner and proceed with the recipe from step 4.

GETTING IT RIGHT:
Not All Pork Loins Can Be Stuffed

Center-cut roasts come in various shapes, some of which are not suited to stuffing. Here's what to look for (and what to avoid).

Long and Thin
This roast is 12 inches long and just 3 inches wide . . .

Too Little Room
. . . so there's not much surface area for the stuffing.

Short and Wide
This roast is just 8 inches long and nearly 5 inches wide . . .

Plenty of Room
. . . so there's more surface area once the roast is opened up.

SAUTÉED SPINACH

WHAT WE WANTED: A method for preventing baby spinach from turning watery and bland once sautéed.

In the test kitchen we've always reserved delicate baby spinach for salads, turning to bigger, mature flat-leaf spinach for cooking. The reason? Tender, young baby spinach releases a lot of liquid when it hits a hot pan, which turns it into a waterlogged, mushy mess. But given how convenient baby spinach is (no stems to remove or grit to rinse out), we thought it was time to give cooking it another try.

In the past we've solved the water problem of the baby green's grownup cousin by wilting it first in a pan, squeezing it with tongs in a colander to remove liquid, and then returning it to the skillet. This tactic failed miserably with the more delicate baby spinach. As soon as the pressed spinach was put back in the pan, it exuded even more juices, which watered down the other ingredients in the dish.

Blanching or steaming the baby spinach first to release liquid, a technique we found successful with sturdier curly-leaf spinach, was also out. Besides the hassle of another pot to wash, why add water to something that you know will get even wetter?

How about microwaving? After all, that's the suggestion offered on the back of the spinach bag. We placed the leaves in a large glass bowl and covered it with a plate. After six minutes, the spinach was warm but still not sufficiently wilted.

We were loath to do it—but would adding just a little water (¼ cup) to the bowl help speed things up? Eureka! After three minutes the spinach had softened and shrunk to half its size, thanks to the release of a great deal of liquid. Yet a nagging problem remained: Pressing the spinach against the colander didn't remove enough of the liquid or eliminate its tissue-like texture.

We found other recipes that called for precooking the spinach before sautéing. A few advocated chopping the wilted vegetable as a way to remove liquid. Taking up a new batch of spinach, we microwaved, pressed, and then roughly chopped it on a cutting board. Not only was the mushy texture gone, but the chopping had released even more of the water pooling around the spinach. With victory in sight, we threw the greens back in the colander for a second squeeze. This chopped and double-pressed spinach was just right: tender, sweet, and ready to be combined with complementary ingredients.

Pairings including almonds and raisins or pecans and feta introduced bold flavors and crunchy textures that enlivened this quick-cooking dish. When all was said and done, we had managed to turn a vegetable usually destined for the salad bowl into a delicious side dish with nary a stem to pick.

WHAT WE LEARNED: Parcook the spinach in the microwave and add a little water to the bowl to hasten wilting the spinach. Press the spinach in a colander to rid it of excess water, chop it (which helps release even more water), and then press it in the colander one final time. Quickly sauté the spinach in a skillet with oil and add complementary seasonings.

SAUTÉED SPINACH WITH ALMONDS AND GOLDEN RAISINS

serves 4

Be sure to toast the almonds for best flavor and good crunch. If you don't have a microwave-safe bowl large enough to accommodate the entire amount of spinach, cook it in a smaller bowl in 2 batches. Reduce the amount of water to 2 tablespoons per batch and cook the spinach for about 1½ minutes.

  3   (6-ounce) bags baby spinach (about 16 cups)
  ¼   cup water
  2   tablespoons extra-virgin olive oil, plus
       2 teaspoons for drizzling
  4   medium garlic cloves, sliced thin crosswise
       (about 2 tablespoons)
  ¼   teaspoon red pepper flakes
  ½   cup golden raisins
       Salt
  2   teaspoons sherry vinegar
  ⅓   cup slivered almonds, toasted

1. Place the spinach and water in a large microwave-safe bowl. Cover the bowl with a large microwave-safe dinner plate (the plate should completely cover the bowl and not rest on the spinach). Microwave on high power until the spinach is wilted and decreased in volume by half, 3 to 4 minutes. Using potholders, remove the bowl from the microwave and keep covered for 1 minute. Carefully remove the plate and transfer the spinach to a colander set in the sink. Using the back of a rubber spatula, gently press the spinach against the colander to release the excess liquid. Transfer the spinach to a cutting board and roughly chop. Return to the colander and press a second time.

2. Heat 2 tablespoons of the oil, the garlic, pepper flakes, and raisins in a 10-inch skillet over medium-high heat. Cook, stirring constantly, until the garlic is light golden brown and beginning to sizzle, 3 to 6 minutes. Add the spinach to the skillet, using tongs to stir and coat with the oil. Sprinkle

with ¼ teaspoon salt and continue stirring with the tongs until the spinach is uniformly wilted and glossy green, about 2 minutes. Sprinkle with the vinegar and almonds; stir to combine. Drizzle with the remaining 2 teaspoons oil and season with salt to taste. Serve immediately.

VARIATIONS

SAUTÉED SPINACH WITH PECANS AND FETA

serves 4

Sweet pecans and salty feta are terrific paired with sautéed spinach. If you don't have a microwave-safe bowl large enough to accommodate the entire amount of spinach, cook it in a smaller bowl in 2 batches. Reduce the amount of water to 2 tablespoons per batch and cook the spinach for about 1½ minutes.

  3   (6-ounce) bags baby spinach (about 16 cups)
  ¼   cup water
  2   tablespoons extra-virgin olive oil, plus
       2 teaspoons for drizzling
  3   large shallots, sliced thin crosswise
       (about 1 cup)
       Salt
  2   teaspoons red wine vinegar
  ⅓   cup chopped pecans, toasted
  1½   ounces feta cheese, crumbled (about ¼ cup)

Follow the recipe for Sautéed Spinach with Almonds and Golden Raisins through step 1. Heat 2 tablespoons of the oil and the shallots in a 10-inch skillet over medium-high heat. Cook, stirring constantly, until the shallots are golden brown, 3 to 5 minutes. Add the spinach to the skillet, using tongs to stir and coat with the oil. Sprinkle with ¼ teaspoon salt and continue stirring with the tongs until the spinach is uniformly wilted and glossy green, about 2 minutes. Sprinkle with the vinegar and pecans; stir to combine. Drizzle with the remaining 2 teaspoons oil and sprinkle with the feta. Season with salt to taste and serve immediately.

SAUTÉED SPINACH WITH CHICKPEAS AND SUN-DRIED TOMATOES

serves 4

Potent sun-dried tomatoes and Parmesan give this variation an Italian flavor, and chickpeas make the dish even heartier. If you don't have a microwave-safe bowl large enough to accommodate the entire amount of spinach, cook it in a smaller bowl in 2 batches. Reduce the amount of water to 2 tablespoons per batch and cook the spinach for about 1½ minutes.

- 3 (6-ounce) bags baby spinach (about 16 cups)
- ¼ cup plus 2 tablespoons water
- 2 tablespoons extra-virgin olive oil, plus 2 teaspoons for drizzling
- 4 medium garlic cloves, sliced thin crosswise (about 2 tablespoons)
- 2 ounces oil-packed sun-dried tomatoes, drained and sliced thin (about ½ cup)
- ¾ cup canned chickpeas, drained and rinsed
  Salt
- 1 ounce Parmesan cheese, grated (about ½ cup)

Follow the recipe for Sautéed Spinach with Almonds and Golden Raisins through step 1. Heat 2 tablespoons of the oil and the garlic in a 10-inch skillet over medium-high heat. Cook, stirring constantly, until the garlic is light golden brown and beginning to sizzle, 3 to 6 minutes. Add the tomatoes, chickpeas, and the remaining 2 tablespoons water; cook, stirring occasionally, until the water evaporates and the tomatoes are softened, 1 to 2 minutes. Add the spinach to the skillet, using tongs to stir and coat with the oil. Sprinkle with ¼ teaspoon salt and continue stirring with the tongs until the spinach is uniformly wilted and glossy green, about 2 minutes. Sprinkle with 2 tablespoons of the Parmesan and stir to combine. Drizzle with the remaining 2 teaspoons oil and sprinkle with the remaining 6 tablespoons Parmesan; season with salt to taste. Serve immediately.

SAUTÉED SPINACH WITH LEEKS AND HAZELNUTS

serves 4

This refined variation would be terrific paired with salmon. If you don't have a microwave-safe bowl large enough to accommodate the entire amount of spinach, cook it in a smaller bowl in 2 batches. Reduce the amount of water to 2 tablespoons per batch and cook the spinach for about 1½ minutes.

- 3 (6-ounce) bags baby spinach (about 16 cups)
- ¼ cup water, plus more if necessary
- 2 tablespoons unsalted butter
- 2 small leeks, white and light green parts halved lengthwise, washed, and sliced thin (about 3 cups)
  Salt
- ½ teaspoon grated zest and 1 tablespoon juice from 1 lemon
- ⅛ teaspoon ground nutmeg
- 2 tablespoons heavy cream
- ⅓ cup chopped hazelnuts, toasted

Follow the recipe for Sautéed Spinach with Almonds and Golden Raisins through step 1. Heat the butter in a 10-inch skillet over medium heat until the foaming subsides. Add the leeks and cook, stirring occasionally, until softened, 10 to 15 minutes, adding 1 teaspoon water to the skillet if the leeks begin to color. Add the spinach to the skillet, using tongs to stir, and coat with the butter. Sprinkle with ¼ teaspoon salt, the lemon zest, and nutmeg; continue stirring with the tongs until the spinach is uniformly wilted and glossy green, about 2 minutes. Drizzle with the lemon juice and cream; stir to combine. Sprinkle with the hazelnuts and season with salt to taste. Serve immediately.

TASTING LAB:
Premium Applewood Bacons

WHILE THERE'S PROBABLY NO SUCH THING AS TERRIBLE bacon, we know from previous tastings that there is definitely better bacon, with mass-market supermarket strips, for example, varying a lot from producer to producer. In recent years we've been hearing about small, artisanal producers crafting premium bacon using old-fashioned curing methods and hand labor. Before you factor in shipping (most of these products are available only through mail order), premium pork can cost double or even triple the price of ordinary bacon. Could such a dramatic difference in price really be worth it?

We bought six artisanal bacons by mail order in a single style—applewood smoked—so we could sample different brands' treatment of this traditional approach that adds a mildly sweet, fruity note to familiar bacon. We then pitted these premium strips against applewood-smoked bacon from the supermarket (we found just two brands, both a cut above true mass-market bacons like Hormel or Oscar Mayer). We cooked them all to a uniform doneness and tasted them blind.

American-style bacon is made from pork bellies that have been cut into slabs, cured, smoked, and sliced. But the similarity between most supermarket bacon and artisanal bacon generally ends there. Mass-produced bacon is made in a matter of hours and by machine. Artisanal bacon is made over days or even weeks, and much of the work is done by hand.

Mass-produced bacon often starts with frozen pork bellies that are thawed and tumbled in a metal drum to soften the meat, then placed on hangers and pumped full of a liquid cure solution. This solution includes curing salts such as sodium erythorbate and sodium nitrite, along with phosphates that bind the water to the cells in the meat, plumping it up (and also causing it to shrink in the pan when cooked). The meat is not actually smoked—liquid smoke and other flavorings such as sweeteners, herbs, and spices are added to the cure. After curing for a few hours, the bellies are often sprayed with more liquid smoke and heated in a thermal processing unit (often referred to as "the smokehouse") to destroy bacteria and infuse smoke flavor throughout the meat. Finally, the slab is quickly chilled, machine-pressed into a uniform shape, sliced, and packaged for sale.

By contrast, artisanal bacon takes much more time, as well as hand labor and real wood smoke. It begins with fresh pork bellies, which artisanal producers say make bacon with superior texture and flavor compared to starting with frozen bellies. While the pork is sometimes soaked in a "wet" cure, it is traditionally dry-cured, which means the meat is hand-rubbed with a dry mixture of herbs, sugars, salt, and curing salts. Artisanal producers leave the bacon to cure for anywhere from a day to a month, then slow-smoke it over wood fires, generally from one to three days, depending on the maker. The extended curing time intensifies the pork flavor and shrinks the meat so that the bacon doesn't shrivel much as it cooks. While most producers in our lineup burn real applewood sawdust or wood chips to create smoke, one burns dried apple pomace, the residue left after squeezing apples for cider.

The ingredients of the cure, the method of smoking, and the timing of each step determine each bacon's unique flavor. The age, gender, and breed of the pig and what it is fed are other factors that determine the final flavor of the bacon. For instance, most bacon producers won't use a sow that has given birth (too tough) or a male that isn't castrated (testosterone can give the meat an off-flavor) and call for a slaughter weight that is not too heavy to keep the bacon fat in proportion to the meat. In contrast to mass-produced bacon, where the pork bellies must be similar in size for machine processing, artisanal bacon has a much more irregular shape.

In spite of the fact that all of the bacons in our lineup were applewood-smoked or apple-flavored, they were remarkably different. Great bacon is all about a balance of sweet, smoky, salty, and meaty—and striking that flavor balance turned out to be the biggest factor for success with our tasters. In fact, tasters downgraded most of the premium mail-order brands for being too much of any one thing—too smoky, too fatty, or too sweet.

Only two of the six achieved enough of a balance to bring genuine raves. Tasters extolled Vande Rose Farms for having it all: a "nice balance of sweetness to salt, great deep complex ham flavor, very meaty." They also singled out Nodine's Smokehouse for its "hulking slices of delectable pork belly, sure to satisfy sweet and smoky fans." In addition

to sharing that desirable balance of sweet, smoky, and salty flavors, both bacons provided the largest, thickest-cut slices of the lineup (33 grams and 37 grams, respectively, compared to other slices that were as slight as 4 grams), which gave our tasters the meaty, substantial bacon texture they preferred.

But in the biggest surprise of the tasting, the next highest-rated bacons were not premium mail-order bacons at all, but our two supermarket brands. Both were a step up from the usual mass-produced bacon, straddling the gap between artisanal and more mainstream supermarket styles. Applegate Farms' Natural Uncured Sunday Bacon is smoked over real hardwood from apple trees. While it is described as "uncured" because the company does not use sodium nitrite (the chemically produced curing salt that creates the deep red color and characteristic flavor of bacon), it is cured just as thoroughly with naturally occurring sodium nitrate from celery juice. Farmland (called Carando in the Northeast) uses its own pigs, which allows it to start the process with fresh, versus frozen, pork bellies that absorb the cure more evenly. Farmland also uses real smoke from applewood chips, not liquid smoke. While these bacons didn't receive quite the raves of the two top-ranked premium bacons, tasters praised them both for good meaty flavor and mild smokiness.

So where does that leave us? As delicious as the best premium pork can be, there's no getting around the fact that mail-order bacon is far more expensive than even higher-end supermarket bacon. Applegate Farms costs about $11 per pound, while Farmland costs just $6. Even after we shopped around for the best price, one 12-ounce package of Vande Rose Farms bacon set us back $13.95 plus $22 in shipping (second-day delivery), adding up to nearly $36 for not even a full pound of bacon. (If you order a few pounds of bacon at the same time, you might get the total cost down to just over $20 per pound—still well over supermarket bacon prices.) Unfortunately for most of us, such a high price tag for what's basically breakfast food is a pretty steep barrier to bringing these bacons home.

Rating Premium Applewood Bacons

TWENTY MEMBERS OF THE AMERICA'S TEST KITCHEN STAFF SAMPLED EIGHT BACONS, SIX MAIL-ORDER ARTISANAL BRANDS and two higher-end brands from the supermarket, all smoked with applewood or cured with apple cider. We cooked them to a uniform doneness on a rimmed baking sheet and rated them on saltiness, sweetness, smokiness, and meatiness, as well as overall appeal. Because pork bellies are an agricultural product, some variation from package to package in flavor and in fat-to-meat ratio could be expected. To ensure that any variation was within an acceptable range, we tasted multiple batches of our two top-rated bacons months apart. Brands are listed in order of preference. See www.americastestkitchen.com for updates to this tasting.

HIGHLY RECOMMENDED

Vande Rose Farms Artisan Dry Cured Bacon, Applewood Smoked

$13.95 for 12 ounces, plus shipping; Size of slice: 33 g

Tasters raved that this bacon—which scored a distinct few notches higher than the rest of the lineup—had it all: "Nice balance of sweetness to salt, great deep complex ham flavor, very meaty."

RECOMMENDED

Nodine's Smokehouse Apple Smoke Flavored Bacon

$8 for 16 ounces, plus shipping; Size of slice: 37 g

"Wow, this is some huge piece of amazing bacon. Slices very wide and thick, and even the fat tastes great."

RECOMMENDED

Applegate Farms Natural Uncured Sunday Bacon

$5.39 for 8 ounces (supermarket); Size of slice: 7 g

One taster praised this nitrite-free supermarket brand for a "subtle smokiness, sweetness of pork, but not sugary. Woodsy but not overly smoky."

RECOMMENDED WITH RESERVATIONS

Farmland/Carando Apple Cider Cured Bacon, Applewood Smoked

$5.99 for 16 ounces (supermarket); Size of slice: 7.5 g

Some found this "sugary" super-market bacon far too sweet: "like cotton candy!" Others enjoyed its "apple-like flavor."

RECOMMENDED WITH RESERVATIONS

Oscar's Smoke House Applewood Smoked Bacon

$9.95 for 16 ounces, plus shipping; Size of slice: 4 g

A few tasters noted an "almost Asian" flavor to this bacon, describing it as "like teriyaki bacon, sweet and tangy," or "soy sauce."

RECOMMENDED WITH RESERVATIONS

North Country Smokehouse Applewood Smoked Bacon

$18.50 for 2 pounds, plus shipping; Size of slice: 12 g

Smoke flavor dominated, according to our tasters. "Pretty smoky, and very meaty and chewy." But the majority disagreed: "Wow, a lot of smoke, like barbecued bacon."

NOT RECOMMENDED

Niman Ranch Applewood Smoked Dry-Cured Bacon

$7.98 for 12 ounces, plus shipping; Size of slice: 15 g

"A fairly average piece of bacon," "thin," "not sweet or deeply flavorful."

NOT RECOMMENDED

Nueske's Applewood Smoked Bacon

$19.95 for 2 pounds, plus shipping; Size of slice: 9 g

Despite the company's claims of using particularly lean hogs, our tasters found this bacon "very fatty," with "hardly any meat."

Chris and Julia take a moment to joke around while the grilled rack of lamb rests. This resting period is essential because the lamb will finish cooking from residual heat. The rest also allows the meat's juices to redistribute so that the lamb is juicy and flavorful throughout.

GRILLED RACK
of lamb dinner

Toward the end of summer, when nights start to cool off, it's time to turn to lamb on the grill. Rich, hearty, and succulent, lamb is a welcome change from the burgers, chicken, and salads we most often associate with summer. And for company, rack of lamb is a terrific choice. But at nearly $20 a pound, it had better be good. Racks aren't easy to cook evenly, and lamb, being very fatty, has its own challenges on the grill, where flare-ups are a concern. We set out to find the secret to achieving a rich crust and pink interior to make the most of this prime cut of meat.

A Provençal-style summer vegetable gratin—thinly sliced fresh summer squash, zucchini, and tomatoes, shingled together with herbs and olive oil in a shallow casserole—partners perfectly with lamb. The heat of the oven intensifies the vegetables' sweet flavor, and the result should be a side dish that tastes as good as it looks. Unfortunately, summer vegetables contain a fair amount of water, so the dish has a tendency to bake up soggy and flavorless. This French casserole deserves better. Join us as we look for ways to guarantee a tender mélange of vegetables with deep, not dull, flavor.

GRILLED RACK OF LAMB

WHAT WE WANTED: Grilled rack of lamb with flavorful, evenly cooked meat and a great crust.

Rack of lamb is like prime rib: You don't cook an expensive cut like this very often, and when you do, you want it to be spectacular. The meat should be pink and juicy, surrounded by a well-caramelized crust that provides a contrast in texture to the lush, ultra-tender interior. Although it's possible to achieve these results in the oven, lamb and the grill have unbeatable chemistry. The intense heat of the coals produces a great crust and melts away the meat's abundance of fat, distributing flavor and tenderness throughout. And grilling imparts a smokiness that's the perfect complement to lamb's rich, gamey flavor. The only hitch: We'd have to figure out how to keep all the rendering fat from creating the meat-scorching flare-ups and sooty flavors that are the surest way to ruin this pricey cut.

Before we looked into the best way to grill the rack, we needed to figure out which type to buy. The racks sold by supermarkets are typically domestic or imported from Australia or New Zealand. Our tasters in the test kitchen preferred the milder domestic lamb to the imported meat, which is bred for gamier flavors. Domestic lamb also has the advantage of coming in bigger sizes. (For more information on the differences between domestic and imported lamb, see "Choosing Lamb," page 236.) We knew that the larger racks would be a challenge to cook evenly, but we also figured a heftier size would translate to a longer stay on the grill, and thus better grilled flavor.

The key to lamb's unique flavor and tenderness is its high proportion of fat, most of which covers one side of the rack like a cap. We knew from experience that leaving on the fat would lead to aggressive flare-ups virtually as soon as we put the lamb over the coals. But removing all of the cap wasn't the solution either. When we did this, the racks ended up dry, with very little of the distinctive lamb flavor

that makes this meat taste superb. As a compromise, we left a thin layer of fat over the loin and removed most of the fat between the bones.

Even trimmed of fat, we knew we couldn't treat lamb like any old piece of chicken or pork cooked directly over the coals the entire time. Lamb still has enough interior fat that it would only be a matter of minutes before the flare-ups started. When grilling fattier meat, we often build a two-level fire by pushing all the coals to one side of the grill to create hot and cool areas. We then brown the meat over the hot coals, sliding it to the cooler side of the grill to finish. When we tried this method, the racks cooked to medium-rare at the center and had decent grilled flavor. However, many tasters found the outer layers of the meat to be overdone and tough. Plus, starting the racks on the hot side of the grill still led to flare-ups if we weren't paying close attention.

It then dawned on us that our order of cooking was reversed. What we should do is start the lamb over indirect heat to allow the fat to render first. Once that fat was sufficiently rendered, we could move the racks to direct heat to brown the exterior. Testing this hypothesis, we had much better results. The only drawback was that because of the lamb's size, we had to crowd the racks on one side of the grill, leaving them catty-corner to the fire, which caused them to cook unevenly. This method also left small pockets of unrendered fat that made the meat taste greasy instead of rich.

To solve this problem, we turned to a solution we devised for other large cuts: Instead of a traditional two-level fire with all the coals on one side, we heaped two smaller mounds on either side of the grill and placed a foil pan in the center to act as a divider. (The pan would also serve as a drip tray to catch rendering fat.) We then positioned our lamb racks over this cooler middle ground. Situated this way, all parts of the meat were exposed to the same amount of heat, allowing the racks to cook more

evenly. And because the heat was more diffuse, the fat also rendered more thoroughly. When the racks were lightly browned and the fat sufficiently rendered, we could then slide them over to the hot sides for just a short while to brown the exterior without fear of flare-ups. (Concerned that this setup might be hard to replicate on a gas grill, we did some quick tests. We found that because of the larger surface area of the gas grill, we could abandon the split-fire method and simply leave one burner on high and turn the others off.)

Our biggest challenge met, we set out to flavor the lamb. Because lamb tastes so good on its own, we wanted to enhance the meat's flavor without overwhelming it. Many recipes call for marinating the lamb before grilling, but the several we tried only succeeded in making the lamb mushy. A dry rub, applied to the racks before they went on the grill, did add some flavor, but with our particular cooking method, much of the spice rub trickled away with the rendering fat, ending up in the drip pan. We tried applying the spice rub partway through cooking, but we just ended up with burnt fingers and the dusty taste of raw spices. Our

best option turned out to be a wet rub consisting of garlic and a couple of robust herbs (rosemary and thyme) mixed with a little oil (just enough to adhere the flavorings to the lamb without causing flare-ups). Brushed on the racks as they browned over the direct heat, the wet rub added just the right note to our perfectly cooked meat.

WHAT WE LEARNED: To prep the lamb for the grill, remove a thin layer of fat over the loin and most of the fat between the bones; leaving some fat on the lamb is essential for flavor and moisture. To cook the lamb evenly as well as to effectively render its fat, place a disposable foil pan in the middle of the grill and heap two small piles of coals on either side of the pan. Place the lamb in the middle of the grill, over the pan (which catches the rendering fat, so flare-ups won't occur), and flip the lamb racks throughout grilling. A wet rub (garlic, rosemary, thyme, and olive oil) is the best bet for flavoring the meat—marinades turn the lamb mushy and dry rubs simply don't work with our grilling method. For a rich crust that isn't charred, apply the wet rub during the last few minutes of grilling.

SHOPPING NOTES: Choosing Lamb

Consumers typically have three choices when shopping for lamb: domestic meat or meat imported from Australia or New Zealand. Lambs in both Australia and New Zealand are pasture-fed on mixed grasses, which leads to their gamier, more pronounced flavor. Lambs raised in the United States begin on a diet of grass but finish with grain, resulting in the milder-tasting meat that our tasters preferred. Diet also accounts for the larger size of American lamb. On average, the domestic racks we used to develop our recipe weighed about 1½ pounds each, whereas the imported racks typically weighed in at just over a pound.

Domestic
American-raised lamb boasts bigger racks and a sweet, mild flavor.

Down Under
Racks from Australia (as well as New Zealand) are smaller and have a stronger, gamier flavor.

CHARCOAL-GRILLED RACK OF LAMB

serves 4

We prefer the milder taste and bigger size of domestic lamb, but you may substitute imported lamb from New Zealand or Australia. Since imported racks are generally smaller, follow the shorter cooking times given in the recipe. Most lamb is sold frenched (meaning part of each rib bone is exposed), but chances are there will still be some extra fat between the bones. Remove the majority of this fat, leaving an inch at the top of the small eye of meat. Also, make sure that the chine bone (along the bottom of the rack) has been removed to ensure that it will be easy to cut between the ribs after cooking. Ask the butcher to do it; it's very hard to cut off at home.

12 by 8-inch disposable foil pan
Vegetable oil for the cooking grate
4 teaspoons olive oil
4 teaspoons chopped fresh rosemary leaves
2 teaspoons chopped fresh thyme leaves
2 medium garlic cloves, minced or pressed through a garlic press (about 2 teaspoons)
2 racks of lamb (about 1½ pounds each), rib bones frenched, meat trimmed of all excess fat (see "Trimming Fat from Rack of Lamb," page 237)
Salt and ground black pepper

1. Light a large chimney starter filled with charcoal (6 quarts, or about 100 briquettes) and allow to burn until the coals

TECHNIQUE: Trimming Fat from Rack of Lamb

1. Peel back the thick outer layer of fat from the racks, along with the thin flap of meat underneath it. Use a boning or paring knife to cut any tissue connecting the fat cap to the rack. (Not all lamb racks will have this cap of fat attached.)

2. Using a sharp boning or paring knife, trim the remaining thin layer of fat that covers the loin, leaving the strip of fat that separates the loin and small eye of meat directly above it.

3. Make a straight cut along the top side of the bones, an inch up from the small eye of meat.

4. Remove any fat above this line and scrape any remaining meat or fat from the exposed bones.

are fully ignited and partially covered with a thin layer of ash, about 20 minutes. Place the foil pan in the center of the grill. Empty the coals into the grill, creating equal-sized piles on each side of the pan. Position the cooking grate over the coals, cover the grill, and heat until the grate is hot, about 5 minutes; scrape the cooking grate clean with a grill brush. The grill is ready when the coals are medium-hot. Lightly dip a wad of paper towels in the oil; holding the wad with tongs, wipe the cooking grate.

2. Combine 3 teaspoons of the olive oil, the rosemary, thyme, and garlic in a small bowl; set aside. Rub the lamb with the remaining 1 teaspoon oil and season generously with salt and pepper. Place the racks, bone side up, on the center of the cooking grate over the foil pan, with the meaty side of the racks very close to, but not quite over, the hot coals. Cover and grill until the meat is lightly browned, faint grill marks appear, and the fat has begun to render, 8 to 10 minutes.

3. Flip the racks over, bone side down, and move to the hotter part of the grill. Grill, without moving, until well browned, 3 to 4 minutes. Brush the racks with the rosemary mixture. Flip the racks so the bone side is up and continue to grill over the hotter parts of the grill until well browned, 3 to 4 minutes. Stand the racks up and lean them against each other; continue to grill over one side of the hotter part of the grill until the bottoms are well browned and an

TECHNIQUE: Grilling Racks of Lamb

1. Build split fire: Place disposable foil pan between two mounds of coals to create cooler center area flanked by 2 hotter areas.

2. Start over indirect heat: Place racks bone side up on cooler center of grill and grill until lightly browned. (On gas grill, place racks on cool side of grill.)

3. Transfer to direct heat: Grill racks, bone side down, over hotter sides of grill for 3 to 4 minutes, and then brush with herb paste.

4. Flip meat: Flip each rack so bone side is up and brown meat.

5. Brown rack bottoms: Stand racks together and brown their bottoms.

instant-read thermometer inserted from the side of a rack into the center, but away from any bones, reads 120 degrees for medium-rare or 125 degrees for medium, 3 to 8 minutes longer.

4. Remove the lamb from the grill and allow to rest, tented with foil, 15 minutes (the racks will continue to cook while resting). Cut between each rib to separate the chops and serve immediately.

VARIATION

GAS-GRILLED RACK OF LAMB

Follow the recipe for Charcoal-Grilled Rack of Lamb, turning all of the burners to high and heating the grill with the lid down until very hot, about 15 minutes. Scrape and oil the cooking grate. Proceed with the recipe from step 2, leaving the primary burner on high and turning off the other burner(s). Grill the lamb, omitting the disposable pan, with the lid down.

SUMMER VEGETABLE GRATIN

WHAT WE WANTED: A foolproof version of the classic French casserole—perfectly cooked summer vegetables, accented with herbs and topped with a browned, cheesy crust.

When summer yields a bumper crop of zucchini and tomatoes, we often consider making a simple, Provençal-style vegetable gratin. We imagine a golden brown, cheesy topping providing a rich contrast to the fresh, bright flavor of the vegetables. Then reality interrupts: As they cook, juicy vegetables exude a torrent of liquid that washes away flavors, turning our idyllic side dish into a squishy, soggy mistake.

There are plenty of vegetable gratin recipes out there, and we spent a day in the test kitchen trying a few, hoping to find the one of our dreams. But it wasn't meant to be—most were so flooded that we had to serve them with a slotted spoon. One even called for half of a loaf of sourdough bread to be layered among the vegetables, presumably to soak up some of the juices. But it didn't work. Even with 4 cups of spongy bread cubes, a deluge of liquid still ruined the dish. And with the release of juices, along went the flavor—the gratins were hopelessly bland and watery.

Before we could outline a dehydration plan, we had to determine exactly which vegetables to include. After some experimentation, we decided to stick with a fairly typical combination of tomatoes, zucchini, and summer squash. The other common choices, eggplant and bell peppers, fell short. Eggplant was simply too mushy and spongy; and red, yellow, and orange bell peppers looked pretty but took on a steamed flavor unless they were roasted before being added to the gratin. (The roasted peppers, on the other hand, tasted great and are worth the extra effort, so we used them in a recipe variation.)

Our first move was to bake the casserole uncovered. The practice of covering the gratin with foil during baking (recommended by most recipes to speed cooking) was keeping too much moisture in. This was a step in the right direction, but our gratin was still waterlogged. To rid the zucchini and squash of some of their liquid, precooking methods such as grilling, broiling, or sautéing came to mind. Although these methods were workable, we didn't want to spend all day at the grill, oven, or stove just to make a mere side dish. Salting, a technique frequently used to draw moisture from vegetables, made more sense. This method worked like a charm on the zucchini and summer squash, drying them out and thoroughly seasoning them as well. The tomatoes, however, were still exuding more liquid than we wanted. Should we go one step further and remove their watery jelly and seeds before salting them?

To our surprise, when we tried this, the gratin lacked deep tomato flavor. We wanted to make sure our results weren't a fluke, so we prepared two gratins—one with salted seedless tomatoes and one with salted tomatoes with the seeds and jelly intact—and tasted them side by side. The gratin made with tomatoes that had jelly and seeds was significantly richer and fuller in flavor than the one made without them. After some research, we learned why: These two components contain far more flavorful glutamate compounds than the tomato flesh (see "Keeping the Taste in Tomatoes," page 242). If we wanted a gratin with intense tomato flavor, it was actually in our best interest to leave the jelly and seeds in, even if it meant a little extra liquid in the dish.

In our testing, we found that the spots where the edges of the tomatoes peeked through the layers of zucchini were particularly good, having taken on the appealing qualities of oven-roasted tomatoes. To capitalize on this effect, we remodeled the architecture of the casserole, moving the tomatoes to a single top layer where they could really roast and caramelize. This worked well, especially when we drizzled the tomatoes with an aromatic garlic-thyme oil. The fragrant oil was so good that we decided to toss the zucchini and squash in it as well.

To add complexity, we inserted a layer of caramelized

onions between the zucchini/squash and tomato layers and sprinkled the gratin with Parmesan bread crumbs. When our gratin came out of the oven leaking very little juice, we knew our rescue mission was a success.

WHAT WE LEARNED: For juicy, but not waterlogged, vegetables (tomatoes, zucchini, and summer squash), salt them prior to assembling the gratin. Salting draws moisture from the vegetables and seasons them as well. Don't seed the tomatoes, as that's where much of the tomato flavor resides. Press the vegetables with paper towels after salting to wick away the excess moisture, and season the vegetables with garlic-thyme oil to further enhance their flavor. To intensify the tomatoes' flavor, layer them on top of the zucchini and summer squash, where they'll stay especially dry, and roast. Include a layer of caramelized onions for richness, and top the gratin with bread crumbs, shallots, and Parmesan for a well-seasoned topping that also provides a crunchy contrast to the baked vegetables.

SUMMER VEGETABLE GRATIN

serves 6 to 8 as a side dish or 4 as a light entrée

The success of this recipe depends on good-quality produce. Buy zucchini and summer squash of roughly the same diameter. We like the visual contrast zucchini and summer squash bring to the dish, but you can also use just one or the other. A similarly sized broiler-safe gratin dish can be substituted for the 13 by 9-inch baking dish. Serve the gratin alongside grilled fish or meat and accompanied by bread to soak up any flavorful juices.

  6 tablespoons extra-virgin olive oil
  1 pound zucchini, ends trimmed and cut crosswise into ¼-inch-thick slices (see note)
  1 pound yellow summer squash, ends trimmed and cut crosswise into ¼-inch-thick slices (see note)
  2 teaspoons salt
 1½ pounds ripe tomatoes (3 to 4 large), cut into ¼-inch-thick slices
  2 medium onions, halved lengthwise and sliced thin pole to pole (about 3 cups)
  ¾ teaspoon ground black pepper
  2 medium garlic cloves, minced or pressed through a garlic press (about 2 teaspoons)
  1 tablespoon minced fresh thyme leaves
  1 large slice good-quality white sandwich bread, torn into quarters
  2 ounces grated Parmesan cheese (about 1 cup)
  2 medium shallots, minced (about ¼ cup)
  ¼ cup chopped fresh basil leaves

1. Adjust an oven rack to the upper-middle position and heat the oven to 400 degrees. Brush a 13 by 9-inch baking dish with 1 tablespoon of the oil; set aside.

2. Toss the zucchini and summer squash slices with 1 teaspoon of the salt in a large bowl; transfer to a colander set over a bowl. Let stand until the zucchini and squash release at least 3 tablespoons of liquid, about 45 minutes. Arrange the slices on a triple layer of paper towels; cover with another triple layer of paper towels. Firmly press each slice to remove as much liquid as possible.

3. Place the tomato slices in a single layer on a double layer of paper towels and sprinkle evenly with ½ teaspoon more salt; let stand 30 minutes. Place a second double layer of paper towels on top of the tomatoes and press firmly to dry the tomatoes.

4. Meanwhile, heat 1 tablespoon more oil in a 12-inch nonstick skillet over medium heat until shimmering. Add the onions, the remaining ½ teaspoon salt, and ¼ teaspoon of the pepper; cook, stirring occasionally, until the onions are softened and dark golden brown, 20 to 25 minutes. Set the onions aside.

5. Combine the garlic, 3 tablespoons more oil, the remaining ½ teaspoon pepper, and thyme in a small bowl. In a large bowl, toss the zucchini and summer squash in half of the oil mixture, then arrange in the greased baking dish. Arrange the caramelized onions in an even layer over the squash. Slightly overlap the tomato slices in a single layer on top of the onions. Spoon the remaining garlic-oil mixture evenly

over the tomatoes. Bake until the vegetables are tender and the tomatoes are starting to brown on the edges, 40 to 45 minutes.

6. Meanwhile, process the bread in a food processor until finely ground, about 10 seconds. (You should have about 1 cup crumbs.) Combine the bread crumbs, remaining 1 tablespoon oil, the Parmesan, and shallots in a medium bowl. Remove the baking dish from the oven and increase the heat to 450 degrees. Sprinkle the bread crumb mixture evenly on top of the tomatoes. Bake the gratin until bubbling and the cheese is lightly browned, 5 to 10 minutes. Sprinkle with the basil and let sit at room temperature 10 minutes before serving.

VARIATION

SUMMER VEGETABLE GRATIN WITH ROASTED PEPPERS AND SMOKED MOZZARELLA

Follow the recipe for Summer Vegetable Gratin, substituting 4 ounces shredded smoked mozzarella cheese (1 cup) for the Parmesan and 3 roasted red peppers, skinned and cut into 1-inch pieces, for the summer squash (do not salt the roasted peppers).

TECHNIQUE: Assembling the Gratin

1. Toss the salted zucchini and squash in half of the garlic-thyme oil, then arrange in a greased baking dish.

2. Spread the caramelized onions in an even layer on top of the zucchini and squash.

3. Slightly overlap the salted tomatoes in a single layer on top of the onions, then top with the remaining garlic-thyme oil.

4. When the vegetables are tender, sprinkle the gratin with the bread crumb mixture, then bake until golden brown.

SCIENCE DESK:
Keeping the Taste in Tomatoes

REMOVING THE SEEDS FROM TOMATOES IS A COMMON practice intended to improve the texture of a finished dish. But how does that affect flavor?

EXPERIMENT
We prepared two gratins, one made with intact tomatoes and another from which the tomato seeds and jelly had been removed.

RESULTS
The gratin with the intact tomatoes had a decidedly richer, deeper flavor than its stripped-down counterpart.

EXPLANATION
According to a study published in the *Journal of Agricultural and Food Chemistry,* the seeds and jelly of tomatoes actually contain three times the amount of flavor-enhancing glutamic acid as the flesh. (This is the compound that supplies the savory quality known as umami in many foods.) So the next time a recipe calls for removing the seeds from tomatoes, you may want to ignore the instructions. You'll be saving time—and flavor.

Stripped Away   **Full of Flavor**

Rating Broiler-Safe Gratin Dishes

WE TESTED THREE BROILER-SAFE BAKING DISHES BY baking a variety of casseroles in them. We rated them on how well the food browned as well as how easily we were able to maneuver the dishes in and out of the oven. Brands are listed in order of preference. See www.americastestkitchen.com for updates to this testing.

HIGHLY RECOMMENDED
Emile Henry 3-Quart Gratin Dish
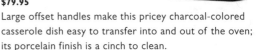
$54.95
This heavy-duty clay casserole dish is a great broiler-safe alternative to Pyrex glassware.

RECOMMENDED
Revol Eclipse 3½-Quart Graphite Baker
$79.95
Large offset handles make this pricey charcoal-colored casserole dish easy to transfer into and out of the oven; its porcelain finish is a cinch to clean.

RECOMMENDED
All-Clad Porcelain 3¼-Quart Baker with Stainless Steel Trivet

$99.95
This shallow porcelain pan browns food nicely and cleans up easily, but without its trivet, the handles are skimpy.

EQUIPMENT CORNER:
Broiler-Safe Gratin Dishes

AS AN ALL-PURPOSE BAKING DISH, PYREX HOLDS ITS own—it was the first dish we turned to for baking our gratin. But it has one main drawback: Pyrex is not broiler-safe, a necessary feature for melting cheese on many casseroles. As alternatives to Pyrex, we tested three broiler-safe baking dishes of similar size (around 3 quarts) made of clay or porcelain. All produced well-browned, evenly cooked food and each sported large, easy-grip handles for trouble-free maneuvering.

Sizzling Garlic Shrimp **page 154**

Simple Italian-Style Meat Sauce **page 30**

Charcoal-Grilled Bone-In Chicken Breasts **page 203**

Charcoal-Grilled Marinated Flank Steak **page 213**

Stuffed Chicken Breasts **page 65**

Crunchy Baked Pork Chops **page 53**

Chicken Saltimbocca **page 131**

Steak Tacos **page 94** with Sweet and Spicy Pickled Onions **page 96**

Daube Provençal **page 143**

Individual Make-Ahead Chocolate Soufflés **page 339**

Oatmeal Cake with Broiled Icing **page 313**

Apple Pandowdy **page 276**

Fluffy Yellow Layer Cake **page 325** with Foolproof Chocolate Frosting **page 328**

Applesauce Snack Cake **page 280**

Blueberry Pie **page 300**

Almost No-Knead Bread **page 263**

BREADMAKING, simplified

We'd always thought that using a bread machine was the only "shortcut" available to home bakers. (And even so, it's not a method we advocate.) So when we read about a no-knead bread recipe, published in the *New York Times,* we took notice. After baking up a few loaves, we were impressed, but the recipe wasn't perfect. The flavor wasn't nearly as complex as a loaf made in the traditional manner. And the shape of the bread was a problem, too—the loaves often turned out misshapen. With dreams of inspiring the uninitiated to try their hand at bread making with an easier approach, we set out to improve this no-fuss bread's bland taste and make it rise high every time.

For beginning bakers, Irish soda bread can be a great place to start. There's no kneading or rising required—this bread relies on a chemical leavener (usually baking soda) for its rise. Even better, this simple bread comes together quickly, so it can be on the table for dinner or breakfast in no time. We set out to create a recipe for authentic soda bread, one with a tender, tight crumb and craggy crust—a loaf that's as good dunked in soup or stew as it is spread with butter and jam.

ALMOST NO-KNEAD BREAD

WHAT WE WANTED: A fresh-baked artisanal-style loaf with a light, moist crumb, fully developed flavor, and crisp crust—and made with a minimum of effort.

In November 2006, *New York Times* writer Mark Bittman published a recipe developed by Jim Lahey of the Sullivan Street Bakery in Manhattan that promised to shake up the world of home baking. The recipe did the seemingly impossible: It allowed the average home cook to bake a loaf of bread that looked like it had been produced in a professional bakery. The recipe, which instantly won legions of followers, was exceedingly simple: Mix a few cups of flour, a tiny amount of yeast, and a little salt together in a bowl; stir in some water until the ingredients just come together; and leave the dough to rise. After 12 to 18 hours, the dough is turned a couple of times, shaped, allowed to rise, and baked in a Dutch oven. An hour later, out comes the most beautiful-looking loaf most people have ever baked at home—and all with no kneading.

At first, it seemed unlikely that there was anything to improve upon here. The no-knead recipe was remarkably easy and worlds better than other no-fuss breads. But threads on our bulletin board and other Web sites turned up some complaints amid all the praise. We decided to give the existing recipe to five inexperienced bakers in order to see what (if any) issues arose.

We noticed a problem even before we sliced into the first loaf. Although all were beautifully browned and crisp, the loaves varied wildly in size and shape, ranging from rounded mounds to flat, irregular blobs. Casting first impressions aside, we cut into each one and tasted a bite. Though the crusts were extraordinary—better than any we'd ever produced—the flavor of the crumb fell flat. It simply did not capture the complex yeasty, tangy flavor of a true artisanal loaf. We wondered if we could make this bread more consistent and better-tasting.

We decided to tackle the problem of shape first. Thanks to the ingenious use of a Dutch oven, the bread always acquired a dark, crisp crust, but the loaves took on a disconcertingly broad range of forms. After observing testers make the recipe a few times, we realized the problem: The wetness of the dough was making it too delicate to handle. Though it was well risen before baking, it was deflating on its way into the pot. In addition, because of its high moisture content, the dough was spreading out over the bottom of the pot before it could firm up properly. We analyzed the no-knead recipe and found that its dough is 85 percent hydrated—meaning that for every 10 ounces of flour, there are 8.5 ounces of water. Most rustic breads, on the other hand, max out at around 80 percent hydration, and standard sandwich breads hover between 60 percent and 75 percent hydration. So what would happen if we reduced the amount of water?

To find out, we made a batch of dough in which we cut the hydration to 70 percent. Sure enough, this dough was much easier to handle and emerged from the oven well risen and perfectly shaped. But unfortunately, the texture was ruined. Instead of an open, airy crumb structure, it was dense and chewy, with rubbery pockets of unleavened flour. So more moisture led to an open but squat loaf, and less moisture led to a high but dense loaf. Was there a way to reconcile these two extremes?

Many bread recipes call for a rest period after water is added to the flour but before the dough is kneaded. This rest is called "autolysis" (although most bakers use the French term *autolyse*). In most recipes, autolysis is just 20 to 30 minutes, but the no-knead bread calls for something completely out of the ordinary: a 12-hour rest. Was there something in the mechanics of such a lengthy autolysis that could help us solve the textural problem? The most common explanation for the autolysis process is simply that it allows time for the flour to hydrate and rest, making the dough easier to manipulate later on. But the word *autolysis* technically refers to the destruction of cells or proteins through enzymatic

action. We decided to have a closer look at what really happens to the dough during the process.

The ultimate goal of making bread dough is to create gluten, a strong network of cross-linked proteins that traps air bubbles and stretches as the dough bakes, creating the bubbly, chewy crumb structure that is the signature of any good loaf. In order to form these cross-links, the proteins in the flour need to be aligned next to each other. Imagine the proteins as bundled-up balls of yarn you are trying to tie together into one longer piece, which you'll then sew together into a wider sheet. In their balled-up state, it's not possible to tie them together; first you have to untangle and straighten them out. This straightening out and aligning is usually accomplished by kneading.

But untangling and stretching out short pieces of yarn is much easier than untangling entire balls. This is where autolysis comes in. As the dough autolyzes, enzymes naturally present in wheat act like scissors, cutting the balled-up proteins into smaller segments that are easier to straighten during kneading. This is why dough that has undergone autolysis requires much less kneading than freshly made dough. And here's where the hydration level comes in: The more water there is, the more efficiently the cut-and-link process takes place.

So this was the explanation for how the no-knead bread recipe published in the *New York Times* worked. With 85 percent hydration and a 12-hour rest, the dough was so wet and had autolyzed for so long that the enzymes had broken the proteins down into extremely small pieces. These pieces were so small that, even without kneading, they could stretch out and cross-link during fermentation and the brief turning step. At 70 percent hydration, there simply was not enough water in our dough for the enzymes to act as efficiently as they had in the original recipe. As a result, many of the proteins in our finished bread were still in a semi-balled-up state, giving our bread the overly chewy texture.

What if the secret to making a better no-knead bread was actually adding in some kneading? We knew that even at a relatively dry 70 percent hydration, the proteins in our dough had already been broken down significantly by the long 12- to 18-hour autolysis. All they probably needed was a little kneading to untangle and create an airy, light crumb. We decided to make the leap.

We took the dough that we had resting from the day before and turned it out onto our board. Trusting that our understanding of autolysis was correct, we gave the dough the bare minimum of kneads—adding just 15 extra seconds to the no-knead recipe—and continued exactly as we had before. The loaf emerged from the oven as beautifully browned and perfectly shaped as any we'd made so far. After letting it cool, we cut into it to reveal an ideal crumb structure: large pockets of air and stretched sheets of gluten. Not only that, we found that since such a small amount of kneading could develop gluten in such a forceful manner, we could actually reduce the minimum time of the rest period from 12 hours to eight. That 15 seconds of kneading had reaped huge benefits.

Now that we had bread with a great shape and texture, we turned our attention to the loaf's lackluster taste. To get a better sense of what specific flavors we were missing, we bought a loaf of bread from a bakery that makes dough the old-fashioned way—with a fermented starter. Because a starter contains a much more varied assortment of yeasts than the ones found in a packet, it yields more complex flavor. Tasting the bakery bread side by side with the no-knead bread confirmed this. But creating a starter is a multiday process. How could we get the flavors that a starter produces without actually having to use one? Could we introduce a little tanginess another way?

Scanning the labels in our dry storage area, we saw that the majority of our bottled vinegars are 5 percent solutions of acetic acid—the same acid produced by bacteria during dough fermentation. Since other vinegars would introduce undesirable flavors to the bread, we experimented with different amounts of distilled white vinegar before settling on a single tablespoon.

Our bread now had tang, but it lacked complexity. What we needed was a concentrated shot of yeasty flavor. We then realized that beyond bread, there is another commonly available substance that relies on yeast for flavor: beer. Would its flavors compare to those produced in dough fermentation?

For the most part, no. We started our testing with dark ales, thinking their rich taste would lead to better flavor. The resulting bread had a strange spicy, fruity aftertaste and smelled like beer. Then we tried a light American-style lager. This time the loaf came out with a distinct "bready" versus "beery" aroma that could fool anyone who had not seen the lager go into the dough. Why is it that the lighter beer produced the better taste? It turns out that the yeast in lagers is treated in a way that closely resembles the way yeast acts in dough, resulting in the production of similar flavor compounds (see "How Beer Boosts Bread's Flavor," page 265).

Through the simplest of tweaks—less hydration, the addition of vinegar and beer, and a few seconds of kneading—we had a loaf of bread that both looked and tasted incredible.

WHAT WE LEARNED: The existing *New York Times* recipe for no-knead bread produced a decent, but not great, loaf, so we set out to improve upon it. For a consistently high-rise, even shape and complex yeasty flavor, we found that a few changes were in order. To ensure that the loaf doesn't turn out misshapen, lower the hydration (the ratio of water to flour)—this makes a less wet dough that holds its shape. Knead the dough briefly (just 15 seconds) to help strengthen it for a consistent shape and better crumb, once baked. For bread with artisanal-quality flavor, add a little vinegar to the dough—vinegar's tang imparts a flavor similar to that of a fermented starter. And for further complexity, add a little mild lager as well—the yeasty quality of the beer mimics the flavor of a loaf made the old-fashioned way.

ALMOST NO-KNEAD BREAD

makes 1 large round loaf

An enameled cast-iron Dutch oven with a tight-fitting lid yields best results, but the recipe also works in a regular cast-iron Dutch oven or heavy stockpot. Use a mild-flavored lager, such as Budweiser (mild nonalcoholic lager also works). The bread is best eaten the day it is baked but can be wrapped in aluminum foil and stored in a cool, dry place for up to 2 days.

3	cups (15 ounces) unbleached all-purpose flour, plus additional for dusting work surface
¼	teaspoon instant or rapid-rise yeast
1½	teaspoons salt
¾	cup plus 2 tablespoons (7 ounces) water, at room temperature
¼	cup plus 2 tablespoons (3 ounces) mild-flavored lager (see note)
1	tablespoon distilled white vinegar

1. Whisk the flour, yeast, and salt together in a large bowl. Add the water, beer, and vinegar. Using a rubber spatula, fold the mixture, scraping up the dry flour from the bottom of the bowl, until a shaggy ball forms. Cover the bowl with plastic wrap and let sit at room temperature for 8 to 18 hours.

1. Mix: Stir the wet ingredients into the dry ingredients with a spatula.

2. Rest: Leave the dough to rest for 8 to 18 hours.

3. Knead: Knead the dough 10 to 15 times and shape it into a ball.

4. Let Rise: Allow the dough to rise for 2 hours in a parchment paper–lined skillet.

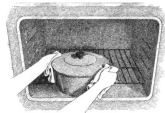

5. Bake: Place the dough in a preheated Dutch oven and bake it until it's deep brown.

2. Lay a 12 by 18-inch sheet of parchment paper inside a 10-inch skillet and spray with vegetable oil spray. Transfer the dough to a lightly floured work surface and knead 10 to 15 times. Shape the dough into a ball by pulling the edges into the middle. Transfer the dough, seam side down, to the parchment-lined skillet and spray the surface of the dough with vegetable oil spray. Cover loosely with plastic wrap and let rise at room temperature until the dough has doubled in size and does not readily spring back when poked with a finger, about 2 hours.

3. About 30 minutes before baking, adjust an oven rack to the lowest position, place a 6- to 8-quart heavy-bottomed Dutch oven (with a lid) on the rack, and heat the oven to 500 degrees. Lightly flour the top of the dough and, using a razor blade or sharp knife, make one 6-inch-long, ½-inch-deep slit along the top of the dough. Carefully remove the pot from the oven and remove the lid. Pick up the dough by lifting the parchment overhang and lower into the pot (let any excess parchment hang over the pot edge). Cover the pot and place in the oven. Reduce the oven temperature to 425 degrees and bake, covered, for 30 minutes. Remove the lid and continue to bake until the loaf is deep brown and an instant-read thermometer inserted into the center registers 210 degrees, 20 to 30 minutes longer. Carefully remove the bread from the pot; transfer to a wire rack and cool to room temperature, about 2 hours, before serving.

VARIATIONS

ALMOST NO-KNEAD BREAD WITH OLIVES, ROSEMARY, AND PARMESAN

Italian flavorings give this bread zesty flavor.

Follow the recipe for Almost No-Knead Bread, adding 4 ounces finely grated Parmesan cheese (about 2 cups) and 1 tablespoon minced fresh rosemary leaves to the flour mixture in step 1. Add ½ cup pitted green olives, chopped, with the water in step 1.

TECHNIQUE: Making a Bread Sling

Transferring dough to a preheated Dutch oven to bake can be tricky. To avoid burnt fingers and help the dough hold its shape, we came up with a novel solution: Let the dough rise in a skillet (its shallow depth makes it better than a bowl) that's been lined with greased parchment paper, then use the paper's edges to pick up the dough and lower it into the Dutch oven. The bread remains on the parchment paper as it bakes.

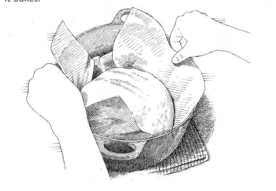

ALMOST NO-KNEAD SEEDED RYE BREAD

This deli favorite makes terrific sandwiches.

Follow the recipe for Almost No-Knead Bread, replacing 1⅜ cups (7 ounces) of the all-purpose flour with 1⅛ cups (7 ounces) rye flour. Add 2 tablespoons caraway seeds to the flour mixture in step 1.

ALMOST NO-KNEAD WHOLE WHEAT BREAD

This hearty loaf is great for sandwiches or toast—try it buttered and drizzled with honey.

Follow the recipe for Almost No-Knead Bread, replacing 1 cup (5 ounces) of the all-purpose flour with 1 cup (5 ounces) whole wheat flour. Stir 2 tablespoons honey into the water before adding it to the dry ingredients in step 1.

ALMOST NO-KNEAD CRANBERRY-PECAN BREAD

This hearty variation is terrific at breakfast.

Follow the recipe for Almost No-Knead Bread, adding ½ cup dried cranberries and ½ cup toasted pecan halves to the flour mixture in step 1.

SCIENCE DESK:
How Beer Boosts Bread's Flavor

DURING A STARTER'S FERMENTATION, YEAST produces alcohol, carbon dioxide, and sulfur compounds, all of which contribute to good bread's unique flavor. These three elements are present together in another location—a bottle of beer. But why choose lager over other types of beer? It's all about the fermentation. Most nonlager beers undergo a process called "top fermentation," whereby yeast floats on top of the wort (grain mashed in hot water), which is exposed to oxygen and kept warm. Oxygen and warmth persuade yeast to produce spicy, astringent flavor compounds called phenols and fruity, floral compounds called esters that are desirable in beer but not in bread. Lagers, on the other hand, undergo "bottom fermentation," where the yeast is kept submerged in the low-oxygen environment at the bottom of the wort at colder temperatures, which causes the yeast to produce fewer phenols and esters, so that the breadier yeast and sulfur flavors come forward.

Beer for Bread

Mild-flavored beer contains flavor compounds similar to those in a dough starter, which gives our bread a taste boost.

IRISH SODA BREAD

WHAT WE WANTED: Authentic Irish soda bread—a simple bread that's tender, crusty, and not too sweet.

Authentic Irish soda bread has a tender, dense crumb and a rough-textured, crunchy crust. It is versatile enough to be served with butter and jam at breakfast, for sandwiches at lunch, or alongside the evening meal.

As we looked over a multitude of recipes for soda bread, we found that they fell into two categories. The American versions contained eggs, butter, and sugar in varying amounts along with caraway seeds, raisins, and a multitude of other flavorings. But recipes from most Irish cookbooks used only four ingredients: flour (white and/or whole wheat), baking soda, salt, and buttermilk.

We decided to begin our investigations with the flour. Because of Ireland's climate, the wheat grown there is a "soft," or low-protein, variety. Although not suitable for strong European-style yeast breads, this flour is perfect for chemically leavened breads. This is basically because flour with a lower protein content produces a finer crumb and more tender product, key for breads that don't have the light texture provided when yeast is used as the leavener.

After suffering through several tough, heavy loaves made with unbleached all-purpose flour, we started exploring different proportions of cake flour—a low-protein flour—as well as all-purpose flour. And, in fact, the bread did become more tender and a little lighter with the addition of some cake flour. As the ratio of cake to all-purpose exceeded 1 to 1, however, the bread became much more compact and heavy, with an undesirable texture: 1 cup of cake flour to 3 cups of unbleached all-purpose flour proved best.

Because the ratio of liquid to dry ingredients is important in determining dough texture and bread moistness, we decided to test buttermilk next. (We also knew that the amount of this acidic liquid would have a direct effect on the amount of baking soda we would be able to use. Baking soda reacts with acids such as those in buttermilk to provide leavening; however, if there is too much soda, some remains intact in the bread, giving it a slightly metallic taste.) As it turned out, bread made with 1¾ or 1⅔ cups of buttermilk produced bread that was doughy, almost gummy. With 1½ cups, the dough was firmer yet still moist—and the resulting bread was no longer doughy. (If you don't have buttermilk on hand, yogurt can be substituted for an equally delicious bread with a slightly rougher crust and lighter texture.)

With the amount of buttermilk decided upon, we were now ready to explore the amount and type of leavener used. After trying various combinations of baking soda, baking powder, and cream of tartar, we found that 1½ teaspoons of soda, combined with an equal amount of cream of tartar, provided just the right amount of lift for a bread that was light but not airy. Relying on the acidity of cream of tartar (rather than the acidity in the buttermilk) to react with the baking soda allows the tangy buttermilk flavor to come through.

Unfortunately, the flavor of these basic loaves was mediocre at best, lacking depth and dimension, and they were also a bit tough. Traditionally, very small amounts of sugar and/or butter are sometimes added to soda bread, so, starting with sugar, we baked loaves with 1 and with 2 tablespoons. Two tablespoons of sugar added just the flavor balance that was needed without making the bread sweet. It was only with the introduction of butter, though, that the loaves began to lose their toughness and become outstanding. Still, we really wanted to maintain the integrity of this basic bread and avoid making it too rich. We tried loaves with from 1 to 4 tablespoons of unsalted butter; the bread made with 2 tablespoons proved a clear winner. This bread was tender but not crumbly, compact but not heavy. Using more than 2 tablespoons of butter began to shift the flavor balance of the bread and add unnecessary richness.

We were getting very close to our goal, but the crust was still too hard, thick, and crumbly. In our research we came upon various techniques for modifying the crust. Some dealt with the way the bread was baked, and others concentrated on how the bread was treated after baking. Trying to inhibit the formation of a thick crust by covering the bread with a bowl during the first 30 minutes of baking helped some, but the resulting bread took longer to bake and was pale and uneven in color. Using a large flowerpot and clay dish to simulate a cloche (a covered earthenware dish specifically designed for baking bread) again gave us a bread that didn't color well, even when we preheated the tray and buttered the dough.

But the next test—which, by no coincidence, closely simulated historical cooking methods for Irish soda bread—was a breakthrough. Baking the loaf in a cast-iron skillet, covered for only the first 30 minutes, produced a well-risen loaf with an even, golden crust that was thin and crisp yet still had a bit of chew.

Finally, make sure that you cool the bread for at least 30 to 40 minutes before serving. If cut when too hot, the bread will be dense and slightly doughy.

WHAT WE LEARNED: For a tender crumb, cut some of the all-purpose flour with low-protein cake flour. The mix of flours mimics Ireland's softer wheat flour. To avoid a doughy bread, use just 1¾ cups of buttermilk, which gives the loaf a subtle tang and moist crumb. For leavening, a combination of baking soda and cream of tartar works perfectly. A modest amount of butter and sugar—just 2 tablespoons of each—gives the bread flavor without making it too rich or distinctly sweet. For a deeply browned crunchy crust, bake the bread in a cast-iron skillet. The even, intense heat of cast iron helps produce a golden, crunchy crust just like loaves baked in Ireland.

SKILLET SODA BREAD

makes 1 loaf

If you do not have a cast-iron skillet, the bread can be baked on a baking sheet, although the crust won't be quite as crunchy. We prefer to use low-fat buttermilk in this bread, but nonfat buttermilk will work as well (though the bread will be a little lighter in texture and flavor). Soda bread is best eaten on the day it is baked but does keep well covered and stored at room temperature for a couple of days, after which time it will become dry.

3	cups (15 ounces) unbleached all-purpose flour
1	cup (4 ounces) cake flour
1½	teaspoons baking soda
1½	teaspoons cream of tartar
1½	teaspoons salt
2	tablespoons sugar
2	tablespoons unsalted butter, softened
1¾	cups buttermilk, preferably low-fat (see note)
1	tablespoon unsalted butter, melted (optional)

1. Adjust an oven rack to the middle position and heat the oven to 400 degrees. Place the flours, baking soda, cream of tartar, salt, and sugar in a large mixing bowl. Add the butter and rub it into the flour using your fingers until it is completely incorporated. Make a well in the center of the flour mixture and add 1½ cups of the buttermilk. Work the buttermilk into the flour mixture using a fork until the dough comes together in large clumps and there is no dry flour in the bottom of the bowl, adding up to ¼ cup more buttermilk, 1 tablespoon at a time, until all the loose flour is just moistened. Turn the dough onto a work surface and pat together to form a 6- to 7-inch round. The dough will still be scrappy and uneven.

2. Place the dough in a 12-inch cast-iron skillet. Score a deep cross on the top of the loaf and place in the oven. Bake until nicely browned and a knife comes out clean when inserted into the center of the loaf, about 40 to 45 minutes. Remove from the oven and brush with the tablespoon of melted butter, if using. Cool for at least 30 minutes before slicing.

VARIATIONS
WHOLE WHEAT SODA BREAD
This variation is known as Brown Bread in Ireland.

Reduce the amounts of all-purpose flour to 1½ cups (7½ ounces) and cake flour to ½ cup (2 ounces). Add 1½ cups (8¼ ounces) whole wheat flour and ½ cup toasted wheat germ. Increase the amount of sugar to 3 tablespoons. The dough will be sticky and you may need to add a small amount of flour as you mix it.

AMERICAN-STYLE SODA BREAD
Increase the amount of sugar to ¼ cup and of butter to ¼ cup. If desired, add 1 cup raisins and 1 tablespoon caraway seeds to the bowl once the butter has been incorporated into the flour. Reduce the amount of buttermilk to 1¼ cups, and along with the buttermilk add 1 large egg, slightly beaten.

TECHNIQUE: Scoring Soda Bread

Use a serrated knife to cut a cross shape in the top of the dough. Each score should be 5 inches long and ¾ inch deep.

SCIENCE DESK:
A Light Hand for Tender Bread

WHILE TESTING THE VARIOUS INGREDIENTS IN OUR Skillet Soda Bread, we discovered that the way the dough is handled while you are mixing it is as crucial as the amount and type of leavener used. Because baking soda begins reacting immediately with cream of tartar and does not provide the big second rise you get with double-acting baking powder, it is important to mix the dough quickly and not too vigorously. If you mix too slowly or too enthusiastically, too much carbon dioxide will be formed and will dissipate during the mixing process; not enough will then be produced during baking to provide the proper rise. Extended kneading also overdevelops the gluten in the flour, toughening the bread. It's no wonder that in Ireland a baker who produces a superior loaf of soda bread is traditionally said to have "a light hand," a great compliment.

EQUIPMENT CORNER: Serrated Knives

SERRATED KNIVES ARE AN INDISPENSABLE PART OF ANY cook's kitchen arsenal, slicing through squishy tomatoes and foods with a hard exterior and soft interior (like bread) that the straight edge of a chef's knife has trouble tackling. But choosing a serrated knife isn't as simple as it sounds. Do you want serrations that are pointed, scalloped, or saw-toothed? Big and spread-out or tiny and crowded? Or maybe a mix of styles and shapes on one knife? Do you want a blade that's forged or stamped? One that sticks straight out from the handle, one that curves—a little or a lot—or even one where the handle is tilted downward from the blade? What about offset serrated knives, where the blade drops down from the handle into an L shape?

And must you buy different serrated knives for different tasks? Can a knife that's good for cutting bread and sandwiches also cut tomatoes, split cake layers, and separate dough for sticky buns? We have always wanted a good serrated knife that can do it all. We bought 12 knives of all shapes and sizes and began cutting into food to see if our frugal dream of the perfect all-purpose tool could be fulfilled.

In contrast to a chef's knife, which works best when its straight edge is pushed through food, a serrated knife relies on a slicing motion in which the blade is dragged across the food's surface as it moves down through it. To excel in our testing, the serrations had to exert just the right amount of grip on the food's surface. In the past, we've found that scalloped edges (also known as reverse serrations) provide too little grip, skidding before biting in; the one model of this type we included in our lineup lived down to this expectation. Pointed serrations, on the other hand, needed to be just the right size—too long, and they had too much grip, snagging and tearing at the soft interiors of the bread, cake, and sandwich; too small, and they were ineffectual (see "Serration Styles," page 270) on the tougher tasks.

But it's not just point size that matters in a serrated knife; blade size is equally important. Blades shorter than 10 inches just couldn't cut across larger foods like 9-inch cake rounds or big loaves of bread without getting lost inside. We were excited about a 14-inch knife, but although its serrations did every task exceptionally well, it was just too much knife—we kept bumping into objects at the back of the countertop as we worked on the cutting board.

Cutlery companies keep tinkering with serrated knife design. We tested offset serrated knives, where the blade is lower than the handle by a few inches, making an L-shaped profile. The idea is to give the cook additional leverage, but these knives didn't offer enough control when cutting through foods; the blades felt too removed from the testers' hands. Another new-style knife sported a downward-sloping handle designed to be more ergonomic and comfortable for the cook. But combined with an offset blade, the sloping handle just gave this knife too many odd angles. In the end, none of the innovations we sampled were improvements over classic serrated knives.

Like chef's knives, serrated knives are manufactured in one of two ways: stamping (cutting the blade out of a sheet of metal) or forging (the age-old technique of heating and hammering a rough shape of metal into a knife). Forged knives tend to have heavier blades, but our longtime favorite 8-inch chef's knife, by Victorinox, is stamped, so we didn't think it would matter whether a serrated knife was forged or stamped. And, for the most part, it didn't—our top two knives were one of each. However, we did appreciate the way the heavier blade and more steeply tapered serrations of our top-rated knife, which is forged, sliced into food with greater power and ease.

Regardless of how they were manufactured, we found that bad serrated knives often failed on opposite extremes: They felt like either blunt instruments or wet noodles. A few knives were so rigid that they were hard to manipulate, making them poorly suited for precise work. With one particularly unbendable blade, if we tried to correct our angle

of attack through a soft cake layer, there was no bringing it back, resulting in a lopsided slice. Both of our top-ranked knives hit a nice middle ground, being slightly bendable for better maneuverability yet firm enough to allow for proper control.

We found that for a knife to be a great all-purpose tool that excelled at cutting bread and soft, ripe tomatoes as well as cake layers and gooey sticky-bun dough, it needed three main traits: a slightly flexible blade between 10 and 12 inches long, with serrations that are both uniformly spaced and moderate in length. We highly recommend two knives that boast all three qualities. Wüsthof's Classic Bread Knife, 10 Inches ($79.95), edged out the competition as the best all-purpose serrated knife, and the Victorinox Forschner 10¼-Inch Curved Blade Bread Knife with Black Fibrox Handle ($24.95) performed almost as well for about a third of the price.

TESTING NOTES: Serration Styles

Good Points

Uniformly spaced, moderately sized serrations, such as those on the Wüsthof Classic, excelled at cutting through all foods.

Too Toothy

The LamsonSharp Wave Edge's overly large pointed serrations snagged and tore at foods.

Too Tiny

Saw-toothed microserrations on the Warther knife struggled to make the cut.

Too Rounded

Scalloped serrations on the MAC knife slid over food too many times before cutting in.

Rating Serrated Knives

WE TESTED 12 SERRATED KNIVES, USING THEM TO SPLIT CAKE LAYERS, SLICE BREAD AND RIPE TOMATOES, AND CUT sticky-bun dough and club sandwiches. Testers included a left-handed cook (serrations tend to pull in the wrong direction for lefties) and cooks with large hands (who prefer blades that are taller and curved, as both qualities help keep their knuckles off the cutting board). Brands are listed in order of preference. See www.americastestkitchen.com for updates to this testing.

HIGHLY RECOMMENDED
Wüsthof Classic Bread Knife, 10 Inches
$79.95; Forged construction, pointed serrations

This well-balanced knife with deeply tapered pointed serrations handled every task with exceptional ease and control.

HIGHLY RECOMMENDED
Victorinox Forschner 10¼-Inch Curved Blade Bread Knife, Black Fibrox Handle
$24.95; Stamped construction, pointed serrations

The comfortable, sharp blade and pointed serrations performed almost as well as our top knife.

RECOMMENDED
Viking 10-Inch Serrated Slicer
$108; Forged construction, pointed serrations

The lethally sharp forged blade feels (and is) expensive and isn't good for lefties or cooks with large hands.

RECOMMENDED WITH RESERVATIONS
Victorinox Forschner 14-Inch Bread/Serrated Slicing Knife, Black Fibrox Handle
$30.95; Stamped construction, pointed serrations

The extra-long blade excelled at tackling a large crusty loaf and splitting a cake round, but its length kept us poking at the back of the kitchen countertop when cutting smaller foods such as tomatoes.

RECOMMENDED WITH RESERVATIONS
MAC Bread/Roast Knife, Superior Series, 10½ Inches
$28; Stamped construction, scalloped ("reverse") serrations

The knife's scallop-shaped serrations slid over bread crust and tomato skin for several strokes before biting in.

RECOMMENDED WITH RESERVATIONS
F. Dick Utility Serrated Edge Knife, 1905 Series, 10 Inches
$74.95; Forged construction, pointed serrations

This thick, forged knife glided through bread but was described as feeling "like an ax" cutting a tomato or splitting a cake.

RECOMMENDED WITH RESERVATIONS
Global 10-Inch Bread Knife, Serrated
$122.95; Forged construction, pointed serrations

The priciest knife in the lineup looks and feels like a chef's knife with serrations. The alleged 10-inch blade is only 9½ inches long.

NOT RECOMMENDED
Warther Serrated Knife, 9-Inch
$48.50; Stamped construction, micro-serrations

This knife's saw-toothed serrations and too-short blade (just 8¾ inches) were not up to tackling big bread loaves or cake rounds.

NOT RECOMMENDED
Messermeister 10-Inch Park Plaza Bread/Serrated Slicing Knife
$39.95; Stamped construction, mixed-shape serrations

An odd mix of wavy, pointed, and rounded serrations lacked bite and held this knife back.

NOT RECOMMENDED
LamsonSharp Forged Offset Bread Knife with Ebony Handle, 9 Inches
$67.95; Forged construction, tiny pointed serrations

Although this knife felt solidly built, its blade was too short and its pointed serrations too tiny.

NOT RECOMMENDED
Ergo Chef 9-Inch Pro-Series Offset Serrated Bread/Multi-Purpose Knife
$79.99; Forged construction, pointed serrations

This knife's downward-tilting handle unnerved testers. It was ranked last for slicing bread.

NOT RECOMMENDED
LamsonSharp 10-Inch Wave Edge Curved Bread Knife
$30; Stamped construction, pointed serrations

This knife snagged and tore the soft sticky-bun dough, chewed up toast, and made a disheveled club sandwich.

Apple Pandowdy boasts a skillet full of juicy sweet apples blanketed with a tender pastry crust. After placing the crust over the filling, we cut the crust into squares so that the pastry bakes up with crisp edges all around.

EASY APPLE
CHAPTER 21
desserts

Biting into a crisp, juicy apple is one of fall's true pleasures. Just as pleasurable is baking with apples. Apple pie is at the top of our list, but sometimes we like to bake something less labor-intensive. Here we turn to two easier apple desserts—apple pandowdy and applesauce cake.

Apple pandowdy is an old-fashioned Yankee dish that promises apple pie appeal without all the fuss. Similar to a crisp, cobbler, or betty, a pandowdy is a baked fruit dessert with a top crust. The crust is broken and pushed down into the filling (during or after baking), a technique that helps tenderize the crust by softening it in the apples' juices. (Pastry in colonial days was much tougher than today's flaky pastry dough.) The method also serves to give the dessert its rustic, "dowdy" appearance. We wanted to bring this apple dessert into the 21st century using today's tender, butter-rich pastry for a less fussy alternative to traditional apple pie.

A homey square of applesauce cake makes a great afternoon snack or rustic dessert. But poor versions of this cake run the gamut from dense, chunky fruitcakes to gummy "health" cakes that are bland and boring. Why can't we have an applesauce cake that tastes like apples? This was the question we'd start with in our quest for a simple, sweet apple cake that we could bake anytime.

MODERNIZING APPLE PANDOWDY

WHAT WE WANTED: An updated version of the colonial-era Yankee apple dessert—one that yields tender, juicy apples and a flaky crust.

Ask the average person what apple pandowdy is, and you'll be met with a blank stare. Most of us are familiar with its popular cousins—crisp, cobbler, and betty—but pandowdy is different. This colonial New England original is essentially an apple pie filling baked with a top crust. During or after baking, the cook breaks the pastry and pushes it into the filling, a technique known as "dowdying." The dish's offbeat name may derive from the fact that this technique leaves it looking untidy, or dowdy.

Despite its rustic looks, this no-frills dessert is a true diamond in the rough. It satisfies like an apple pie but is free from pie's challenges: There's no fussy crimping, no filling that must be finessed to make it sliceable, and no bottom crust that can get soggy.

We wondered if we could make apple pandowdy by simply putting an apple pie filling in a baking dish and topping it with dough. We decided to try this with the test kitchen's favorite apple pie filling, which incorporates sweet and tart apples, sugar, and lemon juice. As for the topping, a traditional pandowdy may be topped with a cake-like batter, biscuit dough, or pie pastry. Because we were drawn to the idea of a simple apple pie, we decided to stick with a pie-pastry topping.

When the dessert came out of the oven, we gave dowdying a try, using the back of a spoon to push the crust into the filling. The results were disappointing. The crust quickly became soggy and bloated—not what we wanted at all. In colonial times, dowdying was likely practiced in order to soften a tough dough with the juice from the apples. Our tender modern dough was much more delicate than its sturdy ancestors, and dowdying just didn't make sense. We made the radical decision to skip the dowdying and pursue a dessert modeled on a one-crust pie.

Even after abandoning the dowdying step, there were adjustments to be made. First and foremost, the apple filling was dry and lacked flavor. We wanted a juicy, rich filling that really tasted like apples. Unlike a pie, which needs to be thick and sliceable (a challenge because apples never cook up the same way twice; see "The Story Behind Mushy Apples," page 277), our pandowdy could afford to be somewhat saucy—and then we could concentrate on building superior flavor without having to worry about sliceability.

Perhaps we could produce a juicier filling by drawing out some of the liquid in the apples? We tried macerating the apples in sugar to coax out moisture (a technique we use in various other fruit desserts), but this was unsuccessful: Apples aren't as juicy as berries or stone fruits. We would have to add some extra liquid to the apples. An additional ½ cup of apple juice made the filling moist but diluted its taste. Simmering a cup of apple juice until it was reduced by half intensified the flavor, but using apple cider was easier—it

provided resonant apple flavor straight from the jug. Our apple filling was now pleasantly juicy and bursting with the taste of apples. We thickened the cider with 2 teaspoons of cornstarch, which yielded a juicy filling with just the right amount of body.

To enhance the flavor of the apples, we experimented with different sweeteners and spices. Pandowdies were originally sweetened with molasses, maple syrup, or brown sugar. Compared with these old-fashioned choices, the granulated sugar that we had been using tasted plain and boring. But not all the traditional sweeteners were equally appealing. Molasses lent the filling a dark color and somewhat overpowering flavor. Both dark and light brown sugars also turned out to be too imposing. One-third of a cup of maple syrup, however, struck the perfect balance, complementing the natural sweetness of the apples without being cloying. As a bonus, the extra moisture from the maple syrup made our juicy filling even juicier. After we tried—and dismissed—a few different spices, tests proved that a classic pinch of cinnamon was a nice optional addition.

At this point we had a succulent, juicy apple filling and could focus on improving the crust. We wanted it to be extra-crisp to stand up to the moist, saucy fruit. After some trial and error, we found that the best approach was to use a standard pie crust that had been brushed with egg white and sprinkled with sugar, then bake the pandowdy in a 500-degree oven on the upper-middle rack. The egg white and sugar combination created a wonderful, crackly finish. But there was a problem: Although the crust was browned and crisp, with a beautiful golden color, the apples were sadly undercooked. Lowering the oven temperature eventually cooked the apples through but left the crust pale.

As we struggled to solve this dilemma, we wondered if colonial American cooks had faced similar problems with this otherwise straightforward dish. We turned to our historical sources again and rediscovered a chief point about early pandowdies: They were cooked in a heavy skillet or pot that was placed directly over the heat source. An intriguing idea began to form in our minds. Could we mimic this old-fashioned technique by starting our pandowdy in a skillet on the stovetop? We could give the apples a head start by sautéing them first, then add the crust and quickly brown it in a hot oven. Envisioning a skillet filled with sizzling, cider-sauced apples topped by an impeccably crisp crust, we headed into the kitchen to test this promising whim.

Eureka! Our new method worked beautifully, yielding apples that were richly flavored and perfectly cooked. In fact, caramelizing the apples before baking them made the filling taste even better than a traditional apple pie filling. The total cooking time was only about 25 minutes (much less than for a pie, which can take an hour or more). In this time, the apples baked evenly, the sauce was nicely thickened and sticky around the edges, and the crust developed a lovely deep brown hue.

As a final touch, we cut the dough into six squares before the pandowdy went into the oven. Prepared this way, each square of pastry baked up with multiple crisp, flaky edges—a delicious, new-fashioned tribute to the broken-up crust of traditional pandowdy. The cider-enriched filling bubbled up and caramelized nicely around the edges of the tender pastry. Move over, apple pie: Updated pandowdy is a cinch!

WHAT WE LEARNED: For an apple filling with bright fruit flavor, add cider to the apples and sweeten the filling with maple syrup. The tart intensity of the cider deepens the apple flavor and maple syrup's rich character adds the right degree of sweetness, without being saccharine. Both additions also make for a pleasantly saucy filling. Parcook the apples in a skillet until caramelized, add the remaining filling ingredients, and then top with the crust before baking. Cut a standard pie crust into squares after rolling it over the fruit—this encourages a multitude of crispy edges that contrast nicely with the tender fruit and recall (in a less dowdy way), the broken-up crusts of a traditional pandowdy. This skillet apple pie approach guarantees perfectly cooked apples and a beautifully browned crust—all in far less time than it takes to bake a traditional apple pie.

APPLE PANDOWDY

serves 6 to 8

If your skillet is not heatproof, precook the apples and stir in the cider mixture as instructed, then transfer the apples to a 13 by 9-inch baking dish. Roll out the dough to a 13 by 9-inch rectangle and bake the pandowdy as instructed. If you do not have apple cider, reduced apple juice may be used as a substitute; simmer 1 cup apple juice in a small saucepan over medium heat until reduced to ½ cup (about 10 minutes). Serve the pandowdy warm or at room temperature with vanilla ice cream or whipped cream. Use a combination of sweet, crisp apples such as Golden Delicious and firm, tart apples such as Cortland or Empire.

crust

1	cup (5 ounces) unbleached all-purpose flour, plus more for dusting work surface
1	tablespoon sugar
½	teaspoon salt
2	tablespoons vegetable shortening, chilled
6	tablespoons (¾ stick) cold unsalted butter, cut into ¼-inch pieces
3–4	tablespoons ice water

filling

½	cup apple cider
⅓	cup maple syrup
2	tablespoons juice from 1 lemon
2	teaspoons cornstarch
⅛	teaspoon ground cinnamon (optional)
2	tablespoons unsalted butter
2½	pounds sweet and tart apples (about 5 medium), peeled, cored, halved, and cut into ½-inch-thick wedges (see note)
1	large egg white, lightly beaten
2	teaspoons sugar

1. FOR THE CRUST: Process the flour, sugar, and salt in a food processor until combined. Add the shortening and pulse until the mixture has the texture of coarse sand, about ten 1-second pulses. Scatter the butter pieces over the flour mixture and pulse until the mixture is pale yellow and resembles coarse crumbs, with the butter bits no larger than small peas, about ten 1-second pulses. Transfer the mixture to a medium bowl.

2. Sprinkle 3 tablespoons of the ice water over the mixture. With the blade of a rubber spatula, use a folding motion to mix. Press down on the dough with the broad side of the spatula until the dough sticks together, adding up to 1 tablespoon more ice water if the dough does not come together. Turn the dough out onto a sheet of plastic wrap and flatten into a 4-inch disk. Wrap the dough and refrigerate 30 minutes, or up to 2 days, before rolling out. (If the dough is refrigerated longer than 1 hour, let stand at room temperature until malleable.)

TECHNIQUE: Keys to a Successful Pandowdy

1. Caramelize the Apples: Precooking the apples in butter in a skillet deepens their flavor.

2. Add Cider: Adding ½ cup apple cider yields a juicy, flavorful filling.

3. Cut Dough Before Baking: Scoring the dough before baking allows the juices to bubble up and caramelize around the edges.

4. Bake in a Hot Oven: Because the apples are precooked, a brief stay in a hot oven is all that's required.

3. FOR THE FILLING: Adjust an oven rack to the upper-middle position (between 7 and 9 inches from the heating element) and heat the oven to 500 degrees. Whisk the cider, syrup, lemon juice, cornstarch, and cinnamon, if using, together in a medium bowl until smooth. Heat the butter in a 12-inch heatproof skillet over medium-high heat. When the foaming subsides, add the apples and cook, stirring 2 or 3 times, until the apples begin to caramelize, about 5 minutes. (Do not fully cook the apples.) Remove the pan from the heat, add the cider mixture, and gently stir until the apples are well coated. Set aside to cool slightly.

4. TO ASSEMBLE AND BAKE: Roll out the dough on a lightly floured work surface, or between 2 large sheets of plastic wrap, to an 11-inch circle. Roll the dough loosely around the rolling pin and unroll over the apple filling. Brush the dough with the egg white and sprinkle with the sugar. With a sharp knife, gently cut the dough into 6 pieces by making 1 vertical cut followed by 2 evenly spaced horizontal cuts (perpendicular to the first cut). Bake until the apples are tender and the crust is a deep golden brown, about 20 minutes. Let cool 15 minutes; serve.

SCIENCE DESK:
The Story Behind Mushy Apples

WHILE DEVELOPING OUR PANDOWDY RECIPE, WE noticed that the apple filling occasionally turned mushy, even after a short baking time. Something wasn't right. After a chat with our science editor, we learned that apples that aren't going to be sold within a few weeks of harvest are placed in refrigerated "controlled atmosphere" (CA) storage. Because apples continue to ripen after harvest, these conditions are designed to halt the ripening process. The problem is that once the apples are removed from CA storage and put on display at the grocery store, they begin an accelerated ripening process. The apple's structure will then quickly break down upon cooking. The longer the apples are kept in CA storage (and they may be stored as long as 10 months), the faster they ripen once removed, and the more likely they are to become mushy during baking.

Because it is impossible to know how long or under what conditions supermarket apples have been stored, your best bet is to use fresh, local apples whenever possible. If you purchase fresh apples, refrigerate and use them as soon as you can.

APPLESAUCE CAKE

WHAT WE WANTED: A moist, rich applesauce cake with pronounced apple flavor and a tender, not gummy, crumb.

With all of its incarnations over the years, it is no surprise that applesauce cake suffers from an identity crisis. Its origins hark back to the chunky medieval fruitcake, but in the years after World War I applesauce cake became a popular way to cut back on such hard-to-get ingredients as eggs, butter, and sugar without giving up dessert. In the health-crazed 1960s, applesauce cake reemerged as a low-fat (applesauce mimics fat in some baked goods) and often flavorless option. More recently it's been offered up as a moist, rich, spice-laden cake. It's this last version that speaks of comfort to us: a simple cake to enjoy alongside a cup of afternoon tea.

But a quick survey of recipes representing this rich and tender style revealed that the applesauce cake still hasn't quite come into its own. Some recipes packed in dried fruit and nuts (a holdover from the fruitcake days?); others overdosed on the dried spices—a ploy to distract from a gummy or wet texture, perhaps. For us, applesauce cake conjures up more than an expectation of moist and tender spice cake: we wanted something that actually tasted like apples.

But before we could inject this cake with a dose of apple flavor, we needed to get the structure right. We started with a simple recipe (omitting any distracting nuts, raisins, or spices) of 1 cup of applesauce, 1½ cups of flour, 1 teaspoon of baking soda, 1 cup of sugar, 2 eggs, and 8 tablespoons of butter. The most common mixing method for these butter-rich cakes was the creaming method, in which the butter and sugar are whipped together until light and fluffy, the eggs are added, and the dry ingredients added alternately with the applesauce. The result was an elegant cake with a refined crumb. Tasters liked it, but it seemed like an awful lot of fuss for such a simple cake.

Could we just melt the butter, dump everything into a bowl, and stir it all by hand? Not unless we wanted a dense, heavy cake, apparently. The next simplest method we tried was the one often used for quick breads and muffins, in which a few extra minutes are spent mixing the wet ingredients separately, before gently adding the dry ingredients—but still by hand. When this cake emerged from the oven, it was clear that this method was a winner. A far cry from the refined crumb produced by creaming in a standing mixer, this cake's texture had a looser, more casual crumb that was better suited to a rustic snack cake.

Despite better structure, the texture remained somewhat gummy. We tried substituting vegetable oil (a common quick-bread ingredient) for melted butter, but our efforts were for naught: The oil did keep the gumminess under control, but tasters were not about to sacrifice buttery flavor for a slightly better texture. We fussed with the type and amount of leavener, adding some baking powder in hopes of quelling the gumminess with a more powerful rise, but the metallic aftertaste wasn't worth the modest improvement. In the end, the solution was about as simple as it gets: reducing the number of eggs by one.

Since apple flavor was the main goal, our first step seemed the most obvious: Increase the amount of applesauce. But as little as an extra ½ cup reintroduced the gumminess. To combat the moisture, we tried both draining the applesauce and cooking off the moisture in a pan (each method released ½ cup of liquid), but to no avail. The flavor of the applesauce was simply less noticeable and bright than before. Apparently, the flavor of applesauce (already cooked once) is a subtle thing—too subtle. The applesauce was doing a fine job of providing the cake with moisture and tenderness, but we would have to eke out more apple flavor from another source.

Fresh apples, whether shredded or diced, added a nice

tart apple flavor, but they also added too much moisture. Apple butter, made from cooking apples down to a smooth, satiny paste, contributed a deep brown color yet disappointingly little flavor. Apple cider was our next bet, but we were wary of adding pure liquid to a recipe prone to being too moist. Reducing it to a syrup as a precautionary measure turned out to be key: The syrup contributed a pleasing sweetness and a slight tang without excess moisture. To compensate for the sweetness the cider added, we adjusted the amount of sugar from 1 cup to just ⅔ cup.

A fellow test cook suggested adding dried apples to accent the apple flavor even further, but we were reminded of the unpleasantly chunky applesauce cakes from our initial tests. We tried grinding them up into tiny pieces and adding them along with the applesauce. The apple flavor was significantly improved, but the bits of dried apple floated to the surface of the cake during baking, creating an odd top layer. Noticing our pan of cider simmering away, we tossed in the dried apples; not only did they absorb the cider, but they became plump and soft. A quick run through the food processor further unified the dried apples, cider, and applesauce. This triple-apple applesauce cake finally had the bright, recognizable taste of apple that we were after—without any compromise in texture.

Although spices can easily become too much of a good thing, their use in moderation was welcome (the nuts and raisins were still out). Some applesauce cakes come adorned with a syrupy glaze or a creamy frosting, but we didn't want this cake to be too sweet or rich. To achieve at least a modicum of textural contrast, we tried topping the cake first with a simple streusel and then with an even simpler topping of granulated sugar. Although we liked the simple, crunchy sugar best, a few tasters preferred the streusel version, so we kept that recipe as a variation.

After peeling away the many guises of applesauce cake, we had hit on an original that was simple in design yet bursting with honest apple flavor and warm spices. Identity crisis—at long last—averted.

WHAT WE LEARNED: For a cake with a rustic, tender crumb, use the quick-bread method for mixing: Stir the wet ingredients together and then add the dry ingredients, all by hand—it couldn't be simpler. For a cake with rich apple flavor, applesauce alone isn't enough; include dried apples cooked in apple cider. Puree the mixture in a food processor to eliminate any dried bits in the cake. Use modest amounts of cinnamon, nutmeg, and cloves to lend the cake warm spice flavor without obscuring the apple flavor. Skip a frosting or glaze for this simple cake—all it needs is a sprinkle of lightly spiced sugar.

APPLESAUCE SNACK CAKE

makes one 8-inch square cake

This recipe can be easily doubled and baked in a 13 by 9-inch baking dish. If doubling the recipe, give the cider and dried apple mixture about 20 minutes to reduce, and bake the cake for about 45 minutes. The cake is very moist, so it is best to err on the side of overdone when testing its doneness. The test kitchen prefers the rich flavor of cider, but apple juice can be substituted. Cooled leftovers can be wrapped in plastic wrap and stored at room temperature for up to 2 days.

¾	cup (2 ounces) dried apples, cut into ½-inch pieces
1	cup apple cider (see note)
1½	cups (7½ ounces) unbleached all-purpose flour
1	teaspoon baking soda
⅔	cup (4¾ ounces) sugar
½	teaspoon ground cinnamon
¼	teaspoon ground nutmeg
⅛	teaspoon ground cloves
1	cup unsweetened applesauce, at room temperature

1	large egg, at room temperature, lightly beaten
½	teaspoon salt
8	tablespoons (1 stick) unsalted butter, melted and cooled slightly
1	teaspoon vanilla extract

GETTING IT RIGHT: Apple Flavor 1-2-3

Sauce
Applesauce added moisture, but its flavor was too faint once the cake was baked.

Cider
Reduced in a saucepan, cider added an apple kick without extra wetness.

Dried
Dried apples infused the cake with flavor without gumming it up.

1. Adjust an oven rack to the middle position and heat the oven to 325 degrees. Cut a 16-inch length parchment paper or aluminum foil and fold lengthwise to a 7-inch width. Spray an 8-inch square baking dish with vegetable oil spray and fit the parchment into the dish, pushing it into the corners and up the sides; allow the excess to overhang the edges of the dish.

2. Bring the dried apples and cider to a simmer in a small saucepan over medium heat; cook until the liquid evaporates and the mixture appears dry, about 15 minutes. Cool to room temperature.

3. Whisk the flour and baking soda in a medium bowl to combine; set aside. In a second medium bowl, whisk together the sugar, cinnamon, nutmeg, and cloves. Measure 2 tablespoons of the sugar-spice mixture into a small bowl and set aside for the topping.

4. In a food processor, process the cooled dried-apple mixture and applesauce until smooth, 20 to 30 seconds, scraping down the sides of the bowl as needed; set aside. Whisk the egg and salt in a large bowl to combine. Add the sugar-spice mixture and whisk continuously until well combined and light colored, about 20 seconds. Add the butter in three additions, whisking after each. Add the applesauce mixture and vanilla and whisk to combine. Add the flour mixture to the wet ingredients; using a rubber spatula, fold gently until just combined and evenly moistened.

5. Turn the batter into the prepared pan, smoothing the top with a rubber spatula. Sprinkle the reserved 2 tablespoons sugar-spice mixture evenly over the batter. Bake until a wooden skewer inserted in the center of the cake comes out clean, 35 to 40 minutes. Cool on a wire rack to room temperature, about 2 hours. Run a knife along the cake edges without parchment to release. Remove the cake from the pan by lifting the parchment overhang and transfer to a cutting board. Cut the cake and serve.

VARIATIONS

GINGER-CARDAMOM APPLESAUCE SNACK CAKE

Follow the recipe for Applesauce Snack Cake, omitting the cinnamon, nutmeg, and cloves. Whisk ½ teaspoon ground ginger and ¼ teaspoon ground cardamom into the sugar in step 3. Measure 2 tablespoons of the sugar-spice mixture into a small bowl, add 1 tablespoon finely chopped crystallized ginger, and set aside for the topping.

APPLESAUCE SNACK CAKE WITH OAT-NUT STREUSEL

Follow the recipe for Applesauce Snack Cake through step 2. In step 3, measure 2 tablespoons of the sugar-spice mixture into a medium bowl. Add 2 tablespoons brown sugar, ⅓ cup chopped pecans or walnuts, and ⅓ cup old-fashioned or quick oats. Work in 2 tablespoons softened unsalted butter by rubbing the mixture between your fingers until fully incorporated. Pinch the mixture into hazelnut-sized clumps and sprinkle evenly over the batter before baking.

EQUIPMENT CORNER: Coffeemakers

IN THIS AGE OF STARBUCKS, AMERICANS HAVE GOTTEN much more sophisticated about the complexities of coffee flavor. Now when we make our coffee at home, that old Mr. Coffee on the countertop—never all that great to begin with—increasingly doesn't measure up. As we looked over the latest models on store shelves, we wondered if manufacturers might have caught up with our coffee obsession and finally developed an automatic drip coffeemaker that can produce a terrific brew.

From previous tests we knew that a thermal carafe would be essential; the usual hot plate under a glass carafe starts turning fresh coffee acrid in a matter of minutes, as chemical compounds called lactones hydrolyze to form free acids. We found eight brands with thermal carafes and at least a 10-cup capacity at prices from $47 to $300. Most were programmable, meaning you can fill them with coffee and water and set the time you want the pot to turn itself on. Two of the more expensive models came with an attached burr-style coffee grinder. With hope—and more than 30 pounds of freshly roasted, house-blend coffee beans from Stumptown Coffee Roasters in Portland, Oregon—we set to work.

Brewing a full pot in each machine, we asked tasters to judge the coffees' aroma, body, complexity of flavor, level of bitterness, and overall appeal. Our hopes for the new generation of coffeemakers were quickly crushed. Most of those eight gleaming stainless steel machines made the same kind of mediocre coffee we've come to expect: bitter, weak, or one-dimensional.

What's the problem? Aside from using fresh, high-quality coffee beans and good-tasting cold water, the two most important factors in making good coffee are the temperature of the water as it passes through the grounds and the length of time the grounds are exposed to the water. These factors determine which of the more than 1,000 volatile flavor and aroma compounds identified in roasted coffee beans make it into your cup, and which get left behind (only a limited number of them—approximately 30—produce the best-tasting coffee). Studies have shown that the most flavorful, aromatic compounds are released by water that is between 195 and 205 degrees Fahrenheit, at a brew time of six minutes, for drip coffeemakers. The ideal cup of coffee contains 18 to 22 percent suspended solids extracted from the ground coffee. Too fast a brew time, and the extraction of solids will be less than 18 percent, and your coffee will be weak; too slow a brew time leads to overextraction (more than 22 percent suspended solids) and a bitter brew. If the coffeemaker is too slow and the water is not sufficiently hot, you can even wind up with coffee that is both weak and bitter.

We set out to make more coffee in each machine, this time measuring the water temperature throughout the brew cycle. And here we made a key discovery: Most of these machines were too cool, spending most of the brewing cycle struggling to bring the water into the right temperature range. Many didn't reach the correct temperature until the last minute or two of brewing—and then kept climbing, scorching the grounds as the last few cups dripped into the carafe.

Next, we timed three pots in each coffeemaker with a stopwatch and averaged the results. Once again, our lousy coffee could be explained: Most of the machines never reached that ideal time frame for water to pass through the coffee grounds, though two came much closer than the rest. The slowest machine took three times as long as it should: 18 minutes to make one pot of very bitter coffee. The fastest took just four minutes, and tasters found its coffee weak, thin, and flat.

How can manufacturers keep on getting away with these crimes against good coffee? They know consumers can't taste the coffee before they buy; most people choose a coffeemaker based on its looks and price. New models are dressed up to be enticing, with graceful carafes, backlit digital displays, sleek buttons, and multiple features. Why can't the flavor match up? "In order to sell their coffeemakers competitively in the market, these machines have to be made as cheaply as possible," said Mane Alves, president of the research firm Coffee Lab International in Waterbury, Vermont, and chair of the technical standards committee for the Specialty Coffee Association of America. "And the most expensive part of the coffeemaker is the heating element."

In the end, only one coffeemaker stood out in our tests as exceptional. The Technivorm Moccamaster (Model KBT741), made in the Netherlands, consistently brewed smooth, full-flavored coffee that our tasters ranked highest. Tellingly, it was the only model to get close to the ideal six-minute brewing time, averaging seven and a half minutes to completely finish dripping, though the water was fully dispensed within six minutes. Unlike any of the other coffeemakers, its internal heating element brought the brewing water to the correct temperature range within seconds and kept it there through the brewing cycle.

It turns out that in contrast to most coffeemaker heating elements, which are made of aluminum, the Technivorm's heating element is made of copper, a very expensive but excellent conductor of heat. Heating elements in coffeemakers work similarly to those of other small appliances, such as toaster ovens: A wire of nickel-chrome alloy responds to electricity by resisting its flow and heating up its aluminum (or copper) housing. In coffeemakers, this hot element usually runs alongside a tube containing water. As the cool water drips down from the tank, it passes through the heated channel, then boils up to the top of the machine, and finally drips down onto the grounds. A copper heating element has higher thermal conductivity than aluminum, meaning it is more responsive and can reach a higher temperature more quickly. The Technivorm is also more powerful, operating at a higher wattage than most coffeemakers—1,400 watts compared to the average 900 watts of the rest of the lineup—making its brew time correspondingly more efficient.

Aside from its sophisticated heating element and greater horsepower, the rest of the Technivorm is simple, with a cone to hold the coffee and a nine-hole sprayer to disperse water evenly. A switch lets you stop the flow of coffee to pour a cup. There's just one problem with the Technivorm: its price. Could we really justify spending $240 on a drip coffeemaker—when we know that great coffee can be had through the far cheaper method favored by many coffee connoisseurs, the French press? Just to make

sure, we compared coffee made in the Technivorm to coffee from a French press (we used the Bodum Chambord, which sells for $39.95). Although our tasters enjoyed the French press coffee's rich aroma and flavor, the Technivorm coffee won the day with even better flavor—and with no need to go through the French press's multiple steps of separately heating the water to 200 degrees, checking it with an instant-read thermometer, then pouring, stirring, waiting four minutes (according to manufacturer instructions), and pressing.

The Technivorm's price tag may be high, but its consistently full-flavored, smooth brew—made with all the convenience of that old Mr. Coffee—will pay for itself when you start skipping a few trips to Starbucks.

Rating Coffeemakers

WE TESTED EIGHT AUTOMATIC DRIP COFFEEMAKERS WITH THERMAL CARAFES AND A CAPACITY OF AT LEAST 10 CUPS. We rated the coffeemakers on performance, ease of use, and flavor—in our ratings, we placed greatest emphasis on the taste of the coffee. Brands are listed in order of preference. See www.americastestkitchen.com for updates to this testing.

HIGHLY RECOMMENDED
Technivorm Moccamaster Coffeemaker, Model KBT741
$239.95

Tasters described this machine's coffee as "very good; robust but smooth." The machine achieved perfect temperatures for brewing and serving and was closest of all the coffeemakers to reaching the ideal brewing time.

RECOMMENDED WITH RESERVATIONS
Krups 10-Cup Programmable Thermal Coffee Machine, Model FMF5
$95.93

This programmable machine is simple to use, but it lost points for too-slow and slightly too-hot brewing. Tasters deemed its coffee "slightly too bitter."

RECOMMENDED WITH RESERVATIONS
Cuisinart Grind & Brew Thermal 12-Cup Automatic Coffeemaker, Model DGB-900BC
$199

This machine's attached burr grinder will wake anyone who isn't already up in the morning. A few tasters called the coffee "mellow," but others deemed it "watery" and "bitter."

RECOMMENDED WITH RESERVATIONS
Black & Decker 10-Cup Thermal Stainless Steel Coffeemaker, Model TCM830
$59.99

Tasters found the coffee "strong" and some remarked on its bitterness. The brewing water remained too cool for most of the cycle, then spiked up too high near the end.

NOT RECOMMENDED
Hamilton Beach Stay or Go Deluxe 10-Cup Thermal Coffeemaker, Model 45238
$89.99

The slowest coffeemaker in the lineup, it took 18 minutes to produce a pot. Tasters found the coffee "strong" but too "bitter."

NOT RECOMMENDED
Mr. Coffee 10-Cup Thermal Programmable Coffee Maker, Model FTTX95
$47.24

An attractive machine, but the water filter is fussy to put in the correct direction, with tiny raised print being the only indication. Tasters found the coffee the most bitter of the lineup, calling it "harsh," "like cowboy coffee."

NOT RECOMMENDED
Bunn-O-Matic Home Brewer, Model BTX
$131.32

This super-fast machine brews a full pot in just four minutes, but the coffee is "weak," "thin," and "flat." You can't see into the water reservoir or check the water level.

NOT RECOMMENDED
Capresso CoffeeTEAM Therm, Model 455
$299

This deluxe machine is enjoyable to watch as the filter fills, then swings over to begin brewing, but for the price, the coffee should taste better, and the machine takes up too much counter space.

A water bath helps ensure that our Crème Caramel has a smooth, silky texture. Here, Chris prepares the water bath by pouring hot water into the roasting pan until it reaches halfway up the sides of the ramekins.

PUDDINGS—
CHAPTER 22
from simple to spectacular

The charm of rice pudding is found not only in its creamy flavor and comforting texture, but in the fact that it can be pulled together from pantry ingredients at a moment's notice for a homey dessert anytime. The best rice pudding has a texture that's not too soft and not too firm. A good balance of flavor is key, too. Some rice puddings take a heavy hand with the dairy or sugar, both of which mute the flavor of the rice; we aimed toward a pudding in which rice takes center stage. Our goal would be to determine the ratio of rice to dairy and sugar, and we wanted to narrow down a method for cooking the rice so the grains would remain intact, but perfectly cooked through.

Crème caramel is pudding that's all grown up. Sleek, sophisticated, and rich, this baked custard is a looker, too. Crème caramel is made by pouring caramel into a mold such as a ramekin. The custard is then poured over the caramel. Once baked and chilled, the ramekin is unmolded and the caramel runs down over the custard, giving it a glossy, amber sheen. Here we had a few questions to address. For a dessert that contains such simple ingredients—sugar, eggs, milk, and cream—what are the ideal proportions for a custard that isn't too sweet or too rich? And what's the best way to ensure a set, but not rubbery, custard? Finally, the caramel is key to this dessert; what is the most foolproof method for making a smooth caramel with a toasty, complex flavor—one that elevates this custard to star status? With these questions in mind, we headed into the test kitchen to find the answers.

STOVETOP RICE PUDDING

WHAT WE WANTED: A straightforward stovetop rice pudding—modestly sweet and creamy—and one in which both the texture and the flavor of the primary ingredient stand out.

At its best, rice pudding is simple and lightly sweet, and it tastes of its primary component: rice. At its worst, the rice flavor is lost to cloying sweetness, condensed dairy, and a pasty, leaden consistency. Right from the start, we agreed on the qualities of an ideal rice pudding: intact, tender grains bound loosely in a subtly sweet, milky sauce.

We turned our attention to the cooking medium and method first. For our first experiment, we prepared eight existing recipes for rice pudding, each using a different combination of water, milk, and cream, and each with varying ratios of rice to liquid. The tasting revealed that cooking the rice in milk or cream obscured the rice flavor, whereas cooking the rice in water emphasized it. The most appealing balance of rice flavor and satisfying yet not too rich consistency was achieved when we cooked 1 cup of rice in 2 cups of water until it was absorbed and then added equal parts (2½ cups each) of whole milk and half-and-half to make the pudding. Whole milk alone made the pudding too thin, but the milk and half-and-half together imparted just the right degree of richness. Eggs, butter, whipped cream, and heavy cream—on their own or in combination—overpowered the flavor of the rice.

We also tried a couple of variations in the cooking method, such as covering the pot or not and using a double boiler. The double boiler lengthened the cooking time by 25 minutes and turned out a pudding that was gummy and too sweet. By far, the best results came from cooking the rice and water in a covered pot, then simmering the cooked rice and dairy mixture uncovered. This technique gave us just what we wanted—distinct, tender grains of rice in a smooth sauce that tasted of milk rather than reduced cream. We found we could cut 10 minutes off the total cooking time by simmering the rice in the water and dairy mixture together from the start, but this approach sacrificed the texture of the grains and resulted in a pudding that our tasters described as overly dense and sweet.

Now it was time to try different kinds of rice. We tested the readily available varieties: supermarket brands of long- and medium-grain white, Arborio (a super-starchy Italian medium-grain white used to make risotto), and basmati (an aromatic long-grain white).

All rice contains two types of starch, called amylose and amylopectin, but they are present in different concentrations in different kinds of rice. Arborio, with its high level of amylopectin, made a stiff, gritty pudding. On the other end of the starch scale, long-grain rice, which is high in amylose, cooked up separate and fluffy. But the puddings made with long-grain rice were a little too thin for our liking, and the flavor of the basmati rice was too perfumey, overwhelming the milk. Medium-grain rice, which has a high proportion of amylopectin (but less than Arborio), cooked up a little more moist and sticky than long-grain rice. This type proved ideal for our pudding, which had a creamy texture and tasted distinctly of rice and milk. As a final test, we made a pudding with cooked rice that had been refrigerated overnight. Unfortunately, the result was liquidy and grainy, without discernible rice flavor.

WHAT WE LEARNED: To preserve the rice flavor, cook the rice in water. Then add dairy in the form of whole milk and half-and-half—this combination gives the pudding enough richness without obscuring the rice flavor. Don't be tempted to cut corners and add all the liquids to the rice at the same time or the result will be mushy, overly sweet rice. Stick to medium-grain (or long-grain) rice—it makes for a creamy pudding with simple rice flavor. And avoid strongly flavored rices such as basmati or jasmine—they taste out of whack with the simple milky profile of the pudding.

STOVETOP RICE PUDDING

serves 6 to 8

We prefer pudding made with medium-grain rice, but long-grain rice works, too. Using a heavy-bottomed saucepan is key to preventing the bottom from burning.

2   cups water
1   cup medium-grain rice
¼   teaspoon salt
2½ cups whole milk
2½ cups half-and-half
⅔   cup (4⅔ ounces) sugar
½   cup raisins
1½ teaspoons vanilla extract
1   teaspoon ground cinnamon

1. Bring the water to a boil in a large, heavy-bottomed saucepan. Stir in the rice and salt, cover, and simmer over low heat, stirring once or twice, until the water is almost fully absorbed, 15 to 20 minutes.

2. Stir in the milk, half-and-half, and sugar. Increase the heat to medium-high and bring to a simmer, then reduce the heat to maintain a simmer. Cook, uncovered and stirring frequently, until the mixture starts to thicken, about 30 minutes. Reduce the heat to low and continue to cook, stirring every couple of minutes to prevent sticking and scorching, until a spoon is just able to stand up in the pudding, about 15 minutes longer.

3. Remove from the heat and stir in the raisins, vanilla, and cinnamon. Serve warm, at room temperature, or chilled. (To store, press plastic wrap directly onto the surface of the pudding and refrigerate for up to 2 days. If serving at room temperature or chilled, stir in up to 1 cup warm milk, 2 tablespoons at a time, as needed to loosen before serving.)

VARIATION

COCONUT RICE PUDDING

To toast the coconut, spread it out on a baking sheet and toast it in a 325-degree oven, stirring often, until light golden, 10 to 15 minutes.

Follow the recipe for Stovetop Rice Pudding, substituting coconut milk for the whole milk and garnishing with 1 cup shredded sweetened coconut, toasted, before serving.

CRÈME CARAMEL

WHAT WE WANTED: A modestly sweet, silky, refined custard with a caramel sauce that boasts a deep, toasted flavor.

Crème caramel is a deceptively simple classic French dessert. Made with just a few ingredients that are readily available (sugar, eggs, and milk or cream), it is similar in construction and flavor to other baked custards. This dessert is slightly lighter and a little less sweet than a standard baked custard, but what really makes it special is the caramel sauce.

For us, though, what makes a perfect crème caramel is texture. Our ideal caramel is delicate enough to melt in the mouth, but firm enough to hold its shape on the plate.

The first thing we discovered in our research was that the most important part of the recipe is the proportion of egg whites to egg yolks. Too many whites produced a custard that was almost solid and rubbery; too few egg whites, on the other hand, made our custard collapse. After much tinkering, we came up with what we consider the ideal ratio: 3 whole eggs to 2 yolks—in other words, 3 whites to 5 yolks. The resulting custard was tender yet not overly rich and firm enough to unmold easily.

Next we examined the question of what liquid to use. Since we were making a classic crème caramel, our choices were limited to milk, heavy cream, light cream, and half-and-half. We made our initial custard using milk alone, but it tasted far too thin. Our custard with heavy cream and milk, on the other hand, was creamy but too rich. Half-and-half was better, yet it left us wanting something slightly richer. Light cream solved our problem. A mixture of equal parts of milk and light cream gave us just that extra edge of richness—creamy enough to satisfy both ourselves and our tasters.

Our experiments with sugar were less extensive, since we had decided at the beginning that a crème caramel custard should be less sweet than a custard meant to be eaten unadorned. To us, that made the dessert more interesting and sophisticated. We initially used 6 tablespoons of sugar for the 3 cups of liquid in the recipe and were quite satisfied, but some tasters felt that this custard was bland. We then tried using ½ cup of sugar for the same amount of liquid. Opinions were divided on this custard. Some palates still wanted an even sweeter custard, so we tried ⅔ cup. This slightly sweeter custard became the new favorite for the majority, but if you prefer a less sweet custard, simply cut the amount of sugar down to ½ cup.

There are basically two methods of making caramel. In the dry method, you use only sugar, cooking it slowly until it melts and caramelizes. The wet method uses a combination of water and sugar. The sugar begins to dissolve in the water, then the mixture is simmered until the water evaporates and the sugar caramelizes. We never successfully produced a smooth caramel with the dry method, so we opted for the wet as a way of increasing the margin of success.

Once our caramel was done, we poured it directly into our molds. Some cookbooks advise buttering the molds, but we found this step both unnecessary and ill-advised: The butter solidified when cold and left the custard greasy. We then followed the common advice to pour the caramel into the molds, coat the bottom evenly, and then tilt the molds to coat the sides. An accident with hot caramel burning our fingers while the molds were tilted caused us to question this particular bit of advice. (A bowl of ice water nearby—a useful thing to have when you are making caramel or any type of candy—saved the day for the burnt finger.) We started to coat only the bottoms of the mold, reasoning that the caramel sinks to the bottom of the mold while baking anyway. When we unmolded the custards, the caramel still poured evenly over the tops of the custards. It was an easier and safer method.

How you bake crème caramel and how long you bake it can make the difference between a great dessert and a

mediocre, or even disappointing, one. After considerable experimentation, we determined that baking the custards at 350 degrees in a *bain-marie,* or water bath, to maintain an even, gentle heating environment, produced custards that were creamy and smooth.

As a final experiment, we decided to try lining the baking pan with a towel before adding the molds or the water. We found this step in a couple of recipes and initially dismissed it as not worth the bother. At this point, however, our testing produced custards that were wonderful, but still had bubbles from overcooking near the bottom. We reasoned that the towel might absorb some of the heat from the bottom, preventing the custards from overcooking in this area. Custards baked with the towel contained significantly fewer bubbles, so we judged it worth the effort.

WHAT WE LEARNED: The key to a silky custard that sets well, but doesn't turn rubbery, is the eggs—use 3 whole eggs and 2 egg yolks. A duo of light cream and whole milk provides just enough rich dairy flavor. Use the wet method for preparing the caramel sauce. This method, in which sugar is dissolved in water and cooked, is easier and safer than the dry method of cooking the sugar in a dry pan. Don't butter the ramekins before adding the custard, or the finished dessert will be greasy. For evenly cooked, delicate crème caramel, bake the ramekins in a water bath (a pan filled with enough water to reach halfway up the sides of the ramekins); the gentle, steady heat ensures a delicate, creamy custard. And place a dish towel on the bottom of the pan, where the heat is most intense, to keep the bottoms of the custards from overcooking.

CLASSIC CRÈME CARAMEL

serves 8

Though you can make one large crème caramel, we find that custards baked in individual ramekins cook faster, are more evenly textured, and unmold more easily. You can vary the amount of sugar in the custard to suit your taste. Most tasters preferred the full ⅔ cup, but you can reduce that amount to as little as ½ cup to create a greater contrast between the custard and the caramel. Cook the caramel in a pan with a light-colored interior, since a dark surface makes it difficult to judge the color of the syrup. Caramel can leave a real mess in a pan, but it is easy to clean. Simply boil lots of water in the pan for 5 to 10 minutes to loosen the hardened caramel.

caramel

⅓	cup water
2	tablespoons light corn syrup
¼	teaspoon juice from 1 lemon
1	cup (7 ounces) sugar

custard

1½	cups whole milk
1½	cups light cream
3	large whole eggs, plus 2 large egg yolks
⅔	cup (4⅔ ounces) sugar (see note)
1½	teaspoons vanilla extract
	Pinch salt

1. FOR THE CARAMEL: Combine the water, corn syrup, and lemon juice in a heavy-bottomed 2- to 3-quart saucepan. Pour the sugar into the center of the saucepan, taking care not to let the sugar granules touch the sides of the pan. Gently stir with a clean spatula to moisten the sugar thoroughly. Bring to a boil over medium-high heat and cook, without stirring, until the sugar is completely dissolved and the liquid is clear, 6 to 10 minutes. Reduce the heat to medium-low and continue to cook (swirling occasionally)

until the caramel turns a honey-caramel in color, 4 to 5 minutes longer. Remove the pan immediately from the heat and, working quickly but carefully (the caramel is above 300 degrees and will burn if it touches your skin), pour a portion of the caramel into each of 8 ungreased 6-ounce ovenproof ramekins. Allow the caramel to cool and harden, about 15 minutes. (The caramel-coated ramekins can be covered with plastic wrap and refrigerated for up to 2 days; return to room temperature before adding the custard.)

2. FOR THE CUSTARD: Adjust an oven rack to the middle position and heat the oven to 350 degrees. Heat the milk and cream in a medium saucepan over medium heat, stirring occasionally, until steam appears and/or an instant-read thermometer held in the liquid registers 160 degrees, 6 to 8 minutes; remove from the heat. Meanwhile, gently whisk the eggs, yolks, and sugar in a large bowl until just combined. Off the heat, gently whisk the warm milk

mixture, vanilla, and salt into the eggs until just combined but not at all foamy. Strain the mixture through a fine-mesh strainer into a large measuring cup or container with a pouring spout; set aside.

3. Bring 2 quarts water to a boil in a kettle. Meanwhile, fold a dish towel to fit the bottom of a large baking dish or roasting pan and position it in the pan. Divide the reserved custard mixture among the ramekins; place the filled ramekins on the towel in the pan (making sure they do not touch) and set the pan on the oven rack. Fill the pan with boiling water to reach halfway up the sides of the ramekins; cover the entire pan loosely with aluminum foil so steam can escape. Bake until a paring knife inserted halfway between the center and the edge of the custards comes out clean, 35 to 40 minutes. Transfer the custards to a wire rack and cool to room temperature. (The custards can be covered with plastic wrap and refrigerated for up to 2 days.)

4. To unmold, slide a paring knife around the perimeter of each ramekin, pressing the knife against the side of the dish. Hold a serving plate over the top of the ramekin and invert; set the plate on the work surface and shake the ramekin gently to release the custard. Serve immediately.

VARIATIONS
LARGE CRÈME CARAMEL
If you don't have ramekins, make this version.

Follow the recipe for Classic Crème Caramel, pouring the caramel and custard into a 1½-quart straight-sided soufflé dish rather than individual ramekins. Fill a roasting pan with boiling water to reach halfway up the sides of the soufflé dish; increase the baking time to 70 to 75 minutes, or until an instant-read thermometer inserted in the center of the custard registers 175 degrees.

ESPRESSO CRÈME CARAMEL
Espresso beans ground in a coffee grinder would be too fine and impart too strong a coffee flavor to the custard. Instead, crush the beans lightly with the bottom of a heavy saucepan.

Follow the recipe for Classic Crème Caramel, heating ½ cup lightly crushed espresso beans with the milk and cream mixture until steam appears and/or an instant-read thermometer held in the liquid registers 160 degrees, 6 to 8 minutes. Off the heat, cover and steep until the coffee flavor has infused the milk and cream, about 15 minutes. Pour the mixture through a fine-mesh strainer to strain out the beans and continue with the recipe, reducing the amount of vanilla extract to 1 teaspoon.

EQUIPMENT CORNER: Electric Kettles

ELECTRIC KETTLES PROMISE TO SHAVE MINUTES OFF THE wait for boiling water and save space on your stovetop, too. We tested eight brands, ranging in price from $9.99 to $89.99, to see if brand makes a difference. All but one (the Proctor Silex K2070; $9.99) beat the time it took to boil water on the powerful gas stovetops we use in the test kitchen. Unfortunately, the Proctor Silex and the other under-$25 model we tested (Melitta MEK17W; $24.95)

also lacked the automatic shutoff/boil-dry safeguards we deem necessary. We preferred models that had a separate base, allowing you to move the kettle away from the heating element, and a window that lets you view the water level. With the exception of the Bodum 5600 Curl (our Best Buy at $49.95), we disliked plastic kettles, which tended to impart an off-flavor to the water.

Of the quickest kettles, we were most impressed by the Capresso Silver H2O Plus Electric Kettle ($59.95). Easy to fill, pour, and clean, its 6-cup glass carafe affords a view of bubbles rising from an orb-like stainless heating element.

Rating Electric Kettles

WE TESTED EIGHT ELECTRIC KETTLES AND RATED THEM ON SPEED, SAFETY, AND EASE OF USE. TIME TO BOIL IS THE average time it took to boil 1 quart of water. Brands are listed in order of preference. See www.americastestkitchen.com for updates to this testing.

RECOMMENDED
Capresso Silver H2O Plus

$59.95; 6-cup capacity; Time to boil: 4 minutes, 39 seconds

This kettle ranked second in speed and won us over with its sleek design and ease of use. Its glass carafe affords a view of bubbles rising from an orb-like stainless heating element and safety features include an automatic shutoff.

RECOMMENDED WITH RESERVATIONS
Krups FLF2-J4

$49.95; 7-cup capacity; Time to boil: 3 minutes, 55 seconds

Although this was the fastest kettle to boil, one of the four models we tested had a flawed switch that turned the kettle off right after we switched it on. The spout cover also seemed superfluous on this model, as the water spilled past it when it was "shut." However, the low exterior temperature, speed, and safety features helped this kettle hold a high ranking.

RECOMMENDED WITH RESERVATIONS
Cuisinart RK-17

$79.95; 7-cup capacity; Time to boil: 5 minutes, 3 seconds

The classic design of this pot contributed to a clean pour. This and its speed kept it near the top of the rankings despite a lid that stuck at times and an exterior that got too hot to touch for even a second. This was the only kettle in the testing that didn't have a viewing panel to monitor the water level.

RECOMMENDED WITH RESERVATIONS
Bodum 5600 Curl

$49.95; 5.8-cup capacity; Time to boil: 4 minutes, 29 seconds

The modest price tag and speedy heating time make the Bodum a good option if you don't mind a few disadvantages: The limited view afforded by the dotted windows makes judging the water level a bit of a guessing game and the carafe's small opening makes cleaning the inside by any conventional method a challenge.

RECOMMENDED WITH RESERVATIONS
Breville ikon 1.7

$69.99; 7-cup capacity; Time to boil: 5 minutes, 42 seconds

The futuristic hydraulic-lift quality of the lid made for a particularly modern and impressive touch. The Breville is a good kettle in terms of design and safety, but it ranked second to last in speed—barely beating the time it takes to boil water on the stove. The stainless steel exterior also reached burn-inducing temperatures.

RECOMMENDED WITH RESERVATIONS
Braun Impressions WK600

$89.95; 7-cup capacity; Time to boil: 5 minutes, 8 seconds

This behemoth made for heavy lifting, but it was an efficient boiler. However, the fast boiling quickly heated the exterior of the metal carafe. The short cord also requires that the Braun model be near the power source.

NOT RECOMMENDED
Melitta MEK17W

$24.95; 7-cup capacity; Time to boil: 5 minutes, 37 seconds

Lack of safety features to prevent the kettle from boiling dry or operating if the lid remains open raised concerns about this kettle. Otherwise, it stayed relatively cool, had an average speed ranking, and poured flawlessly.

NOT RECOMMENDED
Proctor Silex K2070

$9.99; 4-cup capacity; Time to boil: 7 minutes, 9 seconds

This kettle took more time to boil water than the stove did, and it boils dry if the lid isn't fully closed, a potential safety hazard. In addition, the water boiled in the plastic carafe had pronounced plastic flavors. A short cord, sloppy pouring, and lack of a power base were also factors that landed this model at the bottom of the bunch.

We thicken our blueberry pie with tapioca and a little grated apple, which is high in pectin, a natural thickener that doesn't obscure the filling's fresh berry flavor.

BEST BLUEBERRY *pie*

A slice of blueberry pie, just warm enough to slowly melt a scoop of vanilla ice cream, is our idea of summer heaven. But as with many berry desserts, an excess of juices can flood the plate once the pie is cut, causing disappointment all around. We wanted a blueberry pie that would slice neatly so that each forkful holds a bite of flaky crust and juicy berry filling. Most recipes load up the filling with a thickener, such as flour, cornstarch, or tapioca, but we've never been satisfied with these approaches. These thickeners often muddy the flavor of the berries, or they give the filling a rubbery texture akin to Jell-O. Is there another way to thicken the filling so that the berries retain their bright flavor? We gathered together pints and pints of berries and a host of thickening ideas to see if we could pull it off.

The only aspect of baking a pie that gives most of us pause is making the crust. Each step can be a land mine—mixing together the dough, rolling it out, and fitting it into the pie plate. One misstep often spells disaster. We wanted to develop a fuss-free, no-stress pie crust that would mix together easily, roll out neatly, and fit into a pie plate without tearing—and most importantly, one that would bake up with a flaky texture and buttery flavor every time.

BEST BLUEBERRY PIE

WHAT WE WANTED: A juicy yet sliceable blueberry pie full of fresh berry flavor.

There's nothing like blueberry pie to shake the confidence of even the most experienced baker. Unlike apple pie, which requires little (if any) starch to thicken the fruit, the filling in blueberry pie needs special attention because the berries are so juicy. The very first slice reveals success or failure. Triumph brings a firm, glistening filling full of fresh, bright flavor and still-plump berries. Defeat can range from a wedge that collapses into a soupy puddle topped by a sodden crust to filling so dense that cutting into it is like slicing through Gummi Bears.

We started our search for a juicy yet sliceable pie by filling our Foolproof Pie Dough (page 308) with a fairly standard mixture of 6 cups of fresh blueberries, ¾ cup of sugar, and our usual thickener for berry pies, tapioca. (We knew to avoid cornstarch and flour; in the test kitchen we've found they mute fresh fruit flavor.) The 6 tablespoons recommended on the back of the tapioca box produced a stiff, congealed mass, so we slowly cut back the amount. At 4 tablespoons, the filling was still too congealed for our tasters' liking, but this amount proved to be the tipping point; any less, and the pie needed to be served with a spoon.

The problem, of course, was the juiciness of the berries. Could we reduce some of their liquid by cooking them before they were baked in the pie shell? We put all 6 cups in a pan. As the berries simmered, we mashed them with a potato masher to release their juices. Excess liquid did indeed boil away—but so did a lot of fresh berry flavor.

After some experimentation, we found that cooking just half of the berries was enough to adequately reduce the liquid. We then folded the remaining raw berries into the mixture, creating a satisfying combination of intensely flavored cooked fruit and bright-tasting fresh fruit that allowed us to cut the tapioca down to 3 tablespoons. Encouraged by this success, we wondered if we could decrease the amount of tapioca even further.

As we watched the blueberries for our pie bubble away in the pot, we thought about blueberry jam. Well-made jam boasts a soft, even consistency that is neither gelatinous nor slippery. The secret to this great texture is pectin, a carbohydrate found in fruit. Blueberries are low in natural pectin, so commercial pectin in the form of a liquid or powder is usually added when making blueberry jam. The only downside to commercial pectin is that it needs the presence of a certain proportion of sugar and acid in order to work. We added an ounce of pectin, which required us to bump up the sugar to 2½ cups. This increase in sugar overpowered the berries, making the filling sickeningly sweet. A test with "no sugar needed" pectin set up properly, but this additive contains lots of natural acid, which compensates for the lack of extra sugar—and its sourness made our tasters wince. We were ready to give up when a colleague offered a suggestion: Since apples contain a lot of natural pectin, could an apple be added to the blueberries to help set the filling?

We folded one peeled and grated Granny Smith apple into a new batch of fresh and cooked berries we had mixed with 2 tablespoons of tapioca. We baked the pie, then waited impatiently while it cooled. When we finally tried a slice, we knew we'd hit on a great solution. Combined with a modest 2 tablespoons of tapioca, the apple provided enough thickening power to set the pie beautifully, and it enhanced the flavor of the berries without anyone guessing our secret ingredient. (For more information, see "Thickening Blueberry Pie," on page 301.) Just as important, it left no evidence of its own texture. To make sure the tapioca was equally unobtrusive—thickening the filling without leaving any telltale pearls—we pulverized it in a spice grinder before adding it to the filling.

Tweaking the crust was the last step. We found that baking the pie on a heated baking sheet on the bottom rack of the oven produced a crisp, golden bottom crust that didn't get soggy. As for the top crust, berry pies are often made with a decorative lattice topping that allows the steam from the berries to gently escape. But after making more than 50 lattice tops, we were determined to find a faster, easier approach. We decided to try making a crust we had seen in our research that had vents in the form of simple round cutouts. After rolling out the dough, we used a small biscuit cutter to cut out circles, then transferred the dough onto the pie. This method saved time and made an attractive, unusual-looking top crust that properly vented the steam from the berry filling as it baked. At long last, our blueberry blues had turned to blueberry bliss.

WHAT WE LEARNED: Simmer and gently mash half of the berries to release their juices and reduce the amount of liquid in the pie. Add a peeled and grated Granny Smith apple to the berries—apples contain a lot of natural pectin, which helps the filling to set. The pectin in the apple provides enough thickening power that you can reduce the amount of tapioca to 2 tablespoons. Bake the pie on a heated baking sheet to ensure a crisp, golden crust, and use a biscuit cutter as an easy way to vent the top crust, allowing plenty of steam to escape.

BLUEBERRY PIE

makes one 9-inch pie

This recipe was developed using fresh blueberries, but unthawed frozen blueberries (our favorite brands are Wyman's and Cascadian Farm) will work as well. In step 2, cook half the frozen berries over medium-high heat, without mashing, until reduced to 1¼ cups, 12 to 15 minutes. Grind the tapioca to a powder in a spice grinder or mini food processor. If using pearl tapioca, reduce the amount to 5 teaspoons.

- 1   recipe Foolproof Pie Dough (page 308)
- 6   cups (about 30 ounces) fresh blueberries (see note)
- 1   Granny Smith apple, peeled and grated on large holes of box grater
- 2   teaspoons grated zest and 2 teaspoons juice from 1 lemon
- ¾   cup (5¼ ounces) sugar
- 2   tablespoons instant tapioca, ground (see note)
      Pinch salt
- 2   tablespoons unsalted butter, cut into ¼-inch pieces
- 1   large egg, lightly beaten with 1 teaspoon water

1. Roll out one of the dough disks on a generously floured (up to ¼ cup) work surface to a 12-inch circle, about ⅛ inch thick. Roll the dough loosely around the rolling pin and unroll into a 9-inch pie plate, leaving at least a 1-inch overhang on each side. Working around the circumference, ease the dough into the plate by gently lifting the edge of the dough with one hand while pressing into the plate bottom with the other hand. Leave the dough that overhangs the plate in place; refrigerate while preparing the filling until the dough is firm, about 30 minutes.

2. Adjust an oven rack to the lowest position, place a rimmed baking sheet on the oven rack, and heat the oven to 400 degrees. Place 3 cups of the berries in a medium

TECHNIQUE: No-Fuss Top Crust

We used a 1¼-inch biscuit cutter to cut holes in the dough, but a spice-jar lid will also do the trick.

saucepan and set over medium heat. Using a potato masher, mash the berries several times to release the juices. Continue to cook, stirring frequently and mashing occasionally, until about half of the berries have broken down and the mixture is thickened and reduced to 1½ cups, about 8 minutes. Let cool slightly.

3. Place the grated apple in a clean kitchen towel and wring dry. Transfer the apple to a large bowl. Add the cooked berries, remaining 3 cups uncooked berries, the lemon zest, lemon juice, sugar, tapioca, and salt; toss to combine. Transfer the mixture to the dough-lined pie plate and scatter the butter pieces over the filling.

4. Roll out the second disk of dough on a generously floured (up to ¼ cup) work surface to an 11-inch circle, about ⅛ inch thick. Using a 1¼-inch round biscuit cutter, cut a round from the center of the dough. Cut another 6 rounds from the dough, 1½ inches from the edge of the center hole and equally spaced around the center hole. Roll the dough loosely around the rolling pin and unroll over the pie, leaving at least a ½-inch overhang on each side.

TESTING NOTES:
Looks Can Be Deceiving

Pretty but Pasty
Too much tapioca (or the wrong thickener, such as flour or cornstarch) results in a filling that holds its shape but tastes gluey and dull.

Fresh but Soupy
With no thickener at all, there is plenty of fresh berry flavor, but the filling is loose and runny.

5. Using kitchen shears, trim the bottom layer of the overhanging dough, leaving a ½-inch overhang. Fold the dough under itself so that the edge of the fold is flush with the outer rim of the pie plate. Flute the edges using your thumb and forefinger or press with the tines of a fork to seal. Brush the top and edges of the pie with the egg mixture. If the dough is very soft, chill in the freezer for 10 minutes.

6. Place the pie on the heated baking sheet and bake 30 minutes. Reduce the oven temperature to 350 degrees and continue to bake until the juices bubble and the crust is deep golden brown, 30 to 40 minutes longer. Transfer the pie to a wire rack; cool to room temperature, at least 4 hours. Cut into wedges and serve.

SCIENCE DESK: Thickening Blueberry Pie

WHEN MAKING OUR BLUEBERRY PIE FILLING, WE FOUND that if we used more than 2 tablespoons of tapioca, the texture of the filling took on a gummy consistency we didn't like. But 2 tablespoons or less resulted in a filling that was too loose. Could we solve this problem with pectin, a gentle thickener that occurs naturally in fruit?

EXPERIMENT
As a control, we thickened one pie with 2 tablespoons of tapioca. We then compared it with a second pie thickened with 2 tablespoons of tapioca and a grated apple, which is high in pectin and has a mild flavor.

RESULTS
The pie thickened with tapioca alone was loose and soupy. But the pie thickened with tapioca plus an apple had a naturally jelled texture that was just right. The apple bits seemed to melt into the berry filling, boosting fruity flavor but leaving no textural sign of their presence.

EXPLANATION
Pectin is a natural substance, found in fruits and vegetables, that creates structure in a plant by helping to bind its cell walls together. This same substance is used to thicken jams and jellies into a set, but soft, mass. Pectin content varies from fruit to fruit. Apples are a great source of pectin because they contain high levels of high-methoxy pectin, the best natural pectin for making gels. By mashing some of the blueberries and then grating the apple, we helped to release the pectin from the fruits' cell walls so that it could thicken the pie filling.

EQUIPMENT CORNER: Baking Sheets

IN THE TEST KITCHEN WE USE BAKING SHEETS for baking cookies, biscuits, scones, and jellyroll cakes, as well as for roasting oven fries and asparagus. With a wire cooling rack set inside, they're good for broiling or roasting meats and holding breaded cutlets before frying. Our baking sheets aren't just for baking—they are true kitchen workhorses.

But you'd be hard-pressed to find these essential pans in most cookware stores. Known as a half-sheet pan in restaurant supply stores, the real thing is made of heavy-gauge metal and measures 18 by 13 inches with a 1-inch rim all around. The closest thing you'll usually find in retail stores is a flimsy, too-small 15 by 10-inch "jellyroll pan."

If you happen to see a roomy rimmed baking sheet, stop and take a look. You want this pan. But are some models more useful and durable than others? After some digging, we found eight heavy-duty, full-sized rimmed baking sheets, priced from $9.95 to $59.95, and put them to the test.

If you glanced at the pans we gathered for this testing, you would be forgiven for wondering if it really matters which one you use. Our very first test convinced us that it does. We prepared a batch of cookies in each of the eight baking sheets. Some pans gave us cookies that rose high and turned an evenly light golden brown across the baking sheet; others turned out burnt cookies—even when we repeated the test several times.

A closer look revealed that these pans are not identical. Rimmed baking sheets are formed by a machine that presses a flat metal sheet into a predetermined shape, maintaining consistent pressure so the metal will flow in without wrinkling or cracking, said Campbell Buchanan, technical manager for United Aluminum in North Haven, Connecticut. They can be made from different alloys and gauges of aluminum, aluminized steel (a thin coat of aluminum over steel), or a tri-ply sandwich of shiny stainless steel with an aluminum core.

We found that solid construction is more important than the choice of materials. A too-flimsy pan warps under high heat. We observed this when the oil pooled at one end of the warping Chicago Metallic baking sheet as we made fries in a 475-degree oven, resulting in uneven browning of the potatoes.

Aluminum sheet pans will soften slightly beginning at temperatures of 400 to 500 degrees, Buchanan said, and the metal will expand and contract. Although steel won't soften significantly below 500 degrees, the combination of metals in aluminized steel can behave differently at high heat, leading to the warping we experienced. The thinner pans also seemed much more prone to warping.

A pan that is too lightweight also can transfer heat too intensely. We saw this with the lightest pan in our lineup (which was also one of the thinnest), by Wilton, which burned batch after batch of cookies. In this pan, oven fries also browned before they were cooked through, and the jellyroll cake finished before the recipe's recommended time. Other pans that overbrowned cookies, Anolon and NordicWare, were also among the thinnest in our testing.

After all the cooking was done, we placed the pans on a countertop and pushed down on one corner of the rim. Some pans remained resolutely flat; others rocked, having been warped by our testing. We grasped the short sides of each pan and twisted. Again, some pans could be flexed easily, and others could not. In general, the less flexible, flatter pans performed better in the kitchen.

So what should you buy? We loved almost everything about the Gourmet Standard pan. It was one of the thickest pans in the lineup and performed admirably in our kitchen tests. But one flaw kept this pan from claiming the top spot: The pan is 2 inches shorter than the competition, so parchment paper and standard cooling racks won't fit. And at $60, this flaw is hard to overlook.

The best rimmed baking sheet turned out to be a restaurant supply item available to retail consumers online. The Lincoln Foodservice Half-Size Heavy Duty Sheet Pan ($15.40) performed flawlessly, is one of the thickest pans we tested, sells at a reasonable price, and is our new favorite.

Rating Baking Sheets

WE TESTED EIGHT BRANDS OF RIMMED BAKING SHEETS, RANGING IN PRICE FROM $9.95 TO $59.95. TESTS INCLUDED baking cookies, making oven fries, and oven-barbecuing pork. Brands are listed in order of preference. See www.americastestkitchen.com for updates to this testing.

HIGHLY RECOMMENDED
Lincoln Foodservice Half-Size Heavy Duty Sheet Pan
$15.40; aluminum alloy (13-gauge); 18" x 13" x 1"; 1 lb., 14 oz.; 1.8 mm thick

This "flawless" pan turned out "perfect" cookies, oven fries, and jellyroll. Pork produced "lots of fat but no worries about spilling— the pan is solid as a rock." The pan can't be twisted and did not warp. "The search is over."

RECOMMENDED
Norpro Heavy Gauge Aluminum Jelly Roll Pan
$17.99; aluminum; 18" x 12" x 1"; 1 lb., 15 oz.; 1.0 mm thick

Oven fries were evenly browned, as were cookies and jellyroll cake, and the pan felt solid when we barbecued pork. However, although it felt sturdy, the pan had warped slightly by the end of testing.

RECOMMENDED
Gourmet Standard Tri-Ply Stainless Steel Jelly Roll Pan
$59.95; two layers of stainless steel sandwiching a layer of aluminum; 16" x 13" x 1"; 3 lb., 5 oz.; 1.8 mm thick

This "pretty but pricey" pan performed all cooking tests well, but its nonstandard size was a handicap: At just 16 inches long (15 inches once rims are discounted), it's too short for a standard wire rack to fit inside, and parchment sheets must be trimmed.

RECOMMENDED
Anolon Commercial Bakeware Jelly Roll Pan
$14.95; aluminized steel; 18" x 13" x 1"; 2 lb., 6 oz.; 0.5 mm thick

This "sturdy" pan produced crisp, evenly cooked fries, released the jellyroll cake easily, and was steady when full of hot barbecued pork and drippings. However, cookies baked up too dark, due to the thinness of the pan.

RECOMMENDED
Vollrath Jelly Roll Pan
$9.95; aluminum alloy; 18" x 13" x 1"; 1 lb., 11 oz.; 1.02 mm thick

Cookies baked well, as did the jellyroll cake, but fries were "a little uneven and not very crisp." The pan bent when full of hot barbecued pork. It was slightly warped after testing.

RECOMMENDED
NordicWare Natural Commercial Bakeware Baker's Half Sheet
$14.99; aluminum; 18" x 13" x 1"; 1 lb., 10 oz.; 0.8 mm thick

Cookies baked evenly, but they were too dark. Oven fries in the middle of the pan were "soggy, wimpy," and underdone, but those around the edges of the pan were too dark. The pan was stable with hot drippings but the soft surface scratched too easily.

RECOMMENDED WITH RESERVATIONS
Chicago Metallic Commercial Cookie/Jelly Roll Pan
$15.25; aluminized steel; 18" x 13" x 1"; 2 lb., 7 oz.; 0.5 mm thick

Cookies and fries browned unevenly. Oil pooled at one end of the pan after it warped under high heat while making fries; the pan buckled a bit with the pork, causing some hot fat to splash out as we moved the pan.

RECOMMENDED WITH RESERVATIONS
Wilton Jelly Roll and Cookie Pan
$13.99; aluminum; 18" x 12" x 1"; 1 lb.; 0.8 mm thick

Light and "flimsy, bendy" ("It's flapping like a sail"), this pan transferred heat too rapidly: Cookies burned; oven fries were still uncooked inside when exteriors were deeply brown. The pan was "quite warped" by the end of testing.

EQUIPMENT CORNER: Wire Racks

A GOOD WIRE RACK SHOULD BE STURDY, ABLE TO withstand a hot broiler, and clean up without warping or damage. It should also fit inside a standard 18 by 13-inch baking pan, which eliminated four of the six brands we purchased. Both the CIA Bakeware 12 by 17 Inch Cooling Rack ($14.95) and the Libertyware Cross Wire Cooling Rack Half Sheet Pan Size ($4.35) performed well. The CIA rack offered extra support, with a central brace and six feet, rather than four, and took top honors. But the inexpensive Libertyware rack is almost as good, and at one-third the price, it's our Best Buy.

Rating Wire Racks

WE RATED SIX BRANDS OF WIRE RACKS FOR THEIR SIZE, STURDINESS, AND ABILITY TO CLEAN UP EASILY. BRANDS ARE listed in order of preference. See www.americastestkitchen.com for updates to this testing.

HIGHLY RECOMMENDED
CIA Bakeware 12 by 17 Inch Cooling Rack
$14.95; chrome-plated steel
This rack fit perfectly inside a standard 18 by 13-inch rimmed baking sheet, offering extra support with a central brace and six feet rather than four. It did not warp in the oven or dishwasher.

RECOMMENDED
Libertyware Cross Wire Cooling Rack Half Sheet Pan Size (16½ by 11¾ inches)
$4.35; nickel-plated steel
Our best buy, this rack fit well inside a standard 18 by 13-inch rimmed baking sheet, supported by four feet. It did not warp in the oven or dishwasher.

NOT RECOMMENDED
Chicago Metallic Commercial Large Chrome Cooling Grid 15½ by 12½ Inch
$16.29; chrome-plated steel
Although it is sturdily constructed, this rack was too wide and too short for a standard 18 by 13-inch rimmed baking sheet and did not fit its own brand of rimmed baking sheet.

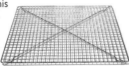

NOT RECOMMENDED
Anolon SureGrip Bakeware 10 by 18-Inch Nonstick Cooling Rack
$12; nonstick coating on carbon steel
The Anolon rack did not fit inside a standard 18 by 13-inch rimmed baking sheet (it is far too long and narrow) or Anolon's own rimmed baking sheet. Heavyweight construction with four support feet.

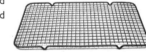

NOT RECOMMENDED
Wilton Cooling Rack (10 by 16 inches)
$8.95; nonstick coating on aluminum
This narrow, short rack supported by four feet did not fit in either a standard 18 by 13-inch rimmed baking sheet or Wilton's own baking sheet. The construction feels lightweight; the grid is large and irregular.

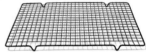

NOT RECOMMENDED
Baker's Secret 10 by 16-Inch Nonstick Cooling Rack, Set of 2
$6.99; chrome
A very lightweight rack; the grid spacing is large and irregular. The rack is too narrow and short for a standard 18 by 13-inch rimmed baking sheet.

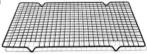

FOOLPROOF PIE DOUGH

WHAT WE WANTED: An easy, foolproof pie dough, one that's tender, flaky, and flavorful—every time.

Pie crust in a nutshell: Mix flour, salt, and sugar together, cut in some fat, add water just until the dough sticks together, roll it out, and bake it. A study in simplicity. Yet it can all go wrong so easily. The dough is almost always too dry and crumbly to roll out successfully. The crust is either flaky but leathery or tender with no flakes. And the results are seemingly random: The recipe that gave you a perfect crust last month resulted in a tough-as-nails crust when you followed it this week.

We wanted to figure out exactly where a crust goes south, so we set out to sort through all the dubious science, purported secret ingredients, and perennial pie crust theories to separate fact from fiction and create a recipe for a crust that not only bakes up tender and flaky every single time, but also rolls out easily.

The first question was what type of fat to use. The test kitchen likes the rich flavor of an all-butter crust. Problem: Butter starts to soften at around 50 degrees and fully melts at around 100 degrees, which means the crust has to be worked very quickly. Also, butter's high water content (about 20 percent; the rest is fat) can lead to leathery crusts, as too much water will stimulate the formation of gluten, the protein matrix that provides structure in baked goods. Enter hydrogenated vegetable shortening, a soft fat that doesn't melt until a relatively high temperature and contains no water, just fat. But although crusts made with shortening are very tender, they have virtually no flavor. We ultimately found that a combination of butter and shortening provided the best balance of flavor and tenderness.

We moved on to the next step: cutting the fat into the flour. Of all the methods we tried (food processor, standing mixer, pastry blender, and by hand), the food processor was the fastest and most consistent. Even so, we ran into our first

major hurdle—some recipes call for cutting the butter into walnut-sized pieces, and others say to incorporate the fat until it resembles wet sand. Which approach is better? And once you determine which method to use, is it possible to produce same-sized pieces of butter time after time?

What if we ran the food processor until the flour and fat were completely combined? This is simple to repeat every time, and there's no way to overprocess it. But dough is supposed to have pockets of fat in it, which melt upon baking to leave behind the gaps that create flaky layers. By fully incorporating the fat, we were left with no pockets, and

sure enough, our dough baked up with no flakes. Our next attempt was to process only a portion of the fat completely into the flour, freeze the rest of the fat, and grate it into the mixed dough to create those fat pockets. Consistent? Yes. But despite the fact that there were plenty of pockets of unmixed fat, our crust still came out flake-free.

While we were testing methods for incorporating the fat into the flour, we had been dealing with the frustrating issue of how much water to add to the dough. Some recipes call for a range of water amounts that can vary by as much as 100 percent, claiming that a hot or humid day can throw measurements off. This excuse seemed a little suspicious, and we were eventually able to dismiss the theory by measuring the effects of humidity on flour. It was time to step back and examine the structure of a pie crust.

When fat is being cut into flour, the flour is separated into two groups. Some of the flour is coated with a layer of fat, which protects it from absorbing any water; the uncoated flour will absorb water and form gluten. When the dough is rolled out, this gluten stretches into sheets separated by pockets of unmixed fat that melt upon baking, leaving behind crisp, separated sheets. The problem is that depending on who's making the crust, the exact temperature of the fat, and even the type of food processor being used, the ratio of fat-coated flour to uncoated flour can change drastically from batch to batch. This means a pie crust recipe that barely absorbed ¼ cup of water one time might readily absorb ½ cup the next. It also explains why the same recipe is flaky one day but not the next: For consistent flakiness, you need the same ratio of fat-coated flour to uncoated flour.

It's not just the chunks of fat that create flakiness. It's also the uncoated flour that mixes with water and forms gluten that guarantees a flaky crust. This explained the failure of the test in which we combined all the flour with some of the butter, then added grated butter to the dough. You need at least some flour that hasn't been coated with butter in the dough in order to create the gluten layers that form flakes. When processing the fat in a traditional crust, leaving some chunks of butter in the dough is a good sign that the dough hasn't been overprocessed (that is, chunks of butter in the dough are an indication that there is enough uncoated flour left to combine with water and create a flaky crust).

What if we measured out the two types of flour—the portion we wanted coated with fat and the portion we wanted to remain uncoated—separately? Rather than starting with all the flour in the processor, we put aside 1 cup of flour, then placed the remaining 1½ cups of flour in the food processor with all of the fat and processed it until it formed a unified paste. We then added the cup of reserved flour back to the bowl and pulsed it just until it was evenly distributed around the bowl. This would guarantee the dough had a constant amount of uncoated flour to mix with the water. After mixing in the water and rolling out the dough, we now theoretically had a dough with two distinct parts: long sheets of gluten separated by a flour-fat paste.

The dough baked up as flaky as could be. And since the stage in which the fat gets processed into the flour was no longer ambiguous, our new crusts came out identically, time and again.

We had guaranteed flakiness, but tenderness was still a crapshoot. Most recipes with 2½ cups of flour call for 6 to 8 tablespoons of ice water. If we kept the water at the lower end of this range, the dough baked up very tender but was dry and hard to roll out. When we used the full 8 tablespoons, the dough was smooth and easy to roll out but baked up tough—too much gluten was forming. We had to figure out a way to tenderize the finished crust without reducing the amount of water we used.

Scanning through recipes for pie crusts turned up a common "miracle ingredient"—acid. Many recipes say that a teaspoon of vinegar or lemon juice can tenderize dough, claiming that gluten formation is inhibited at lower pH values. But after consulting our science editor, we learned that gluten formation is actually increased in slightly acidic environments (a pH of between 5 and 6) and doesn't begin to decrease until the pH drops below 5. Achieving this level required replacing nearly half the water with lemon juice,

by which point the pie crust was inedibly sour.

What about using lower-protein cake or pastry flour? No good. The crusts baked up sandy and too short. What about adding cream cheese or sour cream? Although they made the crust more tender, it had a strange, soft chewiness.

Let's review: In order to roll easily, dough needs more water, but more water makes crusts tough. Therefore, we needed something that's not water but is still wet. As the aromas from a nearby pan of reducing wine reached our noses, the answer hit us like a bottle to the head: alcohol.

Eighty-proof vodka is essentially 40 percent ethanol and 60 percent water. As it happens, gluten cannot form in alcohol, which means that for every tablespoon of vodka we added, only 60 percent of it contributed to gluten development.

We made a batch of pie dough with 4 tablespoons each of cold vodka and water. The resulting dough was as smooth as Play-Doh, and we couldn't have made it crack even if we'd wanted to. We were tempted to toss it, thinking it would bake up tough as leather, but giving good science the benefit of the doubt, we baked it anyway. It was an unparalleled success. The dough baked up every bit as tender and flaky as any crust we'd ever had, without a hint of booziness to give away its secret. One hundred forty-eight pie crusts later, we'd finally come up with a recipe that is 100 percent reliable.

WHAT WE LEARNED: Use a combination of butter and shortening to provide the best balance of flavor and tenderness. To ensure that the right amount of flour gets coated with fat while the rest remains uncoated (essential to flakiness), fully process a portion of the flour with the butter and shortening until it forms a unified paste, then gently incorporate the remaining flour. For maximum tenderness, replace a portion of the water with vodka—vodka adds moisture (making the dough easy to roll out) while allowing less gluten development (too much results in a tough crust).

FOOLPROOF PIE DOUGH

makes enough for one 9-inch double-crust pie

Vodka is essential to the texture of the crust and imparts no flavor—do not substitute. This dough will be moister and more supple than most standard pie doughs and will require more flour to roll out (up to ¼ cup).

2½ cups (12½ ounces) unbleached all-purpose flour
1 teaspoon salt
2 tablespoons sugar
12 tablespoons (1½ sticks) cold unsalted butter, cut into ¼-inch slices
½ cup cold vegetable shortening, cut into 4 pieces
¼ cup cold vodka
¼ cup cold water

1. Pulse 1½ cups of the flour, salt, and sugar in a food processor until combined, about two 1-second pulses. Add the butter and shortening and process until a homogeneous dough just starts to collect in uneven clumps, about 15 seconds (the dough will resemble cottage cheese curds and there should be no uncoated flour). Scrape down the bowl with a rubber spatula and redistribute the dough evenly around the processor blade. Add the remaining 1 cup flour and pulse until the mixture is evenly distributed around the bowl and the mass of dough has been broken up, 4 to 6 quick pulses. Empty the mixture into a medium bowl.

2. Sprinkle the vodka and water over the mixture. With a rubber spatula, use a folding motion to mix, pressing down on the dough until the dough is slightly tacky and sticks together. Divide the dough into two even balls and flatten each into a 4-inch disk. Wrap each in plastic wrap and refrigerate at least 45 minutes or up to 2 days.

TECHNIQUE:
Key Steps to Foolproof Pie Dough

1. Make a Fat and Flour Paste: Completely blending part of the flour with all of the butter and shortening ensures a consistent amount of fat-coated flour in the final dough.

2. Add More Flour: Pulsing in the final cup of flour ensures a consistent amount of uncoated flour in the final dough.

3. Add Water and Vodka: Sprinkling with water and vodka ensures even distribution. No need to skimp—unlike water, vodka won't make the dough tough.

SCIENCE DESK:
Pie Dough's Secret Ingredient

PIE DOUGH GETS ITS STRUCTURE FROM GLUTEN, LONG chains of protein that form when flour mixes with water. But too much gluten will make pie dough tough. That's why traditional pie doughs are so stingy with the water. We discovered that vodka lets you add more liquid (so the dough is easy to roll out) without toughening the crust. Why?

Eighty-proof vodka consists of 60 percent water and 40 percent ethanol. Gluten forms readily in water, but it does not form in ethanol. Thus, our recipe, which contains 4 tablespoons each of cold water and vodka, gets the benefits of 8 tablespoons of liquid (supple, easy-to-roll dough) but actually has the equivalent of about 6½ tablespoons of water—an amount that limits gluten formation and ensures tenderness. As for the alcohol? It vaporizes in the oven.

Dough Tenderizer

TESTING NOTES: Why Traditional Pie Dough Fails

Traditional pie dough is cold and dry, making it difficult to handle and leading to imperfect results.

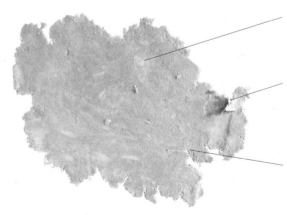

Problem: Dough Rolls Out Unevenly
Dough must be chilled (so the butter won't melt), but cold dough is hard to roll out into an even circle.

Problem: Dough Sticks and Tears
Most recipes call for using as little flour on the work surface as possible. As a result, butter sticks to the work surface and the dough sticks and tears.

Problem: Dough Cracks
Too much water makes the crust tough, so most recipes call for the bare minimum. As a result, the dough cracks at the edges.

Butter adds rich flavor and moisture to our snack cakes. Test Cook Suzannah McFerran measures out the butter that will be used in our Oatmeal Cake with Broiled Icing and our Spice Cake with Cream Cheese Frosting.

OLD-FASHIONED
CHAPTER 24
snack cakes

A generous square of snack cake can bring a smile
to anyone's face. Simple and homey, snack cakes are terrific packed into
a lunch box, served with tea in the afternoon, or brought to a potluck
supper. We loved the simple, old-fashioned appeal of two snack cakes,
oatmeal cake and spice cake, and aimed to create foolproof versions of
each one.

Oats provide lightly spiced oatmeal cake with a toasty flavor and
interesting texture, but it's the broiled icing—a sugary blend of shredded
coconut and chopped pecans—that really makes this cake so addictive.
We wanted the ultimate oatmeal cake—one that didn't suffer the pitfalls
of existing recipes (gummy texture and achingly sweet icing that can
often be greasy)—and we also wanted a foolproof method for broiling
the icing, so that it would be perfectly crunchy, not charred, and boast
the right balance of buttery, sweet flavor.

A great spice cake should be tender and airy with a convincing
spice flavor that stands up to a rich cream cheese frosting. Too often,
we've found that spice cakes are bland and leaden. Spices are anything
but bland, so what's going on? We'd need to zero in on the right spices,
the right proportions, and a method for infusing the cake with assertive
but balanced spice flavor. Next, we'd need to correct the cake's texture
so that it would still be moist, but tender. In short, we wanted a spice
cake that would deliver on all fronts.

OATMEAL CAKE

WHAT WE WANTED: A moist yet light and crumbly oatmeal cake, topped with a crisp and chewy coconut-pecan icing, perfect for an afternoon snack or casual dessert.

The informal title "snack cake" is applied to a broad range of simple cakes that come together with a few minutes' effort using pantry staples, making them ideal for after-school snacks, bake sales, and surprise visitors. One of the more interesting of the bunch is an oatmeal cake with a unique coconut- and pecan-studded broiled icing (broiled, that is, on top of the baked and slightly cooled cake).

After baking up a few test recipes, we were disappointed with the results. We assumed the cake would be moist, but instead we found it dense, gummy, and bland. The broiled icing, however, won us over: We loved its combination of chewy coconut and crunchy nuts and its butterscotch-like flavor, despite a saccharine sweetness and tendency toward greasiness. We decided that if we could make a moist (but not dense) cake and fix the icing's foibles, then we might hop on the bandwagon, too.

In each of the recipes we collected, a cup or so of old-fashioned rolled oats were hydrated in water and folded into a basic batter leavened with both baking powder and baking soda. The biggest difference among recipes—outside of base ratios of ingredients—was the type of fat specified: vegetable oil, shortening, or butter. The first two provided no flavor, making butter the obvious choice. Of the recipes that called for butter, most specified a surprisingly small amount: 6 tablespoons or less. Such a scant amount of butter seemed light for a cake of this style. But with all the hydrated oats in the batter, a mere 4 tablespoons of butter was all it took to produce a cake that tasters felt was plenty moist (albeit gummy), with buttery undertones.

Oats contribute starch and fiber to the cake, but little of the gluten needed for structure. For support, recipes typically include moderate amounts of all-purpose flour, usually in a 1-to-1 ratio with the oats. To create a lighter cake, could we use less flour than oats? Reducing the amount of flour from 1 cup (the amount of oats we had been using) to ¾ cup helped, but the cake still wasn't light enough to suit tasters. But if we used any less flour, the cake collapsed into crumbs when we sliced it. We'd have to look elsewhere for a solution.

In most recipes the cake is sweetened with 1 cup or more of brown sugar. We hazarded a guess that the sugar's dampness contributed to the cake's density. We cut the brown sugar by half (to ½ cup) and compensated with an equal amount of granulated sugar. The cake was now sufficiently light, and its more moderate sweetness was actually better suited to the sugary icing. Still, a less dense cake did not mean a less gummy cake. It was time to address the elephant in the room: the oats.

To mitigate their gumminess, we tried both toasting the oats and changing the amounts of oats and water in the batter, all to no avail. If changing the amount of oats wouldn't work, perhaps using a different type would. Chewy steel-cut oats made little sense here, but instant and quick-cooking rolled oats both did. The former bombed (precooked instant oats mostly dissolve when combined with boiling water, making the cake gluey), but the latter was a marked improvement. The cake was perceptibly less gummy, though not yet perfect.

Irrespective of type, the soaked oats were a sticky mess when we stirred them into the batter. Was that contributing to the gummy texture of the final cake? Would simply folding in dried oats suffice? No dice: The dried oats never fully hydrated, and they tasted raw and chewy in the finished cake. A chat with our science editor gave us a different idea: The hotter the water in which the oats are soaked, the more starches they release and the gluier they become (see "Getting Rid of Gumminess," page 315). So why not soak the oats in room-temperature, rather than boiling, water? We poured tepid tap water over a new batch of quick-cooking oats. Within a few minutes they had absorbed the water but weren't nearly as sticky or starchy as oats "cooked" in boiling water. We baked the cake, and the results were the best yet: delightfully moist yet enticingly crumbly, and entirely free of that once-persistent gumminess.

It was time to tackle the topping. The ingredients were the same in all recipes we found: sweetened, shredded coconut; pecans; light brown sugar; and butter. First we cut back on the amount of brown sugar to make the icing less sweet. Then we examined technique. Some recipes instruct you to cream the butter and sugar until fluffy before stirring in the coconut and pecans; others have you simply melt the butter before stirring the ingredients together. We determined that any fluffiness achieved by creaming the butter was lost once the frosting went under the broiler, so we took the easier route and used melted butter. This produced a stiffer icing than did the creaming method, but that was easily remedied by adding a splash of milk.

After we'd charred a few cakes under the broiler, we realized that placing the cake about 9 inches from the heating element evenly browned the icing in the time it took for the texture to turn "crun-chewy." We were finally ready to give this quick, delicious, and unique cake rave reviews.

WHAT WE LEARNED: For an oatmeal cake that's moist, not dense and gummy, use a small amount of butter (a modest 4 tablespoons), use quick-cooking rolled oats, and soak the oats in room-temperature water (they release less starch than if soaked in hot water). Switching out half the brown sugar for an equal amount of granulated sugar further prevents the cake from being dense and also helps moderate its sweetness. No need to cream the butter and sugar for the frosting—simply add melted butter to the sugar (and add a little milk to keep the icing from becoming too stiff).

OATMEAL CAKE WITH BROILED ICING

makes one 8-inch square cake

Do not use old-fashioned or instant oats for this recipe. Be sure to use a metal baking dish; glass pans are not recommended when broiling. If you have a drawer-style broiler (underneath the oven), position the rack as far as possible from the broiler element and monitor the icing carefully as it cooks in step 5. A vertical sawing motion with a serrated knife works best for cutting through the crunchy icing and tender crumb.

cake

1	cup (3 ounces) quick-cooking oats (see note)
¾	cup water, room temperature
¾	cup (3¾ ounces) unbleached all-purpose flour
½	teaspoon baking soda
½	teaspoon baking powder
½	teaspoon salt
¼	teaspoon ground cinnamon
⅛	teaspoon ground nutmeg
4	tablespoons (½ stick) unsalted butter, softened
½	cup (3½ ounces) granulated sugar
½	cup packed (3½ ounces) light brown sugar
1	large egg, at room temperature
½	teaspoon vanilla extract

broiled icing

- ¼ cup packed (1¾ ounces) light brown sugar
- 3 tablespoons unsalted butter, melted and cooled
- 3 tablespoons milk
- ¾ cup sweetened, shredded coconut
- ½ cup (2½ ounces) pecans, chopped

1. FOR THE CAKE: Adjust an oven rack to the middle position and heat the oven to 350 degrees. Cut two 16-inch lengths aluminum foil and fold both lengthwise to 5-inch widths. Spray an 8 by 8-inch metal baking dish with vegetable oil spray. Following illustration 1 on page 315, fit the foil pieces into the baking dish, one overlapping the other, pushing them into the corners and up the sides of the pan; allow the excess to overhang the pan edges. Spray the foil lightly with vegetable oil spray.

2. Combine the oats and water in a medium bowl and let sit until the water is absorbed, about 5 minutes. In another medium bowl, whisk the flour, baking soda, baking powder, salt, cinnamon, and nutmeg together.

3. In the bowl of a standing mixer, beat the butter and sugars on medium speed until combined and the mixture has the consistency of damp sand, 2 to 4 minutes, scraping down the bowl with a rubber spatula halfway through mixing. Add the egg and vanilla; beat until combined, about 30 seconds. Add the flour mixture in 2 additions and mix until just incorporated, about 30 seconds. Add the soaked oats and mix until combined, about 15 seconds.

4. Give the batter a final stir with a rubber spatula to make sure it is thoroughly combined. Transfer the batter to the prepared pan and lightly tap it against the countertop 3 or 4 times to dislodge any large air bubbles; smooth the surface

---

TECHNIQUE: Finishing the Cake

1. Cool the cake at least 10 minutes, then spread the icing evenly over the cake.

2. Broil the cake until the icing is bubbling and golden brown.

---

with the spatula. Bake the cake until a toothpick inserted into the center comes out with a few crumbs attached, 30 to 35 minutes, rotating the pan halfway through baking. Let the cake cool slightly in the pan, at least 10 minutes.

5. FOR THE BROILED ICING: While the cake cools, adjust an oven rack about 9 inches from the broiler element and heat the broiler. In a medium bowl, whisk together the brown sugar, melted butter, and milk; stir in the coconut and pecans. Spread the mixture evenly over the warm cake. Broil until the topping is bubbling and golden, 3 to 5 minutes.

6. Let the cake cool in the pan 1 hour. Following illustration 2 on page 315, transfer the cake to a serving platter, then discard the foil. Cut the cake into squares and serve.

SCIENCE DESK:
Getting Rid of Gumminess

THE UNIQUE MOIST YET CRUMBLY TEXTURE OF OUR oatmeal cake is largely the result of the inclusion of oats hydrated in water. Although most recipes for this cake specify old-fashioned oats soaked in boiling water, we found these cakes to be gummy and dense. We produced a cake with a much lighter texture by switching to quick-cooking oats soaked in room-temperature water. How did such a seemingly small alteration so greatly improve the cake's crumb?

It turns out that the extent to which the starch and fibers in oats absorb water is directly related to temperature: The hotter the water in which the oats are soaked, the more starches are hydrated (and subsequently released into the mix) and the more gluey the oats become. In the case of our snack cake, all those released starches weighed down the cake's batter.

Soaking raw old-fashioned oats in tap water accomplishes little at all: Being raw, they need heat to effectively hydrate. Quick-cooking oats, however, have been steamed and then rolled into thin flakes, giving them the ability to readily absorb water at any temperature. So our success was a compromise of sorts: The quick-cooking oats absorb water and release some of their starches and fibers to moisten the cake, but not nearly as much as old-fashioned oats steeped in boiling water.

TECHNIQUE: Making a Double Foil Sling

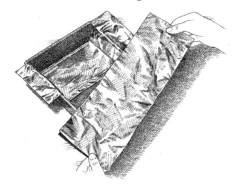

1. To transfer our exceptionally tender cake to a platter without it crumbling, we devised a novel solution. Cut two 16-inch pieces of aluminum foil and fold them into 5-inch widths. Press one piece of foil into the pan. Repeat with the second piece, overlapping the pieces by about 1 inch.

2. Once the cake has cooled, pick up the overhanging edges of the foil and transfer the cake to a flat surface or platter. Gently push the side of the cake with a knife and remove the foil, one piece at a time.

SPICE CAKE

WHAT WE WANTED: An exceptional spice cake—light but with a substantial crumb, fragrant with warm spices, and topped with an irresistible cream cheese frosting.

The spice cakes we remember most vividly are from our childhood. Usually baked in a rectangular pan, these cakes were light and airy and more akin to a layer cake than the heavy, dense snack cakes that all too often define the genre today. And spice cake was company cake, something too special to serve every day. It was moist and substantial, with spices that were warm and bold without being overpowering, and its layer of rich cream cheese frosting was the perfect complement. We wanted to return to this classic, but no one in the kitchen seemed to have a recipe fixed in writing.

We decided to do a little research in our library, where we found as many variations on the spice cake theme as there are cooks to make them. We found Bundt cakes with raisins and nuts; squat, square versions that resembled gingerbread or carrot cake; cakes that incorporated everything from apples and stewed figs to chocolate chips and pumpkin puree. Some had spice overload, tasting gritty and dusty. Others were so lacking in spice flavor that it seemed as if a cinnamon stick had only been waved in their general direction. In fact, other than a mixture of warm spices, there were few common denominators linking any of these desserts. And, unfortunately, not one had the old-fashioned simplicity of the frosted spice cake from our childhood. We would have to begin from scratch.

We started by simply adding spices to a basic yellow cake, but that didn't work. The cake crumbled under the heavy frosting, and the spice flavor was overwhelming. To add volume and heft, we replaced the cake flour we had used with all-purpose flour. The switch made for a slightly tougher, drier cake. Adding more yolks to the batter increased the cake's tenderness; so did switching from milk to buttermilk, which also enriched the cake's flavor.

Doubling the amount of dairy from ½ cup to 1 cup was enough to fix the dryness issue.

But the most important adjustment we made involved the mixing technique. We make yellow cake by reversing the usual order of things and mixing butter into the dry ingredients before adding the liquids, which yields a cake with a very fine-grained texture. We wanted a more open and substantial crumb, so we used the standard method of beating the softened butter with the sugar, incorporating the eggs, and adding flour and liquid alternately in small amounts.

We knew that simply adding more spice to something does not lead to increased spiciness. Most of what we experience when we consume a food containing spice is not actually the spice's taste but its aroma. These aromas are produced by volatile oils found within the spice cells. When spices are ground, these aromatic oils are released, which is why freshly ground whole spices are much "tastier" (i.e., more aromatic) than packaged ground spices (especially those that have been sitting on the shelf awhile). But in addition to being too much work, individually grinding the five spices we'd chosen for the recipe always imparted a faint but discernible grittiness to the cake, no matter how much time they spent in the spice grinder.

What about using techniques from the test kitchen to get the most out of the spices already in our cupboard? We knew from preparing curries and chili that heating spices (either through dry-toasting them or blooming them in hot oil) intensifies their aroma. This is because heat drives moisture out of the spice, carrying the aromatic oils along with it. Both techniques created a fuller-flavored cake, but dry-toasting the spices was not as successful as blooming them in oil. Toasting allows more of the piquant aromas to escape into the air, but because the aromatic oils are soluble in cooking oil, blooming the spices was a more effective way of making sure the oils made it into the cake.

Up to this point, we had been using ground cinnamon, cloves, cardamom, allspice, and nutmeg. Although the mixture contributed a respectable spiciness to the cake, we wanted more complexity. A coworker suggested steeping crushed fresh ginger in the buttermilk to extract maximum flavor. This brought slightly more depth of flavor to the cake but not enough to justify the extra work. A tablespoon of grated fresh ginger added directly to the batter, on the other hand, added noticeable zing. For yet another flavor dimension, we replaced the oil we had been using to bloom our spices with browned butter, which imparted a faint nuttiness and filled out the overall taste of the cake. As a finishing touch, we incorporated a couple of tablespoons of molasses into the batter—just enough to balance the spices with a slight bittersweet nuance without turning the cake into gingerbread.

All that remained was to create just the right frosting. Almost every frosting recipe for spice cake we'd come across in our initial research consisted of confectioners' sugar, cream cheese, and butter in varying amounts. To create a light, creamy frosting that would work well with the cake's tender crumb, we used a little less butter than called for in most of these recipes. When we frosted the cake, however, we were disappointed. The two elements lacked harmony and needed something to pull them into balance. Why shouldn't that be spice? We added ½ teaspoon of the spice mixture from the cake to the frosting, which lent a subtle yet perceptible flavor that made the two work beautifully together. This was the cake we all remembered from our childhood.

WHAT WE LEARNED: All-purpose flour makes the cake sturdier, and extra yolks and buttermilk ensure tenderness and add rich flavor. Use the standard mixing method (beating butter and sugar together, adding eggs, then adding flour and liquid alternately) to give the cake an open and substantial crumb. Bloom the spices in browned butter to enhance their flavor and impart a welcome nutty taste, and add fresh ginger and molasses for just the right amount of complexity. Add just a hint of spice to the cream cheese frosting to tie the elements of this old-fashioned dessert together.

SPICE CAKE WITH CREAM CHEESE FROSTING
serves 12 to 14

To save time, let the eggs, buttermilk, and butter come up to temperature while the browned butter and spice mixture cools. To prevent unsightly air holes in the finished cake, be sure to follow the instructions for removing air bubbles in the batter (see the illustrations on page 319). Leftover cake can be stored, covered with plastic wrap, in the refrigerator for up to 2 days. The cake should be brought to room temperature before serving.

cake

2¼	cups (11¼ ounces) unbleached all-purpose flour, plus extra for dusting pan
1	tablespoon ground cinnamon
¾	teaspoon ground cardamom
½	teaspoon ground allspice
½	teaspoon ground cloves
¼	teaspoon ground nutmeg
16	tablespoons (2 sticks) unsalted butter, softened
½	teaspoon baking powder
½	teaspoon baking soda
½	teaspoon salt
2	large whole eggs plus 3 large egg yolks, at room temperature
1	teaspoon vanilla extract
1¾	cups (12¼ ounces) granulated sugar
2	tablespoons light or mild molasses
1	tablespoon grated fresh ginger
1	cup buttermilk, at room temperature

frosting

5	tablespoons unsalted butter, cut into 5 pieces, softened
1¼	cups (5 ounces) confectioners' sugar
8	ounces cream cheese, cut into 4 pieces, softened
½	teaspoon vanilla extract
¾	cup coarsely chopped walnuts, toasted (optional)

GETTING IT RIGHT:
Keys to Spice Flavor

1. Browned Butter:
Browning the butter imparts a faint nuttiness that deepens the cake's spice flavor.

2. Bloomed Spices:
Blooming the spices in the browned butter brings out their volatile oils, boosting their impact.

3. Molasses:
Molasses adds a bittersweet note that underscores the warm flavor of the spices.

4. Grated Ginger:
Finely grated ginger adds a fresh, zesty quality to the cake that dried ginger can't provide.

1. FOR THE CAKE: Adjust an oven rack to the middle position and heat the oven to 350 degrees. Grease and flour a 13 by 9-inch baking pan. Combine the spices in a small bowl; reserve ½ teaspoon for the frosting.

2. Heat 4 tablespoons of the butter in an 8-inch skillet over medium heat until melted, 1 to 2 minutes. Continue to cook, swirling the pan constantly, until the butter is light brown and has a faint nutty aroma, 2 to 4 minutes. Add the spices and continue to cook, stirring constantly, 15 seconds. Remove from the heat and cool to room temperature, about 30 minutes.

3. Whisk together the flour, baking powder, baking soda, and salt in a medium bowl. In a small bowl, gently whisk the eggs, yolks, and vanilla to combine. In a standing mixer fitted with the paddle attachment, cream the remaining 12 tablespoons butter with the sugar and molasses at medium-high speed until pale and fluffy, about 3 minutes, scraping down the sides and bottom of the bowl twice with a rubber spatula. Reduce the mixer speed to medium and add the cooled butter and spice mixture, ginger, and half of the egg mixture; mix until incorporated, about 15 seconds. Repeat with the remaining egg mixture; scrape down the bowl again. Reduce the mixer speed to low; add about one-third of the flour mixture, followed by half of the buttermilk, mixing until just incorporated after each addition, about 5 seconds. Repeat using half of the remaining flour mixture and all of the remaining buttermilk. Scrape down the bowl and add the remaining flour mixture; mix at medium speed until the batter is thoroughly combined, about 15 seconds. Remove the bowl from the mixer and fold the batter once or twice with the rubber spatula to incorporate any remaining flour.

TECHNIQUE:
Removing Trapped Air Bubbles

In cakes with a thick batter, such as spice cake or carrot cake, trapped air bubbles can lead to a finished cake with unsightly holes. Here's how to get rid of them:

1. Run the tip of a metal spatula through the batter in a zigzag motion, pulling the batter to the edges of the pan.

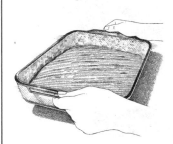

2. Gently tap the pan against the countertop three or four times to release any air bubbles that have risen to the surface.

4. Transfer the batter to the prepared pan; following the illustrations above, zigzag the tip of a metal spatula through the batter, pulling it to the pan edges. Lightly tap the pan against the countertop 3 or 4 times to dislodge any large air bubbles; smooth the surface with the spatula.

5. Bake until a toothpick inserted in the center of the cake comes out clean, 32 to 37 minutes. Cool the cake to room temperature in the pan on a wire rack, about 2 hours.

6. FOR THE FROSTING: In the bowl of a standing mixer fitted with the paddle attachment, beat the butter, sugar, and reserved ½ teaspoon spice mixture at medium-high speed until light and fluffy, 1 to 2 minutes. Add the cream cheese one piece at a time, beating thoroughly after each addition. Add the vanilla and beat until no lumps remain, about 30 seconds.

7. Run a paring knife around the edge of the cake to loosen from the pan. Using a spatula, spread the frosting evenly over the surface of the cake. Sprinkle the cake with the walnuts, if using. Cut into squares and serve.

VARIATION

SPICE CAKE WITH ORANGE CREAM CHEESE FROSTING

Follow the recipe for Spice Cake with Cream Cheese Frosting, adding 1½ teaspoons finely grated zest from 1 orange to the frosting with the vanilla in step 6. Substitute toasted slivered almonds or roughly chopped hazelnuts for the walnuts in step 7.

EQUIPMENT CORNER:
Dry Measuring Cups

FOR SUCH A SIMPLE TOOL, DRY MEASURING CUPS COME in a tremendous range of materials, shapes, weights, and prices. We rounded up 11 sets, in plastic and stainless steel, to compare them. Our first test focused on accuracy. Although a dry measuring cup will never rival a scale for perfect measuring, we wanted ours to be within 5 percent of its corresponding weight. We knew better than to use flour to test accuracy, but instead filled each cup to the brim with water. (We have found that eyeballing fluid in a cup yields a more precise measurement than filling it with a dry ingredient, where the amount can vary by as much as 10 percent, depending on who is doing the measuring.) Except for the sets by Anolon ($19.95) and Fox Run ($8.99), both of which were off by more than 6 percent, the rest measured up.

As for design, testers preferred stainless steel for heft, balance, and durability (plastic can get scratched, and markings fade in the dishwasher over time), though a seven-piece plastic set from OXO ($7.95) fared especially well for accuracy and durability. They also preferred long handles that extend straight out and are level with the brim of the cup; angled or raised handles obstruct our preferred "dip and sweep" measuring method when drawing a straight edge across the rim, and dropped handles sometimes collect a little extra flour or sugar. Our winner, a four-piece stainless steel set from Amco ($9.95), met all these criteria at an economical price.

Rating Dry Measuring Cups

WE TESTED 11 SETS OF MEASURING CUPS AND EVALUATED THEM FOR ACCURACY, COMFORT, EASE OF USE, AND durability. Brands are listed in order of preference. See www.americastestkitchen.com for updates to this testing.

HIGHLY RECOMMENDED
Amco Stainless Steel 4-Piece Measuring Cup Set

$9.95; metal; cups included: ¼, ⅓, ½, 1

This stainless steel set measured with perfect—truly perfect—accuracy and offered moderate weight, great balance, and long, level, clearly marked handles.

RECOMMENDED
OXO Good Grips 7-Piece Soft Handled Measuring Cup Set

$7.95; plastic; cups included: ¼, ⅓, ½, ⅔, ¾, 1, plus egg separator

Of the plastic sets, this was our favorite. Accuracy was good—off by less than 1 percent—and we liked the colorful measurement marks and comfortable handles.

RECOMMENDED
Zyliss Perfect Pour Measuring Cup Set

$7.95; plastic; cups included: ¼, ⅓, ½, 1, plus a leveling knife

This set earned positive comments across the board for comfort, easy sweep, and clear markings, but the plastic scratched easily, and the white cups showed stains even after washing.

RECOMMENDED
OXO 4-Piece Stainless Steel Measuring Cups

$21.95; metal; cups included: ¼, ⅓, ½, 1

Great weight balance and exceptionally long, well-marked handles made these cups quite user-friendly, except that the slanted handles blocked a clean sweep motion for leveling off an ingredient.

RECOMMENDED WITH RESERVATIONS
Norpro Stainless Steel 5-Piece Measuring Cup Set

$19.99; metal; cups included: ⅛, ¼, ⅓, ½, 1

These cups were disliked by all but a few testers for their "shovel-like" oval shape. The measurement marks were also hard to read.

RECOMMENDED WITH RESERVATIONS
Cuisinart 5-Piece Measuring Cup Set

$6.99; plastic; cups included: ¼, ⅓, ½, 1, plus a leveling knife

These cups with clear measurement marks on the handles would have won more fans had their slightly offset handles not disrupted the "dip and sweep" motion when leveling off an ingredient.

NOT RECOMMENDED
Calphalon Set of 4 Stainless Steel Measuring Cups

$19.99; metal; cups included: ¼, ⅓, ½, 1

We liked the shape of these perfectly weighted cups, but their accuracy was off by more than 4 percent.

NOT RECOMMENDED
Cuisipro Stainless Steel Oval Measuring Cups

$29.95; metal; cups included: ¼, ⅓, ½, 1

This cup set was a disappointment; accuracy was off by nearly 3 percent.

NOT RECOMMENDED
All-Clad Measuring Cups

$49.95; metal; cups included: ¼, ⅓, ½, ⅔, 1

Have you ever wanted to measure out ingredients with miniature saucepans? Neither have we. These cups were off by more than 4 percent in accuracy.

NOT RECOMMENDED
Anolon Measuring Cup Set

$19.95; metal; cups included: ¼, ⅓, ½, 1

These short-handled scoopers were inaccurate by more than 6 percent.

NOT RECOMMENDED
Fox Run Set of Four Stainless Steel Measuring Cups with Colored Handles

$8.99; metal; cups included: ¼, ⅓, ½, 1

Color-coded handles are a good idea, but these cups were inaccurate by more than 6 percent.

Here, Julia shows Chris how to gauge when egg whites have reached stiff peaks—they should stand tall on the tip of a beater. Properly beaten egg whites are essential for cake that rises high and boasts a light crumb.

EVERYONE'S

CHAPTER 25

favorite cake

Chances are that the birthday cake you were often served as a child was a yellow cake with chocolate frosting. This was a cake that everyone liked—and it never disappointed. And unless your mother had loads of time to bake, she probably used a boxed cake mix that baked up light and fluffy every time. There's something to be said for the convenience of a cake mix, but mixes contain additives and preservatives. And the resulting flavor just can't compete with that of a fresh, homemade cake made naturally—with butter, eggs, sugar, and flour. The problem with homemade cakes is their texture; they can sometimes turn out dense and dry. Could we develop a yellow cake that offers the best of both worlds—a feathery light, moist texture and great flavor? We were ready to find out.

Silky, rich chocolate buttercream is the perfect frosting for our fluffy yellow cake, but it can be a hassle to pull off. Traditional buttercream starts with boiling sugar syrup, a tricky operation that requires the use of a candy thermometer. Next, egg yolks and butter must be incorporated correctly, so the frosting turns out smooth, not curdled. Is there an easier way? We're familiar with shortcut buttercreams, but they often fall short in texture (too grainy) and flavor (muted chocolate flavor). We wanted a no-hassle frosting that would require no special equipment and would turn out thick and fluffy. And most important, it would need to taste chocolaty enough to light up the faces of children and adults alike.

FLUFFY YELLOW CAKE

WHAT WE WANTED: A yellow cake with the ultra-light, fluffy texture of cake made from a mix, but without the artificial flavors, chemicals, and additives.

When the first Betty Crocker boxed cake mix hit store shelves shortly after World War II, it introduced Americans to a convenience food many have never lost their taste for. It also introduced the country to a whole new kind of cake—one so light, soft, and moist that it practically melted on the tongue. As kids, we could never get enough of this chemically engineered confection, so different was it from the dense and crumbly cakes our mothers baked from scratch. Eventually, of course, we came to our senses and could no longer tolerate the box cake's cloying artificial flavors. But one thing we've never gotten over is its supreme fluffiness. We wondered: Without the help of mono- and diglycerides, cellulose gum, and other additives, was it possible to create a yellow layer cake with the same ethereal texture but also the great flavor of natural ingredients?

To answer that question, we began by researching recipes for basic yellow butter cake, the prototype after which the box-mix yellow version is modeled. Very quickly we made a surprising discovery: Yellow cake with the kind of soft and fluffy texture we were looking for doesn't actually exist. Of the half-dozen yellow or gold layer cakes we tested, not one had the super-moist lightness we wanted. The best of the bunch was a rich yellow cake we'd developed years ago; but although this cake was definitely worthy of its name, it was still more dense—and rich—than the box-mix version.

It was time to step back and really think about the mechanics of cake making. We knew that along with the ingredients, mixing methods play a major role in cake volume and texture. To achieve their relative lightness and tenderness, the yellow butter cakes we tested relied on one of two methods: conventional creaming and reverse creaming (also known as the two-stage method). With conventional creaming, butter and sugar are whipped together before any other ingredients are added, creating lots of air bubbles that produce lightness and volume in the cake. Reverse creaming has a different impact on texture: Soft butter is blended with the flour (and other dry ingredients) to coat the flour proteins with fat and prevent them from forming tough gluten, leading to a more tender cake.

What if we widened our net beyond yellow cake and tested a chiffon cake, which uses a large quantity of whipped egg whites, instead of a creaming method, to get its mile-high volume and feathery texture? First, the batter is made as if for pancakes, with the dry ingredients (flour, sugar, leavener) dumped into a bowl with the liquid ingredients (yolks, water, oil). The egg whites are then aerated through vigorous whipping and folded into the batter, creating height and super fluffiness. The test kitchen's chiffon cake is especially weightless, springy, and moist. Unfortunately, with its five whipped egg whites (in addition to two whole eggs), the cake had too much of a good thing—it was too ethereal and light. It would never be a proper substitute for a layer cake that could stand up to a serious slathering of frosting.

Besides employing a different mixing method, butter cakes differ from chiffon cakes by using butter as their fat, fewer eggs (usually three or four, left whole), a greater proportion of flour, and a liquid, usually some type of dairy. On a whim, we decided to see what would happen if we took these butter cake ingredients and combined them using a chiffon cake technique: We would separate our eggs; mix the rest of our ingredients together, except the whites; and then whip the whites and fold them in at the end. The only other change: Since we needed a liquid fat, we would use melted butter instead of solid. This mixing of chiffon cake method and butter cake ingredients worked beautifully. After adding extra egg yolks to enrich the crumb, we had a light, porous cake that still had enough heft to hold a frosting.

Our cake now had the fluffiness we were after, but it still didn't have the moistness we wanted. We knew that oil, even more than butter, can be a key factor in the moisture level of a cake. (Butter contains about 20 percent water, which can evaporate in the oven and leave a cake dry.) Could we use a combination of both types of fat? After testing different proportions of each, we found that 10 tablespoons of butter plus 3 tablespoons of oil kept our butter flavor intact and improved the moistness of the cake. But could we get it even more soft and tender?

Adding more sugar was our first thought. Sugar is well known for increasing tenderness in cakes by attracting and bonding with water, thus preventing the water from hydrating the proteins in the flour. With less liquid available to them, fewer proteins can link together, resulting in weaker gluten. We found that an additional ½ cup of sugar did the trick. Our cake was very moist and now had nice caramelization on its sides and bottom. Tasters also liked its sweeter flavor.

Up to now we had been using milk in our working recipe, but yellow cake recipes often call for buttermilk, sour cream, or yogurt. In the end, buttermilk was tasters' clear favorite, producing a crumb that was slightly porous and so fine it was almost downy. The buttermilk's tang also brought a new flavor dimension to our cake—an added bonus. With acidic buttermilk in our recipe, we needed to replace some of the baking powder with a little baking soda to ensure an even rise.

A slight tweaking of the salt and vanilla was all that was needed to finish the recipe. We now had a cake that was so moist and fluffy that we could almost patent it. Of course, there would be no way to patent its fresh, all-natural taste.

WHAT WE LEARNED: For yellow cake that's fluffy, but sturdy enough to hold up to a thick layer of frosting, use butter cake ingredients (butter, eggs, flour, and liquid) and the chiffon cake technique of separating the eggs, whipping the whites, and folding them in at the end. Supplement the butter with a little oil to help keep the cake moist, add some extra sugar to make it especially tender, and use buttermilk for the dairy to add a welcome tang.

FLUFFY YELLOW LAYER CAKE

makes two 9-inch cake layers

Vegetable oil spray can be used for greasing the pans (proceed with flouring as directed). Bring all the ingredients to room temperature before beginning. Frost the cake with our Foolproof Chocolate Frosting (page 328) or your favorite topping.

2½	cups (10 ounces) cake flour, plus extra for dusting pans
1¼	teaspoons baking powder
¼	teaspoon baking soda
¾	teaspoon salt
1¾	cups (12¼ ounces) sugar
10	tablespoons (1¼ sticks) unsalted butter, melted and cooled slightly
1	cup buttermilk, at room temperature
3	tablespoons vegetable oil
2	teaspoons vanilla extract
6	large egg yolks plus 3 large egg whites, at room temperature

1. Adjust an oven rack to the middle position and heat the oven to 350 degrees. Grease two 9-inch-wide by 2-inch-high round cake pans and line the bottoms with parchment paper. Grease the paper rounds, dust the pans with flour, and knock out the excess. Whisk the flour, baking powder, baking soda, salt, and 1½ cups of the sugar together in a large bowl. In a 4-cup liquid measuring cup or medium bowl, whisk together the melted butter, buttermilk, oil, vanilla, and yolks.

2. In the clean bowl of a standing mixer fitted with the whisk attachment, beat the egg whites at medium-high speed until foamy, about 30 seconds. With the machine running, gradually add the remaining ¼ cup sugar; continue to beat until stiff peaks just form, 30 to 60 seconds (the whites should hold a peak but the mixture should appear moist). Transfer to a bowl and set aside.

3. Add the flour mixture to the now-empty mixing bowl. With the mixer, still fitted with the whisk attachment, running at low speed, gradually pour in the butter mixture and mix until almost incorporated (a few streaks of dry flour will remain), about 15 seconds. Stop the mixer and scrape the whisk and the sides of the bowl. Return the mixer to medium-low speed and beat until smooth and fully incorporated, 10 to 15 seconds.

4. Using a rubber spatula, stir one-third of the whites into the batter to lighten, then add the remaining whites and gently fold into the batter until no white streaks remain. Divide the batter evenly between the prepared cake pans. Lightly tap the pans against the countertop 2 or 3 times to dislodge any large air bubbles.

5. Bake until the cake layers begin to pull away from the sides of the pans and a toothpick inserted into the center comes out clean, 20 to 22 minutes. Cool the cakes in the pans on a wire rack for 10 minutes. Loosen the cakes from the sides of the pans with a small knife, then invert onto a greased wire rack and peel off the parchment. Invert the cakes again and cool completely on the rack, about 1½ hours. Frost with our Foolproof Chocolate Frosting or your favorite frosting and serve.

GETTING IT RIGHT:
Turning Up the Volume

High
The chief hallmark of a box-mix cake is a feather-light (and chemical-laden) crumb.

Higher
Our Fluffy Yellow Layer Cake has an even more ethereal texture—and it tastes good, too.

SCIENCE DESK:
The Miracle of Yellow Cake Mix

CAKE MIXES CONTAIN ALL THE SAME INGREDIENTS AS a from-scratch cake, plus a whole lot of additives that help ensure that each cake is a replica of the one that came before it, with the same look, taste, and texture. Chief among them are a slew of chemically engineered emulsifiers and leavening agents that work in tandem to guarantee a mix that is virtually foolproof—no matter if the cook overbeats, adds too much or too little water, or pours the batter into the wrong-sized pan.

Emulsifiers like mono- and diglycerides help incorporate more air into the batter than do the eggs that are the sole emulsifiers in homemade cakes, as well as holding all the ingredients together. The emulsifiers also work to improve the effectiveness of the leaveners (baking soda or powder along with monocalcium and dicalcium phosphates) by helping the batter hold more of the gas these agents produce, which in turn ensures greater volume and lightness in the cake. Beyond these additives, cake mix contains hydrogenated fats and artificial food coloring—the latter imparting a deep golden hue that hasn't been common in all-natural yellow cake since mass-produced eggs with uniformly pale yolks began dominating supermarket shelves decades ago.

We'll stick with the fresh, honest flavors of an all-natural cake.

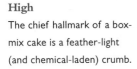

CHOCOLATE FROSTING

WHAT WE WANTED: A simple, foolproof chocolate frosting that won't curdle, deflate—or take an hour to set.

In the world of chocolate frosting, rich, dense ganaches and billowy buttercreams are the archetypes you turn to when you want to impress. But they're also the frostings you steer clear of when you're looking for something fast and foolproof. Ganache involves whisking hot cream into chopped chocolate and waiting at least an hour for the warm mixture to set. Traditional buttercream requires you to stand over a pot of boiling sugar syrup with a candy thermometer, keeping your fingers crossed that things will go well when you mix it with egg yolks and butter.

At the other end of the spectrum are quick chocolate buttercreams. Simple and no-nonsense, these call for beating butter with cooled, melted chocolate and confectioners' sugar—and they're ready to spread. But such frostings also have their flaws: Confectioners' sugar gives them an underlying graininess and blunts their chocolate flavor. Worse, they often deflate or harden a few hours after they're made.

We had several goals for a chocolate frosting. We wanted it to be easy and foolproof and require no special equipment. We wanted it to have a light, satiny consistency that would spread like a dream. We wanted to be able to use it immediately—or to know that it wouldn't harden or deflate if we left it sitting on the countertop for an hour or two. And above all, we wanted it to have deep chocolate flavor.

We began our testing on the quick buttercream end of things, with a base of butter, confectioners' sugar, and 8 ounces of melted chocolate—the fairly modest standard amount in most recipes we'd come across. Our first task was to bump up the chocolate flavor. Could this be as simple as adding a few ounces more? No. As we mixed in more melted chocolate, our frosting became gooey, waxy, and too thin to spread.

Up to this point we had been avoiding cocoa powder. Graininess was already an issue because of the confectioners' sugar, and we feared adding more powdery solids would make the problem even worse. But with no other options for intensifying chocolate flavor, we decided to give it a try. We began cautiously, with a few tablespoons, then added a few tablespoons more until we'd incorporated ¾ cup. To our surprise, the cocoa powder remained undetectable, except for its rich flavor. When we checked with our science editor, we found out why: The cocoa butter crystals in cocoa powder blend with the fat in butter (we were using two and a half sticks) to coat and lubricate particles of cocoa powder, helping mask any grittiness.

The ¾ cup of cocoa powder combined with 8 ounces of melted chocolate gave us the big chocolate boost we were looking for. It was time to tackle the graininess that the confectioners' sugar was causing. A little research revealed the reason: Confectioners' sugar is soluble only in water, not fat, and our recipe had very little water (in the butter). Was there a liquid ingredient that could sweeten the frosting? We thought back to traditional buttercreams and how they use boiled sugar syrup to achieve their luxuriously silky texture. We already had a type of dissolved sugar syrup sitting right in the pantry—corn syrup. Simply swapping one sweetener for the other was not an option; too much corn syrup would have made our frosting runny. After testing a few amounts, our tasters agreed that replacing 1 cup of the confectioners' sugar with ¾ cup of corn syrup was the right proportion. And because of the water content in the syrup, the confectioners' sugar could at least partially dissolve. Our frosting was now smooth, glossy, and practically grainless.

All that was left to figure out was how to keep the frosting from separating and turning greasy as the ingredients were whipped together and from deflating after all was done—problems common to both quick and traditional

buttercreams as well as the whipped form of ganache. Our working recipe followed the typical buttercream protocol of beating the ingredients together in a standing mixer. With a mixer, care must be taken to not overbeat, or friction will make the butter break down and melt. Overbeating can also pump in too much air, causing the frosting to become frothy and unstable. We needed a technique that could blend our ingredients quickly without melting the butter and without incorporating too much air.

We thought back to some of the frosting recipes we'd come across that used a food processor instead of a mixer—a faster method that creates less aeration. Would this method help our frosting? The proof was in the waiting: Three hours after processing, the frosting still looked perfectly smooth and fluffy.

Easy, foolproof, with a rich chocolate flavor and a light, satiny texture, this frosting was truly the icing on the cake—whether we used it right out of the processor bowl or chose to wait.

WHAT WE LEARNED: For frosting with a serious chocolate punch, supplement the chocolate with ¾ cup of cocoa powder. To avoid a grainy texture, replace some of the confectioners' sugar with corn syrup. Use a food processor (rather than a standing mixer) to combine the ingredients; it ensures the frosting will remain smooth and fluffy (it incorporates less air, which makes the frosting more stable and less likely to deflate).

FOOLPROOF CHOCOLATE FROSTING

makes about 3 cups, enough to frost one 9-inch 2-layer cake

This frosting may be made with milk, semisweet, or bittersweet chocolate. For our Fluffy Yellow Layer Cake (page 325), we prefer a frosting made with milk chocolate. Cool the chocolate to between 85 and 100 degrees before adding it to the butter mixture. The frosting can be made 3 hours in advance. For longer storage, refrigerate the frosting, covered, and let it stand at room temperature for 1 hour before using.

20   tablespoons (2½ sticks) unsalted butter, softened
     (60 to 65 degrees)
 1   cup (4 ounces) confectioners' sugar
 ¾   cup (2¼ ounces) Dutch-processed cocoa
     Pinch salt
 ¾   cup light corn syrup
 1   teaspoon vanilla extract
 8   ounces chocolate, melted and cooled slightly
     (see note)

In a food processor, process the butter, sugar, cocoa, and salt until smooth, about 30 seconds, scraping down the sides of the bowl as needed. Add the corn syrup and vanilla and process until just combined, 5 to 10 seconds. Scrape down the sides of the bowl, then add the chocolate and pulse until smooth and creamy, 10 to 15 seconds. The frosting can be used immediately or held (see note).

TASTING LAB: Dark Chocolates

JUST A FEW YEARS AGO, SELECTING DARK CHOCOLATE for your dessert recipe seemed pretty simple: You went to the supermarket and bought a bar of baking chocolate. These days, there are dozens of choices, and you can spend hours poring over the cacao percentages and exotic provenances on the labels. You can pay a lot more, too. But does any of it really matter? Does spending more get you better chocolate flavor? And can your choice of chocolate change your baking results?

First, we looked into the definition of "dark chocolate" and discovered it's a pretty loose term. The U.S. Food and Drug Administration doesn't distinguish between bittersweet and semisweet chocolate; it simply requires that products by either name contain at least 35 percent cacao (the cocoa solids and cocoa butter from the cacao bean). Companies use the names *cacao* and *cocoa* interchangeably, but in general, when there is more cacao in the chocolate, there is less sugar, and bittersweet chocolate tends to be less sweet and have more cacao than semisweet. Even darker chocolates, with higher cacao percentages, are correspondingly less sweet (100 percent cacao chocolate is completely unsweetened).

Any number of variables—the type of bean, where it's grown, and when it's harvested; the length and conditions of fermentation; the roasting and grinding methods; and the quality and quantity of any additives (such as vanilla)—can contribute to differences in flavor and texture. Chocolate makers claim that every detail is critical—and are loath to share too many specifics.

We'd heard a lot about the type of cacao bean being extremely important. There are only three types. The most prized (and expensive) bean, the *criollo,* grown mainly in the Caribbean and Central America, makes up less than 2 percent of the world's cacao. Most chocolate is made from *forastero* beans, generally from Africa. These beans are harvested from hardier trees, which makes them cheaper. The third, *trinitario,* is a hybrid of the other two beans and comprises about 5 percent of the total harvest.

To choose chocolate for our testing lineup, we ignored "bittersweet" or "semisweet" nomenclature and concerned ourselves with chocolate containing roughly 60 percent cacao—the type that most recipes calling for dark chocolate have been developed to use. We asked 24 members of the America's Test Kitchen staff to taste 12 dark chocolates, sampled plain, in chocolate pots de crème, and baked into brownies.

So which chocolates won favor with our tasters? The results were surprising. The chocolate with the fanciest pedigree in our lineup, El Rey, made exclusively from Venezuelan criollo beans, wound up in the lower half of the rankings. The other single-origin sample, produced by Lindt from criollo and trinitario beans grown in Madagascar, came in last. The two top-rated chocolates, Callebaut and Ghirardelli, came from blends relying primarily on the inexpensive forastero bean. Both were purchased at the supermarket, and they cost just 53 cents and 75 cents per ounce, respectively.

Our second discovery also defied expectations. We assumed that if one brand of chocolate is 60 percent cacao, it would be pretty similar in sweetness, chocolate intensity, and creaminess to another brand's 60 percent cacao chocolate. Not so. When chocolate makers grind shelled cacao beans, known as nibs, to create the thick paste called chocolate liquor, this paste contains both cocoa solids and cocoa butter. Most manufacturers then add even more cocoa butter, in varying amounts, to help create the texture of the final chocolate. A few, like the maker of our winner, also add extra cocoa solids to intensify the chocolate flavor. Ultimately, however, the cacao percentage on the label of a chocolate bar is a total that includes both cocoa solids and cocoa butter—meaning that different chocolates can have different proportions of each and still share the 60 percent cacao designation. As our lab tests showed, the cocoa solids in our lineup ranged from about 17 percent of a bar's total weight to more than 30 percent, and fat content ranged from a third of the weight to nearly half of it. Sugar levels varied by nearly 20 percent as well.

So would the chocolate with the most cocoa butter make the biggest splash, bringing richer, extra-creamy flavor to your desserts? No. In fact, our lab results revealed that the

chocolate with the lowest fat won the day, whereas the one with the most fat came in dead last. And would having the most cocoa solids make a chocolate superior? Again, no. Our tasters preferred chocolates with only a moderate amount. Sweetness wasn't the explanation, either: Chocolates in the middle range of sugar levels were preferred over those with the most sugar, though overall the top half of the rankings had more sugar than the bottom half.

In the end, we preferred dark chocolate that achieved the best balance of all three major components—cocoa butter, cocoa solids, and sugar. Callebaut Intense Dark Chocolate was favored for its rich chocolate flavor, moderate sugar and cocoa solids, and comparatively low fat. It excelled in every application. San Francisco–based Ghirardelli's Bittersweet Chocolate Baking Bar came in a close second. It also demonstrated that balanced chocolate flavor derived from moderate levels of sugar, cocoa solids, and cocoa butter.

Rating Dark Chocolates

TWENTY-FOUR MEMBERS OF THE AMERICA'S TEST KITCHEN STAFF TASTED 12 BRANDS OF CHOCOLATE, ALL CONTAINING around 60 percent cacao. Chocolates were tasted plain, in chocolate pots de crème, and baked into brownies. Note that many of these brands are manufactured in giant slabs; purveyors break up the chocolate into more manageable pieces, typically wrapped in plastic, and priced by the ounce. Brands are listed in order of preference. See www.americastestkitchen.com for updates to this tasting.

RECOMMENDED

Callebaut Intense Dark Chocolate, L-60-40NV

53 cents per ounce; 60 percent cacao; Belgium

"Complex flavor, creamy and thick," with a "rich cocoa flavor" and "a nice balance of sweetness and bitterness." This chocolate baked into "what a brownie should be."

RECOMMENDED

Ghirardelli Bittersweet Chocolate Baking Bar

75 cents per ounce; 60 percent cacao; USA

Tasters discerned "coffee, smoke, and dried fruit" in this chocolate. In brownies, it had "quintessential brownie flavor."

RECOMMENDED

Dagoba Organic Semisweet Dark Chocolate

$1.30 per ounce; 59 percent cacao; USA

"Fairly sweet" (a few said "cloyingly" so), with "great chocolate flavor," it had "hints of fruit." In pots de crème, it was "very buttery and chocolaty." In brownies: "a good one all-around."

RECOMMENDED

Michel Cluizel Noir de Cacao Dark Chocolate

$1.43 per ounce; 60 percent cacao; France

"Creamy, not bitter," but tasters were reminded of "olive oil" or "mayonnaise." It made "very smooth and well balanced" brownies and "super-creamy" pots de crème.

RECOMMENDED

Valrhona Le Noir Semisweet Chocolate

$1.37 per ounce; 56 percent cacao; France

This chocolate was "well balanced" and "creamy," with "a sharp chocolate flavor" and "not much aftertaste." In pots de crème, it was "super-smooth and cushiony."

RECOMMENDED WITH RESERVATIONS

E. Guittard Tsaratana Pure Semisweet Dark Chocolate

$1.45 per ounce; 61 percent cacao; USA

"Fruity and spicy," this "very creamy" chocolate had slightly "odd" flavors, including banana, tobacco, and leather. Some observed that it made drier, cakier brownies and slightly "chalky" pots de crème.

RECOMMENDED WITH RESERVATIONS

Hershey's All-Natural Extra Dark Pure Dark Chocolate

63 cents per ounce; 60 percent cacao; USA

Many tasters decried a "chalky" texture, both when eaten plain and in brownies. In pots de crème, it was "dark and glossy," but "gummy and dense."

RECOMMENDED WITH RESERVATIONS

El Rey Mijao Dark Chocolate, Venezuelan Single Bean, Carenero Superior

50 cents per ounce; 61 percent cacao; Venezuela

"Not very complex" with a slightly "sour" aftertaste, it was "sweet and buttery" in pots de crème and "kinda flat" in brownies.

RECOMMENDED WITH RESERVATIONS

Scharffen Berger Fine Artisan Semisweet Dark Chocolate

$1.03 per ounce; 62 percent cacao; USA

"Lots of fruit" here: Tasters noted cherry (some said "cough syrup"), grape, raspberry, raisins, and prunes. "Gluey" in pots de crème, it had a "roasty" quality in brownies.

RECOMMENDED WITH RESERVATIONS

Nestlé Chocolatier Premium Baking Chocolate Bittersweet Chocolate Bar

56 cents per ounce; 62 percent cacao; USA

"Dry and chalky," "grainy," and "gritty," agreed tasters when it was sampled plain and in pots de crème. In brownies, it was "rich" and "fudgy," but again "a bit grainy."

RECOMMENDED WITH RESERVATIONS

Baker's Semi-Sweet Baking Chocolate Squares

44 cents per ounce; 54 percent cacao; USA

"Very sweet; you can almost taste the sugar granules." It rated poorly when tasted plain and in pots de crème due to its granular texture, but shone in brownies as "very moist, chewy" and "fudgy."

RECOMMENDED WITH RESERVATIONS

Lindt Excellence Madagascar Extra Fine Mild Dark Chocolate

$1.08 per ounce; 65 percent cacao; Switzerland

Tasters noted a "very creamy" but "waxy" texture. In pots de crème, it was "creamy, but strange and acidic." In brownies, it was "funky."

Our easy, make-ahead chocolate soufflés can be assembled and stored in the freezer for up to one month before baking. Once baked, they will rise dramatically and taste just as rich and creamy as a fresh-made soufflé.

A GRAND, SWEET *finale*

CHAPTER 26

Soufflés show us that beauty is more than skin deep.

This "ultimate" dessert may be unabashedly dramatic and a bit show-offy, but if it wasn't also so melt-in-your-mouth creamy and light, we would never bother to bake one. Here we look at two approaches to the soufflé: first, a citrusy Grand Marnier soufflé, made in the traditional manner; and second, a make-ahead chocolate soufflé for those times when you don't want to bother with any last-minute fuss.

It's no secret that soufflés are temperamental, but could we streamline our Grand Marnier soufflé so that we could easily turn it out without breaking a sweat? We aimed for a soufflé with just the right amount of richness—not too airy and not too eggy, with an appealingly sweet, citrus flavor. And, of course, we wanted the soufflé to rise high and stay set long enough to make an impression on everyone at the table.

A make-ahead soufflé makes sense for anyone who struggles with coordinating all the last-minute details a dinner party requires. (And yes, we count ourselves among that group.) Our goal was to create a chocolate soufflé with rich chocolaty flavor and a light, creamy texture. And as for the make-ahead aspect of our soufflé, we really meant it: We wanted a freezer- (or fridge-) to-oven dessert, so that all we'd need to do the night of the party would be to slide the soufflés effortlessly into the oven for a spectacular ending to a meal everyone would remember.

IN THIS CHAPTER

THE RECIPES

Grand Marnier Soufflé
Grand Marnier Soufflé with
    Grated Chocolate

Individual Make-Ahead Chocolate
    Soufflés
Individual Make-Ahead Mocha
    Soufflés

EQUIPMENT CORNER

Balloon Whisks

SCIENCE DESK

Do Copper Bowls Make a
    Difference?

GRAND MARNIER SOUFFLÉ

WHAT WE WANTED: A foolproof soufflé, with a dramatic rise and a pleasing contrast between the light, crisp exterior and the rich, creamy interior.

When was the last time you made a soufflé? Perhaps about the same time you prepared quiche, carved a swan out of an apple, or spent hours turning carrots into perfect miniature footballs. Many of us have never made one, relegating them to the category of "restaurant dessert," difficult to assemble and quick to deflate. The reality of soufflés, as we quickly learned, is entirely different. They are easy to make, unlikely to fall, and, when made properly, are nothing like the foamy, flavorless concoctions you may have had at third-rate ersatz French restaurants.

At its best, a soufflé rises dramatically above its rim to create a light but substantial and crusty top layer cushioned by a luxurious, creamy center that flows slowly across the tongue, richly saucing the taste buds. This contrast between exterior and interior is the essence of a great soufflé; lesser versions have a light, foamy texture throughout. A first-class soufflé must also convey a true mouthful of flavor, bursting with the bright, clear taste of the main ingredient rather than obscuring it with an eggy aftertaste. There are several types of soufflé—liqueur-flavored, chocolate, fruit, cheese, savory—and each requires a slightly different approach. For the purposes of this investigation, we decided to focus on a classic Grand Marnier soufflé, with variations to come after the initial recipe was perfected.

The first question was how to prepare the base, which is the thick, flavored mixture into which the beaten egg whites are folded. In a Grand Marnier soufflé, the base is often a *béchamel,* a classic French sauce made from butter, flour, and milk. Pastry cream is often used as a base as well, as is a *bouillie,* a paste made from flour and milk. It is similar to a béchamel without butter. The test kitchen prepared a blind tasting using each of these three methods. Although past experience led us to expect the béchamel version to win, the bouillie soufflé had the creamiest, richest texture and it seemed to set the best. It did, however, taste a bit like scrambled eggs. To solve this problem, we added 2 tablespoons of butter to the bouillie, which eliminated the eggy aftertaste. (Although our bouillie now contained the same three ingredients as a béchamel, the two are made quite differently.)

Our tastings also confirmed that most recipes produce foamy rather than creamy soufflés. Part of the solution to this problem was to increase the amount of flour used in the base from 3 tablespoons per cup of milk to 5. We also wondered if milk was the right choice as opposed to heavy cream, half-and-half, or a mixture of milk and heavy cream. When all were tested, tasters preferred milk, which made for a livelier flavor than any of the other versions.

The next issue was determining the proper ratio of egg whites to egg yolks. We tried four variations, starting with 8 whites to 5 yolks, working our way down to 5 whites and 5 yolks. The latter (5 each of whites and yolks) made the best soufflé, producing a rich and creamy texture rather than merely a mouthful of foam. As it turned out, however, the method of beating the whites would also be critical to our success.

The objective in beating egg whites for a soufflé is to create a strong, stable foam that rises well and is not prone to collapse during either folding or baking. Cookbooks often begin this discussion by warning against the use of cold egg whites, the theory being that cold whites do not whip up as well as those at room temperature. When we tested this, however, we discovered that the difference between egg whites that had been whipped when cold and those whipped when warm was negligible after they

because of its superior rise. Timing is also important. Most of the sugar, it turned out, must be added not at the outset of whipping but after the whites break up and become foamy. In addition, the sugar must be added gradually. Sugar added all at the outset produced a soufflé with an uneven, shorter rise and a bit of an overly sweet taste.

We wondered if any other ingredient should be added to the whites as they are beaten to improve stability and cooking properties. Knowing that cream of tartar is often recommended as an additive, we tested this and found it beneficial, producing a more stable soufflé with a bigger rise.

Just to satisfy our curiosity, we also made soufflés using powdered and pasteurized egg whites. The former produced a horrible-tasting soufflé, and the whites deflated quickly during the folding process. Pasteurized egg whites had a curious effect on the baked soufflé—the edges were crunchy and overcooked, yet the interior was almost raw. We also tried adding a bit of water to the whites during beating—a trick we use to increase the moisture content of certain sponge-style cakes—but there is insufficient fat in a soufflé recipe to support the water. The result? A dense, watery mess.

Next to be considered was oven temperature. Although we had been convinced that 375 degrees was the best temperature, when tested head-to-head against a 400-degree oven, the latter won hands down. The higher temperature provided for a more dramatic rise and more contrast between the cooked exterior and the creamy, saucy interior. If your oven runs a bit hot, though, beware that 400 degrees is pushing the outer envelope; the top crust can start to burn around the edges. We then tested the notion of using a water bath (placing the baking dish in a roasting pan half-filled with hot water) with the hope that this might moderate the heat around the dish and result in a more delicate soufflé. In all cases, the outside of the soufflé turned out wet and gelatin-like, a true disaster.

had been baked—so go ahead and use eggs right out of the refrigerator.

The next issue was whether sugar should be added to the whites during beating and, if so, how. We found that egg whites became more stable when beaten with even a small amount of sugar. This made them more resilient to a heavy hand during folding and less apt to fall quickly after being pulled from the oven. The question then became which is better, granulated or powdered? Granulated won this round

Now we had just a few more variables to test. We found that a 1½-quart dish works best; a 2-quart baking dish is so large that you don't get that nice, high rise and creamy, moist center. Freezing the buttered and sugared soufflé dish before adding the mixture and baking produced a dramatic high-rise soufflé, but the outside and top crust were inferior, so this idea was voted down. We also found that a soufflé should be baked in the upper-middle portion of the oven. When placed on the lowest rack, it burns on the bottom. When placed on the top rack, a soufflé can rise right up into the heating element or the top can simply overcook, turning black around the edges.

Finally, and most important of all, never overcook a soufflé. It should be very creamy in the middle and firm around the outside, almost like a pudding cake. The center should not be liquid but still quite loose and very moist. Once you can smell a soufflé baking in the oven, it's about ready to come out.

WHAT WE LEARNED: For a rich, creamy soufflé, start with a bouillie—a paste of flour and milk. Add a little butter to the bouillie to help keep the soufflé from tasting eggy. To prevent a foamy texture, increase the ratio of flour to milk and use an equal number of egg whites and yolks. Whip the egg whites with a little sugar and cream of tartar to produce a more stable soufflé. Bake the soufflé in a 1½-quart dish at 400 degrees (on the upper-middle rack) for the highest rise and creamiest interior.

GRAND MARNIER SOUFFLÉ

serves 6 to 8

Make the soufflé base and immediately begin beating the whites before the base cools too much. Once the whites have reached the proper consistency, they must be used at once. Do not open the oven door during the first 15 minutes of baking time; as the soufflé nears the end of its baking, you may check its progress by opening the oven door slightly. (Be careful here; if your oven runs hot, the top of the soufflé may burn.) A quick dusting of confectioners' sugar is a nice finishing touch, but a soufflé waits for no one, so be ready to serve it immediately.

soufflé dish preparation

- 1 tablespoon unsalted butter, softened
- ¼ cup (1¾ ounces) granulated sugar
- 2 teaspoons sifted cocoa

soufflé

- 5 tablespoons unbleached all-purpose flour
- ½ cup (3½ ounces) granulated sugar
- ¼ teaspoon salt
- 1 cup whole milk
- 2 tablespoons unsalted butter, at room temperature
- 5 large eggs, separated
- 1 tablespoon grated zest from 1 medium orange
- 3 tablespoons Grand Marnier
- ⅛ teaspoon cream of tartar

1. Adjust an oven rack to the upper-middle position and heat the oven to 400 degrees. Grease a 1½-quart porcelain soufflé dish with the butter, making sure to coat all of the interior surfaces. Stir together the sugar and cocoa in a small bowl; pour into the buttered soufflé dish and shake to coat the bottom and sides with a thick, even coating. Tap out the excess and set the dish aside.

2. FOR THE SOUFFLÉ: Whisk the flour, ¼ cup of the sugar, and salt in a small, heavy-bottomed saucepan. Gradually whisk in the milk, whisking until smooth and no lumps remain. Bring the mixture to a boil over high heat, whisking constantly, until thickened and the mixture pulls away from the sides of the pan, about 3 minutes. Scrape the mixture into a medium bowl; whisk in the butter until combined. Whisk in the yolks until incorporated; stir in the orange zest and Grand Marnier.

3. In the bowl of a standing mixer fitted with the whisk attachment, beat the egg whites, cream of tartar, and 1 teaspoon of the sugar at medium-low speed until combined, about 10 seconds. Increase the speed to medium-high and beat until frothy and no longer translucent, about 2 minutes. With the mixer running, sprinkle in half of the remaining sugar; continue beating until the whites form soft, billowy peaks, about 30 seconds. With the mixer still running, sprinkle in the remaining sugar and beat until just combined, about 10 seconds. The whites should form soft peaks when the beater is lifted but should not appear Styrofoam-like or dry.

4. Using a rubber spatula, immediately stir one-quarter of the beaten whites into the soufflé base to lighten until almost no white streaks remain. Scrape the remaining whites into the base and fold in the whites with a balloon whisk until the mixture is just combined, gently flicking the whisk after scraping up the side of the bowl to free any of the mixture caught in the whisk. Gently pour the mixture into the prepared dish and run your index finger through the mixture, tracing the circumference about ½ inch from the side of the dish, to help the soufflé rise properly. Bake until the surface of the soufflé is deep brown, the center jiggles slightly when shaken, and the soufflé has

risen 2 to 2½ inches above the rim of the dish, 20 to 25 minutes. Serve immediately.

VARIATION

GRAND MARNIER SOUFFLÉ WITH GRATED CHOCOLATE

A rotary cheese grater is the perfect tool for grating the chocolate, though a box grater works well, too.

Finely grate ½ ounce bittersweet chocolate (you should have about ⅓ cup). Follow the recipe for Grand Marnier Soufflé, folding the grated chocolate into the soufflé base along with the beaten whites.

SCIENCE DESK:
Do Copper Bowls Make a Difference?

DESPITE THE FACT THAT ALMOST NOBODY HAS LARGE copper bowls anymore, we are slaves to any sort of investigation, so we decided to find out whether copper bowls are better for whisking egg whites. We discovered that copper bowls do not produce a larger volume of beaten egg whites, but they do have a contribution to make; the flavor of the baked soufflé is brighter, the soufflé is less eggy and dense, and the crust has a beautiful brown color. (The copper ions combine with conalbumin, an egg white protein, to slow the coagulation process. This means that the foam can better tolerate expansion in the oven, which in turn results in greater volume in the final product.) We also discovered that the best results were achieved by giving the bowl a spare coating of white wine vinegar and coarse salt before beating the whites. That said, very good results can also be achieved in stainless steel bowls using the techniques developed for our soufflé, so copper is nice, but not necessary.

MAKE-AHEAD CHOCOLATE SOUFFLÉS

WHAT WE WANTED: A chocolate soufflé that can be made ahead (with no last-minute fuss) and still have all the qualities of a great chocolate soufflé—dramatic rise, creamy interior, and intense chocolate flavor.

For most people, soufflés are the cooking equivalent of a high-wire act—better left to the deft and practiced hands of a professional. You might order one in a restaurant, but you would never think about adding one (and the stress that accompanies it) to your own menu at home, right? Timing is essential, and anxiety about last-minute whisking and fallen soufflés abounds. But the truth is, they are really not that hard to execute—especially if you eliminate the last-minute hurdles like whipping and gently folding in the egg whites. But the idea of making one ahead still seemed totally out of the question—which meant we wanted to find a way to do it. Determined, we headed into the kitchen to develop a make-ahead chocolate soufflé.

But first we needed to define the perfect soufflé. A quick poll in the test kitchen and some mouthwatering conversation portrayed a soufflé with a crusty exterior packed with flavor, a dramatic rise above the rim, an airy but substantial outer layer, and a rich, loose center that is not completely set. A great soufflé must also convey a true mouthful of flavor, bursting with the taste of the main ingredient. In a chocolate soufflé, the chocolate high notes should be clear and strong. A balancing act among egg whites, chocolate, yolks, and butter is the essence of a great chocolate soufflé.

A primary consideration when trying to create such a soufflé is what to use as the base—the mixture that gives substance and flavor to the soufflé, as opposed to the airiness and "lift" provided by the whipped egg whites. The base can be a *béchamel* (a classic French sauce made with equal amounts of butter and flour, whisked with milk over heat), a *bouillie* (a paste of flour and milk), pastry cream (egg yolks beaten with sugar and then heated with milk), or flour cooked with milk or water until thickened. After

trying several versions of each of these options, we liked the béchamel base the best. We thought we might prefer the bouillie version, as that's what we liked for our Grand Marnier Soufflé (page 336), but it made a stiffer, denser soufflé—no doubt due to the chocolate, which already sets fairly firm. The only problem with the béchamel base is that the milk in it was muting the chocolate. Taking a new approach, we removed both the milk and the flour from our recipe and reduced the amount of butter. We then more than doubled the amount of chocolate and added six egg yolks (the egg whites were already being folded into the chocolate as part of our working recipe). This approach resulted in a base of egg yolks beaten with sugar until thick. This gave the soufflé plenty of volume and, because we had eliminated the milk, the chocolate now took center stage. Our chocolate soufflé now had the intense flavor we had been looking for. But we still weren't completely happy with the texture, which was a bit cakey on the outside. After several more experiments, we discovered that an additional two egg whites solved the problem, giving the soufflé more lift and a better texture.

We now moved on to check oven temperatures. For most recipes a 25-degree variance in oven temperature is not crucial, so we were surprised to discover the dramatic impact it had on our soufflé. Our initial oven temperature was 400 degrees, but to be sure this temperature was optimum, we tested both 375 and 425 degrees as well. The higher oven temperature resulted in an overcooked exterior and an undercooked interior, and the lower temperature did not brown the exterior enough to provide good flavor and also produced a texture that was too even—a proper soufflé should have a nice contrast between the loose center and slightly crusty exterior. We decided to stick with 400 degrees.

During the course of all this testing, we found a chocolate soufflé will give you three indications for doneness: You can smell the chocolate, the soufflé stops rising, and only the very center of the top jiggles when gently shaken. Of course, these are all imprecise methods. If you are not sure if your soufflé is done, simply take two spoons, pull open the top of the soufflé, and peek inside. If the center is still soupy, simply put the dish back in the oven! Much to our surprise, this in no way harmed the soufflé.

With our ideal soufflé recipe in hand, we turned our attention to the real challenge. We tried both refrigerating and freezing the soufflé batter in a single soufflé dish and in individual ramekins—and discovered that individual soufflés hold up much better in the refrigerator or freezer than a full recipe held in a soufflé dish. As we suspected, the refrigerated soufflés were a disaster when we baked them (they hardly rose at all and were very wet inside). But much to our amazement, the frozen versions worked fairly well—though they were cake-like and lacked the requisite loose center.

We tried adding 2 tablespoons of confectioners' sugar to the whites. This version was a great success, producing a soufflé that was light and airy with an excellent rise and a nice moist center. The actual texture of the whites changed as they were beaten, becoming more stable so they held up better during freezing. We did find that these soufflés ended up with a domed top, but by wrapping foil around each ramekin to form a "collar," we were able to get our soufflés to bake up picture-perfect. Your guests may not believe you made these soufflés ahead of time, but we guarantee they will be impressed with the results.

WHAT WE LEARNED: Use a base of egg yolks beaten with sugar, with no flour or milk, to give the soufflé plenty of volume while allowing the chocolate flavor to remain front and center. Add a little confectioners' sugar to the egg whites to make them more stable and to ensure the soufflés will be light and airy (rather than cakey). Freeze, don't refrigerate, the soufflé mixture to make the dessert ahead of time. Wrap a foil "collar" around each ramekin to allow the soufflés to rise with a nice, flat top. Bake in a 400-degree oven, which will result in the best contrast of creamy interior and slightly crisp exterior.

INDIVIDUAL MAKE-AHEAD CHOCOLATE SOUFFLÉS

serves 6 to 8

The yolk whipping time in step 3 depends on the type of mixer you use; a standing mixer will take about 3 minutes, and a hand-held mixer will take about 8 minutes. If using 6-ounce ramekins, reduce the cooking time to 20 to 22 minutes. See our tip on page 340 for making a collar for the ramekins.

ramekin preparation

2 tablespoons unsalted butter, softened
2 tablespoons granulated sugar

soufflés

8 ounces bittersweet or semisweet chocolate, chopped coarse
4 tablespoons (½ stick) unsalted butter, cut into ½-inch pieces
⅛ teaspoon salt
½ teaspoon vanilla extract
1 tablespoon Grand Marnier
6 large egg yolks
⅓ cup (2⅓ ounces) granulated sugar
8 large egg whites
¼ teaspoon cream of tartar
2 tablespoons (½ ounce) confectioners' sugar

1. FOR THE RAMEKINS: Grease the inside of eight 8-ounce ramekins with the softened butter, then coat the inside of each dish evenly with the sugar.

2. FOR THE SOUFFLÉS: Melt the chocolate and butter in a medium heatproof bowl set over a saucepan filled with 1 inch of barely simmering water, stirring frequently until smooth. Remove from the heat and stir in the salt, vanilla, and liqueur; set aside.

3. Using an electric mixer, whip the yolks and the granulated sugar at medium speed until the mixture triples in volume and is thick and pale yellow, 3 to 8 minutes (see note). Fold the yolk mixture into the chocolate mixture. Thoroughly clean and dry the mixing bowl and the beaters.

TECHNIQUE: Making a Foil Collar

Baking our individual chocolate soufflés from the freezer yields a high rise and a domed top, just as we like them. But placing a collar around the ramekins yields an even higher rise with a flat, perfectly iconic rise. To get this look, make a foil collar by securing a strip of foil that has been sprayed with vegetable oil spray (or use nonstick foil) around each ramekin so that it extends about 2 inches above the rim (this is easiest to do after the ramekins have been filled). You can tape the foil collar to the soufflé dish as necessary to prevent it from slipping.

---

4. Using the clean beaters, whip the egg whites at medium-low speed until frothy, 1 to 2 minutes. Add the cream of tartar, increase the mixer speed to medium-high, and whip until soft peaks form when the beaters are lifted, 1 to 2 minutes. Add the confectioners' sugar and continue to whip at medium-high speed to stiff peaks, 2 to 4 minutes (do not overwhip). Whisk the last few strokes by hand, making sure to scrape any unwhipped whites from the bottom of the bowl.

5. Vigorously stir one-quarter of the whipped egg whites into the chocolate mixture. Gently fold the remaining whites into the chocolate mixture until just incorporated. Carefully spoon the mixture into the prepared ramekins almost to the rim, wiping the excess filling from the rims with a wet paper towel. (To serve right away, bake as directed in step 7, reducing the baking time to 12 to 15 minutes.)

6. TO STORE: Cover each ramekin tightly with plastic wrap and then foil and freeze for at least 3 hours or up to 1 month. (Do not thaw before baking.)

7. TO BAKE AND SERVE: Adjust an oven rack to the lower-middle position and heat the oven to 400 degrees. Unwrap the ramekins and spread them out over a baking sheet. Bake the soufflés until fragrant, fully risen, and the exterior is set but the interior is still a bit loose and creamy, about 25 minutes. (To check the interior, use 2 spoons to pull open the top of one and peek inside.) Serve immediately.

VARIATION

INDIVIDUAL MAKE-AHEAD MOCHA SOUFFLÉS

Follow the recipe for Individual Make-Ahead Chocolate Soufflés, adding 1 tablespoon instant coffee or espresso powder dissolved in 1 tablespoon hot water to the melted chocolate with the vanilla in step 2.

EQUIPMENT CORNER: Balloon Whisks

EVERYONE KNOWS THE FASTEST WAY TO WHIP CREAM is with a stand mixer, but when only a cup or so is needed, is it really necessary to haul out the heavy machinery? To find out, we whipped 1 cup of heavy cream to stiff peaks with five balloon-style whisks, and compared their performances—whipping time and user-friendliness—to our favorite French whip from Best ($9.36) and a stand mixer.

Long and svelte, the all-purpose French whip performed fine, but fatigued our arms after 3 minutes of whipping cream—and we still had another half-minute to go to finish the job. Not surprisingly, the whisk attachment on the Cuisinart 5.5 Quart Stand Mixer ($349) was pulling up stiff, smooth peaks in 1 minute, 55 seconds—and at no expense to our biceps. We figured a good balloon whisk would possess similar features: a bulbous shape no smaller than 2½ inches at the widest point, with flexible yet sturdy tines woven in layers. Gimmicky features only slowed whipping times: A Zyliss model ($7.95) introduced non-crossing tines to prevent clogging; another from Cuisipro ($17.99) contained a trapped wire ball with a marble inside to boost air incorporation. Plus, these two models offered only 16 tines each, compared to the 20-24 on more traditional balloon whisks from Rösle ($27), OXO ($9.99), and Best ($19.12)—though this latter model was larger and better-suited for cooks with a strong arm. The Rösle whisk whipped cream in a record 2 minutes, 22 seconds and included a handy hook for storage, but most testers favored the OXO for its particularly comfortable handle, efficiency (2 minutes, 58 seconds), and wallet-friendly price. With a small amount of cream—and a little elbow grease—this one whips up just fine.

Rating Balloon Whisks

WE TESTED FIVE BALLOON WHISKS AGAINST AN all-purpose French whip and a stand mixer to see how well they would whip a small amount of cream. Brands are listed in order of preference. See www.americastestkitchen.com for updates to this testing.

RECOMMENDED
OXO Steel 11" Balloon Whisk
$9.99; 20 tines; Time to whip cream: 2 minutes, 58 seconds
Testers considered this the best overall whisk for its under-3-minute whipping time, a particularly comfortable handle, and lightweight design.

RECOMMENDED
Rösle Balloon Whisk/Beater
$27; 24 tines; Time to whip cream: 2 minutes, 22 seconds
This Rolls Royce of balloon whisks sported 24 tines and holds the record for whipping cream in under 2½ minutes. The only drawbacks? A slightly heavy handle and a price that makes your wallet shudder.

RECOMMENDED
Best 14" Piano Wire Balloon Whip
$19.12; 20 tines; Time to whip cream: 2 minutes, 37 seconds
Though on the large side for most testers, this 14-inch whisk brought up stiff peaks of heavy cream in near-record time and offered nice weight balance for those with stronger arms.

RECOMMENDED WITH RESERVATIONS
Cuisipro Duo Whisk with Wire Ball
$17.99; 16 tines; Time to whip cream: 4 minutes, 37 seconds
"Seems like a tool a cat would enjoy," remarked one tester about this whisk with an inner wire ball encasing a rattling marble. Unfortunately, this innovation failed to boost speed; in fact, whipping cream took just over 4½ minutes.

RECOMMENDED WITH RESERVATIONS
Zyliss Quick Blend Whisk
$7.95; 16 tines; Time to whip cream: 4 minutes, 49 seconds
Relatively few, unwoven tines did not solve any clogging problems; instead, it was the caboose, whipping the cream in just under 5 minutes.

A NOTE ON CONVERSIONS

SOME SAY COOKING IS BOTH A SCIENCE AND AN ART. We would say that geography has a hand in it, too. Flour milled in the United Kingdom and elsewhere will feel and taste different from flour milled in the United States. So we cannot promise that the loaf of bread you bake in Canada or England will taste the same as a loaf baked in the States, but we can offer guidelines for converting weights and measures. We also recommend that you rely on instincts when making our recipes. Refer to the visual cues provided. If the bread dough hasn't "come together in a ball," as described, you may need to add more flour—even if the recipe doesn't tell you so. You be the judge. For more information on conversions and ingredient equivalents, visit our Web site at www.cooksillustrated.com and type "conversion chart" in the search box.

The recipes in this book were developed using standard U.S. measures following U.S. government guidelines. The charts below offer equivalents for U.S., metric, and Imperial (U.K.) measures. All conversions are approximate and have been rounded up or down to the nearest whole number. For example:

1 teaspoon = 4.9292 milliliters, rounded up to 5 milliliters

1 ounce = 28.3495 grams, rounded down to 28 grams

Volume Conversions

U.S.	METRIC
1 teaspoon	5 milliliters
2 teaspoons	10 milliliters
1 tablespoon	15 milliliters
2 tablespoons	30 milliliters
¼ cup	59 milliliters
⅓ cup	79 milliliters
½ cup	118 milliliters
¾ cup	177 milliliters
1 cup	237 milliliters
1¼ cups	296 milliliters
1½ cups	355 milliliters
2 cups	473 milliliters
2½ cups	592 milliliters
3 cups	710 milliliters
4 cups (1 quart)	0.946 liter
1.06 quarts	1 liter
4 quarts (1 gallon)	3.8 liters

Weight Conversions

OUNCES	GRAMS
½	14
¾	21
1	28
1½	43
2	57
2½	71
3	85
3½	99
4	113
4½	128
5	142
6	170
7	198
8	227
9	255
10	283
12	340
16 (1 pound)	454

Conversions for Ingredients Commonly Used in Baking

Baking is an exacting science. Because measuring by weight is far more accurate than measuring by volume, and thus more likely to achieve reliable results, in our recipes we provide ounce measures in addition to cup measures for many ingredients. Refer to the chart below to convert these measures into grams.

INGREDIENT	OUNCES	GRAMS
1 cup all-purpose flour*	5	142
1 cup whole wheat flour	5½	156
1 cup granulated (white) sugar	7	198
1 cup packed brown sugar (light or dark)	7	198
1 cup confectioners' sugar	4	113
1 cup cocoa powder	3	85
Butter†		
4 tablespoons (½ stick, or ¼ cup)	2	57
8 tablespoons (1 stick, or ½ cup)	4	113
16 tablespoons (2 sticks, or 1 cup)	8	227

* U.S. all-purpose flour, the most frequently used flour in this book, does not contain leaveners, as some European flours do. These leavened flours are called self-rising or self-raising. If you are using self-rising flour, take this into consideration before adding leavening to a recipe.

† In the United States, butter is sold both salted and unsalted. We generally recommend unsalted butter. If you are using salted butter, take this into consideration before adding salt to a recipe.

Oven Temperatures

FAHRENHEIT	CELSIUS	GAS MARK (IMPERIAL)
225	105	¼
250	120	½
275	130	1
300	150	2
325	165	3
350	180	4
375	190	5
400	200	6
425	220	7
450	230	8
475	245	9

Converting Temperatures from an Instant-Read Thermometer

We include doneness temperatures in many of our recipes, such as those for poultry, meat, and bread. We recommend an instant-read thermometer for the job. Refer to the above table to convert Fahrenheit degrees to Celsius. Or, for temperatures not represented in the chart, use this simple formula:

Subtract 32 degrees from the Fahrenheit reading, then divide the result by 1.8 to find the Celsius reading.

EXAMPLE:

"Roast until the juices run clear when the chicken is cut with a paring knife or the thickest part of the breast registers 160 degrees on an instant-read thermometer." To convert:

160°F − 32 = 128°
128° ÷ 1.8 = 71°C (rounded down from 71.11)

INDEX

L

Ladyfingers
  dried, buying, 136
  Tiramisù, 134–37
  Tiramisù with Cooked Eggs, 138

Lamb
  domestic, flavor of, 236
  imported, flavor of, 236
  Rack of, Charcoal-Grilled, *109,* 234–38
  Rack of, Gas-Grilled, 238
  rack of, trimming fat from, 237

Large Crème Caramel, 293

Latino-Style Chicken and Rice, 156–58
  with Bacon and Roasted Red Peppers, 159
  with Ham, Peas, and Orange, 159

Leeks and Hazelnuts, Sautéed Spinach with, 228

Lo Mein, Pork, *111,* 164–66

M

Main dishes (meat)
  Charcoal-Grilled Marinated Flank Steak, 212–14, *246*
  Charcoal-Grilled Pork Loin with Apple-Cranberry Filling, *112,* 222–25
  Charcoal-Grilled Rack of Lamb, *109,* 234–38
  Crunchy Baked Pork Chops, 52–54, *248*
  Crunchy Baked Pork Chops with Prosciutto and Asiago Cheese, 55
  Daube Provençal, 142–45, *251*
  Gas-Grilled Marinated Flank Steak, 214
  Gas-Grilled Pork Loin with Apple-Cranberry Filling, 225
  Gas-Grilled Rack of Lamb, 238
  Glazed Spiral-Sliced Ham, 190–92

Main dishes (meat) *(cont.)*
  Inexpensive Roast Beef, 76–79, *104*
  Pork Lo Mein, *111,* 164–66
  Steak Tacos, 91–94, *250*
  Stir-Fried Beef with Snap Peas and Red Peppers, *107,* 170–71
  Stir-Fried Red Curry Beef with Eggplant, 172–73
  Tangerine Stir-Fried Beef with Onions and Snow Peas, 171–72
  Teriyaki Stir-Fried Beef with Green Beans and Shiitakes, 168–70

Main dishes (pasta)
  Pasta with Creamy Tomato Sauce, 32–34
  Simple Italian-Style Meat Sauce, 28–31, *244*

Main dishes (poultry)
  Charcoal-Grilled Bone-In Chicken Breasts, 202–4, *245*
  Chicken Saltimbocca, 130–32, *249*
  Enchiladas Verdes, 86–90, *99*
  French Chicken in a Pot, 116–18
  Gas-Grilled Bone-In Chicken Breasts, 204
  Herbed Roast Turkey, 180–82
  Latino-Style Chicken and Rice, 156–58
    with Bacon and Roasted Red Peppers, 159
    with Ham, Peas, and Orange, 159
  Stuffed Chicken Breasts, 64–67, *247*

Main dishes (seafood)
  Crunchy Oven-Baked Fish, 45–48, *106*
  Poached Salmon
    with Bourbon and Maple, 43–44
    with Dill and Sour Cream Sauce, 44
    with Herb and Caper Vinaigrette, 40–43, *103*
  Sizzling Garlic Shrimp, 152–55, *243*

Main dishes (stews)
  Daube Provençal, 142–45, *251*
  Hearty Tuscan Bean Stew, 18–21, *100*
  Hearty Tuscan Bean Stew with Sausage and Cabbage, 21
  Quick Hearty Tuscan Bean Stew, 21
  Vegetarian Hearty Tuscan Bean Stew, 21

Mandolines, ratings of, 125–27

Mango and Lime Curry Vinaigrette, Cherry Tomato Salad with, 209

Maple and Bourbon, Poached Salmon with, 43–44

Maple-Orange Glaze, 192

Marinades
  garlic flavor in, 155
  Wet Paste, Garlic-Chile, 215
  Wet Paste, Garlic-Ginger-Sesame, 215
  Wet Paste, Garlic-Shallot-Rosemary, 215

Mascarpone
  Tiramisù, 134–37
  Tiramisù with Cooked Eggs, 138

Mashed Potatoes
  Fluffy, 186
  and Root Vegetables, 81–83
  and Root Vegetables with Bacon and Thyme, 83
  and Root Vegetables with Paprika and Parsley, 83

Measuring cups
  dry, ratings of, 320–21
  liquid, deluxe, ratings of, 22

Meat. *See* Beef; Lamb; Pork

Meat pounders, ratings of, 67

Meat-probe thermometers, ratings of, 79–80

Meringue Cookies, 146–48
  adding cornstarch to, 148–49
  Chocolate, 148
  Orange, 148
  Toasted Almond, 148